T0374723

PLINY

LETTERS AND PANEGYRICUS

I

LCL 55

PLINY

LETTERS, BOOKS 1–7
PANEGYRICUS

WITH AN ENGLISH TRANSLATION BY
BETTY RADICE

HARVARD UNIVERSITY PRESS
CAMBRIDGE, MASSACHUSETTS
LONDON, ENGLAND

ISBN 978-0-674-99061-6

*Printed on acid-free paper and bound by
The Maple-Vail Book Manufacturing Group*

CONTENTS

PREFACE

My first thanks are to the Clarendon Press for permission to base my translation of Pliny on the Oxford Classical Texts of Sir Roger Mynors, and to Penguin Books for permission to reprint, with some changes, my translation of the *Letters* first published by them in 1963. I have listed in a Bibliography books and articles which I have found particularly helpful, from which it is clear how much I owe to the published work of Sir Ronald Syme and Mr. A. N. Sherwin-White. Sir Roger Mynors has given me generous help with text and interpretation at all stages, and so has Mr. Sherwin-White; Professors Ernst Badian, G. W. Bowersock, and W. S. Maguinness, Dr. A. Birley, Dr. E. M. Smallwood, and Mr. G. E. M. de Ste. Croix have been equally kind in giving advice and encouragement on special points. The mistakes which remain are, of course, my own.

In compiling the Index I have tried to supply information on the many persons who figure in Pliny's correspondence by reference to parallel literary sources or to inscriptions. I have had in mind readers who find it more encouraging to work from accessible and manageable reference books; consequently inscriptions quoted have been referred

PREFACE

either to the Selections of Dessau (ILS) or to those of McCrum and Woodhead (MW) and E. M. Smallwood (S). Many will judge this inadequate, but I fancy they will know where to look for further evidence when they need it.

B.R.

INTRODUCTION

THE younger Pliny was in a position to provide essential information for historians of a poorly-documented period, the reigns of Domitian, Nerva, and Trajan. He had a successful senatorial career; he was an active advocate in the Roman Chancery court and was in the habit of publishing his speeches in revised form; he had a large circle of friends both personal and professional to whom he addressed the letters from which he made a selection for publication. (He also dabbled in light verse, not very successfully, to judge by the few extant specimens.) Nine books of his personal letters (247 in all) survive, as well as his official correspondence with the emperor Trajan, posthumously published and later added as a tenth book. Of his speeches, only the one of thanks to Trajan for his consulship in A.D. 100 survives in greatly expanded form, known as the *Panegyricus.*

The details of Pliny's background and career are well known from the *Letters,* and also from some personal inscriptions.[1] He was the son of Lucius Caecilius of Comum, and both the Caecilii and his mother's family, the Plinii, owned considerable properties in the region, to which several letters refer.[2] As he was seventeen at the time of the eruption of Vesuvius in August 79[3] he must have been

---

[1] The most important are listed in Appendix A.
[2] II. 1. 8; II. 15; IX. 7.   [3] VI. 20. 5.

born in late 61 or early 62. His education followed
the normal pattern of study under a *grammaticus* at
Comum, followed by lectures in Rome under Quintilian and the Greek rhetorician, Nicetes Sacerdos.[1]
After his father's early death he had Verginius
Rufus for guardian, and in Rome came into closer
contact with his distinguished uncle, his mother's
brother. He and his mother were both at Misenum
with the elder Pliny at the time of the eruption. At
his uncle's death he inherited the full estate, and a
change of name indicates his adoption by will as a
son.[2] His full official title henceforth was Gaius
Plinius Luci filius Caecilius Secundus.[3] Soon after
this, still at the age of eighteen, he began his career
with a success in the Centumviral Court,[4] which was
to be his special sphere throughout his active life at
the bar. With the support of his older consular
friends he started on his senatorial *cursus* with a minor
magistracy, as one of the *decemviri stlitibus iudicandis*[5]
presiding over the panels of the Centumviral Court.
Next came the routine military tribunate, probably
for no more than the minimum six months, during
which Pliny served with the Third Gallic legion in
Syria as auditor of the auxiliary forces' accounts.[6]
After another minor office (*sevir equitum Romanorum*)[7]
he was *quaestor Caesaris* and then *tribunus plebis*,[8] and
during the latter period of service felt it his duty to
suspend his practice in the courts.[9] Domitian allowed

[1] VI. 6. 3.
[2] V. 8. 5.
[3] App. A. 1.
[4] V. 8. 8; I. 18. 3.
[5] App. A. 1.
[6] III. 11. 5; VII. 31. 2.
[7] App. A. 1.
[8] VII. 16. 2.
[9] I. 23. 2.

him to proceed to the praetorship without the statutory year's interval,[1] probably in 93, and in the same year he appeared for the prosecution of Baebius Massa by the province of Baetica.[2] Massa was convicted, but retaliated by charging Pliny's colleague in the case, Herennius Senecio, with *maiestas*. This brought Pliny into closer contact with the so-called "Stoic opposition," of which Senecio was one of the leaders, and later on he made a point of recalling the dangers he faced during the reign of terror in the later part of 93.[3] In fact his career does not seem to have suffered; indeed, he was given a three-year appointment by Domitian as *curator aerarii militaris*.[4] Soon after Domitian's assassination in 96 he came forward to vindicate the name of Helvidius Priscus, one of the Stoics executed in 93, by denouncing his prosecutor Publicius Certus, and a letter written some years afterwards vividly recalls the feeling of uncertainty in the Senate in the early months of Nerva's reign.[5] Pliny accordingly had to content himself with the fact that Certus did not proceed to the consulship he expected after his post at the *aerarium Saturni*—a post which fell to Pliny himself when Certus died soon after the trial. This too was a three-year appointment, and Pliny and his colleague Cornutus Tertullus held it up to the day when they were suffect consuls in September–October 100.[6] Pliny's official speech of thanks for his appointment was the *Panegyricus* in its original, shorter form.

[1] VII. 16. 2.   [2] VI. 29. 8; VII. 33. 4.
[3] III. 11. 3.   [4] App. A. I.
[5] IX. 13.   [6] V. 14. 5; *Pan.* 91–2.

INTRODUCTION

At the end of his treasury and consular duties Pliny continued to be active in the Centumviral Court and the Senate, and also frequently acted as assessor in the *consilium* of the City prefect's court or to Trajan himself,[1] though he looked forward increasingly to honourable retirement. His reward for distinguished public service did not come until 103, when he was elected augur to fill the vacancy left by the death of Julius Frontinus;[2] Trajan's response to an earlier request for a priesthood[3] is not known. The following year he was appointed to another three-year office, as *curator alvei Tiberis et riparum et cloacarum urbis*[4] on the Tiber Conservancy Board, a post which must have appealed to Pliny's practical nature. He may still have been holding it when he was chosen by Trajan to go out as the emperor's special representative (*legatus propraetore consulari potestate*) to the province of Bithynia-Pontus.[5] He was well equipped for this commission by his expert knowledge of finance, and still more by his handling of several important public cases involving provincial governors since the one which convicted Baebius Massa. In 99–100 he had secured the conviction of Marius Priscus on behalf of the province of Africa, and in 101 had prosecuted another governor of Baetica, Caecilius Classicus. Moreover, he had gained an inside knowledge of Bithynian affairs during his defence of the proconsular governors Julius Bassus in 102–3 and Varenus Rufus in 106–7.[6] The mere fact that the province had brought these cases against its senatorial governors showed that its

[1] IV. 22; VI. 11. 1; VI. 31.   [2] IV. 8.   [3] X. 13.
[4] V. 14. 2.   [5] App. A. 1.   [6] VI. 29. 8 ff.

affairs, both political and financial, were in urgent need of overhauling. Pliny was to tour the cities, report on his findings and settle what he could on the spot.

This he proceeded to do with commendable energy and good sense, undaunted by the multiplicity of the problems awaiting him—political disorders, municipal bankruptcy arising out of unregulated and dishonest public spending, ignorance of legal procedure, and personal animosities of many kinds. The letters published in Book X make fascinating reading, ranging as they do from a detailed report on the problems presented by practising Christians[1] to the importance of covering an open sewer in the interests of public health.[2] Pliny addressed no more than sixty-one letters to Trajan in a period of less than two years, and some of these are testimonials or formal letters of congratulation. We have no idea how much he settled on his own initiative, and his requests for guidance seem reasonable and are treated by Trajan as such. Some of the replies are presumably drafted by the imperial secretariat,[3] while others sound like Trajan replying in person; the tone may be terse, but is very rarely impatient.[4] In the past Pliny has been unfairly represented as lacking in initiative and consulting Trajan on too many details, but considering the problems he found and his desire to obtain more satisfactory general rulings than the outdated code of Pompey or previous emperors' rescripts to the proconsular governors, it cannot be said that he made undue use of the diplomatic bag.

Pliny evidently died in the province with his work

[1] X. 96–7. [2] X. 98.
[3] *e.g.* X. 101; 103. [4] *e.g.* X. 38; 95.

unfinished, but the exact date is unknown. He had arrived in time for Trajan's birthday celebrations on 18 September[1] in a year which could be 109, 110, or 111, and as there is no mention of similar celebrations for the start of his third year we assume that he died before then, perhaps while on tour in Pontus. His old friend and colleague, Cornutus Tertullus, was sent out with similar powers later in Trajan's reign.

The only details of this career of public service not supplied by the *Letters* are the two early minor posts of decemvirate and sevirate, a priesthood in honour of the deified emperor Titus held at Comum,[2] and presumably bestowed by Pliny's native town, and his post at the military treasury given him by Domitian. These are known only from inscriptions. The last omission is surely significant. Pliny was friendly with several members of the " Stoic opposition " who had either been executed (Arulenus Rusticus, Helvidius Priscus, Herennius Senecio) or exiled (Junius Mauricus, Fannia, and the younger Arria)[3] in the

---

[1] X. 17a. [2] App. A. 3.
[3] The leaders of the opposition, spanning several generations, were close related, and, like Pliny, of Cisalpine origin: Thrasea Paetus was a native of Padua.

Caecina Paetus = Elder Arria

Thrasea Paetus = Younger Arria

(1) = Helvidius Priscus = (2) Fannia

Helvidius = Anteia

Helvidius   2 daughters

purge of 93, and he admired their courage, perhaps the more so as he was aware that he himself was not cut out for political martyrdom. It may well have been an embarrassment to him for the exiles to return and find him, for all his protests, well advanced in his career, and so he deliberately suppressed anything he owed to the Emperor he consistently portrays as a monster of tyranny and caprice.

Pliny was married three times, but nothing is known of his first wife, and of his second, only the bare fact of her death just before the attack on Certus in 97,[1] though Pliny remained on friendly terms with his mother-in-law, Pompeia Celerina, and seems to have managed her affairs for her. His third wife, Calpurnia, was the orphaned granddaughter of Calpurnius Fabatus of Comum, a wealthy landowner and a somewhat testy old gentleman. Pliny's devotion to Calpurnia is undisguised, as is his disappointment at her subsequent miscarriage and consequent sterility, and the *ius trium liberorum* conferred on him by Trajan can have brought him little consolation.

It was natural for him to marry into the provincial gentry, for at heart this is very much what he remained. Though his visits to Comum could never be frequent, he remained sentimentally attached to the lake and his properties in the region, and was far from being a typical absentee landlord. He took as keen a personal interest in the proper management of the farm at Comum as he did in his estates in Tuscany and in his *suburbanum* household near Ostia. He was a generous benefactor to his native town; Comum had a library built and endowed, one-third of

[1] IX. 13. 4.

a resident teacher's salary paid, provision for needy children from a rent charge on Pliny's property, and received more than two million sesterces by his will.[1] He also kept up his friendships with several north-erners, the lawyer Annius Severus, his business adviser and town councillor Calvisius Rufus, old school friends Atilius Crescens and Romatius Firmus, giving substantial financial help where it was needed and furthering their careers as he in his turn had been supported by Verginius Rufus and Vestricius Spurinna. These friends of his are substantial, re-sponsible citizens, often unknown outside the *Letters*, so that Pliny provides valuable information about municipal life in Cisalpine Gaul and the part played by its people when, like himself, they moved to Rome.[2]

The correspondence with Trajan, posthumously published (by Suetonius perhaps, or another of Pliny's literary friends after Trajan's death), is pre-sumably unrevised and provides essential information which exists nowhere else for the workings of Roman bureaucracy. The personal letters, carefully revised and selected though they are, must also be regarded as genuine first-hand documentation, and are indeed the best social commentary we have on the Roman empire at the turn of the first century. They provide the normal, if more humdrum pattern of life to be set against the more highly-coloured pages of Pliny's contemporaries, Juvenal, Martial, Suetonius, and Tacitus. Pliny and his circle are very far from being irresponsible aristocrats or idle sycophants, and it is

[1] I. 8. 2; IV. 13. 5; VII. 18. 2; App. A. 1.
[2] See G. E. F. Chilver, *Cisalpine Gaul*, pp. 95 ff.

from him we learn how many people truly cared for
the proper administration of justice in the courts,
the dignity of the Senate as a deliberative assembly,
the education of the rising generation, and all the
human decencies of behaviour without which life
for the common man would be intolerable.

The *Letters* leave us in no doubt about the sort of
man Pliny was himself, and he is a man one would like
to have known—an affectionate husband, loyal friend,
considerate master, and conscientious public servant.
But he is not lightly to be dismissed as a prig and a
pedant—the lawyer's caution is less in evidence in
Bithynia than the practical administrator's common
sense, and he is tolerant of other people's foibles as
well as being capable of smiling at his own. He is
free from petty jealousies, and his personal integrity
and professional honesty are beyond question. The
one person he cannot tolerate is M. Aquilius Regulus
—whose flamboyant affectations and unscrupulous
ambitions are the exact antithesis of Pliny's solid
principles and unaffectedness. He is certainly a poor
critic of his own work, but he is well aware that his
talents are not of the first order and that Tacitus is
by far his superior;[1] and beside the poverty of his
poetic efforts must be set his observant eye for
natural phenomena and his excellence as a descriptive writer.

More than one hundred persons have letters addressed to them, and many more are referred to by
name in the letters. Some of them (Caninius Rufus,
for example) emerge fairly clearly from the letters
but are unknown elsewhere. Some are well known

[1] VII. 20.

in literary sources, such as Verginius Rufus or Titius
Aristo, the jurist often quoted in the *Digest*, or their
careers can be confirmed or amplified from the inscriptions of the period, as in the case of Valerius
Maximus or Julius Ferox.[1] Some of Pliny's closest
friends (Calestrius Tiro, Voconius Romanus, or even
Suetonius) are slow to achieve distinction, and other
names he mentions show no promise of the successes
they gained long after his death—Bruttius Praesens
and Erucius Clarus, for example.[2] Others (Colonus,
Mustius, Sardus, Venator) remain as yet totally
obscure and have defeated all efforts to establish their
identity. But it is only through the work done on
independent sources[3] that we can begin to understand the true value of the correspondence, both for
what it contains and what it omits. Several names one
might have expected to find, but there is no mention
of literary figures like Statius (though he and Pliny
had at least one acquaintance in common in Vibius
Maximus),[4] nor Juvenal who perhaps had no patience
with Pliny's poetic aspirations. (It has even been
suggested that Juvenal satirizes Pliny's circle in some
of his pseudonyms.)[5] And even if Pliny did not
openly express his dislike of snobbery, it would be
clear from the gaps in the list of correspondents that
he is no snob himself. He rejoices to see the " noble
families " of Republican and Augustan times living

[1] ILS 1018 and 5930 (S. 235 and 381).
[2] See Index for their careers.
[3] See especially R. Syme, *Tacitus* (referred to as " Syme ")
and articles listed in Bibliography, p. xxxii; A. N. Sherwin-
White, The *Letters of Pliny* (referred to as S-W).
[4] See Statius, *Silvae*, IV. 7.
[5] See Gilbert Highet, *Juvenal the Satirist*, pp. 291 ff.

up to their illustrious names, but publishes no letter
addressed to any of their descendants.[1] Julius
Frontinus is mentioned several times, but receives
nothing, and one feels that had Pliny been interested
in name-dropping he could surely have found a note
addressed to Frontinus to add to his published selection. Neratius Marcellus would also have been a
name worth having; and the famous Javolenus
Priscus has no more than a surprisingly uncompli-
mentary reference.[2] All this suggests that the correspondents genuinely represent Pliny's circle of
friends, and also that his interest in publishing his
correspondence was primarily literary.

The opening letter of Book I implies that out of an
accumulated mass of material Pliny proposes to select
the letters " composed with some care " and to put
them together " as they come to hand " rather than
in chronological order. In actual fact, his arrangement is as careful as his writing. Each book contains
letters on a variety of themes, political and legal
topics, literary criticism, appreciations of great men,
advice and recommendation to his friends, domestic
news, descriptions of natural phenomena, courtesy
notes, and jokes, arranged so as to provide a lively
variation of tone. These are, of course, literary
letters, far removed in kind from the only collection
comparable in bulk, that of Cicero; the genre is more
that of the verse epistles of Horace or Statius, while
some of the shorter trifles recall the epigrams of
Martial. In general he follows the principle that a
letter should deal with a single theme, though there
are some which follow the scholastic " rule of three ".

[1] Syme, *Tacitus*, pp. 87 and 666.   [2] VI. 15. 2.

INTRODUCTION

Revision for publication must have led to some omission of material; practical letters ordering marble for a temple or a pedestal for a statue would surely have originally contained actual measurements.[1] Sometimes too we can see that an introductory paragraph has been added to give the context, and there are many letters in which the formal opening gives the gist of the letter Pliny is answering.[2]

The order of the nine books is chronological (though that of the letters within them is not), and the firm dates range from 97 (the death of Verginius Rufus in II. 1) to 108/9 (Valerius Paulinus, addressed in IX. 37, was suffect consul in September–December 107). No one would now follow Mommsen in dating publication from 97 onwards, a book a year, and it is generally agreed that the books were published in groups, certainly before Pliny's departure for Bithynia, and probably none before the death of Regulus in 104. The time after Pliny's treasury posts and consulship and his important cases in the Senate would certainly seem more likely for him to be free to give meticulous attention to the task of selection and revision.[3] Book IX suggests an increase of leisure for literary pursuits, and one letter (IX. 2) rather implies that retirement from an active professional life might mean the drying up of worth-while material, but there is no formal ending to the series. Probably it was cut short by Pliny's appointment to the post in Bithynia.

---

[1] III. 6; IX. 39.

[2] See the list in Sherwin-White, *Letters*, p. 6 ff.

[3] See Syme, *Tacitus*, *App.* 21; Sherwin-White, *Letters*, p. 20 ff.

INTRODUCTION

As a stylist in the Letters Pliny shows himself to be a true pupil of his master Quintilian, following the general rules of oratorical prose for *clausulae* and the advice given in *Institutio Oratoria* IX. iv. 19, that *oratio soluta* is suitable to letters unless they deal with political or philosophical themes. He himself distinguishes between the kind of letters he writes (*epistulae curatius scriptae* though they are), and the Senecan type of essay in letter form, the *scholasticae litterae* mentioned in *Ep.* IX. 2. 3. In VII. 9. 8 he recommends letter-writing as a means of developing *pressus sermo purusque*, and this conciseness and simplicity is marked when he is presenting a narrative story—the dolphin of Hippo, the ghost stories, the account of the eruption—or a piece of objective description like that of the floating islands of Lake Vadimon or the springs of the Clitumnus, both masterpieces of prose style. Sometimes he allows himself a more poetic vocabulary: his debt to Virgil in the account of the harbour being built at Centum Cellae has often been noted. He has a light conversational touch for his *ioca*, and something much nearer formal oratory for the indignant outburst about Pallas or the trial of the Vestal Virgin; while in some of his courtesy notes to friends or addresses to Trajan he is a master at expressing polite formalities in elegant style. It is here that the influence of Martial is most apparent. A modern reader may well wonder why some of these trifles were included in a selection, and though some of them may come under the heading of *officia* conventionally expected for *beneficia* received, these prose epigrams, with their scholarly allusions and conceits or the effortless unwinding of an artfully

balanced period, doubtless gave both Pliny and their recipients great pleasure for the sheer virtuosity of their style. In the main, apart from a liking for diminutives and a rapid succession of verbs for dramatic effect, Pliny has no marked characteristics of style; but his versatility is a perpetual delight, and at his best he can certainly stand second to Tacitus.

Pliny mentions with some amusement the Greek tragedy he wrote at the age of fourteen,[1] and he was proud of his facility in writing hexameters and elegiacs, but the examples he quotes of these are embarrassingly banal.[2] Nothing of his hendecasyllables has survived, perhaps mercifully; his judgements on poetry do not really inspire confidence, and the value of the collective opinion of the company present at the literary reading-parties condemned by Juvenal[3] is highly dubious. He toys with the idea of writing history,[4] but probably never had time to do so. The short memoir he wrote of Spurinna's son[5] is lost, and of the many speeches he revised for publication only the *Panegyricus* remains as " the solitary specimen of Latin eloquence from the century and a half that had elapsed since the death of Cicero."[6] It is by this that we must judge Pliny as an orator, though he discusses style in oratory in two long letters (I. 20 and IX. 26) and makes it clear that his preference is for something fuller and richer than the " Attic " style, with its rather barren ideals of brevity and correctness;

[1] VII. 4. 2. [2] VII. 4. 6 and 9. 11.
[3] Juvenal, *Sat.* I. 1–13; VII. 39–47.
[4] V. 8. [5] III. 10.
[6] Syme, *Tacitus*, p. 114.

though elsewhere he criticizes the flamboyance of
the true " Asian " rhetoric as exemplified in Regulus
or the volubility of a Bithynian advocate pouring out
" a torrent of long monotonous periods without taking
breath."[1] Quintilian (*Inst. Orat.* XII. x) had made a
threefold classification of style, and the mixed or
middle one would best fit Pliny.

The *Panegyricus* was, of course, considerably expanded for publication, possibly to three times its
original length; a reading to an invited audience
filled three sessions, estimated at $1\frac{1}{2}$–2 hours each.[2]
(Whether Trajan ever read or heard it in its expanded
form we cannot know.) Some of its additions are
obvious—the drought in Egypt, for instance (Ch.
30–2) or the anticipation of Trajan's triumph (Ch.
17), but on the whole the paragraphs are expanded
after a striking opening sentence with considerable
technical skill. There are even some descriptive
passages which are not unworthy of Tacitus—notably
the chapters on Domitian (48–9) and the brief description of the atmosphere in the Senate under
Domitian (Ch. 76). The prototype for the treatment
of the subject was the praise of Caesar in Cicero's
Pro Marcello, but Pliny's style and method are quite
different. It was his personal achievement to create
out of the brief official *gratiarum actio* something
which was to serve as a model for later, less gifted,
imitators. The title was not his; it comes from the
collection known as the *XII Panegyrici* in which

---

[1] V. 20. 4.
[2] Sherwin-White, *Letters*, p. 251. But as Pliny originally
intended to read on two days (III. 18. 4), he may have been
reading long extracts, not continuously.

INTRODUCTION

Pliny's was placed first, though it antedated the earliest of the others by some two hundred years.

But the faults of the speech are many, and for most readers who have struggled on to the last, ninety-fifth chapter, the general effect is stupefying, as every possible rhetorical figure is called into play, and the positive facts (such as the details of Trajan's taxation reforms in Ch. 36–40) have somehow to be extracted from a plethora of eulogistic verbiage. Historically it is of great importance, supplying the few scraps of information we have about Trajan's career before his accession (Ch. 14–15), confirming Dio's account of the disturbed state of the country just before Trajan's adoption (Ch. 6. 3; Dio LXVIII. iii. 3), and giving specific detail about election procedure. Historians have also recognized its political importance: Pliny's avowed intent was that *boni principes quae facerent recognoscerent, mali quae facere deberent* (Ch. 4. 1), and the emphasis throughout the speech is on the *obsequium* of the *optimus princeps* to his people. It represents the Senate's ideal of the constitutional ruler, and is a tactful way of telling Trajan what his grateful subjects would have him be.

That this was the main reason why Pliny enlarged the original speech in the way he did is clear from *Ep.* III. 18. 2 where he says explicitly that he expanded it *primum ut imperatori nostro virtutes suae veris laudibus commendarentur, deinde ut futuri principes non quasi a magistro sed tamen sub exemplo praemonerentur, qua potissimum via possent ad eandem gloriam niti*, and the reception it received from his invited audience gave him every reason to be proud of it. Yet editors and commentators alike have tended to treat the *Panegy-*

INTRODUCTION

ricus as something quite separate from Pliny, or else
to dismiss it as doing " no good to the reputation of
its author or the taste of the age."[1] But to do him
justice we should surely recognize that for all its
prolixity and lapses into absurdity the expanded
speech was his own creation, and the idea behind it
was his only sustained piece of political thinking.
The other speeches referred to in the *Letters* were
those of the Chancery Court and of the big public
trials[2] which were to occupy so much of his time until
his services were needed in Bithynia.

It was Pliny's pride and pleasure to hear his name
linked with that of Tacitus and his hope that posterity
would remember them together, but his immediate
fate was apparently to be forgotten. The *Letters*
were certainly not well known until the later part of
the fourth century when the ten books of the correspondence of Q. Aurelius Symmachus were published
in a form like Pliny's, nine books of private and one of
official letters. In the second half of the fifth century
Sidonius Apollinaris, Bishop of Auvergne, collected
and revised his own letters and published them in
nine books, and as he is the first writer to quote directly
and widely from Pliny's letters, the traditional view
is that he virtually rediscovered them, and that before
his time Pliny was confused with his uncle.[3] But
the well-known reference in Tertullian to the correspondence on the Christians in Bithynia,[4] and two
quotations in St. Jerome's letters of a single letter

[1] Syme, *Tacitus*, p. 114.   [2] See VI. 29. 8–11.
[3] See S. E. Stout, " The Coalescence of the Two Plinies,"
Trans. Am. Phil. Ass., LXXXVI (1955).
[4] Tertullian, *Apology* II. 6–10; Eusebius, *Hist. Eccl.* III. 33.

of Pliny's[1] imply that these two people, at any rate, knew his work before Symmachus and Sidonius.[2] In the writings of the Middle Ages he leaves no trace.

NOTE ON THE TEXT

The text of Books I to IX of the *Letters* rests on three manuscript traditions, the 9-book, the 10-book and the 8-book, known as α, β, γ in the Oxford text and as X, Z, Y in the text of S. E. Stout.

α covers all the text, with a few gaps, but after Book IV is represented by a single MS (M). A sub-division θ is also recognized. β now contains nothing in MS beyond V. 6, though the source was complete.

γ contains I to VII. 33 and IX, with nothing from VIII.

Where two traditions combine, their reading is generally preferred to that of the third, and on the whole editors have agreed in establishing an acceptable text.

For Book X there are considerable difficulties. The original source was a 10-book Paris MS of the sixth century (P) now lost, though the " Morgan fragment " (π) was copied from it and pages covering II. 20. 13 to III. 5. 4 survive in New York. Any text of Book X depends on the early editions, notably those of Avantius (A) and of Aldus (a) published in

[1] St. Jerome, *Ep.* LIII. 1. 3 and 2. 2, quoting Pliny, *Ep.* II. 3.
[2] See A. Cameron, " The Fate of Pliny's Letters in the Late Empire," *C.Q.*, XV. 2 (1965).

INTRODUCTION

1502 and 1508. Avantius first printed X. 1–40 from
a copy which must have derived from P. P is also
known to have been copied in Paris by Fra Giocondo
of Verona, an Italian architect working for Louis XII,
and the copy was given to Aldus. In 1508 the
Venetian ambassador in Paris, Aloisius Mocenigo,
brought P itself to Venice, so that Aldus had the
original to compare with the copy from which he prepared the edition which he dedicated to Mocenigo.
That he often did his work inaccurately is proved
from the additions (I) and the corrections (i) made
by the scholar Budaeus in his copy of Avantius's edition, and by the 1498 edition of Beroaldus, which he
bound together in the book now in the Bodleian.
The two editions by Catanaeus of 1508 and 1518 can
also be used as a check.

The text of the *Panegyricus* was preserved as the
first of twelve *Panegyrici Latini*, in no way connected
with the private or the official correspondence of
Pliny, and first known from the MS (M) found at
Mainz in 1432 by Johannes Aurispa, and now lost.
This is considered to be the source for the many
Italian MSS (X) and the Harley MS (H) in London,
discovered by E. Baehrens in 1875. There are also
a few pages of a palimpsest MS (R) of the sixth
century, from an unknown source. The editions of
Puteolanus and Livineius of 1482 and 1599 and later
editors can often supply a correction, but on the whole
the text rests on the evidence of the lost M, as supplied by X and/or H.

The translation throughout is based on the Oxford
texts of Sir R. A. B. Mynors of 1963 and 1964;
textual references are given only where there is

serious disagreement between MSS or editors. The fullest authoritative discussion on the text is in the prefaces to the two Oxford volumes, while S. E. Stout's *Scribe and Critic at work in Pliny's Letters* describes the methods of textual evaluation which produced his own text in 1962.

BIBLIOGRAPHY

Texts

R. A. B. Mynors: *Letters* I–X. Oxford, 1963
(Oxford Classical Text).
  XII *Panegyrici Latini*. Oxford, 1964 (Oxford
Classical Text).
M. Schuster, revised R. Hanslik: *Letters and Panegyricus*. Teubner, 1958.
S. E. Stout: *Letters* I–X. Indiana, 1962.
A-M. Guillemin: *Lettres* I–IX (with notes and French
translation) 3 vols. Budé edition, Paris, 1927–8.
M. Durry: *Lettres X et Panégyrique* (with notes and
French translation). Budé edition, Paris, 1959.

Commentaries

M. Durry: *Pline le Jeune: Panégyrique de Trajan.*
Paris, 1938.
E. G. Hardy: *Pliny's Correspondence with Trajan.*
London, 1889.
A-M. Guillemin: *Notes in Budé edition* (see above).
A. N. Sherwin-White: *The Letters of Pliny.* Oxford,
1966. (S-W)

The following lists are selective, containing generally accessible books and recent articles in which information relative to Pliny can be found.

BIBLIOGRAPHY

Books

Cambridge Ancient History Vol. XI: *The Imperial Peace.* Cambridge, 1936 (esp. Ch. V by R. P. Longden " Nerva and Trajan ").

J. Carcopino: *Daily Life in Ancient Rome.* London, 1941 (Paperback edition).

G. E. F. Chilver: *Cisalpine Gaul.* Oxford, 1941.

J. Crook: *Consilium Principis.* Cambridge, 1955.

H. Dessau: *Inscriptiones Latinae Selectae.* Berlin, 1892–1916. (ILS)

A-M. Guillemin: *Pline et la Vie littéraire de son Temps.* Paris, 1929.

G. Highet: *Juvenal the Satirist.* Oxford, 1954.

A. H. M. Jones: *The Greek City.* Oxford, 1940.

H. Mattingly: *Catalogue of Roman Coins in the British Museum.* Vol. III. Nerva-Trajan. 1936.

M. McCrum and A. G. Woodhead: *Documents of the Flavian Emperors.* Cambridge, 1961. (MW)

A. N. Sherwin-White: *Roman Citizenship.* Oxford, 1939.

Roman Society and Roman Law in the New Testament. Oxford, 1963.

E. M. Smallwood: *Documents of Nerva, Trajan and Hadrian.* Cambridge, 1966. (S)

S. E. Stout: *Scribe and Critic at work in Pliny's Letters.* Indiana, 1954.

R. Syme: *Tacitus.* 2 Vols. Oxford, 1958. (Syme).

Articles

T. D. Barnes: " Legislation against the Christians," *JRS* LVIII, 1968.

BIBLIOGRAPHY

P. A. Brunt: " Charges of Provincial Maladministration," *Historia* X, 1961.

" The Revolt of Vindex and Fall of Nero," *Latomus* XVIII, 1959.

R. T. Bruère: " Tacitus and Pliny's Panegyricus," *Class. Phil.* XLIX, 1954.

A. Cameron: " The Fate of Pliny's letters in the late Empire," *C.Q.* XV, 1965.

" Pliny's Letters in the Later Empire: an Addendum," *C.Q.* XVII. 2. 1967.

R. Duncan-Jones: " The Finances of the Younger Pliny," *PBSR* XXXIII, 1965.

G. P. Goold: Review of O.C.T. of *Letters*, *Phoenix* XVIII, 1964.

J. C. Hainsworth: " Verginius and Vindex," *Historia* XI, 1962.

M. Hammond: " Pliny the Younger's views on government," *Class. Phil.* XLIX, 1954.

T. F. Higham: " Dolphin Riders, " *Greece & Rome* VII. 1, 1960.

S. Jameson: " Cornutus Tertullus and the Plancii of Perge," *JRS* LV, 1965.

C. P. Jones: Review of Sherwin-White's *Letters of Pliny*, Phoenix XXII, 1968.

" Julius Naso and Julius Secundus," *Class. Phil.* LXXII, 1968.

" Sura and Seneco," *JRS* LX, 1970.

C. J. Kraemer: " Pliny and the early church service," *Class. Phil.* XXIX, 1934.

H. Last: " The study of the persecutions," *JRS* XXVII, 1937.

BIBLIOGRAPHY

R. P. Longden: " Notes on the Parthian campaigns of Trajan," *JRS* XXI, 1931.

Wm. C. McDermott: " Pliniana, " *AJP* XC, 3, 1969.

" Fabricius Veiento, " *AJP* XCI, 2, 1970.

F. Millar: reviews A. N. S.-W. *Letters of Pliny*, *JRS* LVII, 1968.

S. L. Mohler: " Bithynian Christians," *Class. Phil.* XXX, 1935.

B. Radice: " A fresh approach to Pliny's letters," *Greece and Rome* IX. 2, 1962.

" Pliny and the Panegyricus," *Greece and Rome* XV, 2, 1968.

G. E. M. de Ste. Croix: " Why were the Early Christians Persecuted ? " *Past and Present*, 26, 1963.

" Rejoinder to A. N. S-W's Amendment," *Past and Present*, 27, 1964.

A. N. Sherwin-White: " The date of Pliny's Praetorship," [1] *JRS* XLVII, 1957.

" Trajan's replies to Pliny: authorship and necessity," *JRS* LII, 1962.

" Early persecutions and the Roman Law, *J. Theol. Studies*, N.S. III (2), 1952.

D. C. A. Shotter: " Tacitus and Verginius Rufus." *C.Q.* XVII. 2, 1967.

S. E. Stout: " The Coalescence of the Two Plinies," *Trans. Am. Phil. Ass.* LXXXVI, 1955.

F. A. Sullivan S. J.: " Pliny *Epistulae* VI. 16 and 20 and modern Volcanology." *Class. Phil.* LXIII. 3, 1968.

[1] Appendices IV and V in *Letters of Pliny*.

BIBLIOGRAPHY

R. Syme: " The Imperial Finances of Domitian,
 Nerva and Trajan," *JRS* XX, 1930.
 " Review of Durry's *Panegyricus*," *JRS* XXVIII,
 1938.
 " The Friend of Tacitus," *JRS* XLVII, 1957.
 " The Lower Danube under Trajan," *JRS* XLIX,
 1959.
 " Pliny's less Successful Friends," *Historia* X, 1961.
 " Pliny and the Dacian Wars," *Latomus* XXIII,
 1964.
 " People in Pliny," *JRS* LVIII, 1968.
G. B. Townend: " The Hippo Inscription and Career
 of Suetonius," *Historia* X, 1961.
H. W. Traub: " Pliny's Treatment of History in
 Epistolary Form," *Trans. Amer. Phil. Ass.*
 LXXXVI, 1955.
K. H. Waters: " The Character of Domitian,"
 Phoenix XVIII, 1964.

THE LETTERS OF PLINY

BOOK I

C. PLINII CAECILII SECUNDI
EPISTULARUM

LIBER PRIMUS

I

C. Plinius Septicio ⟨Claro⟩ Suo S.

1 Frequenter hortatus es ut epistulas, si quas paulo curatius[1] scripsissem, colligerem publicaremque. Collegi non servato temporis ordine (neque enim historiam componebam), sed ut quaeque in manus 2 venerat. Superest ut nec te consilii nec me paeniteat obsequii. Ita enim fiet, ut eas quae adhuc neglectae iacent requiram et si quas addidero non supprimam. Vale.

II

C. Plinius ⟨Maturo⟩ Arriano Suo S.

1 Quia tardiorem adventum tuum prospicio, librum quem prioribus epistulis promiseram exhibeo. Hunc

---

[1] curatius γ: accuratius β: cura maiore α.

---

[1] Brief information about persons is given in the Index, Volume II, p. 557.

THE LETTERS OF PLINY

BOOK I

I

To Septicius Clarus [1]

You have often urged me to collect and publish
any letters of mine which were composed with some
care. I have now made a collection, not keeping to
the original order as I was not writing history, but
taking them as they came to my hand. It remains
for you not to regret having made the suggestion and
for me not to regret following it; for then I shall set
about recovering any letters which have hitherto been
put away and forgotten, and I shall not suppress any
which I may write in future.[2]

II

To Maturus Arrianus

I see that your arrival is going to be later than I
expected, so I am presenting you with the speech

[2] A dedicatory letter, comparable with Quintilian's to the
librarian Trypho, and those of Statius to each book of the
Silvae.

rogo ex consuetudine tua et legas et emendes, eo
magis quod nihil ante peraeque eodem ζήλῳ scripsisse
2 videor. Temptavi enim imitari Demosthenen semper tuum, Calvum nuper meum, dumtaxat figuris
orationis; nam vim tantorum virorum, 'pauci quos
3 aequus . . .' adsequi possunt. Nec materia ipsa
huic (vereor ne improbe dicam) aemulationi repug-
navit: erat enim prope tota in contentione dicendi,
quod me longae desidiae indormientem excitavit, si
4 modo is sum ego qui excitari possim. Non tamen
omnino Marci nostri ληκύθους fugimus, quotiens
paulum itinere decedere non intempestivis amoeni-
tatibus admonebamur: acres enim esse non tristes
5 volebamus. Nec est quod putes me sub hac excep-
tione veniam postulare. Nam quo magis intendam
limam tuam, confitebor et ipsum me et contubernales
ab editione non abhorrere, si modo tu fortasse errori
6 nostro album calculum adieceris. Est enim plane
aliquid edendum—atque utinam hoc potissimum
quod paratum est! audis desidiae votum—edendum
autem ex pluribus causis, maxime quod libelli quos
emisimus dicuntur in manibus esse, quamvis iam
gratiam novitatis exuerint; nisi tamen auribus nostris
bibliopolae blandiuntur. Sed sane blandiantur, dum
per hoc mendacium nobis studia nostra commendent.
Vale.

---

[1] C. Calvus, the poet often linked with Catullus, here cited
as a model for the " pure " Attic style of oratory; cf. Cicero,
Brutus 283.

which I promised you in my last letter. Please read and correct it as you always do, and the more so because I don't think I have written before with quite so much spirit. I have tried to model myself on Demosthenes, as you always do, and lately on my favourite Calvus,[1] though only in figures of speech; for the fire of great men like these can only be caught by " the favoured few." [2] If I may venture to say so, the subject-matter actually encouraged my ambitious effort; for I had to fight my way most of the time,[3] and this shook me out of my usual lazy habits, as far as anything can shake up a man like me. However, I didn't altogether abandon the "lavish colouring "[4] of our master Cicero whenever I felt like making a pleasant deviation from my main path, for I did not want the force of my argument to lack all light relief.

You must not think that I am asking you to be indulgent on this account. To sharpen your critical powers I must confess that my friends and I are thinking of publishing it, if only you cast your vote for the proposal, mistaken though it may be. I must publish something, and I only hope and pray that the most suitable thing is what is ready now—there's laziness for you! But I want to publish for several reasons, and above all because the books which I have already sent out into the world are still said to find readers although they have lost the charm of novelty. Of course, the booksellers may be flattering me; well, let them, as long as their deception makes me think well of my own work.

[2] Virgil, *Aeneid* VI. 129.
[3] Perhaps this is the forensic speech referred to in II. 5.
[4] Cicero, *Ep. ad Att.* I. 14. 5; Horace, *Ars Poet.* 97.

III

C. Plinius Caninio Rufo Suo S.

1 Quid agit Comum, tuae meaeque deliciae? quid
suburbanum amoenissimum, quid illa porticus verna
semper, quid platanon opacissimus, quid euripus
viridis et gemmeus, quid subiectus et serviens lacus,
quid illa mollis et tamen solida gestatio, quid balineum illud quod plurimus sol implet et circumit, quid
triclinia illa popularia illa paucorum, quid cubicula
diurna nocturna? Possident te et per vices parti-
2 untur? an, ut solebas, intentione rei familiaris
obeundae crebris excursionibus avocaris? Si possident, felix beatusque es; si minus, "unus ex multis".
3 Quin tu (tempus enim) humiles et sordidas curas
aliis mandas, et ipse te in alto isto pinguique secessu
studiis adseris? Hoc sit negotium tuum hoc otium;
hic labor haec quies; in his vigilia, in his etiam
4 somnus reponatur. Effinge aliquid et excude, quod
sit perpetuo tuum. Nam reliqua rerum tuarum post
te alium atque alium dominum sortientur, hoc num-
5 quam tuum desinet esse si semel coeperit. Scio
quem animum, quod horter ingenium; tu modo
enitere ut tibi ipse sis tanti, quanti videberis aliis si
tibi fueris. Vale.

6

III

To Caninius Rufus

I wonder how our darling Comum is looking, and your lovely house outside the town, with its colonnade where it is always springtime, and the shady plane trees, the stream with its sparkling greenish water flowing into the lake below, and the drive over the smooth firm turf. Your baths which are full of sunshine all day, the dining-rooms for general or private use, the bedrooms for night or the day's siesta—are you there and enjoying them all in turn, or are you as usual for ever being called away to look after your affairs? If you are there, you are a lucky man to be so happy; if not, you do no better than the rest of us.

But isn't it really time you handed over those tiresome petty duties to someone else and shut yourself up with your books in the complete peace and comfort of your retreat? This is what should be both business and pleasure, work and recreation, and should occupy your thoughts awake and asleep! Create something, perfect it to be yours for all time; for everything else you possess will fall to one or another master after you are dead, but this will never cease to be yours once it has come into being. I know the spirit and ability I am addressing, but you must try now to have the high opinion of yourself which the world will come to share if you do.

IV

C. Plinius Pompeiae Celerinae Socrui S.

1 Quantum copiarum in Ocriculano, in Narniensi, in Carsulano, in Perusino tuo, in Narniensi vero etiam balineum! Ex epistulis meis, nam iam tuis opus 2 non est: una illa brevis et vetus sufficit. Non mehercule tam mea sunt quae mea sunt, quam quae tua; hoc tamen differunt, quod sollicitius et intentius tui me quam mei excipiunt. Idem fortasse 3 eveniet tibi, si quando in nostra deverteris. Quod velim facias, primum ut perinde nostris rebus ac nos tuis perfruaris, deinde ut mei expergiscantur aliquando, qui me secure ac prope neglegenter exspec4 tant. Nam mitium dominorum apud servos ipsa consuetudine metus exolescit; novitatibus excitantur, probarique dominis per alios magis quam per ipsos laborant. Vale.

V

C. Plinius Voconio Romano Suo S.

1 Vidistine quemquam M. Regulo timidiorem humiliorem post Domitiani mortem? sub quo non minora flagitia commiserat quam sub Nerone sed tectiora. Coepit vereri ne sibi irascerer, nec falle-

---

[1] All in Umbria (Otricoli, Narni, Consigliano), on the Via Flaminia.

[2] In Etruria (Perugia), on the way to P.'s house at Tifernum.

[3] M. Aquilius Regulus, a leading advocate of his day,

IV

To Pompeia Celerina, his mother-in-law

What treasures you have in your house at Ocriculum, Narnia, Carsulae,[1] and Perusia[2]—even baths at Narnia! All I have to do is to send a letter, and there is no need for you to write after the short note you sent there some time ago. In fact your property seems more mine than my own, but with this difference: I have better service and attention from your servants than I do from mine. Perhaps you will have the same experience if you ever stay with us, as I hope you will for two reasons; you could enjoy our possessions as if they were yours, and my household would have to bestir itself at long last—it is unconcerned to the point of indifference in the way it treats me. Slaves lose all fear of a considerate master once they are used to him, but they wake up at the sight of new faces and try to win his favour by giving his guests the service due to him.

V

To Voconius Romanus

Have you seen anyone so abject and nervous as Regulus[3] since Domitian's death? It has put an end to his misdeeds (which were as bad as in Nero's day, though latterly better concealed), and made him afraid I was annoyed with him, and rightly so; I *was*

admired by some of his contemporaries but consistently attacked by P.; see Martial II. 74; VI. 38.

2 batur: irascebar. Rustici Aruleni periculum foverat,
exsultaverat morte; adeo ut librum recitaret publi-
caretque, in quo Rusticum insectatur atque etiam
" Stoicorum simiam " adpellat, adicit " Vitelliana
cicatrice stigmosum " (agnoscis eloquentiam Reguli),
3 lacerat Herennium Senecionem tam intemperanter
quidem, ut dixerit ei Mettius Carus " Quid tibi cum
meis mortuis? Numquid ego Crasso aut Camerino
molestus sum? " quos ille sub Nerone accusaverat.
4 Haec me Regulus dolenter tulisse credebat, ideoque
etiam cum recitaret librum non adhibuerat. Praeterea reminiscebatur, quam capitaliter ipsum me
5 apud centumviros lacessisset. Aderam Arrionillae
Timonis uxori, rogatu Aruleni Rustici; Regulus
contra. Nitebamur nos in parte causae sententia
Metti Modesti optimi viri: is tunc in exsilio erat,
a Domitiano relegatus. Ecce tibi Regulus " Quaero,"
inquit, " Secunde, quid de Modesto sentias." Vides
quod periculum, si respondissem " bene "; quod
flagitium si " male ". Non possum dicere aliud tunc
mihi quam deos adfuisse. " Respondebo " inquam
" si de hoc centumviri iudicaturi sunt." Rursus ille:
" Quaero, quid de Modesto sentias." Iterum ego:
6 " Solebant testes in reos, non in damnatos interro-
gari." Tertio ille: " Non iam quid de Modesto, sed
7 quid de pietate Modesti sentias quaero." " Quaeris "

---

[1] For the " Stoic Opposition " see p. xiv.
[2] As praetor in 69 Rusticus had led a deputation from

annoyed. He had helped with the prosecution of
Arulenus Rusticus[1] and proclaimed his delight in
Rusticus's death by giving a public reading of his
speech against him (which he afterwards published)
where he used the words "Stoics' ape" "branded
with Vitellius's mark."[2] (You will recognize his
style of rhetoric.) Then he took to abusing Herennius Senecio with such violence that Mettius Carus
said to him "What are my dead men to you? Have
I ever attacked Crassus or Camerinus?"[3] (two
of Regulus's victims in Nero's time). Guessing
how strongly I felt about all this, Regulus did not
even invite me to his reading. He must have remembered too the deadly trap he laid for me in the
Centumviral Court, when Arulenus Rusticus had
asked me to support Arrionilla, Timon's wife, with
Regulus against me. Part of our case depended
on the opinion of Mettius Modestus, the eminent
senator who had been banished by Domitian and
was still in exile. Up gets Regulus: "Tell me,
Pliny, what is your opinion of Modestus?" Now you
can see the danger if I gave a good one, and the disgrace if I did not. I can only say the gods must have
been with me then. "I will give my opinion," said
I, "if the court is to pass judgement on this man."
He then repeated his request for my opinion.
"Witnesses used to be cross-examined about persons
on trial," I replied, "not on those already convicted."
"Never mind then, what you think of Modestus," he

the Senate to the Flavians after the defeat of Vitellius:
Tacitus, *Hist.* III. 80.
 [3] For M. Licinius Crassus Frugi and Q. Sulpicius Camerinus,
see Index.

inquam " quid sentiam; at ego ne interrogare quidem fas puto, de quo pronuntiatum est." Conticuit;
me laus et gratulatio secuta est, quod nec famam
meam aliquo responso utili fortasse, inhonesto tamen
laeseram, nec me laqueis tam insidiosae interrogation-
is involveram.

8   Nunc ergo conscientia exterritus adprehendit
Caecilium Celerem, mox Fabium Iustum; rogat ut
me sibi reconcilient. Nec contentus pervenit ad
Spurinnam; huic suppliciter, ut est cum timet
abiectissimus: " Rogo mane videas Plinium domi,
sed plane mane (neque enim ferre diutius sollicitudinem possum), et quoquo modo efficias, ne mihi iras-
catur." Evigilaveram; nuntius a Spurinna: " Venio
9 ad te." " Immo ego ad te." Coimus in porticum
Liviae,[1] cum alter ad alterum tenderemus. Exponit
Reguli mandata, addit preces suas, ut decebat
optimum virum pro dissimillimo, parce. Cui ego:
" Dispicies   ipse   quid   renuntiandum   Regulo
10 putes. Te decipi a me non oportet. Exspecto
Mauricum " (nondum ab exsilio venerat): " ideo
nihil alterutram in partem respondere tibi possum,
facturus quidquid ille decreverit; illum enim esse
11 huius consilii ducem, me comitem decet." Paucos

---

[1] Built by Augustus on the slopes of the Esquiline, where
P. had his town house, III. 21. 5.

said (as a third effort). " I want your opinion of his loyalty." " I know you do," said I, " but I think it is quite improper even to put questions about a man on whom sentence has been passed." That silenced him. Afterwards I received praise and congratulations for not damaging my reputation by saving myself with an expedient but dishonourable reply, and for not falling into the trap of such a treacherous question.

So then he was terrified by the realization of what he had done, seized Caecilius Celer and Fabius Justus, and begged them to reconcile me to him. Not content with this, he called on Spurinna and implored his help—he can be very humble when he is afraid. " Please see Pliny at his home in the morning—early in the morning, please, I can't bear the suspense any longer—and somehow stop him being angry with me." I was awake when the message came from Spurinna that he was on the way, and sent back to say *I* would call on *him*; so we met in the colonnade of Livia,[1] each making for the other. Spurinna repeated Regulus's request and put in a plea of his own, but being an honest man acting on behalf of a dishonest, said little. " You must decide yourself what answer to take back to Regulus," I said. " I can only tell you frankly that I am waiting for Mauricus "[2] (who had not yet returned from exile), " and so can't give you an answer either way, since I must do what he decides. The decision must be his, and I shall abide by it."

A few days after this Regulus and I met on an

[2] Junius Mauricus, brother of Junius Arulenus Rusticus. He returned in 97.

post dies ipse me Regulus convenit in praetoris officio; illuc persecutus secretum petit; ait timere se ne animo meo penitus haereret, quod in centumvirali iudicio aliquando dixisset, cum responderet mihi et Satrio Rufo: "Satrius Rufus, cui non est cum Cicerone aemulatio et qui contentus est eloquentia
12 saeculi nostri." Respondi nunc me intellegere maligne dictum quia ipse confiteretur, ceterum potuisse honorificum existimari. "Est enim" inquam "mihi cum Cicerone aemulatio, nec sum
13 contentus eloquentia saeculi nostri; nam stultissimum credo ad imitandum non optima quaeque proponere. Sed tu qui huius iudicii meministi, cur illius oblitus es, in quo me interrogasti, quid de Metti Modesti pietate sentirem?" Expalluit notabiliter, quamvis palleat semper, et haesitabundus: "Interrogavi non ut tibi nocerem, sed ut Modesto." Vide hominis crudelitatem, qui se non dissimulet exsuli
14 nocere voluisse. Subiunxit egregiam causam: "Scripsit" inquit "in epistula quadam, quae apud Domitianum recitata est: 'Regulus, omnium bipedum nequissimus'"; quod quidem Modestus veris-
15 sime scripserat. Hic fere nobis sermonis terminus; neque enim volui progredi longius, ut mihi omnia libera servarem dum Mauricus venit. Nec me praeterit esse Regulum δυσκαθαίρετον; est enim locuples factiosus, curatur a multis, timetur a pluri-
16 bus, quod plerumque fortius amore est. Potest tamen fieri ut haec concussa labantur; nam gratia malorum tam infida est quam ipsi. Verum, ut idem saepius

official visit to the praetor;[1] he came up to me and asked to see me alone. He said he was afraid that something he had once said in court in reply to Satrius Rufus and myself was still rankling in my mind: " Satrius Rufus, who makes no attempt to copy Cicero, and is satisfied with the standard of oratory today." I replied that now that he admitted it, I realized that the remark was offensive, but that it could have been taken as a compliment. " Personally I do try to copy Cicero," I said, " and am *not* satisfied with the oratory of today. It seems to me foolish not to model oneself on the highest standards. But if you remember this case, why have you forgotten the one where you asked me for my opinion of Mettius Modestus's loyalty? " He grew noticeably even paler than usual, and then stammered out, " The question was meant to damage Modestus, not you." (See the cruelty of the man who admits he intended to damage someone in exile.) Then he proffered a fine reason: " He said in a letter which was read out before Domitian that Regulus was ' the vilest of two-legged creatures.' " Modestus never wrote a truer word!

This practically ended our conversation, for I did not wish to prolong it and have to commit myself before Mauricus arrived. I am well aware that Regulus is hard to come to grips with; he is rich, influential, backed by many people and feared by more, and fear usually brings more support than popularity. However, it is quite possible that these props may collapse and let him down, for a bad man's popularity

[1] The ceremonial opening to the praetor's term of office on 1 January, similar to that of the consul referred to in IX. 37.

dicam, exspecto Mauricum. Vir est gravis prudens, multis experimentis eruditus, et qui futura possit ex praeteritis providere. Mihi et temptandi aliquid et
17 quiescendi illo auctore ratio constabit. Haec tibi scripsi, quia aequum erat te pro amore mutuo non solum omnia mea facta dictaque, verum etiam consilia cognoscere. Vale.

VI

C. PLINIUS CORNELIO TACITO SUO S.

1 RIDEBIS, et licet rideas. Ego, ille quem nosti, apros tres et quidem pulcherrimos cepi. "Ipse?" inquis. Ipse; non tamen ut omnino ab inertia mea et quiete discederem. Ad retia sedebam; erat in proximo non venabulum aut lancea, sed stilus et pugillares; meditabar aliquid enotabamque, ut si
2 manus vacuas, plenas tamen ceras reportarem. Non est quod contemnas hoc studendi genus; mirum est ut animus agitatione motuque corporis excitetur; iam undique silvae et solitudo ipsumque illud silentium quod venationi datur, magna cogitationis inci-
3 tamenta sunt. Proinde cum venabere, licebit auctore me ut panarium et lagunculam sic etiam pugillares feras: experieris non Dianam magis montibus quam Minervam inerrare. Vale.

---

¹ This letter appears to have been written before P.'s speech in the Senate in vindication of Helvidius Priscus in 97; cf. IX. 13. He decided against attacking Regulus.

is as fickle as himself. But let me repeat, I am waiting for Mauricus. His opinions carry weight and his wisdom is gained from experience, so that he can judge the future by the past. My own plans for attack or withdrawal will depend on his decision,[1] but I am writing all this to you because, as a good friend, you ought to hear about my intentions as well as anything I have said and done.

VI

To Cornelius Tacitus

I know you will think it a good joke, as indeed you may, when I tell you that your old friend has caught three boars, very fine ones too. Yes, I really did, and without even changing any of my lazy holiday habits. I was sitting by the hunting nets with writing materials by my side instead of hunting spears, thinking something out and making notes, so that even if I came home emptyhanded I should at least have my notebooks filled. Don't look down on mental activity of this kind, for it is remarkable how one's wits are sharpened by physical exercise; the mere fact of being alone in the depths of the woods in the silence necessary for hunting is a positive stimulus to thought. So next time you hunt yourself, follow my example and take your notebooks along with your lunch-basket and flask; you will find that Minerva walks the hills just as much as Diana.[2]

[2] Written from his home in the Apennines; cf. V. 6.

VII

C. Plinius Octavio Rufo Suo S.

1 Vide in quo me fastigio collocaris, cum mihi idem
potestatis idemque regni dederis quod Homerus
Iovi Optimo Maximo: τῷ δ᾽ ἕτερον μὲν ἔδωκε πατήρ,
2 ἕτερον δ᾽ ἀνένευσεν. Nam ego quoque simili nutu
ac renutu respondere voto tuo possum. Etenim,
sicut fas est mihi, praesertim te exigente, excusare
Baeticis contra unum hominem advocationem, ita nec
fidei nostrae nec constantiae quam diligis convenit,
adesse contra provinciam quam tot officiis, tot
laboribus, tot etiam periculis meis aliquando devin-
3 xerim. Tenebo ergo hoc temperamentum, ut ex
duobus, quorum alterutrum petis, eligam id potius,
in quo non solum studio tuo verum etiam iudicio
satisfaciam. Neque enim tantopere mihi consideran-
dum est, quid vir optimus in praesentia velis, quam
4 quid semper sis probaturus. Me circa idus Octobris
spero Romae futurum, eademque haec praesentem
quoque tua meaque fide Gallo confirmaturum; cui
tamen iam nunc licet spondeas de animo meo ἦ καὶ
5 κυανέῃσιν ἐπ᾽ ὀφρύσι νεῦσε. Cur enim non usque-
quaque Homericis versibus agam tecum? quatenus
tu me tuis agere non pateris, quorum tanta cupiditate
ardeo, ut videar mihi hac sola mercede posse corrum-
6 pi, ut vel contra Baeticos adsim. Paene praeterii,

---

[1] Homer, *Iliad* XVI. 250.
[2] *e.g.* he prosecuted Baebius Massa on behalf of the Baetici
in 93, assisted by Herennius Senecio who was afterwards
executed by Domitian. VI. 29. 8; VII. 33.
[3] *Iliad* I. 528. The individual mentioned here is unknown.

VII

To Octavius Rufus

See what a pinnacle you have set me on, giving me
the same power and majesty as Homer gives to
Jupiter Best and Highest: "And part the Father
granted him, but part denied."[1] You see I can use the
same mixture of assent and denial in answer to your
plea. I can very properly agree, especially as you
ask me, not to act for the Baetici against a single
individual; but it would hardly be consistent with
the unfailing sense of duty you admire in me to act
against them, when I have formed a close connexion
with their province through so many different services
rendered and all the risks I have run on their behalf at
various times.[2] I shall therefore have to steer a
middle course, and choose from the alternatives you
offer something which will satisfy your good judgement as well as your inclinations. It is not your
present wishes which I have to consider so much as
your high standards for what will have your permanent approval.

I hope to be in Rome round the middle of October
when I can explain my position to Gallus in person,
with you to support me; but meanwhile you may
assure him of my intentions, " he spoke and bowed his
dark brows in assent."[3] I feel like addressing you in
Homeric verses whenever I can, as long as you will not
let me quote your own[4]—a privilege I covet so much
that I believe it would be the only bribe which would
induce me to act against the Baetici.

[4] cf. II. 10.

quod minime praetereundum fuit, accepisse me careo-
tas optimas, quae nunc cum ficis et boletis certandum
habent.   Vale.

VIII

C. Plinius Pompeio Saturnino Suo S.

1   Peropportune mihi redditae sunt litterae tuae
quibus flagitabas, ut tibi aliquid ex scriptis meis
mitterem, cum ego id ipsum destinassem.   Addidisti
ergo calcaria sponte currenti, pariterque et tibi
veniam recusandi laboris et mihi exigendi verecun-
2   diam sustulisti.   Nam nec me timide uti decet eo
quod oblatum est, nec te gravari quod depoposcisti.
Non est tamen quod ab homine desidioso aliquid
novi operis exspectes.   Petiturus sum enim ut rursus
vaces sermoni quem apud municipes meos habui
3   bibliothecam dedicaturus.   Memini quidem te iam
quaedam adnotasse, sed generaliter; ideo nunc
rogo ut non tantum universitati eius attendas, verum
etiam particulas qua soles lima persequaris.   Erit
enim et post emendationem liberum nobis vel publi-
4   care vel continere.   Quin immo fortasse hanc ipsam
cunctationem nostram in alterutram sententiam
emendationis ratio deducet, quae aut indignum

---

[1] P. was a generous benefactor to Comum; cf. *App.* A. I,
S. 230.

I have nearly left out the most important thing: thank you for your excellent dates, which are now having to compete with my own figs and mushrooms.

VIII

To Pompeius Saturninus

Your letter asking me to send you one of my recent compositions reached me at a good moment, when I had just decided to do that very thing. So you have spurred on a willing horse and removed any excuse you had for refusing the trouble of reading my work as well as my scruples about asking you to do so; I can hardly be expected to hesitate about availing myself of your offer, nor can you feel this a burden when you asked for it yourself. All the same, you must not expect anything new from a lazy man like me. I intend to ask you to spare another look at the speech I delivered to my fellow-citizens at the official opening of the library at Comum.[1] I have not forgotten that you have already made some general comments on it, so this time will you please apply your usual critical eye to the details as well as to the work as a whole. I can then revise it before committing myself whether to publish or suppress it, and possibly the very process of revision will force me to make up my mind at last, and frequent rehandling will either show the speech is not yet fit for publication or actually make it so.

And yet it is the actual subject-matter rather than my treatment of it which is holding me back in this way. It makes me seem rather carried away by my own praises, and this will increase my diffidence even

editione dum saepius retractat inveniet, aut dignum
5 dum id ipsum experitur efficiet. Quamquam huius
cunctationis meae causae non tam in scriptis quam
in ipso materiae genere consistunt: est enim paulo
quasi gloriosius et elatius. Onerabit hoc modestiam
nostram, etiamsi stilus ipse pressus demissusque
fuerit, propterea quod cogimur cum de munificentia
6 parentum nostrorum tum de nostra disputare. An-
ceps hic et lubricus locus est, etiam cum illi necessitas
lenocinatur. Etenim si alienae quoque laudes parum
aequis auribus accipi solent, quam difficile est obtin-
ere, ne molesta videatur oratio de se aut de suis
disserentis! Nam cum ipsi honestati tum aliquanto
magis gloriae eius praedicationique invidemus,
atque ea demum recte facta minus detorquemus et
carpimus, quae in obscuritate et silentio reponuntur.
7 Qua ex causa saepe ipse mecum, nobisne tantum,
quidquid est istud, composuisse an et aliis debeamus.
Ut nobis, admonet illud, quod pleraque quae sunt
agendae rei necessaria, eadem peracta nec utilitatem
parem nec gratiam retinent.
8 Ac, ne longius exempla repetamus, quid utilius fuit
quam munificentiae rationem etiam stilo prosequi?
Per hoc enim adsequebamur, primum ut honestis
cogitationibus immoraremur, deinde ut pulchritudinem illarum longiore tractatu pervideremus, postremo ut subitae largitionis comitem paenitentiam
caveremus. Nascebatur ex his exercitatio quaedam
9 contemnendae pecuniae. Nam cum omnes homines
ad custodiam eius natura restrinxerit, nos contra
multum ac diu pensitatus amor liberalitatis communibus avaritiae vinculis eximebat, tantoque
laudabilior munificentia nostra fore videbatur, quod

22

if I keep to a terse and unassuming style, especially as I am obliged to dwell on my own generosity as well as that of my relatives. This puts me in a very difficult and delicate position, though somewhat justified by being inevitable. Even disinterested praise is very rarely well received, and it is all the harder to avoid a bad reception when a speaker refers to himself and his family. We feel resentment against merit unadorned, and still more when pride publishes it abroad; in fact it is only when good deeds are consigned to obscurity and silence that they escape criticism and misconstruction. For this reason I have often asked myself whether I ought to have written this speech, such as it is, for an audience at all; or done so only for my own benefit, seeing that there are many features which are essential when a matter is still in the process of preparation but lose their value and power to please once it is completed. To take the present case as an example of this: nothing could have been more valuable to me than to set out the reasons for my generosity. I was therefore enabled first to dwell on noble sentiments, then to discern their virtue by prolonged reflection, and so finally to avoid the reaction which follows on an impulsive handing-out of gifts. Thus too I trained myself to some extent to think less of my riches, for though we all seem to be born slaves to money-saving, my love of liberal giving, long and deeply reasoned, has freed me from these besetting bonds of avarice, and my generosity seems likely to win more praise because

ad illam non impetu quodam, sed consilio trahebâ-
10 mur. Accedebat his causis, quod non ludos aut
gladiatores sed annuos sumptus in alimenta ingenuorum pollicebamur. Oculorum porro et aurium voluptates adeo non egent commendatione, ut non tam
11 incitari debeant oratione quam reprimi; ut vero
aliquis libenter educationis taedium laboremque
suscipiat, non praemiis modo verum etiam exquisitis
12 adhortationibus impetrandum est. Nam si medici
salubres sed voluptate carentes cibos blandioribus
adloquiis prosequuntur, quanto magis decuit publice
consulentem utilissimum munus, sed non perinde
populare, comitate orationis inducere? praesertim
cum enitendum haberemus, ut quod parentibus
dabatur et orbis probaretur, honoremque paucorum
13 ceteri patienter et exspectarent et mererentur. Sed
ut tunc communibus magis commodis quam privatae
iactantiae studebamus, cum intentionem effectum-
que muneris nostri vellemus intellegi, ita nunc in
ratione edendi veremur, ne forte non aliorum
utilitatibus sed propriae laudi servisse videamur.

14 Praeterea meminimus quanto maiore animo honestatis fructus in conscientia quam in fama reponatur.
Sequi enim gloria, non adpeti debet, nec, si casu
aliquo non sequatur, idcirco quod gloriam meruit
15 minus pulchrum est. Ii vero, qui benefacta sua

---

[1] A further benefaction; cf. VII. 18. 2 and S. 230; and
Nerva's alimentary foundation in the Table of Velia, S. 436.

24

I was led to it from principle and not out of mere impulse.

I had also to consider the fact that in addition I was not paying for public games or a show of gladiators but making an annual contribution towards the maintenance of free-born children.[1] Pleasures for the ear and eye need no recommendation (in fact they are better restrained than encouraged in a public speech) but carefully chosen and persuasive words as well as material rewards are needed to prevail on anyone to submit willingly to the tedium and hard work involved in bringing up children. Doctors use soothing words to recommend a diet which will bring their patients better health though they may find it dull; still more had anyone acting in the public interest to find attractive phrases to introduce a beneficial service which would not be particularly popular. My own special difficulty was to make the childless appreciate the benefits gained by parents, so that the majority would be willing to wait and prove worthy of the privileges granted to a few. At the time, I was considering the general interest rather than my own self-glorification when I wished the purpose and effect of my benefaction to be known, but my present idea of publishing the speech may perhaps make me seem to be furthering my own reputation instead of benefiting others. I am also well aware that a nobler spirit will seek the reward of virtue in the consciousness of it, rather than in popular opinion. Fame should be the result, not the purpose of our conduct, and if for some reason it fails to follow, there is no less merit in cases where it was deserved. But, when people accompany their generous deeds with

verbis adornant, non ideo praedicare quia fecerint,
sed ut praedicarent fecisse creduntur. Sic quod
magnificum referente alio fuisset, ipso qui gesserat
recensente vanescit; homines enim cum rem des-
truere non possunt, iactationem eius incessunt. Ita
si silenda feceris, factum ipsum, si laudanda non
16 sileas, ipse culparis. Me vero peculiaris quaedam
impedit ratio. Etenim hunc ipsum sermonem non
apud populum, sed apud decuriones habui, nec in
17 propatulo sed in curia. Vereor ergo ut sit satis
congruens, cum in dicendo adsentationem vulgi
adclamationemque defugerim, nunc eadem illa
editione sectari, cumque plebem ipsam, cui consule-
batur, limine curiae parietibusque discreverim, ne
quam in speciem ambitionis inciderem, nunc eos
etiam, ad quos ex munere nostro nihil pertinet praeter
exemplum, velut obvia ostentatione conquirere.
18 Habes cunctationis meae causas; obsequar tamen
consilio tuo, cuius mihi auctoritas pro ratione sufficiet.
Vale.

IX

C. Plinius Minicio[1] Fundano Suo S.

1 Mirum est quam singulis diebus in urbe ratio aut
constet aut constare videatur, pluribus iunctisque

---

[1] Minicio *Mommsen*: Minucio β: *om.* αγ.

words, they are thought not to be proud of having performed them but to be performing them in order to have something to be proud of. So what would win a glowing tribute from an independent opinion soon loses it if accompanied by self-praise, for when men find an action unassailable they will criticize the doer for his pride in it; hence either your conduct is blamed for anything in it which is best passed over in silence, or you can be blamed just as much yourself for not keeping silent about your merits.

I have besides my individual difficulties. This was delivered not as a public speech in the open, but before the town council in their senate-house, so that I am afraid that it is hardly consistent at this point to court by publication the popular favour and applause which I avoided when I was speaking. I put the doors and walls of the senate-house between myself and the populace whom I was trying to benefit, so as not to appear to court their favour; but now I feel that I am going out of my way to display my powers and thus win over those whose sole concern with my benefaction rests in the example it sets.

These then are my reasons for hesitating in this way; but I know I can always depend on your good advice and should like to take it now.

IX

To Minicius Fundanus

It is extraordinary how, if one takes a single day spent in Rome, one can give a more or less accurate account of it, but scarcely any account at all of several

THE LETTERS OF PLINY

2 non constet. Nam si quem interroges " Hodie quid
egisti?," respondeat: " Officio togae virilis interfui,
sponsalia aut nuptias frequentavi, ille me ad signandum testamentum, ille in advocationem, ille in

3 consilium rogavit." Haec quo die feceris, necessaria,
eadem, si cotidie fecisse te reputes, inania videntur,
multo magis cum secesseris. Tunc enim subit
recordatio: " Quot dies quam frigidis rebus ab-

4 sumpsi!" Quod evenit mihi, postquam in Laurentino
meo aut lego aliquid aut scribo aut etiam corpori

5 vaco, cuius fulturis animus sustinetur. Nihil audio
quod audisse, nihil dico quod dixisse paeniteat;
nemo apud me quemquam sinistris sermonibus
carpit, neminem ipse reprehendo, nisi tamen me cum
parum commode scribo; nulla spe nullo timore sollici-
tor, nullis rumoribus inquietor: mecum tantum et

6 cum libellis loquor. O rectam sinceramque vitam!
O dulce otium honestumque ac paene omni negotio
pulchrius! O mare, o litus, verum secretumque
μουσεῖον, quam multa invenitis, quam multa dicta-

7 tis! Proinde tu quoque strepitum istum inanemque
discursum et multum ineptos labores, ut primum
fuerit occasio, relinque teque studiis vel otio trade.

8 Satius est enim, ut Atilius noster eruditissime simul et
facetissime dixit, otiosum esse quam nihil agere.
Vale.

---

[1] Senators with legal training were often in demand to
support the magistrates or the Emperor; cf. IV. 22; V. 1. 5.

28

days put together. If you ask anyone what he did that day, the answer would be: " I was present at a coming-of-age ceremony, a betrothal, or a wedding. I was called on to witness a will, to support someone in court or to act as assessor."[1] All this seems important on the actual day, but quite pointless if you consider that you have done the same sort of thing every day, and much more pointless if you think about it when you are out of town. It is then that you realize how many days you have wasted in trivialities.

I always realize this when I am at Laurentum,[2] reading and writing and finding time to take the exercise which keeps my mind fit for work. There is nothing there for me to say or hear said which I would afterwards regret, no one disturbs me with malicious gossip, and I have no one to blame—but myself— when writing doesn't come easily. Hopes and fears do not worry me, and I am not bothered by idle talk; I share my thoughts with myself and my books. It is a good life and a genuine one, a seclusion which is happy and honourable, more rewarding than almost any "business" can be. The sea and shore are truly my private Helicon, an endless source of inspiration. You should take the first opportunity yourself to leave the din, the futile bustle and useless occupations of the city and devote yourself to literature or to leisure. For it was wise as well as witty of our friend Atilius to say that it is better to have no work to do than to work at nothing.

[2] In Latium, near Ostia, at Vicus Augustanus; described in detail in II. 17.

X

C. Plinius Attio Clementi Suo S.

1 Si quando urbs nostra liberalibus studiis floruit,
2 nunc maxime floret. Multa claraque exempla sunt;
sufficeret unum, Euphrates philosophus. Hunc ego
in Syria, cum adulescentulus militarem, penitus et
domi inspexi, amarique ab eo laboravi, etsi non erat
laborandum. Est enim obvius et expositus, plenus-
3 que humanitate quam praecipit. Atque utinam
sic ipse quam spem tunc ille de me concepit impleve-
rim, ut ille multum virtutibus suis addidit! aut ego
4 nunc illas magis miror quia magis intellego. Quamquam ne nunc quidem satis intellego; ut enim de
pictore scalptore fictore nisi artifex iudicare, ita
5 nisi sapiens non potest perspicere sapientem. Quantum tamen mihi cernere datur, multa in Euphrate
sic eminent et elucent, ut mediocriter quoque doctos
advertant et adficiant. Disputat subtiliter graviter
ornate, frequenter etiam Platonicam illam sublimitatem et latitudinem effingit. Sermo est copiosus et
varius, dulcis in primis, et qui repugnantes quoque
6 ducat impellat. Ad hoc proceritas corporis, decora
facies, demissus capillus, ingens et cana barba; quae
licet fortuita et inania putentur, illi tamen plurimum

---

[1] For Euphrates, see Index.

X

To Attius Clemens

If Rome has ever given a home to the liberal arts, they can be said to flourish there today; from among the many distinguished persons who are proof of this I need only name the philosopher Euphrates.[1] When I was a young man doing my military service in Syria I came to know him well; I visited his home and took pains to win his affection, though that was hardly necessary as he has always been accessible and ready to make overtures, and is full of the courteous sympathy he teaches. I only wish I could have fulfilled the hopes he formed of me at that time in the same way that I feel he has increased his virtues; or perhaps it is my admiration which has increased now that I appreciate them better. I cannot claim to appreciate them fully even now, for if it takes an artist to judge painting, sculpture and modelling, only one philosopher can really understand another. But it is plain to my limited judgement that Euphrates has many remarkable gifts which make their appeal felt even by people of no more than average education. His arguments are subtle, his reasoning profound, and his words well-chosen, so that he often seems to have something of the sublimity and richness of Plato. He talks readily on many subjects with a special charm which can captivate and so convince the most reluctant listener. He is moreover tall and distinguished to look at, with long hair and a flowing white beard, and though these may sound like natural advantages of no real importance, they help to make

7 venerationis adquirunt. Nullus horror in cultu,
nulla tristitia, multum severitatis; reverearis occursum, non reformides. Vitae sanctitas summa;
comitas par: insectatur vitia non homines, nec
castigat errantes sed emendat. Sequaris monentem
attentus et pendens, et persuaderi tibi etiam cum
8 persuaserit cupias. Iam vero liberi tres, duo mares,
quos diligentissime instituit. Socer Pompeius Iulia-
nus, cum cetera vita tum vel hoc uno magnus et
clarus, quod ipse provinciae princeps inter altissi-
mas condiciones generum non honoribus principem,
sed sapientia elegit.

9 Quamquam quid ego plura de viro quo mihi frui
non licet? an ut magis angar quod non licet? Nam
distringor officio, ut maximo sic molestissimo:
sedeo pro tribunali, subnoto libellos, conficio tabulas,
10 scribo plurimas sed inlitteratissimas litteras. Soleo
non numquam (nam id ipsum quando contingit!)
de his occupationibus apud Euphraten queri. Ille
me consolatur, adfirmat etiam esse hanc philosophiae
et quidem pulcherrimam partem, agere negotium
publicum, cognoscere iudicare, promere et exercere
11 iustitiam, quaeque ipsi doceant in usu habere. Mihi
tamen hoc unum non persuadet, satius esse ista
facere quam cum illo dies totos audiendo discendoque

---

[1] Either at the *aerarium militare* or *aerarium Saturni.*

him widely respected. His dress is always neat, and his serious manner makes no show of austerity, so that your first reaction on meeting him would be admiration rather than repulsion. He leads a wholly blameless life while remaining entirely human; he attacks vices, not individuals, and aims at reforming wrongdoers instead of punishing them. You would follow his teaching with rapt attention, eager for him to continue convincing you long after you are convinced.

He has moreover three children, two of them sons whom he has brought up with the greatest care; and his father-in-law, Pompeius Julianus, who has had a career of great distinction as a leading citizen of his province, has particularly to his credit the fact that from among many excellent offers he chose a son-in-law who was outstanding rather for his learning than for any official position.

I don't know why I say so much about a man whose company I am never free to enjoy, unless it is to chafe the more against my loss of freedom. My time is taken up with official duties,[1] important but none the less tiresome. I sit on the bench, sign petitions, make up accounts, and write innumerable—quite unliterary—letters. Whenever I have the chance I complain about these duties to Euphrates, who consoles me by saying that anyone who holds public office, presides at trials and passes judgement, expounds and administers justice, and thereby puts into practice what the philosopher only teaches, has a part in the philosophic life and indeed the noblest part of all. But of one thing he can never convince me—that doing all this is better than spending whole days listening to his teaching and learning from him.

consumere. Quo magis te cui vacat hortor, cum in urbem proxime veneris (venias autem ob hoc maturius), illi te expoliendum limandumque permit-
12 tas. Neque enim ego ut multi invideo aliis bono quo ipse careo, sed contra: sensum quendam voluptatemque percipio, si ea quae mihi denegantur amicis video superesse. Vale.

XI

C. Plinius Fabio Iusto Suo S.

1 Olim mihi nullas epistulas mittis. Nihil est, inquis, quod scribam. At hoc ipsum scribe, nihil esse quod scribas, vel solum illud unde incipere priores
2 solebant: " Si vales, bene est; ego valeo." Hoc mihi sufficit; est enim maximum. Ludere me putas? serio peto. Fac sciam quid agas, quod sine sollicitudine summa nescire non possum. Vale.

XII

C. Plinius Calestrio Tironi Suo S.

1 Iacturam gravissimam feci, si iactura dicenda est tanti viri amissio. Decessit Corellius Rufus et quidem sponte, quod dolorem meum exulcerat. Est enim luctuosissimum genus mortis, quae non ex
2 natura nec fatalis videtur. Nam utcumque in illis qui morbo finiuntur, magnum ex ipsa necessitate solacium est; in iis vero quos accersita mors aufert,

---

[1] For L. Fabius Justus, see Index.
[2] The formula S.V.B.E.E.V., common in Cicero and by P.'s time outmoded.

All the more then do I urge you to let him take you in hand and polish you up next time you are in town; you do have time for this, and the prospect should speed up your coming. For unlike many people, I don't grudge others the advantages which I cannot have myself: on the contrary, I feel a real sense of pleasure if I see my friends enjoying the plenty which is denied to me.

XI

To Fabius Justus [1]

I have not heard from you for a long time, and you say you have nothing to write about. Well, you can at least write *that*—or else simply the phrase our elders used to start a letter with: " If you are well, well and good; I am well." [2] That will do for me— it is all that matters. Don't think I am joking; I mean it. Let me know how you are; if I don't know I can't help worrying a lot.

XII

To Calestrius Tiro

I have lost a very great man, if " loss " is the right word for such a bereavement. Corellius Rufus has died, and died by his own wish, which distresses me even more; for death is most tragic when it is not due to fate or natural causes. When we see men die of disease, at least we can find consolation in the knowledge that it is inevitable, but, when their end is self-sought, our grief is inconsolable because we feel that

hic insanabilis dolor est, quod creduntur potuisse diu
3 vivere. Corellium quidem summa ratio, quae
sapientibus pro necessitate est, ad hoc consilium compulit, quamquam plurimas vivendi causas habentem,
optimam conscientiam optimam famam, maximam
auctoritatem, praeterea filiam uxorem nepotem
4 sorores, interque tot pignora veros amicos. Sed
tam longa, tam iniqua valetudine conflictabatur, ut
haec tanta pretia vivendi mortis rationibus vinceren-
tur. Tertio et tricensimo anno, ut ipsum audiebam,
pedum dolore correptus est. Patrius hic illi; nam
plerumque morbi quoque per successiones quasdam
5 ut alia traduntur. Hunc abstinentia sanctitate,
quoad viridis aetas, vicit et fregit; novissime cum
senectute ingravescentem viribus animi sustinebat,
cum quidem incredibiles cruciatus et indignissima
6 tormenta pateretur. Iam enim dolor non pedibus
solis ut prius insidebat, sed omnia membra pervagaba-
tur. Veni ad eum Domitiani temporibus in subur-
7 bano iacentem. Servi e cubiculo recesserunt (habebat hoc moris, quotiens intrasset fidelior amicus);
quin etiam uxor quamquam omnis secreti capacis-
8 sima digrediebatur. Circumtulit oculos et " Cur "
inquit " me putas hos tantos dolores tam diu susti-
nere? ut scilicet isti latroni vel uno die supersim."
Dedisses huic animo par corpus fecisset quod optabat.
Adfuit tamen deus voto, cuius ille compos ut iam

their lives could have been long. Corellius, it is true, was led to make his decision by the supremacy of reason, which takes the place of inevitability for the philosophers; but he had many reasons for living, a good conscience and reputation, and wide influence, besides a wife and sisters living and a daughter and grandchild: and, as well as so many close relatives, he had many true friends. But he suffered so long from such a painful affliction that his reasons for dying outweighed everything that life could give him.

At the age of thirty-two, I have heard him say, he developed gout in the feet, just as his father had done; for like other characteristics, most diseases are hereditary. As long as he was young and active he could keep it under control by temperate living and strict continence, and latterly when he grew worse with advancing age, he bore up through sheer strength of mind, even when cruelly tortured by unbelievable agony; for the disease was now no longer confined to his feet as before, but was spreading through all his limbs. I went to see him in Domitian's time as he lay ill in his house outside Rome. His servants left the room, as they always had to when one of his more intimate friends came in, and even his wife went out, though she was well able to keep any secret. He looked all round the room before speaking and then: " Why do you suppose I endure pain like this so long ? " he said. " So that I can outlive that robber if only by a single day." Had his body been equal to his spirit he would have made sure that he had his desire.

However, the gods heard his prayer; and knowing it was granted he relaxed and felt free to die. He

securus liberque moriturus, multa illa vitae sed
9 minora retinacula abrupit.   Increverat valetudo,
quam temperantia mitigare temptavit; perseveran-
tem constantia fugit.   Iam dies alter tertius quartus:
abstinebat cibo.   Misit ad me uxor eius Hispulla
communem amicum C. Geminium cum tristissimo
nuntio, destinasse Corellium mori nec aut suis aut
filiae precibus inflecti; solum superesse me, a quo
10 revocari posset ad vitam. Cucurri. Perveneram in
proximum, cum mihi ab eadem Hispulla Iulius
Atticus nuntiat nihil iam ne me quidem impetraturum: tam obstinate magis ac magis induruisse.
Dixerat sane medico admoventi cibum: Κέκρικα,
quae vox quantum admirationis in animo meo tan-
11 tum desiderii reliquit. Cogito quo amico, quo viro
caream.   Implevit quidem annum septimum et
sexagensimum, quae aetas etiam robustissimis satis
longa est; scio. Evasit perpetuam valetudinem;
scio. Decessit superstitibus suis, florente re publica,
12 quae illi omnibus carior erat; et hoc scio. Ego
tamen tamquam et iuvenis et firmissimi mortem
doleo, doleo autem (licet me imbecillum putes) meo
nomine. Amisi enim, amisi vitae meae testem
rectorem magistrum.   In summa dicam, quod recenti
dolore contubernali meo Calvisio dixi: " Vereor ne
13 neglegentius vivam." Proinde adhibe solacia mihi,
non haec: " Senex erat, infirmus erat " (haec enim
novi), sed nova aliqua, sed magna, quae audierim
numquam, legerim numquam. Nam quae audivi

38

broke off all his links with life, now unable to hold
him, for his disease had progressed although he tried
to check it by his strict regimen; and, as it grew
steadily worse, he made up his mind to escape. Two
days passed, then three, then four, but he refused all
food. His wife, Hispulla, sent our friend Gaius
Geminius to me with the sad news that Corellius was
determined to die, and nothing she or her daughter
could say would dissuade him; I was the only person
left who might be able to recall him to life. I hurried
to him, and was nearly there when Julius Atticus
brought me another message from Hispulla that
even I could do nothing now as he had become more
and more fixed in his resolve. Indeed, when the
doctor offered him food he had only said " I have
made up my mind "; and these words bring home to
me how much I admired him and how I shall miss him
now. I keep thinking that I have lost a great friend
and a great man. I know he had lived to the end of
his sixty-seventh year, a good age even for a really
sound constitution: I know that he escaped from perpetual illness: I know too that he left a family to outlive him, and his country (which was still dearer to
him) in a prosperous state: and yet I mourn his death
as if he were a young man in full health. I mourn,
too, on my own account, though you may think this a
sign of weakness, for I have lost the guardian and
mentor who watched over my life. In short, as I said
to my friend Calvisius in my first outburst of grief, I
am afraid I shall be less careful how I live now.

Send me some words of comfort, but do not say that
he was an old man and ill; I know this. What I need
is something new and effective which I have never

legi sponte succurrunt, sed tanto dolore superantur.
Vale.

XIII

C. PLINIUS SOSIO SENECIONI SUO S.

1 MAGNUM proventum poetarum annus hic attulit:
toto mense Aprili nullus fere dies, quo non recitaret
aliquis. Iuvat me quod vigent studia, proferunt se
ingenia hominum et ostentant, tametsi ad audien-
2 dum pigre coitur. Plerique in stationibus sedent
tempusque audiendi fabulis conterunt, ac subinde sibi
nuntiari iubent, an iam recitator intraverit, an dixerit
praefationem, an ex magna parte evolverit librum;
tum demum ac tunc quoque lente cunctanterque
veniunt, nec tamen permanent, sed ante finem
recedunt, alii dissimulanter et furtim, alii simpliciter
3 et libere. At hercule memoria parentum Claudium
Caesarem ferunt, cum in Palatio spatiaretur audis-
setque clamorem, causam requisisse, cumque dictum esset recitare Nonianum, subitum recitanti
4 inopinatumque venisse. Nunc otiosissimus quisque
multo ante rogatus et identidem admonitus aut non
venit aut, si venit, queritur se diem (quia non per-
5 didit) [1] perdidisse. Sed tanto magis laudandi

----

[1] perdidit *Gierig*: perdiderit αβγ.

----

[1] M. Servilius Nonianus, the famous orator and patron of
Persius; cf. Tacitus *Ann.* XIV. 19.

heard nor read about before, for everything I have heard or read comes naturally to my aid, but is powerless against grief like this.

XIII

To Sosius Senecio

This year has raised a fine crop of poets; there was scarcely a day throughout the month of April when someone was not giving a public reading. I am glad to see that literature flourishes and there is a show of budding talent, in spite of the fact that people are slow to form an audience. Most of them sit about in public places, gossiping and wasting time when they could be giving their attention, and give orders that they are to be told at intervals whether the reader has come in and has read the preface, or is coming to the end of the book. It is not till that moment—and even then very reluctantly—that they come dawdling in. Nor do they stay very long, but leave before the end, some of them trying to slip away unobserved and others marching boldly out. And yet people tell how in our fathers' time the Emperor Claudius was walking on the Palatine when he heard voices and asked what was happening; on learning that Nonianus [1] was giving a reading he surprised the reader by joining the audience unannounced. Today the man with any amount of leisure, invited well in advance and given many a reminder, either never comes at all, or, if he does, complains that he has wasted a day—just because he has not wasted it. The more praise and honour then is due to those

41

probandique sunt, quos a scribendi recitandique
studio haec auditorum vel desidia vel superbia non
retardat. Equidem prope nemini defui. Erant
sane plerique amici; neque enim est fere quisquam,
6 qui studia, ut non simul et nos amet. His ex causis
longius quam destinaveram tempus in urbe con-
sumpsi. Possum iam repetere secessum et scribere
aliquid, quod non recitem, ne videar, quorum recitationibus adfui, non auditor fuisse sed creditor. Nam
ut in ceteris rebus ita in audiendi officio perit gratia
si reposcatur. Vale.

XIV

C. PLINIUS IUNIO MAURICO SUO S.

1   PETIS ut fratris tui filiae prospiciam maritum;
quod merito mihi potissimum iniungis. Scis enim
quanto opere summum illum virum suspexerim
dilexerimque, quibus ille adulescentiam meam exhortationibus foverit, quibus etiam laudibus ut
2 laudandus viderer effecerit. Nihil est quod a te
mandari mihi aut maius aut gratius, nihil quod
honestius a me suscipi possit, quam ut eligam iuvenem, ex quo nasci nepotes Aruleno Rustico deceat.
3 Qui quidem diu quaerendus fuisset, nisi paratus et
quasi provisus esset Minicius Acilianus, qui me ut
iuvenis iuvenem (est enim minor pauculis annis)
4 familiarissime diligit, reveretur ut senem. Nam ita

42

whose interest in writing and reading aloud is not damped by the idleness and conceit of their listeners.

Personally I have failed scarcely anyone, though I admit that most of the invitations came from my friends; for there are very few people who care for literature without caring for me too. That is why I stayed in town longer than I intended, but now I can return to my country retreat and write something myself. I shall not read it to my friends, for I don't want it to seem that I went to hear them with the intention of putting them in my debt. Here as elsewhere a duty performed deserves no gratitude if a return is expected.

XIV

To Junius Mauricus

You ask me to look out for a husband for your brother's daughter, a responsibility which I feel is very rightly mine; for you know how I have always loved and admired him as the finest of men, and how his advice was an influence on my early years and his praise made me appear to deserve it. You could not entrust me with anything which I value or welcome so much, nor could there be any more befitting duty for me than to select a young man worthy to be the father of Arulenus Rusticus's grandchildren.

I should have had a long search if Minicius Acilianus were not at hand, as if he were made for us. He loves me as warmly as one young man does another (he is a little younger than I am), but respects me as his elder, for he aspires to be influenced

43

formari a me et institui cupit, ut ego a vobis solebam.
Patria est ei Brixia,[1] ex illa nostra Italia quae multum
adhuc verecundiae frugalitatis, atque etiam rustici-
5 tatis antiquae, retinet ac servat. Pater Minicius
Macrinus, equestris ordinis princeps, quia nihil altius
voluit; adlectus enim a divo Vespasiano inter prae-
torios honestam quietem huic nostrae—ambitioni
6 dicam an dignitati?—constantissime praetulit. Habet
aviam maternam Serranam Proculam e municipio
Patavio.[2] Nosti loci mores: Serrana tamen Patavinis
quoque severitatis exemplum est. Contigit et
avunculus ei P. Acilius gravitate prudentia fide
prope singulari. In summa nihil erit in domo tota,
7 quod non tibi tamquam in tua placeat. Aciliano
vero ipsi plurimum vigoris industriae, quamquam in
maxima verecundia. Quaesturam tribunatum prae-
turam honestissime percucurrit, ac iam pro se tibi
8 necessitatem ambiendi remisit. Est illi facies
liberalis, multo sanguine multo rubore suffusa, est
ingenua totius corporis pulchritudo et quidam
senatorius decor. Quae ego nequaquam arbitror
neglegenda; debet enim hoc castitati puellarum
9 quasi praemium dari. Nescio an adiciam esse patri
eius amplas facultates. Nam cum imaginor vos
quibus quaerimus generum, silendum de facultatibus

---

[1] In Transpadane Italy (Brescia).
[2] Padua. For its provincial virtue, see Martial XI. 16;

and guided by me, as I was by you and your brother. His native place is Brixia,[1] one of the towns in our part of Italy which still retains intact much of its honest simplicity along with the rustic virtues of the past. His father is Minicius Macrinus, who chose to remain a leading member of the order of knights because he desired nothing higher; the deified Emperor Vespasian would have raised him to praetorian rank, but he has always steadfastly preferred a life of honest obscurity to our status—or, shall I say, to our struggles to gain it. His maternal grandmother, Serrana Procula, comes from the town of Patavium,[2] whose reputation you know; but Serrana is a model of propriety even to the Patavians. His uncle, Publius Acilius, is a man of exceptional character, wisdom and integrity. You will in fact find nothing to criticize in the whole household, any more than in your own.

Acilianus himself has abundant energy and application, but no lack of modesty. He has held the offices of quaestor, tribune and praetor with great distinction, thus sparing you the necessity of canvassing on his behalf. He has a frank expression, and his complexion is fresh and high-coloured; his general good looks have a natural nobility and the dignified bearing of a senator. (I personally think these points should be mentioned, as a sort of just return for a bride's virginity.) I am wondering whether to add that his father has ample means; for if I picture you and your brother for whom we are seeking a son-in-law, I feel no more need be said on the subject;

and perhaps Livy's *patavinitas* in Quintilian *Inst. Orat.* I. v. 56; VIII. i. 3.

puto; cum publicos mores atque etiam leges civitatis
intueor, quae vel in primis census hominum spectan-
dos arbitrantur, ne id quidem praetereundum videtur.   Et sane de posteris et his pluribus cogitanti, hic
quoque in condicionibus deligendis ponendus est
10 calculus.   Tu fortasse me putes indulsisse amori
meo, supraque ista quam res patitur sustulisse.   At
ego fide mea spondeo futurum ut omnia longe am-
pliora quam a me praedicantur invenias.   Diligo
quidem adulescentem ardentissime sicut meretur;
sed hoc ipsum amantis est, non onerare eum laudibus.
Vale.

XV

C. Plinius Septicio Claro Suo S.

1 Heus tu! promittis ad cenam, nec venis?   Dicitur
ius: ad assem impendium reddes, nec id modicum.
2 Paratae erant lactucae singulae, cochleae ternae,
ova bina, halica cum mulso et nive (nam hanc quoque computabis, immo hanc in primis quae perit in
ferculo), olivae betacei cucurbitae bulbi, alia mille
non minus lauta.   Audisses comoedos vel lectorem
3 vel lyristen vel (quae mea liberalitas) omnes.   At tu
apud nescio quem ostrea vulvas echinos Gaditanas
maluisti.   Dabis poenas, non dico quas.   Dure feci-
ti: invidisti, nescio an tibi, certe mihi, sed tamen et

---

[1] P. may be thinking of the senatorial census of 1,000,000
HS.

but in view of the prevailing habits of the day and the laws of the country which judge a man's income to be of primary importance,[1] perhaps after all it is something which should not be omitted. Certainly if one thinks of the children of the marriage, and subsequent generations, the question of money must be taken into account as a factor influencing our choice.

It may seem to you that I have been indulging my affection, and going further than the facts allow, but I assure you on my honour that you will find the reality far better than my description. I do indeed love the young man dearly, as he deserves, but, just because I love him, I would not overload him with praise.

XV

To Septicius Clarus

Who are you, to accept my invitation to dinner and never come? Here's your sentence, and you shall pay my costs in full, no small sum either. It was all laid out, one lettuce each, three snails, two eggs, wheat-cake, and wine with honey chilled with snow (you will reckon this too please, and as an expensive item, seeing that it disappears in the dish), besides olives, beetroots, gherkins, onions, and any number of similar delicacies. You would have heard a comic play, a reader or singer, or all three if I felt generous. Instead you chose to go where you could have oysters, sow's innards, sea-urchins, and Spanish dancing-girls. You will suffer for this—I won't say how. It was a cruel trick done to spite one of us—yourself or most likely me, and possibly both of us, if you think what a

tibi. Quantum nos lusissemus risissemus studuis-
4 semus! Potes adparatius cenare apud multos, nusquam hilarius simplicius incautius. In summa ex-
perire, et nisi postea te aliis potius excusaveris,
mihi semper excusa. Vale.

XVI

C. Plinius Erucio Suo S.

1 Amabam Pompeium Saturninum (hunc dico nostrum) laudabamque eius ingenium, etiam antequam
scirem, quam varium quam flexibile quam multiplex
esset; nunc vero totum me tenet habet possidet.
2 Audivi causas agentem acriter et ardenter, nec
minus polite et ornate, sive meditata sive subita pro-
ferret. Adsunt aptae crebraeque sententiae, gravis
et decora constructio, sonantia verba et antiqua.
Omnia haec mire placent cum impetu quodam et
3 flumine pervehuntur, placent si retractentur. Sen-
ties quod ego, cum orationes eius in manus sumpseris,
quas facile cuilibet veterum, quorum est aemulus,
4 comparabis. Idem tamen in historia magis satis-
faciet vel brevitate vel luce uel suavitate vel splen-
dore etiam et sublimitate narrandi. Nam in con-
tionibus eadem quae in orationibus vis est, pressior
5 tantum et circumscriptior et adductior. Praeterea

---

[1] The father, M. Erucius Clarus, rather than his son, Sex.
Erucius Clarus.

feast of fun, laughter and learning we were going to
have. You can eat richer food at many houses, but
nowhere with such free and easy enjoyment. All I
can say is, try me; and then, if you don't prefer to
decline invitations elsewhere, you can always make
excuses to me.

XVI

To Erucius Clarus[1]

I was always much attached to Pompeius Saturninus (I mean that friend of ours), and admired his
talents long before I knew how versatile, sensitive
and comprehensive they were. Now I am truly his,
to have and to hold.

I have heard him plead in court with subtlety and
fervour, and his speeches have the same finish and
distinction when impromptu as when they are prepared. His aphorisms are apt and ready, his periods
rounded with a formal dignity, his vocabulary im
pressive and classical. All of this I find peculiarly
satisfying when it is carried along on the full stream of
his oratory, and no less so when examined afresh.
You will feel the same when you have a chance to
handle his speeches and compare them with any one
of the older orators to whose standards he aspires.
His histories will please you even more by their conciseness and clarity, the charm and brilliance of their
style and their power of exposition, for the words he
puts into the mouths of his characters are as vivid as
his own public speeches, though condensed into a
simpler and terser style.

facit versus, quales Catullus meus aut Calvus, re
vera quales Catullus aut Calvus. Quantum illis
leporis dulcedinis amaritudinis amoris! inserit sane,
sed data opera, mollibus levibusque duriusculos
6 quosdam; et hoc quasi Catullus aut Calvus. Legit
mihi nuper epistulas; uxoris esse dicebat. Plautum
vel Terentium metro solutum legi credidi. Quae sive
uxoris sunt ut adfirmat, sive ipsius ut negat, pari
gloria dignus, qui aut illa componat, aut uxorem
quam virginem accepit, tam doctam politamque
7 reddiderit. Est ergo mecum per diem totum; eundem antequam scribam, eundem cum scripsi, eundem
etiam cum remittor, non tamquam eundem lego.
8 Quod te quoque ut facias et hortor et moneo; neque
enim debet operibus eius obesse quod vivit. An si
inter eos quos numquam vidimus floruisset, non solum
libros eius verum etiam imagines conquireremus,
eiusdem nunc honor praesentis et gratia quasi
9 satietate languescit? At hoc pravum malignumque
est, non admirari hominem admiratione dignissimum, quia videre adloqui audire complecti, nec laudare tantum verum etiam amare contingit. Vale.

---

[1] Catullus and Calvus are coupled as models also in IV.
27.4.

He also writes verses in the style of my favourite
Catullus and Calvus [1] which might indeed be theirs,
for these are full of wit and charm, bitterness and
passion; and, though he sometimes strikes a harsher
note in the even flow of his measures, it is done deliberately and in imitation of his models. He has
recently read me some letters which he said were
written by his wife, but sounded to me like Plautus
or Terence being read in prose. Whether they are
all really his wife's as he says, or his own (which he
denies), one can only admire him either for what he
writes or for the way he has cultivated and refined
the taste of the girl he married.

So all my time is spent with him. If I have something of my own to write I read him first, and again
afterwards; I read him also for recreation, and he
never seems the same. I do urge you to read him too.
The fact that he is still alive should not detract from
his work. If he had been one of the writers before
our own time we should be collecting his portraits as
well as his books; are we then to let him languish
without honour or popularity, as if we saw too much of
him, just because he is living today? It is surely
perverse and ungenerous to refuse recognition to one
so deserving because we have the good fortune to
enjoy his company and conversation, and can demonstrate our affection for the man as well as our appreciation of his work.

XVII

C. Plinius Cornelio Titiano Suo S.

1 Est adhuc curae hominibus fides et officium, sunt
qui defunctorum quoque amicos agant. Titinius
Capito ab imperatore nostro impetravit, ut sibi liceret
2 statuam L. Silani[1] in foro ponere. Pulchrum et
magna laude dignum amicitia principis in hoc uti,
quantumque gratia valeas, aliorum honoribus ex-
3 periri. Est omnino Capitoni in usu claros viros
colere; mirum est qua religione quo studio imagines
Brutorum Cassiorum Catonum[2] domi ubi potest
habeat. Idem clarissimi cuiusque vitam egregiis
4 carminibus exornat. Scias ipsum plurimis virtutibus
abundare, qui alienas sic amat. Redditus est Silano
debitus honor, cuius immortalitati Capito prospexit
pariter et suae. Neque enim magis decorum et
insigne est statuam in foro populi Romani habere
quam ponere. Vale.

XVIII

C. Plinius Suetonio Tranquillo Suo S.

1 Scribis te perterritum somnio vereri ne quid adversi
in actione patiaris; rogas ut dilationem petam, et

---

[1] L. Junius Silanus Torquatus, executed by Nero in 65;
Tacitus, *Ann.* XVI. 7–9.

[2] For a similar attitude to Brutus and Cassius, see Tacitus,
Ann. IV. 34; Suetonius, *Nero* 37.

XVII

To Cornelius Titianus

There is still a sense of loyalty and duty alive in the world, and men whose affection does not die with their friends. Titinius Capito has obtained permission from the Emperor to set up a statue in the forum to Lucius Silanus.[1] To make use of one's friendly relations with the Emperor for such a purpose, and to test the extent of one's influence by paying tribute to others is a graceful gesture which deserves nothing but praise. It is indeed Capito's practice to show respect to famous men, and one must admire the reverence with which he cares for the family busts of Brutus, Cassius,[2] and Cato which he has set up in his own home, not being able to do so elsewhere. He also celebrates the lives of his greatest heroes in excellent verse, and you may be sure that his love of the virtues of others means he has no lack of them himself. In his recognition of what is due to Lucius Silanus, Capito has won immortality for himself as well, for to erect a statue in the forum of Rome is as great an honour as having one's own statue there.

XVIII

To Suetonius Tranquillus [3]

So you have had an alarming dream which makes you fear that the case which is coming on may go against you; and you want me to apply for an

[3] The historian and biographer of the Caesars.

pauculos dies, certe proximum, excusem. Difficile
est, sed experiar, καὶ γάρ τ' ὄναρ ἐκ Διός ἐστιν.
2 Refert tamen, eventura soleas an contraria somniare.
Mihi reputanti somnium meum istud, quod times tu,
3 egregiam actionem portendere videtur. Suscepe-
ram causam Iuni Pastoris, cum mihi quiescenti visa
est socrus mea advoluta genibus ne agerem obse-
crare; et eram acturus adulescentulus adhuc,
eram in quadruplici iudicio, eram contra potentissi-
mos civitatis atque etiam Caesaris amicos, quae
singula excutere mentem mihi post tam triste som-
4 nium poterant. Egi tamen λογισάμενος illud εἷς
οἰωνὸς ἄριστος ἀμύνεσθαι περὶ πάτρης. Nam mihi
patria, et si quid carius patria, fides videbatur.
Prospere cessit, atque adeo illa actio mihi aures
5 hominum, illa ianuam famae patefecit. Proinde
dispice an tu quoque sub hoc exemplo somnium istud
in bonum vertas; aut si tutius putas illud cautissimi
cuiusque praeceptum " Quod dubites, ne feceris," id
6 ipsum rescribe. Ego aliquam stropham inveniam
agamque causam tuam, ut istam agere tu cum voles
possis. Est enim sane alia ratio tua, alia mea fuit.
Nam iudicium centumvirale differri nullo modo, istuc
aegre quidem sed tamen potest. Vale.

---

[1] *Iliad* I. 63.
[2] The Roman Chancery Court, a civil court of justice con-
sisting of 180 judges who normally sat in four panels and dealt
with the more important cases of wills and inheritances. It
was to remain P.'s special sphere (VI. 12).
[3] For the *amici principis* who formed the *consilium* of the

adjournment to get you off for a few days, or one day
at least. It isn't easy but I will try, "for a dream
comes from Zeus."[1] But it makes a difference
whether your dreams usually come true or not, for to
judge by a dream of my own, the one which has
frightened you might well foretell that you will be
successful. I had undertaken to act on behalf of
Junius Pastor when I dreamed that my mother-in-
law came and begged me on her knees to give up the
case. I was very young at the time and I was about
to plead in the Centumviral Court[2] against men of
great political influence, some of them also friends of
the Emperor;[3] any one of these considerations could
have shaken my resolve after such a depressing
dream, but I carried on, believing that "The best and
only omen is to fight for your country ".[4] (For my
pledged word was as sacred to me as my country or
as anything dearer than that.) I won my case, and
it was that speech which drew attention to me and
set me on the threshold of a successful career.

See then if you can follow my example, and give a
happy interpretation to your dream; but if you still
think there is more safety in the warning given by all
cautious folk, "when in doubt do nothing," you can
write and tell me. I will find some way out and deal
with the case so that you can take it up when you
wish. I admit that your position is different from
mine; adjournments are never granted in the Centumviral Court, but in your case it is possible though
not easy.

emperors, cf. the Elder Pliny (III. 5. 7), Suetonius, *Titus* 7. 2:
Juvenal, *Sat.* IV.
[4] *Iliad* XII. 243.

XIX

C. Plinius Romatio Firmo Suo S.

1 Municeps tu meus et condiscipulus et ab ineunte
aetate contubernalis, pater tuus et matri et avunculo meo, mihi etiam quantum aetatis diversitas
passa est, familiaris: magnae et graves causae, cur
2 suscipere augere dignitatem tuam debeam. Esse
autem tibi centum milium censum, satis indicat quod
apud nos decurio es. Igitur ut te non decurione
solum verum etiam equite Romano perfruamur,
offero tibi ad implendas equestres facultates trecenta
3 milia nummum. Te memorem huius muneris amicitiae nostrae diuturnitas spondet: ego ne illud
quidem admoneo, quod admonere deberem, nisi
scirem sponte facturum, ut dignitate a me data quam
4 modestissime ut a me data utare. Nam sollicitius
custodiendus est honor, in quo etiam beneficium
amici tuendum est. Vale.

XX

C. Plinius Cornelio Tacito Suo S.

1 Frequens mihi disputatio est cum quodam docto
homine et perito, cui nihil aeque in causis agendis ut
2 brevitas placet. Quam ego custodiendam esse con-
fiteor, si causa permittat: alioqui praevaricatio est
transire dicenda, praevaricatio etiam cursim et

---

¹ This letter might have been written while Tacitus was
writing his *Dialogus*.

56

XIX

To Romatius Firmus

You and I both come from the same town, went to the same school, and have been friends since we were children. Your father was a close friend of my mother and uncle, and a friend to me too, as far as our difference in age allowed; so there are sound and serious reasons why I ought to try to improve your position. You are a town-councillor of Comum, which shows that your present capital is 100,000 sesterces, so I want to give you another 300,000 to make up your qualification for the order of knights. I can then have the pleasure of seeing you in that position as well as in your present one. The length of our friendship is sufficient guarantee that you will not forget this gift, and I shall not even remind you to enjoy your new status with becoming discretion, because it was received through me; as I ought to, did I not know that you will do so unprompted. An honourable position has to be maintained with special care if it is to keep alive the memory of a friend's generous gift.

XX

To Cornelius Tacitus[1]

I am always having arguments with a man of considerable learning and experience, who admires nothing in forensic oratory so much as brevity. I admit that this is desirable if the case permits, but if it means that points which should be made are

breviter attingere quae sint inculcanda infigenda
3 repetenda. Nam plerisque longiore tractatu vis
quaedam et pondus accedit, utque corpori ferrum, sic
oratio animo non ictu magis quam mora imprimitur.
4 Hic ille mecum auctoritatibus agit ac mihi ex Graecis
orationes Lysiae ostentat, ex nostris Gracchorum
Catonisque, quorum sane plurimae sunt circumcisae
et breves: ego Lysiae Demosthenen Aeschinen
Hyperiden multosque praeterea, Gracchis et Catoni
Pollionem Caesarem Caelium, in primis M. Tullium
oppono, cuius oratio optima fertur esse quae maxima.
Et hercule ut aliae bonae res ita bonus liber melior
5 est quisque quo maior. Vides ut statuas signa pic-
turas, hominum denique multorumque animalium
formas, arborum etiam, si modo sint decorae, nihil
magis quam amplitudo commendet. Idem orationibus evenit; quin etiam voluminibus ipsis auctoritatem
quandam et pulchritudinem adicit magnitudo.
6   Haec ille multaque alia, quae a me in eandem
sententiam solent dici, ut est in disputando incom-
prehensibilis et lubricus, ita eludit ut contendat hos
ipsos, quorum orationibus nitar, pauciora dixisse
7 quam ediderint. Ego contra puto. Testes sunt
multae multorum orationes et Ciceronis pro Murena
pro Vareno, in quibus brevis et nuda quasi subscriptio
quorundam criminum solis titulis indicatur. Ex his
adparet illum permulta dixisse, cum ederet omisisse.

---

[1] *Pro Cluentio.*

omitted, or hurried over when they should be impressed and driven home by repetition, one can only end by betraying one's client. Most points gain weight and emphasis by a fuller treatment, and make their mark on the mind by alternate thrust and pause, as a swordsman uses his steel.

At this point he produces his authorities, and quotes me the Greek Lysias and our own Romans, the brothers Gracchus and Cato. It is true that most of their speeches are short and concise, but I counter Lysias with Demosthenes, Aeschines, Hyperides, and many others, and the Gracchi and Cato with Pollio, Caesar, Caelius, and above all Cicero, whose longest speech is generally considered his best.[1] Like all good things, a good book is all the better if it is a long one; and statues, busts, pictures and drawings of human beings, many animals and also trees can be seen to gain by being on a large scale as long as they are well-proportioned. The same applies to speeches; and when published they look better and more impressive in a good-sized volume.

He parries this and the other examples I usually cite to support my opinion, for he is too nimble in argument for me to come to grips with him. Then he insists that the speeches I instance were shorter when delivered than they are in their published form. This I deny. Several speeches by various authors confirm my opinion, notably two of Cicero's in defence of Murena and Varenus, where some sections are no more than a bare summary of certain charges which are indicated merely by headings. It is obvious from this that the published speech leaves out a great deal of what Cicero said in court. He also

8 Idem pro Cluentio ait se totam causam vetere in-
stituto solum perorasse, et pro C. Cornelio quadri-
duo egisse, ne dubitare possimus, quae per plures dies
(ut necesse erat) latius dixerit, postea recisa ac
repurgata in unum librum grandem quidem unum
9 tamen coartasse. At aliud est actio bona, aliud
oratio. Scio nonnullis ita videri, sed ego (forsitan
fallar) persuasum habeo posse fieri ut sit actio bona
quae non sit bona oratio, non posse non bonam
actionem esse quae sit bona oratio. Est enim oratio
10 actionis exemplar et quasi ἀρχέτυπον. Ideo in optima quaque mille figuras extemporales invenimus, in
iis etiam quas tantum editas scimus, ut in Verrem:
" artificem quem? quemnam? recte admones; Poly-
clitum esse dicebant." Sequitur ergo ut actio sit
absolutissima, quae maxime orationis similitudinem
expresserit, si modo iustum et debitum tempus
accipiat; quod si negetur, nulla oratoris maxima
11 iudicis culpa est. Adsunt huic opinioni meae leges,
quae longissima tempora largiuntur nec brevitatem
dicentibus sed copiam (hoc est diligentiam) suadent;
quam praestare nisi in angustissimis causis non potest
12 brevitas. Adiciam quod me docuit usus, magister
egregius. Frequenter egi, frequenter iudicavi, frequenter in consilio fui: aliud alios movet, ac plerum-

---

¹ In Verrem II. 4. 3.

makes it clear that in accordance with the customs of
his day he conducted the entire defence of Cluentius
by himself, and actually took four days over his
defence of Gaius Cornelius. There can be no doubt
then that if he had to take several days to deliver his
speeches in full he must have subsequently pruned
and revised them in order to compress them into a
single volume, though admittedly a large one.

Then it is argued that there is a great difference
between a good speech as delivered and the written
version. This is a popular view I know, but I feel
convinced (if I am not mistaken) that, though some
speeches may sound better than they read, if the
written speech is good it must also be good when
delivered, for it is the model and prototype for the
spoken version. That is why we find so many
rhetorical figures, apparently spontaneous, in any
good written speech, even in those which we know
were published without being delivered; for example,
in Cicero's speech against Verres: " An artist—now
who was he? thank you for telling me; people said
it was Polyclitus."[1] It follows then that the perfect
speech when delivered is that which keeps most
closely to the written version, so long as the speaker
is allowed the full time due to him; if he is cut short
it is no fault of his, but a serious error on the part of
the judge. The law supports my view, for it allows
speakers any amount of time and recommends not
brevity but the full exposition and precision which
brevity cannot permit, except in very restricted cases.
Let me add what I have learned from the best of all
teachers, experience. On the many occasions when I
have been counsel, judge or assessor, I have found

que parvae res maximas trahunt. Varia sunt hominum iudicia, variae voluntates. Inde qui eandem
causam simul audierunt, saepe diversum, interdum
13 idem sed ex diversis animi motibus sentiunt. Praeterea suae quisque inventioni favet, et quasi fortis-
simum amplectitur, cum ab alio dictum est quod ipse
praevidit. Omnibus ergo dandum est aliquid quod
14 teneant, quod agnoscant. Dixit aliquando mihi
Regulus, cum simul adessemus: "Tu omnia quae
sunt in causa putas exsequenda; ego iugulum statim
video, hunc premo." Premit sane quod elegit, sed in
15 eligendo frequenter errat. Respondi posse fieri, ut
genu esset aut talus, ubi ille iugulum putaret. At
ego, inquam, qui iugulum perspicere non possum,
omnia pertempto, omnia experior, πάντα denique
16 λίθον κινῶ. Utque in cultura agri non vineas tantum, verum etiam arbusta, nec arbusta tantum
verum etiam campos curo et exerceo, utque in ipsis
campis non far aut siliginem solam, sed hordeum
fabam ceteraque legumina sero, sic in actione plura
quasi semina latius spargo, ut quae provenerint
17 colligam. Neque enim minus imperspicua incerta
fallacia sunt iudicum ingenia quam tempestatum
terrarumque. Nec me praeterit summum oratorem
Periclen sic a comico Eupolide laudari:

> πρὸς δέ γ᾽ αὐτοῦ τῷ τάχει
> πειθώ τις ἐπεκάθητο τοῖσι χείλεσιν.
> οὕτως ἐκήλει, καὶ μόνος τῶν ῥητόρων
> τὸ κέντρον ἐγκατέλειπε τοῖς ἀκρωμένοις.

that people are influenced in different ways, and that small points often have important consequences. Men's powers of judgement vary with their temperaments; thus they can listen to the same case but reach different conclusions, or perhaps the same one by a different emotional reaction. Moreover, everyone is prejudiced in favour of his own powers of discernment, and he will always find an argument most convincing if it leads to the conclusion he has reached for himself; everyone must then be given something he can grasp and recognize as his own idea.

Regulus once said to me when we were appearing in the same case: "You think you should follow up every point in a case, but I make straight for the throat and hang on to that." (He certainly hangs on to whatever he seizes, but he often misses the right place.) I pointed out that it might be the knee or the heel he seized when he thought he had the throat. "I can't see the throat," I said, "so my method is to feel my way and try everything—in fact I 'leave no stone unturned.'" On my farms I cultivate my fruit trees and fields as carefully as my vineyards, and in the fields I sow barley, beans and other legumes, as well as corn and wheat; so when I am making a speech I scatter various arguments around like seeds in order to reap whatever crop comes up. There are as many unforeseen hazards and uncertainties to surmount in working on the minds of judges as in dealing with the problems of weather and soil. Nor have I forgotten the words of the comic poet Eupolis in praise of the great orator Pericles: "Speed marked his words, and persuasion sat upon his lips. Thus he could charm, yet alone among orators left his sting

63

18 Verum huic ipsi Pericli nec illa πειθὼ nec illud ἐκήλει brevitate vel velocitate vel utraque (differunt enim) sine facultate summa contigisset. Nam delectare persuadere copiam dicendi spatiumque desiderat, relinquere vero aculeum in audientium animis is
19 demum potest qui non pungit sed infigit. Adde quae de eodem Pericle comicus alter:

> ἤστραπτ᾽, ἐβρόντα, συνεκύκα τὴν Ἑλλάδα.

Non enim amputata oratio et abscisa, sed lata et magnifica et excelsa tonat fulgurat, omnia denique
20 perturbat ac miscet. " Optimus tamen modus est ": quis negat? sed non minus non servat modum qui infra rem quam qui supra, qui adstrictius quam qui
21 effusius dicit. Itaque audis frequenter ut illud: " immodice et redundanter," ita hoc: " ieiune et infirme." Alius excessisse materiam, alius dicitur non implesse. Aeque uterque, sed ille imbecillitate hic viribus peccat; quod certe etsi non limatioris,
22 maioris tamen ingeni [1] vitium est. Nec vero cum haec dico illum Homericum ἀμετροεπῆ probo, sed hunc:

> καὶ ἔπεα νιφάδεσσιν ἐοικότα χειμερίῃσιν,

non quia non et ille mihi valdissime placeat:

> παῦρα μέν, ἀλλὰ μάλα λιγέως·

si tamen detur electio, illam orationem similem nivibus hibernis, id est crebram et adsiduam sed et
23 largam, postremo divinam et caelestem volo. " At

---

[1] ingeni *Brakman*: ingenii αβγ.

---

[1] Eupolis, *Frag.* 94.
[2] Aristophanes, *Acharnians* 531; cf. Plutarch, *Pericles* 8. 3.
[3] *Iliad* II. 212.   [4] *Iliad* III. 222.

behind in his hearers."¹ But "speed" alone (whether by that is meant brevity or rapidity or both, for they are different things) could not have given Pericles his power to persuade and charm had he not also possessed a supreme gift of eloquence. Charm and persuasion require fullness of treatment and time for delivery, and a speaker who leaves his sting in the minds of his hearers does not stop at pricking them, but drives his point in. And again, another comic poet² said of Pericles that "he flashed lightning, thundered and confounded Greece." It is no curtailed and restricted style but a grand oratory, spacious and sublime, which can thunder, lighten, and throw a world into tumult and confusion.

"All the same, the mean is best." No one denies it, but to fall short through over-compression is to miss the mean just as much as to be diffuse and go beyond it. The criticism "spiritless and feeble" is heard as often as "excessive and redundant," when one speaker does not cover his ground and another goes outside it. Both fail, through weakness or vitality, but the latter is at least the fault of a more powerful talent, if a less polished one. In saying this I do not mean to praise Homer's Thersites, "unbridled of tongue," ³ but Odysseus with his "words like flakes of winter snow"; ⁴ and I can also very much admire Menelaus who spoke "at no great length but very clearly." ⁵ But, if I were given my choice, I prefer the speech like the winter snows, one which is fluent and vigorous, but also expansive, which is in fact divinely inspired.⁶

⁵ *Iliad* III. 224.
⁶ See IX. 26 for further discussion on the same theme.

est gratior multis actio brevis." Est, sed inertibus
quorum delicias desidiamque quasi iudicium respicere ridiculum est. Nam si hos in consilio habeas,
non solum satius breviter dicere, sed omnino non
dicere.

24 Haec est adhuc sententia mea, quam mutabo si
dissenseris tu; sed plane cur dissentias explices rogo.
Quamvis enim cedere auctoritati tuae debeam, rectius
tamen arbitror in tanta re ratione quam auctoritate
25 superari. Proinde, si non errare videor, id ipsum
quam voles brevi epistula, sed tamen scribe (con-
firmabis enim iudicium meum); si erraro, longissimam
para. Num corrupi te, qui tibi si mihi accederes
brevis epistulae necessitatem, si dissentires longis-
simae imposui? Vale.

XXI

C. Plinius Plinio Paterno Suo S.

1 Ut animi tui iudicio sic oculorum plurimum tribuo,
non quia multum (ne tibi placeas) sed quia tantum quantum ego sapis; quamquam hoc quoque
2 multum est. Omissis iocis credo decentes esse
servos, qui sunt empti mihi ex consilio tuo. Superest
ut frugi sint, quod de venalibus melius auribus quam
oculis iudicatur. Vale.

" But a lot of people like a short speech." So they do, if they are lazy, but it is absurd to take their idle whim as a serious opinion; if you followed their advice you would do best not in a short speech but saying nothing at all.

This is the view I have held up to now, though I can modify it if you disagree; only please give me your reasons if you do. I know I should bow to your authority, but on an important question like this I would rather yield to a reasoned argument than to authority alone. So if you think I am right, you need only tell me so in as short a letter as you like, as long as you will write to corroborate my opinion. If you think me wrong, make it a long one, and I only hope this does not look like bribery—to demand a short letter if you agree with me, and a very long one if you don't.

XXI

To Plinius Paternus

I HAVE the highest possible opinion of your judgement and critical eye, not because your taste is so *very* good (don't flatter yourself) but because it is as good as mine. Joking apart, I think the slaves you advised me to buy look all right, but it remains to be seen if they are honest; and here one can't go by a slave's looks, but rather by what one hears of him.

XXII

C. PLINIUS CATILIO SEVERO SUO S.

1   Diu iam in urbe haereo et quidem attonitus.
Perturbat me longa et pertinax valetudo Titi
Aristonis, quem singulariter et miror et diligo.
Nihil est enim illo gravius sanctius doctius, ut mihi
non unus homo sed litterae ipsae omnesque bonae
artes in uno homine summum periculum adire videan-
2 tur. Quam peritus ille et privati iuris et publici!
quantum rerum, quantum exemplorum, quantum
antiquitatis tenet! Nihil est quod discere velis quod
ille docere non possit; mihi certe quotiens aliquid
3 abditum quaero, ille thesaurus est. Iam quanta
sermonibus eius fides, quanta auctoritas, quam pressa
et decora cunctatio! quid est quod non statim sciat?
Et tamen plerumque haesitat dubitat, diversitate
rationum, quas acri magnoque iudicio ab origine
4 causisque primis repetit discernit expendit. Ad hoc
quam parcus in victu, quam modicus in cultu! Soleo
ipsum cubiculum illius ipsumque lectum ut imaginem
5 quandam priscae frugalitatis adspicere. Ornat haec
magnitudo animi, quae nihil ad ostentationem, omnia
ad conscientiam refert recteque facti non ex populi
6 sermone mercedem, sed ex facto petit. In summa
non facile quemquam ex istis qui sapientiae studium
habitu corporis praeferunt, huic viro comparabis.

XXII

To Catilius Severus

I HAVE been kept in town for a long time in an appalling state of mind. I am exceedingly worried about Titius Aristo, a man I particularly love and admire, who has been seriously ill for some time. He has no equal in moral influence and wisdom, so that I feel that it is no mere individual in danger, but that literature itself and all the moral virtues are endangered in his person. His experience of civil and constitutional law, his knowledge of human affairs and the lessons of history are such that there is nothing you might wish to learn which he could not teach. I certainly find him a mine of information whenever I have an obscure point to consider. He is genuine and authoritative in conversation, and his deliberate manner is firm and dignified; there can be few questions to which he cannot provide a ready answer, and yet he often pauses to weigh up the many alternative arguments which his keen and powerful intellect derives from their fundamental source and then selects with fine discrimination.

Moreover, his habits are simple and his dress is plain, and his bedroom and its bed always seem to me to give a picture of bygone simplicity. It has its adornment in his greatness of mind, which cares nothing for show but refers everything to conscience, seeking reward for a good deed in its performance and not in popular opinion. In fact none of those people who parade their pursuit of knowledge by their personal appearance can easily be compared with a

Non quidem gymnasia sectatur aut porticus, nec
disputationibus longis aliorum otium suumque delectat, sed in toga negotiisque versatur, multos advo-
7 catione plures consilio iuvat. Nemini tamen istorum
castitate pietate iustitia, fortitudine etiam primo
loco cesserit.

Mirareris si interesses, qua patientia hanc ipsam
valetudinem toleret, ut dolori resistat, ut sitim
differat, ut incredibilem febrium ardorem immotus
8 opertusque transmittat. Nuper me paucosque mecum, quos maxime diligit, advocavit rogavitque, ut
medicos consuleremus de summa valetudinis, ut si
esset insuperabilis sponte exiret e vita; si tantum
9 difficilis et longa, resisteret maneretque: dandum
enim precibus uxoris, dandum filiae lacrimis, dandum
etiam nobis amicis, ne spes nostras, si modo non
10 essent inanes, voluntaria morte desereret. Id ego
arduum in primis et praecipua laude dignum puto.
Nam impetu quodam et instinctu procurrere ad
mortem commune cum multis, deliberare vero et
causas eius expendere, utque suaserit ratio, vitae
mortisque consilium vel suscipere vel ponere ingentis
11 est animi. Et medici quidem secunda nobis polli-
centur: superest ut promissis deus adnuat tandemque
me hac sollicitudine exsolvat; qua liberatus Laurentinum meum, hoc est libellos et pugillares, studio-
sumque otium repetam. Nunc enim nihil legere,

man like Aristo. He does not haunt the gymnasia
and public colonnades, nor does he entertain himself
and his friends in their leisure hours with long dis-
sertations, but he plays an active part in the business
of civil life, helping many people professionally and
still more by his personal advice. Yet none of those
who rank high as philosophers can attain his high
standard of virtue, duty, justice and courage.

His patience throughout this illness, if you could
only see it, would fill you with admiration; he fights
against pain, resists thirst, and endures the unbelievable heat of his fever without moving or throwing off his coverings. A few days ago, he sent for me
and some of his intimate friends, and told us to ask
the doctors what the outcome of his illness would be,
so that if it was to be fatal he could deliberately put
an end to his life, though he would carry on with the
struggle if it was only to be long and painful; he
owed it to his wife's prayers and his daughter's tears,
and to us, his friends, not to betray our hopes by a
self-inflicted death so long as these hopes were not
vain. This I think was a particularly difficult decision to make, which merits the highest praise. Many
people have his impulse and urge to forestall death,
but the ability to examine critically the arguments for
dying, and to accept or reject the idea of living or not,
is the mark of a truly great mind. The doctors are in
fact reassuring in their promises; it only remains for
the gods to confirm these and free me at long last
from my anxiety. If they do, I can then return to
Laurentum, to my books and notes and freedom for
work. At present I am always sitting by Aristo's
bedside or worrying about him, so that I have neither

nihil scribere aut adsidenti vacat aut anxio libet.
12 Habes quid timeam, quid optem, quid etiam in
posterum destinem: tu quid egeris, quid agas, quid
velis agere invicem nobis, sed laetioribus epistulis
scribe. Erit confusioni meae non mediocre solacium,
si tu nihil quereris. Vale.

XXIII

C. Plinius Pompeio Falconi Suo S.

1 Consulis an existimem te in tribunatu causas
agere debere. Plurimum refert, quid esse tribunatum putes, inanem umbram et sine honore nomen an
potestatem sacrosanctam, et quam in ordinem cogi
2 ut a nullo ita ne a se quidem deceat. Ipse cum
tribunus essem, erraverim fortasse qui me esse
aliquid putavi, sed tamquam essem abstinui causis
agendis: primum quod deforme arbitrabar, cui adsur-
gere cui loco cedere omnes oporteret, hunc omnibus
sedentibus stare, et qui iubere posset tacere quemcumque, huic silentium clepsydra indici, et quem
interfari nefas esset, hunc etiam convicia audire et si
inulta pateretur inertem, si ulcisceretur insolentem
3 videri. Erat hic quoque aestus ante oculos, si forte
me adpellasset vel ille cui adessem, vel ille quem

time nor inclination for reading or writing anything.

There you have my fears, hopes, and plans for the future; in return, give me news of your own doings, past, present and intended, but please make your letter more cheerful than mine. It will be a great comfort in my trouble if you have no complaints.

XXIII

To Pompeius Falco

You want to know what I think about your continuing to practice in the law courts while you hold the office of tribune. It depends entirely on the view you take of the tribunate—an " empty form " and a " mere title," or an inviolable authority which should not be called in question by anyone, not even the holder. When I was tribune myself, I acted on the assumption (which may have been a wrong one) that my office really meant something. I therefore gave up all my court work, for I thought it unsuitable for a tribune to stand while others were seated, when it was really every man's duty to rise and give place to him; to be cut short by the water-clock though he had the power to command anyone's silence; and, although it was sacrilege to interrupt him, to be exposed to insults which he could not pass over without an appearance of weakness, nor counter without seeming to abuse his power. I had also to face the anxiety of how to react if my client or my opponent were to appeal to me as tribune, whether to lend my

contra, intercederem et auxilium ferrem an quies-
cerem sileremque, et quasi eiurato magistratu priva-
4 tum ipse me facerem. His rationibus motus malui
me tribunum omnibus exhibere quam paucis advocatum. Sed tu (iterum dicam) plurimum interest
quid esse tribunatum putes, quam personam tibi
imponas; quae sapienti viro ita aptanda est ut
perferatur. Vale.

XXIV

C. Plinius Baebio Hispano Suo S.

1 Tranquillus contubernalis meus vult emere agel-
2 lum, quem venditare amicus tuus dicitur. Rogo
cures, quanti aequum est emat; ita enim delectabit
emisse. Nam mala emptio semper ingrata, eo maxi-
3 me quod exprobrare stultitiam domino videtur. In
hoc autem agello, si modo adriserit pretium, Tranquilli mei stomachum multa sollicitant, vicinitas
urbis, opportunitas viae, mediocritas villae, modus
4 ruris, qui avocet magis quam distringat. Scholasticis
porro dominis, ut hic est, sufficit abunde tantum
soli, ut relevare caput, reficere oculos, reptare per
limitem unamque semitam terere omnesque viteculas
suas nosse et numerare arbusculas possint. Haec
tibi exposui, quo magis scires, quantum esset ille
mihi ego tibi debiturus, si praediolum istud, quod
commendatur his dotibus, tam salubriter emerit ut
paenitentiae locum non relinquat. Vale.

aid by interposing my veto, or to keep silent as if
I had laid down my office and resumed my status
of private citizen. For these reasons I chose to be
tribune to all rather than give my professional services
to a few; but your own decision, as I said before, can
only depend on your idea of the tribunate and the
part you intend to play: a wise man will choose one
within his capacity to play to the end.

XXIV

To Baebius Hispanus

My friend Suetonius Tranquillus wishes to buy a
small property which I hear a friend of yours is trying
to sell. Please see that he has it at a fair price, so
that he will be pleased with his purchase. A bad bar-
gain is always annoying, and especially because it
seems to reproach the owner for his folly. There is
indeed much about this property to whet Tranquillus's appetite if only the price suits him: easy access
to Rome, good communications, a modest house, and
sufficient land for him to enjoy without taking up too
much of his time. Scholars turned landowners, like
himself, need no more land than will suffice to clear
their heads and refresh their eyes, as they stroll
around their grounds and tread their single path,
getting to know each one of their precious vines and
counting every fruit tree.

I am writing this to show you how much he will be
in my debt and I in yours if he is able to buy this
small estate with all its advantages at a reasonable
price which will leave him no room for regrets.

75

BOOK II

LIBER SECUNDUS

I

C. Plinius Romano Suo S.

1 Post aliquot annos insigne atque etiam memorabile
populi Romani oculis spectaculum exhibuit publicum
funus Vergini Rufi, maximi et clarissimi civis, perinde
2 felicis.   Triginta annis gloriae suae supervixit; legit
scripta de se carmina, legit historias et posteritati
suae interfuit.   Perfunctus est tertio consulatu, ut
summum fastigium privati hominis impleret, cum
3 principis noluisset.   Caesares quibus suspectus atque
etiam invisus virtutibus fuerat evasit, reliquit incolumem optimum atque amicissimum, tamquam ad
hunc ipsum honorem publici funeris reservatus.
4 Annum tertium et octogensimum excessit in altissima
tranquillitate, pari veneratione.   Usus est firma valetudine, nisi quod solebant ei manus tremere, citra
dolorem tamen.   Aditus tantum mortis durior
5 longiorque, sed hic ipse laudabilis.   Nam cum vocem
praepararet acturus in consulatu principi gratias, liber

---

[1] See VI. 10 and IX. 19. As legate in Upper Germany he had
put down the revolt of Vindex in 68 and refused to be made
Emperor both then and after the death of Otho. Whether he
was loyal to Nero is uncertain.   Cf. Syme, pp. 178–9: J. C.
Hainsworth, *Historia*, 1962, p. 86: D. C. A. Shotter, C.Q. 1967,
p. 370.

78

BOOK II

I

To Voconius Romanus

It is some years since Rome has had such a splendid sight to remember as the public funeral of Verginius Rufus, one of our greatest and most distinguished citizens whom we can also count a fortunate one. For thirty years after his hour of glory[1] he lived on to read about himself in history and verse, so that he was a living witness of his fame to come. He was three times consul, and thus attained the highest distinction short of the imperial power itself; for this he had refused. His virtues had been suspected and resented by certain of the Emperors, but he had escaped arrest and lived to see a truly good and friendly ruler safely established; so that he might have been reserved for the honour of his public funeral we have just seen. He had reached the age of eighty-three, living in close retirement and deeply respected by us all, and his health was good, apart from a trembling of the hands, not enough to trouble him. Only death when it came was slow and painful, though we can only admire the way he faced it. He was rehearsing the delivery of his address of thanks[2] to the Emperor[3]

[2] P.'s own *Panegyricus*, before revision and expansion, was a similar address.
[3] Nerva, in 97.

quem forte acceperat grandiorem, et seni et stanti
ipso pondere elapsus est. Hunc dum sequitur colligit-
que, per leve et lubricum pavimentum fallente
vestigio cecidit coxamque fregit, quae parum apte
collocata reluctante aetate male coiit.

6   Huius viri exsequiae magnum ornamentum principi
magnum saeculo magnum etiam foro et rostris attu-
lerunt. Laudatus est a consule Cornelio Tacito;
nam hic supremus felicitati eius cumulus accessit,
7 laudator eloquentissimus. Et ille quidem plenus annis
abit, plenus honoribus, illis etiam quos recusavit:
nobis tamen quaerendus ac desiderandus est ut exemplar aevi prioris, mihi vero praecipue, qui illum non
8 solum publice quantum admirabar tantum diligebam;
primum quod utrique eadem regio, municipia finitima,
agri etiam possessionesque coniunctae, praeterea
quod ille mihi tutor relictus adfectum parentis exhibuit. Sic candidatum me suffragio ornavit; sic ad
omnes honores meos ex secessibus accucurrit, cum
iam pridem eiusmodi officiis renuntiasset; sic illo die
quo sacerdotes solent nominare quos dignissimos
9 sacerdotio iudicant, me semper nominabat. Quin
etiam in hac novissima valetudine, veritus ne forte
inter quinqueviros crearetur, qui minuendis publicis
sumptibus iudicio senatus constituebantur, cum
illi tot amici senes consularesque superessent, me

---

[1] The manuscript scroll must have unrolled, and Verginius
fell while trying to gather it up (*colligere*).

[2] See *Pan.* 62. 2, and note.

for his election to his third consulship, when he had
occasion to take up a heavy book, the weight of which
made it fall out of his hands, as he was an old man and
standing at the time.[1] He bent down to pick it up,
and lost his footing on the slippery polished floor, so
that he fell and fractured his hip. This was badly
set, and because of his age it never mended properly.

Such was the man whose funeral does credit to the
Emperor and our times, to the forum and its speakers.
His funeral oration was delivered by the consul,
Cornelius Tacitus, a most eloquent orator, and his
tribute put the crowning touch to Verginius's good
fortune. He died too when full of years and rich in
honours, even those which he refused; and it is left to
us to miss him and feel his loss as a figure from a past
age. I shall feel it more than anyone, since my
admiration for his public qualities was matched by
personal affection. I had many reasons to love him;
we came from the same district and neighbouring
towns, and our lands and property adjoined each
other; and then he was left by will as my guardian,
and gave me a father's affection. So when I was a
candidate for office, he gave me the support of his
vote, and when I entered upon my duties, he left his
retirement to hasten to my side although he had long
since given up social functions of that kind; and on
the day when the priests nominate those they judge
suitable for a priesthood, he always nominated me.
Even during this last illness, when he was anxious not
to be selected for the Board of Five set up by senatorial decree to reduce public expenditure,[2] in spite
of my youth he chose me to make his official excuses
(although many of his friends and contemporaries of

huius aetatis per quem excusaretur elegit, his quidem
verbis: " Etiam si filium haberem, tibi mandarem."

10 Quibus ex causis necesse est tamquam immaturam
mortem eius in sinu tuo defleam, si tamen fas est aut
flere aut omnino mortem vocare, qua tanti viri

11 mortalitas magis finita quam vita est. Vivit enim
vivetque semper, atque etiam latius in memoria
hominum et sermone versabitur, postquam ab oculis

12 recessit. Volo tibi multa alia scribere, sed totus animus in hac una contemplatione defixus est. Verginium cogito, Verginium video, Verginium iam vanis
imaginibus, recentibus tamen, audio adloquor teneo;
cui fortasse cives aliquos virtutibus pares et habemus
et habebimus, gloria neminem. Vale.

II

C. PLINIUS PAULINO SUO S.

1 IRASCOR, nec liquet mihi an debeam, sed irascor.
Scis, quam sit amor iniquus interdum, impotens saepe
μικραίτιος semper. Haec tamen causa magna est,
nescio an iusta; sed ego, tamquam non minus iusta
quam magna sit, graviter irascor, quod a te tam diu

2 litterae nullae. Exorare me potes uno modo, si nunc
saltem plurimas et longissimas miseris. Haec mihi
sola excusatio vera, ceterae falsae videbuntur. Non
sum auditurus " non eram Romae " uel " occupatior

---

[1] For the sentiment, see Tacitus *Agr*. 46. 1 and 4.

consular rank were still living), and told me that he would have entrusted this to me even if he had had a son of his own.

Hence I must ask you to bear with my grief at his death as if he had died before his time; if indeed it is right to grieve or even to give the name of death to what has ended the mortal existence rather than the life of so great a man. For he lives and will live for ever, and in a wider sense in our memories and on our lips, now that he has left our sight.[1]

I intended to write to you about many other things, but Verginius takes up all my thoughts. I see him in my mind's eye, and in these dreams, so vivid and so vain, I speak to him, he answers, and I feel his presence near. There may be some citizens with us now who can equal his merits, and there will be others, but none will win his fame.

II

To Valerius Paulinus

I am furious with you, rightly or not I don't know, but it makes no difference. You know very well that love is sometimes unfair, often violent, and always quick to take offence, but I have good reason, whether or not it is a just one, to be as furious as I would be in a just cause. It is so long since I have had a letter from you. The only way to placate me is to write me a lot of letters now, at long last—lengthy ones, too. That is how you can honestly win my forgiveness; I shall not hear of anything else. Don't say you were not in Rome or were too busy because I shan't listen,

eram"; illud enim nec di sinant, ut "infirmior".
Ipse ad villam partim studiis partim desidia fruor,
quorum utrumque ex otio nascitur. Vale.

III

C. PLINIUS NEPOTI SUO S.

1 MAGNA Isaeum fama praecesserat, maior inventus
est. Summa est facultas copia ubertas; dicit semper
ex tempore, sed tamquam diu scripserit. Sermo
Graecus, immo Atticus; praefationes tersae graciles
2 dulces, graves interdum et erectae. Poscit con-
troversias plures; electionem auditoribus permittit,
saepe etiam partes; surgit amicitur incipit; statim
omnia ac paene pariter ad manum, sensus reconditi
occursant, verba—sed qualia!—quaesita et exculta.
3 Multa lectio in subitis, multa scriptio elucet. Pro-
hoemiatur apte, narrat aperte, pugnat acriter,
colligit fortiter, ornat excelse. Postremo docet
delectat adficit; quid maxime, dubites. Crebra
ἐνθυμήματα crebri syllogismi, circumscripti et
effecti, quod stilo quoque adsequi magnum est.
Incredibilis memoria: repetit altius quae dixit ex

---

¹ On ἐνθυμήματα, see Quintilian, *Inst. Orat.* V. x. 1; xiv. 1.
and 25.

84

only for heaven's sake don't tell me you were ill. I am in the country, dividing my time between the two pleasures of a holiday—reading and relaxation.

III

To Maecilius Nepos

Isaeus's great reputation had reached Rome ahead of him, but we found him to be even greater than we had heard. He has a remarkably eloquent style, rich in variety, and though he always speaks extempore his speeches sound as though he had spent time on preparing them. He expresses himself in Greek, Attic to be precise; his introductory remarks have a neatness and polish which is very attractive, and can also be impressive in the grand style. His method is to ask his audience for a subject, leaving the choice and often the side he is to take with them; then he rises, wraps his cloak round him, and begins to speak. Whatever the subject he is ready at once, with every latent implication clear to him and expressed in words which are accurate and well-chosen; so that the extent of his reading and his practice in composition are apparent in his extempore efforts. He comes straight to the point in his opening words, he is clear in exposition and penetrating in argument, he draws his conclusions boldly and expresses himself with dignity; it is in fact difficult to choose between his powers to instruct, to charm, or to move his hearers. He is ready with rhetorical figures[1] and syllogisms, such as could not easily be worked out so concisely even in writing, and has an amazing memory, so that he can

85

4 tempore, ne verbo quidem labitur. Ad tantam ἕξιν studio et exercitatione pervenit; nam diebus et noctibus nihil aliud agit nihil audit nihil loquitur.

5 Annum sexagensimum excessit et adhuc scholasticus tantum est: quo genere hominum nihil aut sincerius aut simplicius aut melius. Nos enim, qui in foro verisque litibus terimur, multum malitiae quamvis

6 nolimus addiscimus: schola et auditorium et ficta causa res inermis innoxia est, nec minus felix, senibus praesertim. Nam quid in senectute felicius, quam

7 quod dulcissimum est in iuventa? Quare ego Isaeum non disertissimum tantum, verum etiam beatissimum iudico. Quem tu nisi cognoscere concupiscis, saxeus

8 ferreusque es. Proinde si non ob alia nosque ipsos, at certe ut hunc audias veni. Numquamne legisti, Gaditanum quendam Titi Livi nomine gloriaque commotum ad visendum eum ab ultimo terrarum orbe venisse, statimque ut viderat abisse? Ἀφιλόκαλον inlitteratum iners ac paene etiam turpe est, non putare tanti cognitionem qua nulla est iucundior, nulla pulchrior, nulla denique humanior. Dices:

9 " Habeo hic quos legam non minus disertos." Etiam; sed legendi semper occasio est, audiendi non semper. Praeterea multo magis, ut vulgo dicitur,

---

[1] Cadiz.

repeat his extempore speeches word for word without
a single mistake, a technique he has developed by
application and constant practice; for night and day
everything he says and hears and does is directed to
this end alone.

He has reached the age of sixty, but has preferred
to remain a teacher of rhetoric, keeping to a profession followed by some of the most genuinely sincere
and honest of men. Those of us whose energies are
wasted on the active litigation in the courts cannot
help learning a good deal of sharp practice, but the
imaginary cases in the schoolroom and lecture-hall do
no harm with their blunted foils and are none the
less enjoyable; especially to the old, who like nothing
so much as to witness the joys of their youth. Consequently it seems to me that Isaeus's gift of eloquence has also brought him very great happiness,
and if you aren't eager to meet him, you must indeed
be iron-willed and stony-hearted. Nothing brings
you to Rome, myself included, but do come to hear
him. Have you never heard the story of the Spaniard
from Gades?[1] He was so stirred by the famous name
of Livy that he came from his far corner of the earth
to have one look at him and then went back again.
Only a boorish ignorance and a degree of apathy
which is really rather shocking could prevent you
from thinking it worth an effort to gain an experience
which will prove so enjoyable, civilized, and rewarding. You may say that you have authors as eloquent
whose works can be read at home; but the fact is that
you can read them any time, and rarely have the
opportunity to hear the real thing. Besides, we are
always being told that the spoken word is much more

viva vox adficit. Nam licet acriora sint quae legas,
altius tamen in animo sedent, quae pronuntiatio
10 vultus habitus gestus etiam dicentis adfigit; nisi
vero falsum putamus illud Aeschinis, qui cum legisset
Rhodiis orationem Demosthenis admirantibus cunctis, adiecisse fertur: τί δέ, εἰ αὐτοῦ τοῦ θηρίου
ἠκούσατε; et erat Aeschines si Demostheni credimus
λαμπροφωνότατος. Fatebatur tamen longe melius
11 eadem illa pronuntiasse ipsum qui pepererat. Quae
omnia huc tendunt, ut audias Isaeum, vel ideo tantum
ut audieris. Vale.

IV

C. PLINIUS CALVINAE SUAE S.

1 Si pluribus pater tuus vel uni cuilibet alii quam
mihi debuisset, fuisset fortasse dubitandum, an adires
2 hereditatem etiam viro gravem. Cum vero ego
ductus adfinitatis officio, dimissis omnibus qui non
dico molestiores sed diligentiores erant, creditor solus
exstiterim, cumque vivente eo nubenti tibi in dotem
centum milia contulerim, praeter eam summam
quam pater tuus quasi de meo dixit (erat enim
solvenda de meo), magnum habes facilitatis meae
pignus, cuius fiducia debes famam defuncti pudoremque suscipere. Ad quod te ne verbis magis quam
rebus horter, quidquid mihi pater tuus debuit, accept-

---

[1] A common story in antiquity. See IV. 5, and Cic. *De Orat.*
III. 213; Pliny, *NH.* VII. 110; Quint. *Inst. Orat.* XI. iii. 7.
St. Jerome, *Ep.* LIII. 2. 2. The speech was *De Corona*.

effective; however well a piece of writing makes its point, anything which is driven into the mind by the delivery and expression, the appearance and gestures of a speaker remains deeply implanted there, unless there is no truth in the tale of Aeschines when he was at Rhodes, who countered the general applause he won for his reading of one of Demosthenes' speeches with the words: "Suppose you had heard the beast himself?"[1] And yet, if we are to believe Demosthenes, Aeschines had a very good voice; all the same, he admitted that the speech had been much better when its author delivered it himself.

All this goes to show that you ought to hear Isaeus—if only to have the satisfaction of having done so.

IV

To Calvina

If your father had died in debt to more than one person, or to anyone other than myself, you might perhaps have hesitated to accept an inheritance which even a man would have found a burden. But I thought it my duty as your relative to pay off anyone who was rather pressing, though not actually offensive, so as to be left sole creditor; and during your father's lifetime I had contributed 100,000 sesterces towards your dowry on marriage in addition to what he had assigned you (which also came indirectly from me, as it could only be paid from his account with me). All this should be a firm guarantee of my generous feelings, and ought to give you confidence to

3 um tibi fieri iubebo. Nec est quod verearis ne sit
mihi onerosa ista donatio. Sunt quidem omnino
nobis modicae facultates, dignitas sumptuosa, reditus propter condicionem agellorum nescio minor an
incertior; sed quod cessat ex reditu, frugalitate
suppletur, ex qua velut fonte liberalitas nostra
4 decurrit. Quae tamen ita temperanda est, ne nimia
profusione inarescat; sed temperanda in aliis, in te
vero facile ei ratio constabit, etiamsi modum
excesserit. Vale.

V

C. Plinius Luperco Suo S.

1 Actionem et a te frequenter efflagitatam, et a me
saepe promissam, exhibui tibi, nondum tamen totam;
2 adhuc enim pars eius perpolitur. Interim quae
absolutiora mihi videbantur, non fuit alienum iudicio
tuo tradi. His tu rogo intentionem scribentis
accommodes. Nihil enim adhuc inter manus habui
cui maiorem sollicitudinem praestare deberem.
3 Nam in ceteris actionibus existimationi hominum
diligentia tantum et fides nostra, in hac etiam pietas

---

[1] As *praefectus aerarii Saturni*.

[2] P.'s fortune has been estimated at 15,000,000 HS, less than
a third of Regulus's wealth (II. 20. 13), and was invested in his
various properties. There are many references to his problems
in farming out his lands: *e.g.* II. 15; III. 19; VIII. 2; IX. 20;
37; X. 8. His gifts appear to be made from income or savings.

defend your late father's honour and reputation; to
provide you with practical as well as verbal encouragement I shall give instructions for his debt to me to be
entered as paid. You need not fear that such a gift
will tax my finances. It is true that my resources as
a whole are not very great and my position is expensive to keep up;[1] being dependent on the way my
property is farmed, my income is small or precarious,
but its deficiencies can be made up by simple living.[2]
This is the spring from which my well of kindness is
supplied, and though I must not draw upon it without
restraint, lest it dry up after too lavish a flow, I can
keep my restraint for others; I can easily make my
accounts balance in your case even if they have passed
their usual figure.

V

To Lupercus

I am sending you the speech[3] which you have often
asked for and I have promised more than once, but
not the whole of it yet, as part is still under revision.
Meanwhile I thought that the more finished portions
might suitably be handed over to you for your
opinion. Please give them your close attention and
write down your comments, for I have never handled
any subject which demanded greater care. In my
other speeches I have submitted to public opinion no
more than my industry and good faith, but here my
patriotic feelings were involved as well. Conse-

[3] Not the speech delivered at the opening of the library at
Comum (I. 8.), which was a *sermo*; this is an *actio*, a forensic
speech.

subicietur.   Inde et liber crevit, dum ornare patriam
et amplificare gaudemus, pariterque et defensioni
4 eius servimus et gloriae.   Tu tamen haec ipsa quantum ratio exegerit reseca.   Quotiens enim ad fasti-
dium legentium deliciasque respicio, intellego nobis
commendationem et ex ipsa mediocritate libri
5 petendam.   Idem tamen qui a te hanc austeritatem
exigo, cogor id quod diversum est postulare, ut in
plerisque frontem remittas.   Sunt enim quaedam
adulescentium auribus danda, praesertim si materia
non refragetur; nam descriptiones locorum, quae in
hoc libro frequentiores erunt, non historice tantum sed
6 prope poetice prosequi fas est.   Quod tamen si quis
exstiterit, qui putet nos laetius fecisse quam orationis
severitas exigat, huius (ut ita dixerim) tristitiam reli-
7 quae partes actionis exorare debebunt.   Adnisi certe
sumus, ut quamlibet diversa genera lectorum per
plures dicendi species teneremus, ac sicut veremur,
ne quibusdam pars aliqua secundum suam cuiusque
naturam non probetur, ita videmur posse confidere, ut
universitatem omnibus varietas ipsa commendet.
8 Nam et in ratione conviviorum, quamvis a plerisque
cibis singuli temperemus, totam tamen cenam laudare
omnes solemus, nec ea quae stomachus noster re-
9 cusat, adimunt gratiam illis quibus capitur.   Atque
haec ego sic accipi volo, non tamquam adsecutum esse
me credam, sed tamquam adsequi laboraverim,
fortasse non frustra, si modo tu curam tuam admoveris
10 interim istis, mox iis quae sequuntur.   Dices te non

quently the text has grown, for I was glad of the opportunity to pay a tribute of admiration to my native place, and at the same time not only to defend its interests but to bring it further fame. But these are the passages I want you to prune down as you think fit, for whenever I think of the whims and fancies of the reading public I realize that I can only win approval by keeping the text within bounds.

As well as this severity I am demanding from you I am compelled to ask for the exact opposite, that is, your indulgence for several passages. Some concessions must be made to a youthful audience, especially if the subject-matter permits; for example, descriptions of places (which are fairly frequent in this speech) may surely introduce a touch of poetry into narrative prose. But, if anyone thinks I have handled this subject too lightly for serious oratory, then his austerity, if I may call it so, will have to find appeasement in the rest of the speech. I have certainly tried to appeal to all the different types of reader by varying my style, and, though I am afraid that some people will disapprove of certain details because of their individual tastes, I still think I can be sure that the speech as a whole will be generally liked because of this variety. At a dinner party we may individually refuse several dishes, but we all praise the whole meal, and the food which is not to our taste does not spoil our pleasure in what we do like.

I hope that you will understand by this not that I believe that I have achieved my aim, but that I have tried to do so; and perhaps my efforts will not have been in vain if you will only give your critical attention to what you have now, and afterwards to what

93

posse satis diligenter id facere, nisi prius totam actionem cognoveris: fateor. In praesentia tamen et ista tibi familiariora fient, et quaedam ex his talia 11 erunt ut per partes emendari possint. Etenim, si avulsum statuae caput aut membrum aliquod inspiceres, non tu quidem ex illo posses congruentiam aequalitatemque deprendere, posses tamen iudicare, 12 an id ipsum satis elegans esset; nec alia ex causa principiorum libri circumferuntur, quam quia existimatur pars aliqua etiam sine ceteris esse perfecta.

13 Longius me provexit dulcedo quaedam tecum loquendi; sed iam finem faciam ne modum, quem etiam orationi adhibendum puto, in epistula excedam. Vale.

VI

C. Plinius Avito Suo S.

1 Longum est altius repetere nec refert, quemadmodum acciderit, ut homo minime familiaris cenarem apud quendam, ut sibi videbatur, lautum et diligen- 2 tem, ut mihi, sordidum simul et sumptuosum. Nam sibi et paucis opima quaedam, ceteris vilia et minuta ponebat. Vinum etiam parvolis lagunculis in tria genera discripserat, non ut potestas eligendi, sed ne ius esset recusandi, aliud sibi et nobis, aliud minoribus amicis (nam gradatim amicos habet), aliud

---

[1] *i.e.* his clients. For their treatment at the tables of their patrons, see Juvenal, *Sat.* V; Martial, VI. 11.

94

follows.   You may say that you need to have seen the whole speech if you are to do this accurately, and I realize this; but for the moment you can familiarize yourself with what I send, and there will be some passages which can be corrected apart from the whole. You could not judge whether the head or a limb of a statue is in proportion and harmonizes with the whole if you examine it detached from the trunk, but you could still decide if it was well formed in itself; and the only reason why books of selected extracts are circulated is because some passages are thought to be complete apart from their context.

It is a pleasure to talk to you, but I have run on too long; I must stop, or this letter will go beyond the bounds I think proper even for a speech.

VI

To Junius Avitus

It would take too long to go into the details (which anyway don't matter) of how I happened to be dining with a man—though no particular friend of his— whose elegant economy, as he called it, seemed to me a sort of stingy extravagance. The best dishes were set in front of himself and a select few, and cheap scraps of food before the rest of the company.   He had even put the wine into tiny little flasks, divided into three categories, not with the idea of giving his guests the opportunity of choosing, but to make it impossible for them to refuse what they were given. One lot was intended for himself and for us, another for his lesser friends[1] (all his friends are graded) and

THE LETTERS OF PLINY

3 suis nostrisque libertis. Animadvertit qui mihi
proximus recumbebat, et an probarem interrogavit.
Negavi. " Tu ergo " inquit " quam consuetudinem
sequeris ? " " Eadem omnibus pono; ad cenam
enim, non ad notam invito cunctisque rebus exaequo,
quos mensa et toro aequavi." "Etiamne libertos?"
4 " Etiam; convictores enim tunc, non libertos puto.'
Et ille: " Magno tibi constat." " Minime." " Qui
fieri potest ? " " Quia scilicet liberti mei non idem
5 quod ego bibunt, sed idem ego quod liberti." Et
hercule si gulae temperes, non est onerosum quo
utaris ipse communicare cum pluribus. Illa ergo
reprimenda, illa quasi in ordinem redigenda est, si
sumptibus parcas, quibus aliquanto rectius tua con-
tinentia quam aliena contumelia consulas.
6 Quorsus haec? ne tibi, optimae indolis iuveni,
quorundam in mensa luxuria specie frugalitatis im-
ponat. Convenit autem amori in te meo, quotiens
tale aliquid inciderit, sub exemplo praemonere, quid
debeas fugere. Igitur memento nihil magis esse
vitandum quam istam luxuriae et sordium novam
societatem; quae cum sint turpissima discreta ac
separata, turpius iunguntur. Vale.

the third for his and our freedmen. My neighbour at table noticed this and asked me if I approved. I said I did not. "So what do you do?" he asked. "I serve the same to everyone, for when I invite guests it is for a meal, not to make class distinctions; I have brought them as equals to the same table, so I give them the same treatment in everything." "Even the freedmen?" "Of course, for then they are my fellow-diners, not freedmen." "That must cost you a lot." "On the contrary." "How is that?" "Because my freedmen do not drink the sort of wine I do, but I drink theirs." Believe me, if you restrain your greedy instincts it is no strain on your finances to share with several others the fare you have yourself. It is this greed which should be put down and " reduced to the ranks " if you would cut down expenses, and you can do this far better by self-restraint than by insults to others.

The point of this story is to prevent a promising young man like yourself from being taken in by this extravagance under guise of economy which is to be found at the table in certain homes. Whenever I meet with such a situation, my affection for you prompts me to quote it as a warning example of what to avoid. Remember then that nothing is more to be shunned than this novel association of extravagance and meanness; vices which are bad enough when single and separate, but worse when found together.

THE LETTERS OF PLINY

VII

C. PLINIUS MACRINO SUO S.

1 HERE a senatu Vestricio Spurinnae principe auctore triumphalis statua decreta est, non ita ut multis, qui numquam in acie steterunt, numquam castra viderunt, numquam denique tubarum sonum nisi in spectaculis audierunt, verum ut illis, qui decus istud 2 sudore et sanguine et factis adsequebantur. Nam Spurinna Bructerum regem vi et armis induxit in regnum, ostentatoque bello ferocissimam gentem, quod est pulcherrimum victoriae genus, terrore 3 perdomuit. Et hoc quidem virtutis praemium, illud solacium doloris accepit, quod filio eius Cottio, quem amisit absens, habitus est honor statuae. Rarum id in iuvene; sed pater hoc quoque merebatur, cuius gravissimo vulneri magno aliquo fomento medendum 4 fuit. Praeterea Cottius ipse tam clarum specimen indolis dederat, ut vita eius brevis et angusta debuerit hac velut immortalitate proferri. Nam tanta ei sanctitas gravitas auctoritas etiam, ut posset senes illos provocare virtute, quibus nunc honore adaequatus est. 5 Quo quidem honore, quantum ego interpretor, non modo defuncti memoriae, dolori patris, verum etiam

---

[1] See also III. 1. Only a reigning Emperor could hold a full triumph. The Emperor here is Nerva.

[2] For the vexed question of when this was and whether it

VII

To Caecilius Macrinus

YESTERDAY on the Emperor's proposal the Senate decreed a triumphal statue to Vestricius Spurinna,[1] an honour granted to many who have never faced a battle, never seen a camp, nor even heard the sound of a trumpet except at the theatre; but Spurinna was one of those heroes whose honours were won by the blood and sweat of action. It was Spurinna who established the chief of the Bructeri in his kingdom by force of arms,[2] and by mere threat of war against a savage people he terrorized it into submission, so winning the finest type of victory. Now he has his reward of merit; and to bring him consolation in grief, the honour of a statue was also granted to Cottius, the son who had died during his absence abroad.[3] This is rarely granted to a young man, but in this case it was also due to the father whose grievous sorrow needed some special remedy to assuage it. Cottius himself had also given such marked indication of his promise that some sort of immortality was required to extend a life thus cut short. His high principles, his sense of duty and influence were such as to make him rival our elders in merit, and he is now raised to be their equal in honour. And indeed, in granting this honour the Senate would seem to me to have had in mind not only Cottius's memory and his father's grief, but also the effect on the public.

was part of the campaign against the Bructeri in 97 (Tacitus, *Germ.* 33) see Syme, *Tacitus*, App. 6, p. 634.

[3] Perhaps as a member of the senatorial delegation sent to congratulate Trajan in autumn 97.

exemplo prospectum est. Acuent ad bonas artes
iuventutem adulescentibus quoque, digni sint modo,
tanta praemia constituta; acuent principes viros ad
liberos suscipiendos et gaudia ex superstitibus et ex
6 amissis tam gloriosa solacia. His ex causis statua
Cotti publice laetor, nec privatim minus. Amavi
consummatissimum iuvenem, tam ardenter quam
nunc impatienter requiro. Erit ergo pergratum
mihi hanc effigiem eius subinde intueri subinde
respicere, sub hac consistere praeter hanc commeare.
7 Etenim si defunctorum imagines domi positae
dolorem nostrum levant, quanto magis hae quibus in
celeberrimo loco non modo species et vultus illorum,
sed honor etiam et gloria refertur! Vale.

VIII

C. Plinius Caninio Suo S.

1 Studes an piscaris an venaris an simul omnia?
Possunt enim omnia simul fieri ad Larium nostrum.
Nam lacus piscem, feras silvae quibus lacus cingitur,
studia altissimus iste secessus adfatim suggerunt.
2 Sed sive omnia simul sive aliquid facis, non possum
dicere " invideo "; angor tamen non et mihi licere,
qui sic concupisco ut aegri vinum balinea fontes.
Numquamne hos artissimos laqueos, si solvere

The granting of such high rewards to the young, provided that they are worthy of them, will spur on our young men to virtue; and with a prospect of happiness if their sons survive, and such splendid consolation if they die, our leading citizens will be encouraged to undertake the responsibility of children.

For these public considerations, then, I am glad about the statue to Cottius, as I am for personal reasons. I loved this excellent young man dearly, so that I miss him now unbearably; it will therefore be a pleasure for me to contemplate his statue from time to time, turn back to look at it, stand at its foot, and walk past it. We seek consolation in sorrow in the busts of our dead we set up in our homes; still more then should we find it in the statues standing in public places, for these can recall men's fame and distinction as well as their forms and faces.

VIII

To Caninius Rufus

Are you reading, fishing, or hunting or doing all three? You can do all together on the shores of Como, for there is plenty of fish in the lake, game to hunt in the woods around, and every opportunity to study in the depths of your retreat. Whether it is everything or only one thing I can't say I begrudge you your pleasures; I am only vexed at being denied them myself, for I hanker after them as a sick man does for wine, baths, and cool springs. I wonder if I shall ever be able to shake off these constricting

3 negatur, abrumpam? Numquam, puto. Nam veteribus negotiis nova accrescunt, nec tamen priora
peraguntur: tot nexibus, tot quasi catenis maius
in dies occupationum agmen extenditur. Vale.

IX

C. PLINIUS APOLLINARI SUO S.

1 ANXIUM me et inquietum habet petitio Sexti
Eruci mei. Adficior cura et, quam pro me sollicitudinem non adii, quasi pro me altero patior; et alioqui
meus pudor, mea existimatio, mea dignitas in dis-
2 crimen adducitur. Ego Sexto latum clavum a
Caesare nostro, ego quaesturam impetravi; meo
suffragio pervenit ad ius tribunatus petendi, quem
nisi obtinet in senatu, vereor ne decepisse Caesarem
3 videar. Proinde adnitendum est mihi, ut talem
eum iudicent omnes, qualem esse princeps mihi
credidit. Quae causa si studium meum non inci-
taret, adiutum tamen cuperem iuvenem probissimum
gravissimum eruditissimum, omni denique laude
4 dignissimum, et quidem cum tota domo. Nam pater
ei Erucius Clarus, vir sanctus antiquus disertus atque
in agendis causis exercitatus, quas summa fide pari
constantia nec verecundia minore defendit. Habet
avunculum C. Septicium, quo nihil verius nihil

---

¹ P. is unable to leave Rome for long because of his duties
at the *aerarium Saturni.*

² C. Septicius Clarus, to whom the Letters are dedicated.

fetters if I am not allowed to undo them, and I doubt if I ever shall. New business piles up on the old before the old is finished, and, as more and more links are added to the chain, I see my work stretching out farther and farther every day.[1]

IX

To Domitius Apollinaris

My friend Sextus Erucius is standing for office, and this is worrying me very much; in fact I feel far more anxious and apprehensive for my " second self " than I ever did on my own account. Besides, my own honour, my reputation, and my position are all at stake, for it was I who persuaded the Emperor to raise Sextus to senatorial rank and grant him a quaestorship, and it is on my nomination that he is now standing for the office of tribune. If he is not elected by the Senate, I am afraid it will look as though I have deceived the Emperor; and so it is essential for me to see that everyone shares the high opinion which I led the Emperor to form.

Even if I had not this incentive I should still be anxious to support a young man of such outstanding merit, whose sense of duty is matched by his accomplishments and who is like all the rest of his family in deserving every form of praise. His father is Erucius Clarus, a model of ancient virtue and a skilled and practised advocate, who conducts all his cases with the utmost honesty and determination, equalled by his discretion. His uncle, Gaius Septicius,[2] is the most genuinely reliable, frank and trustworthy man I

5 simplicius nihil candidius nihil fidelius novi. Omnes
me certatim et tamen aequaliter amant, omnibus nunc
ego in uno referre gratiam possum. Itaque prenso
amicos, supplico, ambio, domos stationesque circum-
eo, quantumque vel auctoritate vel gratia valeam,
precibus experior, teque obsecro ut aliquam oneris
6 mei partem suscipere tanti putes. Reddam vicem
si reposces, reddam et si non reposces. Diligeris
coleris frequentaris: ostende modo velle te, nec
deerunt qui quod tu velis cupiant. Vale.

X

C. Plinius Octavio Suo S.

1 Hominem te patientem vel potius durum ac paene
crudelem, qui tam insignes libros tam diu teneas!
2 Quousque et tibi et nobis invidebis, tibi maxima
laude, nobis voluptate? Sine per ora hominum
ferantur isdemque quibus lingua Romana spatiis
pervagentur. Magna et iam longa exspectatio est,
3 quam frustrari adhuc et differre non debes. Enotue-
runt quidam tui versus, et invito te claustra sua
refregerunt. Hos nisi retrahis in corpus, quandoque
4 ut errones aliquem cuius dicantur invenient. Habe
ante oculos mortalitatem, a qua adserere te hoc uno
monimento potes; nam cetera fragilia et caduca
non minus quam ipsi homines occidunt desinuntque.

know. The family is united in its affection for me, though each member tries to show it most, and now is my chance to show my gratitude to them all by helping one of them. Consequently I am approaching all my friends to beg their support, and going the round of private houses and public places, testing what influence and popularity I have by my entreaties; and I do beg you to think it worth while to relieve me of a part of my burden. I will do the same for you, asked or unasked. You are popular, admired, and much sought after; you have only to make your wishes plain, and there will be no lack of people positively anxious to think as you do.

X

To Octavius Rufus

Is it indifference, obstinacy, or a sort of cruelty which makes you withhold works of such distinction so long? How much longer will you deny us our pleasure and yourself your crowning glory? They should be on all our lips, to travel as widely as the speech of Rome. Our hopes have long been high, and you ought not still to cheat and defer them. Some of your verses have broken free in spite of you and have become more widely known; unless you recall them to be incorporated in the whole, like runaway slaves they will find someone else to claim them. Bear in mind that you are bound by man's mortality, but that this one memorial of yourself can set you free: everything else is fragile and fleeting like man himself, who dies and is no more. You will

5 Dices, ut soles: " Amici mei viderint." Opto
equidem amicos tibi tam fideles tam eruditos tam
laboriosos, ut tantum curae intentionisque suscipere
et possint et velint, sed dispice ne sit parum providum,
6 sperare ex aliis quod tibi ipse non praestes. Et de
editione quidem interim ut voles: recita saltem quo
magis libeat emittere, utque tandem percipias
gaudium, quod ego olim pro te non temere praesumo.
7 Imaginor enim qui concursus quae admiratio te, qui
clamor quod etiam silentium maneat; quo ego, cum
dico vel recito, non minus quam clamore delector, sit
modo silentium acre et intentum, et cupidum ulteriora
8 audiendi. Hoc fructu tanto tam parato desine
studia tua infinita ista cunctatione fraudare; quae
cum modum excedit, verendum est ne inertiae et
desidiae vel etiam timiditatis nomen accipiat. Vale.

XI

C. Plinius Arriano Suo S.

1 Solet esse gaudio tibi, si quid acti est in senatu
dignum ordine illo. Quamvis enim quietis amore
secesseris, insidet tamen animo tuo maiestatis
publicae cura. Accipe ergo quod per hos dies actum
est, personae claritate famosum, severitate exempli
106

give your usual answer: that your friends can see to this. I only hope that you *have* friends who combine learning with loyalty and industry so that they are able as well as willing to undertake such a difficult and laborious task; but ask yourself whether it is not-ill-advised to expect from others a service which you will not perform for yourself.

As for publication—do as you like for the present, as long as you give some readings. You may then feel more inclined to publish, and will at least have the pleasure which I have long been confidently anticipating for you. I picture to myself the crowds, the admiration and applause which await you, and the hushed stillness—for I personally like this as much as applause when I am speaking or reading, as long as it indicates a keen attentiveness and eagerness to hear what follows. A great reward awaits you, and you must stop denying your work its due by your interminable hesitation; for whenever this goes too far there is a danger that it will be given another name—idleness, indolence, or possibly timidity.

XI

To Maturus Arrianus

You are always glad to hear of anything taking place in the Senate which is in keeping with its dignity, for though you have chosen to live in retirement in search of a quiet life, you have kept your interest in the honour of the State. So here is the news of the last days—a case which has attracted attention because of the celebrity of the defendant,

2 salubre, rei magnitudine aeternum. Marius Priscus accusantibus Afris quibus pro consule praefuit, omissa defensione iudices petiit. Ego et Cornelius Tacitus, adesse provincialibus iussi, existimavimus fidei nostrae convenire notum senatui facere excessisse Priscum immanitate et saevitia crimina quibus dari iudices possent, cum ob innocentes condemnandos, interficiendos etiam, pecunias accepisset.

3 Respondit Fronto Catius deprecatusque est, ne quid ultra repetundarum legem quaereretur, omniaque actionis suae vela vir movendarum lacrimarum peritissimus quodam velut vento miserationis im-

4 plevit. Magna contentio, magni utrimque clamores aliis cognitionem senatus lege conclusam, aliis liberam solutamque dicentibus, quantumque admisis-

5 set reus, tantum vindicandum. Novissime consul designatus Iulius Ferox, vir rectus et sanctus, Mario quidem iudices interim censuit dandos, evocandos autem quibus diceretur innocentium poenas vendi-

6 disse. Quae sententia non praevaluit modo, sed omnino post tantas dissensiones fuit sola frequens, adnotatumque experimentis, quod favor et misericordia acres et vehementes primos impetus habent, paulatim consilio et ratione quasi restincta considunt.

---

[1] The second of the five big public trials in which P. took part; cf. VI. 29. 9; *Pan.* 76. 1. Marius Priscus was provisionally assigned a board of *recuperatores* to assess the money he was to repay, but later summoned to stand trial with his accomplices and finally convicted in January 100.

has set an example of severity which will do a great deal of good, and is unlikely to be forgotten because of the importance of the issue involved.

A charge was brought by the province of Africa against their ex-governor, Marius Priscus.[1] He pleaded guilty and applied for a commission to assess compensation to be paid. Cornelius Tacitus and I were instructed to act for the provincials, and accordingly thought it our duty to inform the Senate that criminal offences of such monstrosity exceeded the powers of a commission, seeing that Priscus had taken bribes to sentence innocent persons to punishment and even to death. Catius Fronto replied in his defence with a plea for the charge to be limited to the question of restitution of money extorted, and, as he is practised in the art of drawing tears, he was able to fill all the sails of his speech with a breeze of pathos. There was a violent argument and an outcry all round, one side arguing that the Senate's judicial powers were limited by law, the other that they were free and unlimited and that the defendant should be punished to the full extent of his guilt. Finally Julius Ferox, the consul-elect, whose integrity always commands respect, proposed that Priscus should be provisionally granted a commission, but that the persons named as having given bribes to him to procure the conviction of the innocent should be summoned as witnesses. Not only was this proposal carried but it was in fact the only one to gain much support after all previous argument; experience has shown that appeals for support and sympathy make an immediate strong impact, but gradually lose their fire and die down under the influence of a reasoned judgement.

7 Unde evenit ut, quod multi clamore permixto tuentur, nemo tacentibus ceteris dicere velit; patescit enim, cum separaris a turba, contemplatio rerum quae
8 turba teguntur. Venerunt qui adesse erant iussi, Vitellius Honoratus et Flavius Marcianus; ex quibus Honoratus trecentis milibus exsilium equitis Romani septemque amicorum eius ultimam poenam, Marcianus unius equitis Romani septingentis milibus plura supplicia arguebatur emisse; erat enim fustibus caesus, damnatus in metallum, strangulatus in
9 carcere. Sed Honoratum cognitioni senatus mors opportuna subtraxit, Marcianus inductus est absente Prisco. Itaque Tuccius[1] Cerialis consularis iure senatorio postulavit, ut Priscus certior fieret, sive quia miserabiliorem sive quia invidiosiorem fore arbitrabatur, si praesens fuisset, sive (quod maxime credo) quia aequissimum erat commune crimen ab utroque defendi, et si dilui non potuisset in utroque puniri.
10 Dilata res est in proximum senatum, cuius ipse conspectus augustissimus fuit. Princeps praesidebat (erat enim consul), ad hoc Ianuarius mensis cum cetera tum praecipue senatorum frequentia celeberrimus; praeterea causae amplitudo auctaque dilatione exspectatio et fama, insitumque mortalibus studium

---

[1] Tuccius αβγ: Tullius *poscunt fasti Potentienses.*

---

[1] *i.e.* out of the regular order of delivering *sententiae.*

Hence the fact that in a general uproar many will support an opinion which no one is prepared to defend when silence is restored, for only when separated from the crowd is it possible to form a clear view of a situation which the crowd hitherto obscured.

The two witnesses, Vitellius Honoratus and Flavius Marcianus, were summoned to appear and duly arrived in Rome. Honoratus was charged with having procured the exile of a Roman knight and the death of seven of the latter's friends for a bribe of 300,000 sesterces, and Marcianus with having paid 700,000 for various punishments inflicted on a Roman knight, who had been cudgelled, condemned to the mines, and finally strangled in prison. However, Honoratus escaped justice at the hands of the Senate by his timely death, and Marcianus appeared in court in the absence of Priscus. Accordingly the ex-consul Tuccius Cerialis exercised the senatorial right to speak[1] by demanding that Priscus be informed, thinking that either he would excite more sympathy or possibly more indignation by his presence, or, more probably to my mind, because it is common justice that a charge made against two persons should be defended by both of them, and both should be convicted if unable to clear themselves.

The hearing was adjourned until the next meeting of the Senate, and this was a most impressive sight. The Emperor presided (being consul), and this was the month of January when there are always large numbers of people and particularly senators in Rome. Then the gravity of the case, the rumours and expectations increased by the adjournment, and the

magna et inusitata noscendi, omnes undique excive-
11 rat. Imaginare quae sollicitudo nobis, qui metus,
quibus super tanta re in illo coetu praesente Caesare
dicendum erat. Equidem in senatu non semel egi,
quin immo nusquam audiri benignius soleo: tunc me
tamen ut nova omnia novo metu permovebant.
12 Obversabatur praeter illa quae supra dixi causae
difficultas: stabat modo consularis, modo septemvir
13 epulonum, iam neutrum. Erat ergo perquam
onerosum accusare damnatum, quem ut premebat
atrocitas criminis, ita quasi peractae damnationis
14 miseratio tuebatur. Utcumque tamen animum co-
gitationemque collegi, coepi dicere non minore audientium adsensu quam sollicitudine mea. Dixi horis
paene quinque; nam duodecim clepsydris, quas
spatiosissimas acceperam, sunt additae quattuor.
Adeo illa ipsa, quae dura et adversa dicturo vide-
15 bantur, secunda dicenti fuerunt. Caesar quidem
tantum mihi studium, tantam etiam curam (nimium
est enim dicere sollicitudinem) praestitit, ut libertum
meum post me stantem saepius admoneret voci
laterique consulerem, cum me vehementius putaret
intendi, quam gracilitas mea perpeti posset. Re-

---

[1] The *septemviri epulonum* responsible for arranging the
sacrificial banquets for the gods. A priesthood at this time was
a decoration conferred for distinguished public service.

[2] See §2. He had been pronounced guilty by the *recuperatores*
on the charge *de repetundis* and was already excluded from the
Senate.

natural curiosity of human nature for anything new and important had attracted members from all parts. You can imagine our nervous anxiety at having to speak on such a subject before the Emperor, and in an assembly of this kind. It is true that I have often addressed the Senate, and nowhere do I receive a more sympathetic hearing, but this time all the unusual features of the case made me unusually nervous. For, as well as the problems I have described, I was confronted with the special difficulties of the case. Before me stood a man who had up till recently been of consular rank and a member of one of the priestly colleges,[1] and was now degraded; as he was thus condemned, it was extremely difficult to make him the subject of a prosecuting speech, for in spite of the weight of the horrible charges against him he had in his favour a certain amount of sympathy aroused by his previous conviction.[2]

However, I managed to pull myself and my thoughts together, and proceeded to speak, meeting with a warm reception to make up for my fears. My speech lasted for nearly five hours, for I was allowed four water-clocks in addition to my original twelve of the largest size; thus all those difficulties I had anticipated in my path were dispelled when I came to speak. The Emperor did indeed show such an attentive and kindly interest in me (I should not like to call it anxiety on my behalf) that more than once, when he fancied I was putting too much strain on my rather delicate physique, he suggested to my freedman [3] standing behind me that I should

[3] His secretary.

spondit mihi pro Marciano Claudius Marcellinus.
16 Missus deinde senatus et revocatus in posterum;
neque enim iam incohari poterat actio, nisi ut noctis
interventu scinderetur.

17 Postero die dixit pro Mario Salvius Liberalis, vir
subtilis dispositus acer disertus; in illa vero causa
omnes artes suas protulit. Respondit Cornelius
Tacitus eloquentissime et, quod eximium orationi
18 eius inest, σεμνῶς. Dixit pro Mario rursus Fronto
Catius insigniter, utque iam locus ille poscebat, plus
in precibus temporis quam in defensione consumpsit.
Huius actionem vespera inclusit, non tamen sic ut
abrumperet. Itaque in tertium diem probationes
exierunt. Iam hoc ipsum pulchrum et antiquum,
senatum nocte dirimi, triduo vocari, triduo contineri.
19 Cornutus Tertullus consul designatus, vir egregius et
pro veritate firmissimus, censuit septingenta milia
quae acceperat Marius aerario inferenda, Mario urbe
Italiaque interdicendum, Marciano hoc amplius
Africa. In fine sententiae adiecit, quod ego et
Tacitus iniuncta advocatione diligenter et fortiter
functi essemus, arbitrari senatum ita nos fecisse ut
20 dignum mandatis partibus fuerit. Adsenserunt consules designati, omnes etiam consulares usque ad
Pompeium Collegam: ille et septingenta milia

---

[1] Cf. *Pan.* 76. 1.

[2] Suffect consul with P., September–October 100.

[3] That Priscus was generally felt to have got off too lightly
is indicated by Juvenal, *Sat.* I. 49; VIII. 120. He lost his
dignitas and gains, but not his civic status and property.

spare my voice and my lungs. Claudius Marcellinus replied on behalf of Marcianus, after which the court adjourned until the following day; any further speech would have had to be cut short at nightfall.

Next day Salvius Liberalis spoke in defence of Priscus. He is a precise and methodical speaker with a forceful command of words, and this case brought all his powers into full play. Cornelius Tacitus made an eloquent speech in reply, with all the majesty which characterizes his style of oratory. Catius Fronto resumed the defence and made an excellent speech, which at this stage he thought best to apply to pleas for mercy rather than defensive arguments. He finished speaking at the end of the day, but did not have to cut short his words. The summing-up was accordingly postponed until the third day, thereby following a good and long-established precedent in the Senate of interrupting proceedings at nightfall and resuming them next day in a continuous three-day session.[1]

Cornutus Tertullus,[2] the consul-elect, who always stands out for his strict adherence to the truth, then proposed that the bribe of 700,000 sesterces which Priscus had taken should be paid by him into the Treasury, that Priscus should be exiled from Rome and Italy,[3] and Marcianus from Rome, Italy, and Africa. He ended his speech by stating on behalf of the Senate that, by our conscientious and courageous handling of the prosecution entrusted to us, Tacitus and I were considered to have correctly carried out the duty assigned us. The consuls-elect supported him and so did all the consulars down to Pompeius Collega, who then proposed that the 700,000 sesterces

aerario inferenda et Marcianum in quinquennium
relegandum, Marium repetundarum poenae quam
21 iam passus esset censuit relinquendum. Erant in
utraque sententia multi, fortasse etiam plures in hac
vel solutiore vel molliore. Nam quidam ex illis
quoque, qui Cornuto videbantur adsensi, hunc qui
22 post ipsos censuerat sequebantur. Sed cum fieret
discessio, qui sellis consulum adstiterant, in Cornuti
sententiam ire coeperunt. Tum illi qui se Collegae
adnumerari patiebantur in diversum transierunt;
Collega cum paucis relictus. Multum postea de
impulsoribus suis, praecipue de Regulo questus est,
qui se in sententia quam ipse dictaverat deseruisset.
Est alioqui Regulo tam mobile ingenium, ut plurimum audeat plurimum timeat.

23 Hic finis cognitionis amplissimae. Superest tamen
λιτούργιον non leve, Hostilius Firminus legatus Mari
Prisci, qui permixtus causae graviter vehementerque
vexatus est. Nam et rationibus Marciani, et sermone quem ille habuerat in ordine Lepcitanorum,
operam suam Prisco ad turpissimum ministerium
commodasse, stipulatusque de Marciano quinquaginta milia denariorum probabatur, ipse praeterea
accepisse sestertia decem milia foedissimo quidem
titulo, nomine unguentarii, qui titulus a vita hominis
compti semper et pumicati non abhorrebat. Placuit
24 censente Cornuto referri de eo proximo senatu; tunc
enim, casu an conscientia, afuerat.

should be paid into the Treasury and Marcianus banished for five years, but that Priscus should receive no sentence beyond the one already passed on him for extorting money. Both proposals found many supporters, especially the second one, being less severe, or if you prefer, more lenient; for there were some who seemed to be in agreement with Cornutus but went over to Collega when he spoke after them. But, when the division was taken, first the members standing by the consuls' chairs proceeded to go over to Cornutus's side, then those who were letting themselves be counted with Collega crossed the floor, so that Collega was left with scarcely anyone. He complained bitterly afterwards about those who had led him on, especially Regulus, who had actually told him what to say and then deserted him. (Regulus's instability generally leads him into rash ventures which he afterwards regrets.)

So ended this important trial. There is still a minor matter, though not unimportant, concerning Priscus's deputy, Hostilius Firminus, who was implicated in the charge and, indeed, very heavily involved. It was proved from the accounts of Marcianus and from a speech made by Firminus in the town-council of Lepcis that he had helped Priscus in a particularly shocking piece of work, and had also bargained with Marcianus to receive 200,000 sesterces; and he had in fact been paid 10,000 under the disgraceful head of " cosmetics "—an entry quite in keeping with his dandified elegance. The Senate adopted Cornutus's proposal to refer his case to the next session; for, either by chance or through knowledge of his guilt, Firminus was not present.

Habes res urbanas; invicem rusticas scribe. Quid arbusculae tuae, quid vineae, quid segetes agunt, quid oves delicatissimae?[1] In summa, nisi aeque longam epistulam reddis, non est quod postea nisi brevissimam exspectes. Vale.

XII

C. PLINIUS ARRIANO SUO S.

1 Λιτούργιον illud, quod superesse Mari Prisci causae proxime scripseram, nescio an satis, circumcisum tamen et adrasum est. Firminus inductus in 2 senatum respondit crimini noto. Secutae sunt diversae sententiae consulum designatorum. Cornutus Tertullus censuit ordine movendum, Acutius Nerva in sortitione provinciae rationem eius non habendam. Quae sententia tamquam mitior vicit, 3 cum sit alioqui durior tristiorque. Quid enim miserius quam exsectum et exemptum honoribus senatoriis, labore et molestia non carere? quid gravius quam tanta ignominia adfectum non in solitudine latere, sed in hac altissima specula conspicien- 4 dum se monstrandumque praebere? Praeterea quid publice minus aut congruens aut decorum? notatum a senatu in senatu sedere, ipsisque illis a quibus sit notatus aequari; summotum a proconsulatu quia se in

---

[1] Perhaps *oves pellitae*, given coats to preserve their fine wool; see Varro, *Rer. Rust.* II. ii. 18; Horace, *Odes* II. vi. 10.

118

So much for the city. Now give me news of the country—how are your fruit trees and your vines, the harvest and your prize sheep?[1] Unless you answer me in as long a letter as this, you can expect nothing in future but the shortest note.

XII

To MATURUS ARRIANUS

THAT " minor matter " which I said in my last letter was left over from the case of Marius Priscus, is polished off and done with, though it could have been better handled. Firminus was summoned before the Senate to answer the charge already known. Then the consuls-elect failed to agree on a sentence; Cornutus Tertullus proposed that he should be expelled from the Senate, but Acutius Nerva thought it sufficient if his claim were not considered when lots were drawn for provinces. This was the opinion which prevailed as being the more lenient, though in another sense it is more cruelly severe. Nothing could be worse than to be stripped of all the privileges of senatorial rank but not to be rid of its toils and troubles, and nothing more humiliating for anyone so disgraced than to remain in his conspicuous position exposed as a marked man to the public gaze instead of hiding himself in retirement. And besides, nothing could be more unsuitable or less conducive to the public interest than for a senator to retain his seat after he has been censured by the Senate, to remain equal in status to those who censured him, and though debarred from a governorship for his

119

legatione turpiter gesserat, de proconsulibus iudicare, damnatumque sordium vel damnare alios vel
5 absolvere! Sed hoc pluribus visum est. Numeran-
tur enim sententiae, non ponderantur; nec aliud in
publico consilio potest fieri, in quo nihil est tam in-
aequale quam aequalitas ipsa. Nam cum sit impar
6 prudentia, par omnium ius est. Implevi promissum
priorisque epistulae fidem exsolvi, quam ex spatio
temporis iam recepisse te colligo; nam et festinanti
et diligenti tabellario dedi, nisi quid impedimenti in
7 via passus est. Tuae nunc partes, ut primum illam,
deinde hanc remunereris litteris, quales istinc redire
uberrimae possunt. Vale.

XIII

C. Plinius Prisco Suo S.

1 Et tu occasiones obligandi me avidissime amplec-
2 teris, et ego nemini libentius debeo. Duabus ergo
de causis a te potissimum petere constitui, quod
impetratum maxime cupio. Regis exercitum amplissimum: hinc tibi beneficiorum larga materia, longum
praeterea tempus, quo amicos tuos exornare potuisti.
3 Convertere ad nostros nec hos multos. Malles tu
quidem multos; sed meae verecundiae sufficit unus

---

¹ If this letter is rightly assigned to Neratius Priscus, he was
in command of three legions as legate in Pannonia in 102–3.
Syme (*Historia* IX, p. 365) prefers Javolenus Priscus, legate
of Syria sometime between 94 and 101.

disgraceful conduct as governor's deputy, to retain his power of passing judgement on other governors, to condemn or acquit them of crimes which he has himself been found guilty. But the majority gave their assent; for votes are counted, their value is not weighed, and no other method is possible in a public assembly. Yet this strict equality results in something very different from equity, so long as men have the same right to judge but not the same ability to judge wisely.

I have kept my word and the promise I made you in my previous letter, which I think must have reached you, judging by the date. I gave it to a fast and reliable courier—unless he has been delayed on the road. Now it is your turn to pay me for both these letters; there can be no lack of news from your part of the world.

XIII

To Neratius (?) Priscus

You would gladly seize any opportunity to oblige me, and there is no one to whom I would rather be in debt than to you. So for two reasons I have singled you out to approach with a request which I am most anxious to be granted. Your command of a large army[1] gives you a plentiful source of benefits to confer, and secondly, your tenure has been long enough for you to have provided for your own friends. Turn to mine—they are not many. You might wish them more, but modesty restricts me to one or two, and the one I have most in mind is Voconius Romanus.

THE LETTERS OF PLINY

4 aut alter, ac potius unus. Is erit Voconius Romanus.
Pater ei in equestri gradu clarus, clarior vitricus,
immo pater alius (nam huic quoque nomini pietate
successit), mater e primis. Ipse citerioris Hispaniae
(scis quod iudicium provinciae illius, quanta sit
5 gravitas) flamen proxime fuit. Hunc ego, cum simul
studeremus, arte familiariterque dilexi; ille meus in
urbe ille in secessu contubernalis, cum hoc seria cum
hoc iocos miscui. Quid enim illo aut fidelius amico
6 aut sodale iucundius? Mira in sermone, mira etiam
7 in ore ipso vultuque suavitas. Ad hoc ingenium
excelsum subtile dulce facile eruditum in causis
agendis; epistulas quidem scribit, ut Musas ipsas
Latine loqui credas. Amatur a me plurimum nec
8 tamen vincitur. Equidem iuvenis statim iuveni,
quantum potui per aetatem, avidissime contuli, et
nuper ab optimo principe trium liberorum ius impetravi; quod quamquam parce et cum delectu
daret, mihi tamen tamquam eligeret indulsit. Haec
9 beneficia mea tueri nullo modo melius quam ut
augeam possum, praesertim cum ipse illa tam grate
interpretetur, ut dum priora accipit posteriora merea-
10 tur. Habes qualis quam probatus carusque sit nobis,
quem rogo pro ingenio pro fortuna tua exornes. In
primis ama hominem; nam licet tribuas ei quantum

---

[1] That of *flamen*, a priesthood widely held in the provinces
and the highest dignity available. P. himself was *flamen divi
Titi* in Comum (App. A. 3.).

[2] The *ius trium liberorum* removed bars on inheriting, permitted offices to be held before the statutory age, and allowed

122

His father was distinguished in the order of knights; even more so was his stepfather, whom I should rather call his second father in view of his kindness to his stepson; his mother comes from a leading family. He himself recently held a priesthood[1] in Hither Spain, a province well known to you for its high principles and good judgement. He was my close and intimate friend when we were students together, my companion in the city and out of it; with him I shared everything, work and play. No one could be a more faithful friend or more delightful companion. His conversation, voice and whole expression have a special charm, and he is gifted besides with a powerful and penetrating intellect, trained by his profession at the bar to express itself with ease and grace. In addition, the letters he writes would make one believe that the Muses speak Latin. I love him dearly, as he does me. Ever since our youth together I have been anxious to do as much for him as my age permitted, and I recently obtained for him from our noble Emperor the privileges granted to parents of three children;[2] the Emperor used to grant this sparingly and after careful selection, but he granted my request as if the choice were his own. The best way for me to confirm my services is by adding to them, especially as Romanus's grateful appreciation in acceptance reveals him as worthy of more.

Now you know the man he is and how much I love and admire him, please provide for him as your generous nature and position permit. What is most important is that you should like him; for though you

priority in holding office and being assigned a province. The Emperor is Nerva, and the letter is prior to X. 4.

amplissimum potes, nihil tamen amplius potes amici-
tia tua; cuius esse eum usque ad intimam familiaritem capacem quo magis scires, breviter tibi studia
11 mores omnem denique vitam eius expressi. Extenderem preces nisi et tu rogari diu nolles et ego tota
hoc epistula fecissem; rogat enim et quidem efficacissime, qui reddit causas rogandi. Vale.

XIV

C. PLINIUS MAXIMO SUO S.

1 VERUM opinaris: distringor centumviralibus causis,
quae me exercent magis quam delectant. Sunt enim
pleraeque parvae et exiles; raro incidit vel persona-
2 rum claritate vel negotii magnitudine insignis. Ad
hoc pauci cum quibus iuvet dicere; ceteri audaces
atque etiam magna ex parte adulescentuli obscuri ad
declamandum huc transierunt, tam inreverenter et
temere, ut mihi Atilius noster expresse dixisse
videatur, sic in foro pueros a centumviralibus causis
auspicari, ut ab Homero in scholis. Nam hic
quoque ut illic primum coepit esse quod maximum est.
3 At hercule ante memoriam meam (ita maiores natu
solent dicere), ne nobilissimis quidem adulescentibus
locus erat nisi aliquo consulari producente: tanta

---

[1] *i.e.* that of *tribunus angusticlavius* in the army, open to
Roman knights. It carried considerable administrative duties.
[2] As recommended by Quintilian in *Inst. Orat.* I. viii. 5.
[3] See Tacitus, *Dial.* 34.

grant him the highest office in your power,[1] you could give him nothing better than your friendship. It was to show you that he is worthy of it and even of your closest intimacy that I have thus briefly described his interests and character, in short his whole life. I would prolong my entreaties did you not dislike long begging letters, of which I am afraid the whole of this letter is one; for to be effective a request must give its reasons.

XIV

To Novius (?) Maximus

You are quite right: cases at the Centumviral Court are taking up all my time, and give me more work than pleasure. Most of them are petty affairs and there is rarely one which stands out for the importance of the issue or the celebrity of the persons involved. There are besides very few people with whom it is any pleasure to appear if you consider the impudence of the rest—mostly unknown youngsters who have arrived in our midst to practise rhetoric: which they do with such effrontery and want of consideration that I think our friend Atilius summed them up well when he said that boys begin their career at the bar with Centumviral cases just as they start on Homer at school. In both places they put the hardest first.[2] But before my time (as our elders always say), believe me, there was no place here for a young man, however well-born, unless a consular senator introduced him; so highly was a noble profession respected.[3] Today the bars of propriety and defer-

4 veneratione pulcherrimum opus colebatur. Nunc
refractis pudoris et reverentiae claustris, omnia
patent omnibus, nec inducuntur sed inrumpunt.
Sequuntur auditores actoribus similes, conducti et
redempti. Manceps convenitur; in media basilica
tam palam sportula quam in triclinio dantur; ex
5 iudicio in iudicium pari mercede transitur. Inde iam
non inurbane Σοφοκλεῖς vocantur,[1] isdem Latinum
6 nomen impositum est Laudiceni; et tamen crescit
in dies foeditas utraque lingua notata. Here duo
nomenclatores mei (habent sane aetatem eorum qui
nuper togas sumpserint) ternis denariis ad laudandum
trahebantur. Tanti constat ut sis disertissimus.
Hoc pretio quamlibet numerosa subsellia implentur,
hoc ingens corona colligitur, hoc infiniti clamores
7 commoventur, cum mesochorus dedit signum. Opus
est enim signo apud non intellegentes, ne audientes
8 quidem; nam plerique non audiunt, nec ulli magis
laudant. Si quando transibis per basilicam et voles
scire, quo modo quisque dicat, nihil est quod tribunal ascendas, nihil quod praebeas aurem; facilis
divinatio: scito eum pessime dicere, qui laudabitur
maxime.
9 Primus hunc audiendi morem induxit Larcius
Licinus, hactenus tamen ut auditores corrogaret.
Ita certe ex Quintiliano praeceptore meo audisse me
10 memini. Narrabat ille: "Adsectabar Domitium
Afrum. Cum apud centumviros diceret graviter et

---

[1] ἀπὸ τοῦ σοφῶς καὶ καλεῖσθαι αβγ: del. *Catanaeus.*

---

[1] Twelve sesterces, a high fee.
[2] The Centumviral Court sat in the Basilica Julia.

erence are down, everything is open to all and sundry,
and no introductions are needed for anyone to burst in.

Audiences follow who are no better than the speakers, being hired and bought for the occasion. They
parley with the contractor, take the gifts offered on
the floor of the court as openly as they would at a
dinner-party, and move on from case to case for the
same sort of pay. The Greek name for them means
" bravo-callers " and the Latin " dinner-clappers ";
witty enough, but both names expose a scandal
which increases daily. Yesterday two of my attendants (who would only just have come of age if they
were citizens) were induced to add their applause for
three denarii[1] each. That is all it costs you to have
your eloquence acclaimed. For this sum seats can be
filled, any number of them, a huge crowd assembled,
and endless cheering raised whenever the chorus-
master gives the signal. (A signal there must be for
people who neither understand nor even hear; most
of them do not listen but cheer as loud as anyone.)
If you happen to be passing the court[2] and want to
know about the speakers, there is no need to come on
to the bench or pay attention to the proceedings;
it is easy to guess—the man who raises most cheers is
the worst speaker.

Larcius Licinus was the first to introduce this way
of getting together an audience, but he went no
further than sending invitations. At least that is
what I remember hearing from my tutor Quintilian.
He used to tell this story: " I was working under
Domitius Afer, who was addressing the Centumviri
in his usual impressive and measured tones when he
heard an extraordinary noise of loud shouting near

lente (hoc enim illi actionis genus erat), audit ex
proximo immodicum insolitumque clamorem. Admiratus reticuit; ubi silentium factum est, repetit
quod abruperat. Iterum clamor, iterum reticuit, et
11 post silentium coepit. Idem tertio. Novissime
quis diceret quaesiit. Responsum est: " Licinus."
Tum intermissa causa " Centumviri," inquit, " hoc
12 artificium perit." ' Quod alioqui perire incipiebat
cum perisse Afro videretur, nunc vero prope funditus
exstinctum et eversum est. Pudet referre quae
quam fracta pronuntiatione dicantur, quibus quam
13 teneris clamoribus excipiantur. Plausus tantum ac
potius sola cymbala et tympana illis canticis desunt:
ululatus quidem (neque enim alio vocabulo potest
exprimi theatris quoque indecora laudatio) large
14 supersunt. Nos tamen adhuc et utilitas amicorum
et ratio aetatis moratur ac retinet; veremur enim ne
forte non has indignitates reliquisse, sed laborem
fugisse videamur. Sumus tamen solito rariores,
quod initium est gradatim desinendi. Vale.

XV

C. Plinius Valeriano Suo S.

1 Quo modo te veteres Marsi tui? quo modo emptio
nova? Placent agri, postquam tui facti sunt? Rarum id quidem; nihil enim aeque gratum est adeptis

---

[1] The region in Latium near Lake Fucinus.

by. He stopped speaking in amazement. Then silence was restored and he resumed his speech where he had broken off. Again the uproar, again he stopped, and when there was silence began again. The same thing happened a third time, and at last he asked who was speaking. ' Licinus,' was the answer. At that he abandoned his case: ' Gentlemen,' he said, ' this means death to our profession.' ' " In fact it was only dying when Afer believed it dead; now its ruin and destruction are almost complete. I am ashamed to describe the speeches of today, the mincing accents in which they are delivered, and the puerile applause they receive. That sort of sing-song needs only the clapping and cymbals and tambourines of Cybele to complete it, for of howling (no other word can express this applause which would be indecent even in the theatre) there is more than enough. However, I still stay on; but only through my wish to be of service to my friends and the thought that if I leave at my age it might look like an escape from work rather than a withdrawal from these disgraceful scenes. But my appearances are less frequent than they used to be, and this is the first step towards a gradual retirement.

XV

To Julius Valerianus

How is your old Marsian[1] place? and the new purchase? Are you pleased with the new property now that it is yours? It rarely happens—nothing is quite so attractive in our possession as it was when

2 quam concupiscentibus. Me praedia materna parum commode tractant, delectant tamen ut materna,
et alioqui longa patientia occallui. Habent hunc
finem adsiduae querellae, quod queri pudet. Vale.

XVI

C. PLINIUS ANNIO SUO S.

1   Tu quidem pro cetera tua diligentia admones me
codicillos Aciliani, qui me ex parte instituit heredem,
pro non scriptis habendos, quia non sint confirmati
2 testamento; quod ius ne mihi quidem ignotum est,
cum sit iis etiam notum, qui nihil aliud sciunt. Sed
ego propriam quandam legem mihi dixi, ut defunctorum voluntates, etiamsi iure deficerentur, quasi per-
fectas tuerer. Constat autem codicillos istos Aciliani
3 manu scriptos. Licet ergo non sint confirmati testamento, a me tamen ut confirmati observabuntur,
4 praesertim cum delatori locus non sit. Nam si
verendum esset ne quod ego dedissem populus
eriperet, cunctantior fortasse et cautior esse deberem; cum vero liceat heredi donare, quod in hereditate subsedit, nihil est quod obstet illi meae legi,
cui publicae leges non repugnant. Vale.

---

[1] Equity was not a recognized principle of Roman Law, but
P. observes it also in IV. 10 and V. 7.

coveted. My mother's property is treating me badly; still I love it for being my mother's, and, besides, long suffering has toughened me. Everlasting complaints come to an end through the shame of complaining at all.

XVI

To Annius Severus (?)

It is like you to be punctilious about reminding me that the codicil left by Acilianus making me heir to part of his property must be held invalid because its existence is not confirmed in his will; but even I am aware of this point of law, which people generally know even if they know no other. I have in fact laid down a private law for myself whereby I treat the wishes of the deceased as formally expressed though they may not be legally binding.[1] It is beyond doubt that this codicil of Acilianus is written in his own hand; therefore I intend to carry out its instructions as if it was confirmed in the will, though in fact it is not, especially as there is no longer any risk of prosecution. For, if I had any reason to fear that a gift I made from this bequest might be officially confiscated, I ought perhaps to pause and act with caution; but an heir is free now to give away what has come to him by inheritance. There is nothing then in the laws of the land in conflict with my private law, so nothing to prevent my acting on it.[2]

[2] A possible reference to the new security for testators in the restored liberty of Trajan's reign; *Pan.* 43.

THE LETTERS OF PLINY

XVII

C. PLINIUS GALLO SUO S.

1 MIRARIS cur me Laurentinum vel (si ita mavis),
Laurens meum tanto opere delectet; desines mirari,
cum cognoveris gratiam villae, opportunitatem loci,
2 litoris spatium. Decem septem milibus passuum ab
urbe secessit, ut peractis quae agenda fuerint salvo
iam et composito die possis ibi manere. Aditur non
una via; nam et Laurentina et Ostiensis eodem
ferunt, sed Laurentina a quarto decimo lapide,
Ostiensis ab undecimo relinquenda est. Utrimque
excipit iter aliqua ex parte harenosum, iunctis paulo
gravius et longius, equo breve et molle. Varia hinc
3 atque inde facies; nam modo occurrentibus silvis via
coartatur, modo latissimis pratis diffunditur et
patescit; multi greges ovium, multa ibi equorum
boum armenta, quae montibus hieme depulsa herbis
et tepore verno nitescunt. Villa usibus capax, non
4 sumptuosa tutela. Cuius in prima parte atrium frugi,
nec tamen sordidum; deinde porticus in D litterae
similitudinem circumactae, quibus parvola sed
festiva area includitur. Egregium hae adversus
tempestates receptaculum; nam specularibus ac
5 multo magis imminentibus tectis muniuntur. Est
contra medias cavaedium hilare, mox triclinium satis

---

[1] See plan, Volume II, p. 554.

XVII

To Clusinius (?) Gallus

You may wonder why my Laurentine place (or my Laurentian, if you like that better) is such a joy to me, but once you realize the attractions of the house itself, the amenities of its situation, and its extensive seafront, you will have your answer.   It is seventeen miles from Rome, so that it is possible to spend the night there after necessary business is done, without having cut short or hurried the day's work, and it can be approached by more than one route; the roads to Laurentum and Ostia both lead in that direction, but you must leave the first at the fourteenth milestone and the other at the eleventh.   Whichever way you go, the side road you take is sandy for some distance and rather heavy and slow-going if you drive, but soft and easily covered on horseback.   The view on either side is full of variety, for sometimes the road narrows as it passes through the woods, and then it broadens and opens out through wide meadows where there are many flocks of sheep and herds of horses and cattle driven down from the mountains in winter to grow sleek on the pastures in the springlike climate.

The house[1] is large enough for my needs but not expensive to keep up.   It opens into a hall [A], unpretentious but not without dignity, and then there are two colonnades, rounded like the letter D, which enclose a small but pleasant courtyard [B].   This makes a splendid retreat in bad weather, being protected by windows and still more by the overhanging

pulchrum, quod in litus excurrit ac si quando Africo
mare impulsum est, fractis iam et novissimis flucti-
bus leviter adluitur. Undique valvas aut fenestras
non minores valvis habet atque ita a lateribus a fronte
quasi tria maria prospectat; a tergo cavaedium porticum aream porticum rursus, mox atrium silvas et
6 longinquos respicit montes. Huius a laeva retractius
paulo cubiculum est amplum, deinde aliud minus
quod altera fenestra admittit orientem, occidentem
altera retinet; hac et subiacens mare longius quidem
7 sed securius intuetur. Huius cubiculi et triclinii
illius obiectu includitur angulus, qui purissimum
solem continet et accendit. Hoc hibernaculum,
hoc etiam gymnasium meorum est; ibi omnes silent
venti, exceptis qui nubilum inducunt, et serenum
8 ante quam usum loci eripiunt. Adnectitur angulo
cubiculum in hapsida curvatum, quod ambitum solis
fenestris omnibus sequitur. Parieti eius in biblio-
thecae speciem armarium insertum est, quod non
9 legendos libros sed lectitandos capit. Adhaeret
dormitorium membrum transitu interiacente, qui
suspensus et tubulatus conceptum vaporem salubri
temperamento huc illuc digerit et ministrat. Reliqua
pars lateris huius servorum libertorumque usibus

---

[1] Laurentum was primarily a winter residence: see IX. 40.

roof. Opposite the middle of it is a cheerful inner
hall [c], and then a dining-room [D] which really is
rather fine: it runs out towards the shore, and whenever the sea is driven inland by the south-west wind
it is lightly washed by the spray of the spent breakers.
It has folding doors or windows as large as the doors
all round, so that at the front and sides it seems to
look out on to three seas, and at the back has a view
through the inner hall, the courtyard with the two
colonnades, then the entrance-hall to the woods and
mountains in the distance.

To the left of this and a little farther back from the
sea is a large bedroom [E], and then another smaller
one [F] which lets in the morning sunshine with one
window and holds the last rays of the evening sun
with the other; from this window too is a view of the
sea beneath, this time at a safe distance. In the
angle of this room and the dining-room is a corner
which retains and intensifies the concentrated warmth
of the sun, and this is the winter-quarters and
gymnasium of my household [G] for no winds can be
heard there except those which bring the rain clouds,
and the place can still be used after the weather has
broken.[1] Round the corner is a room built round in
an apse to let in the sun as it moves round and shines
in each window in turn, and with one wall fitted with
shelves like a library to hold the books which I read
and read again [H]. Next comes a bedroom-wing [I]
on the other side of a passage which has a floor raised
and fitted with pipes to receive hot steam and
circulate it at a regulated temperature. The remaining rooms on this side of the house are kept
for the use of my slaves and freedmen, but most

detinetur, plerisque tam mundis, ut accipere hos-
10 pites possint. Ex alio latere cubiculum est politissi-
mum; deinde vel cubiculum grande vel modica
cenatio, quae plurimo sole, plurimo mari lucet; post
hanc cubiculum cum procoetone, altitudine aestivum,
munimentis hibernum; est enim subductum omnibus
ventis. Huic cubiculo aliud et procoeton communi
11 pariete iunguntur. Inde balinei cella frigidaria
spatiosa et effusa, cuius in contrariis parietibus duo
baptisteria velut eiecta sinuantur, abunde capacia si
mare in proximo cogites. Adiacet unctorium, hypocauston, adiacet propnigeon balinei, mox duae cellae
magis elegantes quam sumptuosae; cohaeret calida
piscina mirifica, ex qua natantes mare adspiciunt,
12 nec procul sphaeristerium quod calidissimo soli
inclinato iam die occurrit. Hic turris erigitur, sub
qua diaetae duae, totidem in ipsa, praeterea cenatio
quae latissimum mare longissimum litus villas amoe-
13 nissimas possidet.[1] Est et alia turris; in hac cubiculum, in quo sol nascitur conditurque; lata post
apotheca et horreum, sub hoc triclinium, quod turbati
maris non nisi fragorem et sonum patitur, eumque
iam languidum ac desinentem; hortum et gesta-
14 tionem videt, qua hortus includitur. Gestatio buxo
aut rore marino, ubi deficit buxus, ambitur; nam

[1] possidet αγ: prospicit β.

of them are quite presentable enough to receive guests [J].

On the other side of the dining-room is an elegantly decorated bedroom [K], and then one which can either be a large bedroom or a moderate-sized dining-room [L] and enjoys the bright light of the sun reflected from the sea; behind is another room with an ante-chamber, high enough to be cool in summer and pro-tected as a refuge in winter, for it is sheltered from every wind. A similar room and antechamber are divided off by a single wall [M]. Then comes the cooling-room of the bath, which is large and spacious and has two curved baths built out of opposite walls; these are quite large enough if you consider that the sea is so near. Next come the oiling-room, the fur-nace-room, and the hot-room for the bath, and then two rest-rooms, beautifully decorated in a simple style [N], leading to the heated swimming-bath [O] which is much admired and from which swimmers can see the sea. Close by is the ball-court [P] which receives the full warmth of the setting sun. Here there is a second storey, with two living-rooms below and two above, as well as a dining-room which com-mands the whole expanse of sea and stretch of shore with all its lovely houses [Q]. Elsewhere another upper storey contains a room which receives both the rising and setting sun, and a good-sized wine-store and granary behind, while below is a dining-room [R] where nothing is known of a high sea but the sound of the breakers, and even that as a dying murmur; it looks on to the garden and the encircling drive.

All round the drive runs a hedge of box, or rose-mary to fill any gaps, for box will flourish extensively

buxus, qua parte defenditur tectis, abunde viret;
aperto caelo apertoque vento et quamquam longin-
15 qua aspergine maris inarescit. Adiacet gestationi in-
teriore circumitu vinea[1] tenera et umbrosa, nudisque
etiam pedibus mollis et cedens. Hortum morus et
ficus frequens vestit, quarum arborum illa vel maxime
ferax terra est, malignior ceteris. Hac non deteriore
quam maris facie cenatio remota a mari fruitur,
cingitur diaetis duabus a tergo, quarum fenestris
subiacet vestibulum villae et hortus alius pinguis et
16 rusticus. Hinc cryptoporticus prope publici operis
extenditur. Utrimque fenestrae, a mari plures, ab
horto singulae sed alternis[2] pauciores. Hae cum
serenus dies et immotus, omnes, cum hinc vel inde
ventis inquietus, qua venti quiescunt sine iniuria
17 patent. Ante cryptoporticum xystus violis odoratus.
Teporem solis infusi repercussu cryptoporticus auget,
quae ut tenet solem sic aquilonem inhibet sum-
movetque, quantumque caloris ante tantum retro
frigoris; similiter africum sistit, atque ita diversis-
simos ventos alium alio latere frangit et finit. Haec
18 iucunditas eius hieme, maior aestate. Nam ante
meridiem xystum, post meridiem gestationis hortique
proximam partem umbra sua temperat, quae, ut dies
crevit decrevitve, modo brevior modo longior hac
19 vel illa cadit. Ipsa vero cryptoporticus tum maxime
caret sole, cum ardentissimus culmini eius insistit.
Ad hoc patentibus fenestris favonios accipit trans-

---

[1] vinea αβγ: vinca a (tuetur Sulze): via Kukula.
[2] singulae sed alternis del. Stout.

---

[1] Not a vineyard for producing grapes; P. makes his wine
in Tuscany, VIII. 2; IX. 16.

where it is sheltered by the buildings, but dries up if exposed in the open to the wind and salt spray even at a distance. Inside the inner ring of the drive is a young and shady vine pergola[1] [s], where the soil is soft and yielding even to the bare foot. The garden itself is thickly planted with mulberries and figs, trees which the soil bears very well though it is less kind to others. On this side the dining-room away from the sea has a view as lovely as that of the sea itself, while from the windows of the two rooms behind [T] it can be seen the entrance to the house and another well-stocked kitchen garden [U].

Here begins a covered arcade [v] nearly as large as a public building. It has windows on both sides, but more facing the sea, as there is one in each alternate bay on the garden side. These all stand open on a fine and windless day, and in stormy weather can safely be opened on one side or the other away from the wind. In front is a terrace [w] scented with violets. As the sun beats down, the arcade increases its heat by reflection and not only retains the sun but keeps off the north-east wind so that it is as hot in front as it is cool behind. In the same way it checks the south-west wind, thus breaking the force of winds from wholly opposite quarters by one or the other of its sides; it is pleasant in winter but still more so in summer when the terrace is kept cool in the morning and the drive and nearer part of the garden in the afternoon, as its shadow falls shorter or longer on one side or the other while the day advances or declines. Inside the arcade, of course, there is least sunshine when the sun is blazing down on its roof, and as its open windows allow the western breezes to enter and

139

mittitque nec umquam aere pigro et manente in-
20 gravescit. In capite xysti, deinceps cryptoporticus
horti, diaeta est amores mei, re vera amores: ipse
posui. In hac heliocaminus quidem alia xystum, alia
mare, utraque solem, cubiculum autem valvis crypto-
21 porticum, fenestra prospicit mare. Contra parietem
medium zotheca perquam eleganter recedit, quae
specularibus et velis obductis reductisve modo adicitur
cubiculo modo aufertur. Lectum et duas cathedras
capit; a pedibus mare, a tergo villae, a capite silvae:
tot facies locorum totidem fenestris et distinguit et
22 miscet. Iunctum est cubiculum noctis et somni.
Non illud voces servolorum, non maris murmur, non
tempestatum motus non fulgurum lumen, ac ne diem
quidem sentit, nisi fenestris apertis. Tam alti
abditique secreti illa ratio, quod interiacens andron
parietem cubiculi hortique distinguit atque ita omnem
23 sonum media inanitate consumit. Adplicitum est
cubiculo hypocauston perexiguum, quod angusta
fenestra suppositum calorem, ut ratio exigit, aut
effundit aut retinet. Procoeton inde et cubiculum
porrigitur in solem, quem orientem statim exceptum
ultra meridiem oblicum quidem sed tamen servat.
24 In hanc ego diaetam cum me recepi, abesse mihi
etiam a villa mea videor, magnamque eius voluptatem praecipue Saturnalibus capio, cum reliqua pars

---

[1] The week starting 17 December.

circulate, the atmosphere is never heavy with stale air.

At the far end of the terrace, the arcade and the garden is a suite of rooms [x] which are really and truly my favourites, for I had them built myself. Here is a sun-parlour facing the terrace on one side, the sea on the other, and the sun on both. There is also a bedroom which has folding doors opening on to the arcade and a window looking out on the sea. Opposite the intervening wall is a beautifully designed alcove which can be thrown into the room by folding back its glass doors and curtains, or cut off from it if they are closed: it is large enough to hold a couch and two arm-chairs, and has the sea at its foot, the neighbouring villas behind, and the woods beyond, views which can be seen separately from its many windows or blended into one. Next to it is a bedroom for use at night which neither the voices of my young slaves, the sea's murmur, nor the noise of a storm can penetrate, any more than the lightning's flash and light of day unless the shutters are open. This profound peace and seclusion are due to the dividing passage which runs between the room and the garden so that any noise is lost in the intervening space. A tiny furnace-room is built on here, and by a narrow outlet retains or circulates the heat underneath as required. Then there is an ante-room and a second bedroom, built out to face the sun and catch its rays the moment it rises, and retain them until after midday, though by then at an angle. When I retire to this suite I feel as if I have left my house altogether and much enjoy the sensation: especially during the Saturnalia[1] when the rest of the roof resounds with festive

tecti licentia dierum festisque clamoribus personat;
nam nec ipse meorum lusibus nec illi studiis meis
25 obstrepunt. Haec utilitas haec amoenitas deficitur
aqua salienti, sed puteos ac potius fontes habet; sunt
enim in summo. Et omnino litoris illius mira
natura: quocumque loco moveris humum, obvius et
paratus umor occurrit, isque sincerus ac ne leviter
26 quidem tanta maris vicinitate corruptus. Suggerunt
adfatim ligna proximae silvae; ceteras copias Ostiensis colonia ministrat. Frugi quidem homini sufficit
etiam vicus, quem una villa discernit. In hoc balinea
meritoria tria, magna commoditas, si forte balineum
domi vel subitus adventus vel brevior mora calfacere
27 dissuadeat. Litus ornant varietate gratissima nunc
continua nunc intermissa tecta villarum, quae
praestant multarum urbium faciem, sive mari sive
ipso litore utare; quod non numquam longa tran-
quillitas mollit, saepius frequens et contrarius
28 fluctus indurat. Mare non sane pretiosis piscibus
abundat, soleas tamen et squillas optimas egerit.
Villa vero nostra etiam mediterraneas copias praestat,
lac in primis; nam illuc e pascuis pecora conveniunt,
si quando aquam umbramve sectantur.
29 Iustisne de causis iam tibi videor incolere inhabi-
tare diligere secessum? quem tu nimis urbanus es
nisi concupiscis. Atque utinam concupiscas! ut
tot tantisque dotibus villulae nostrae maxima commendatio ex tuo contubernio accedat. Vale.

---

[1] Vicus Augustanus. See R. Meiggs, *Roman Ostia*, p. 69,
and map, p. 112.

cries in the holiday freedom, for I am not disturbing
my household's merrymaking nor they my work.

Only one thing is needed to complete the amenities
and beauty of the house—running water; but there
are wells, or rather springs, for they are very near the
surface. It is in fact a remarkable characteristic
of this shore that wherever you dig you come upon
water at once which is pure and not in the least
brackish, although the sea is so near. The woods
close by provide plenty of firewood, and the town of
Ostia supplies us with everything else. There is also
a village,[1] just beyond the next house, which can
satisfy anyone's modest needs, and here there are
three baths for hire, a great convenience if a sudden
arrival or too short a stay makes us reluctant to heat
up the bath at home. The sea-front gains much
from the pleasing variety of the houses built either in
groups or far apart; from the sea or shore these
look like a number of cities. The sand on the shore
is sometimes too soft for walking after a long spell of
fine weather, but more often it is hardened by the
constant washing of the waves. The sea has admittedly few fish of any value, but it gives us excellent
soles and prawns, and all inland produce is provided
by the house, especially milk: for the herds collect
there from the pastures whenever they seek water
and shade.

And now do you think I have a good case for making this retreat my haunt and home where I love to
be? You are too polite a townsman if you don't
covet it! But I hope you will, for then the many
attractions of my treasured house will have another
strong recommendation in your company.

XVIII

C. Plinius Maurico Suo S.

1 Quid a te mihi iucundius potuit iniungi, quam ut
praeceptorem fratris tui liberis quaererem? Nam
beneficio tuo in scholam redeo, et illam dulcissimam
aetatem quasi resumo: sedeo inter iuvenes ut solebam, atque etiam experior quantum apud illos
2 auctoritatis ex studiis habeam. Nam proxime
frequenti auditorio inter se coram multis ordinis
nostri clare iocabantur; intravi, conticuerunt;
quod non referrem, nisi ad illorum magis laudem quam
ad meam pertineret, ac nisi sperare te vellem posse
3 fratris tui filios probe discere. Quod superest, cum
omnes qui profitentur audiero, quid de quoque sentiam scribam, efficiamque quantum tamen epistula con-
4 sequi potero, ut ipse omnes audisse videaris. Debeo
enim tibi, debeo memoriae fratris tui hanc fidem hoc
studium, praesertim super tanta re. Nam quid
magis interest vestra, quam ut liberi (dicerem tui,
nisi nunc illos magis amares) digni illo patre, te
patruo reperiantur? quam curam mihi etiam si non
5 mandasses vindicassem. Nec ignoro suscipiendas
offensas in eligendo praeceptore, sed oportet me non

---

[1] Arulenus Rusticus; see I. 14.

XVIII

To Junius Mauricus

There is nothing you could ask me to do which I should like better than to look for a tutor for your brother's[1] children. Thanks to you I have gone back to school and seem to be reliving the happiest days of my life. I take my seat among the young men as I did in my youth: I am even finding how much consideration my own work has brought me from the younger generation. Only the other day, in a full lecture-room, they were joking loudly among themselves in the presence of several senators. Then I came in and there was silence. I only mention this because it reflects more on their credit than on mine, and I want you to feel confident that there is no reason why your nephews should not be well-behaved students.

It remains for me to write and give you my opinion on each of the lecturers when I have heard them all, and, as far as a letter can, to make you feel you have heard them all yourself. My loyalty and devotion are yours to command in the service of your brother's memory, especially in a decision of such importance; for nothing could be of graver concern to you both than that these children (I should call them your children, did you not already love them more than your own) should be found worthy of the father he was and the uncle you are to them now. It is a duty I should have claimed myself, had you not entrusted it to me. I know very well the risk of giving offence in choosing a tutor, but that I must accept—and also

modo offensas, verum etiam simultates pro fratris tui
filiis tam aequo animo subire quam parentes pro
suis. Vale.

XIX

C. PLINIUS CERIALI SUO S.

1 HORTARIS ut orationem amicis pluribus recitem.
Faciam quia hortaris, quamvis vehementer addubi-
2 tem. Neque enim me praeterit actiones, quae
recitantur, impetum omnem caloremque ac prope
nomen suum perdere, ut quas soleant commendare
simul et accendere iudicum consessus, celebritas
advocatorum, exspectatio eventus, fama non unius
actoris, diductumque in partes audientium studium,
ad hoc dicentis gestus incessus, discursus etiam omnibusque motibus animi consentaneus vigor corporis.
3 Unde accidit ut ii qui sedentes agunt, quamvis illis
maxima ex parte supersint eadem illa quae stantibus,
tamen hoc quod sedent quasi debilitentur et depri-
4 mantur. Recitantium vero praecipua pronuntiationis
adiumenta, oculi manus, praepediuntur. Quo minus
mirum est, si auditorum intentio relanguescit, nullis
extrinsecus aut blandimentis capta aut aculeis
5 excitata. Accedit his quod oratio de qua loquor
pugnax et quasi contentiosa est. Porro ita natura
comparatum est, ut ea quae scripsimus cum labore,

---

[1] Public readings of speeches were evidently less common at
this time than readings of history, drama and poetry; cf. VII.
17. The speech may be P.'s *In Priscum.*

the possibility of making enemies for myself—on behalf of your brother's children as cheerfully as parents do for their own.

XIX

To Tuccius (?) Cerialis

You urge me to give a reading of my speech[1] to a group of friends. I will since you ask it, but with many misgivings. I know very well that speeches when read lose all their warmth and spirit, almost their entire character, since their fire is always fed from the atmosphere of court: the bench of magistrates and throng of advocates, the suspense of the awaited verdict, reputation of the different speakers, and the divided enthusiasm of the public; and they gain too from the gestures of the speaker as he strides to and fro, the movements of his body corresponding to his changing passions. (Hence the loss to anyone who delivers his speech sitting down—he is at a real disadvantage by the mere fact of being seated, though he may be as gifted generally as the speakers who stand.) Moreover, a man who is giving a reading has the two chief aids to his delivery (eyes and hands) taken up with his text, so it is not surprising if the attention of his audience wavers when there is no adventitious attraction to hold it nor stimulus to keep it aroused.

Furthermore, this is a fighting speech, disputatious if you like, and it is besides natural for us to think that what we found an effort to write will also demand an effort on the part of our hearers. There

6 cum labore [1] etiam audiri putemus. Et sane quotus quisque tam rectus auditor, quem non potius dulcia haec et sonantia quam austera et pressa delectent? Est quidem omnino turpis ista discordia, est tamen, quia plerumque evenit ut aliud auditores aliud iudices exigant, cum alioqui iis praecipue auditor adfici de-
7 beat, quibus idem si foret iudex, maxime permovere-tur. Potest tamen fieri ut quamquam in his difficultatibus libro isti novitas lenocinetur, novitas apud nostros; apud Graecos enim est quiddam quamvis ex
8 diverso, non tamen omnino dissimile. Nam ut illis erat moris, leges quas ut contrarias prioribus legibus arguebant, aliarum collatione convincere, ita nobis inesse repetundarum legi quod postularemus, cum hac ipsa lege tum aliis colligendum fuit; quod nequaquam blandum auribus imperitorum, tanto maiorem apud doctos habere gratiam debet, quanto
9 minorem apud indoctos habet. Nos autem si placuerit recitare adhibituri sumus eruditissimum quemque. Sed plane adhuc an sit recitandum examina tecum, omnesque quos ego movi in utraque parte calculos pone, idque elige in quo vicerit ratio. A te enim ratio exigetur, nos excusabit obsequium. Vale.

[1] cum labore *alterum om.* αγ, *post* etiam β; *correxit Postgate.*

are certainly very few members of an audience sufficiently trained to prefer a stiff, close-knit argument to fine-sounding words. Such a disparity shocks, but it exists; for in general a bench of magistrates and an audience have very different demands, though a listener should really be influenced most by what would convince him if he were called on to pronounce judgement. However, it may be that in spite of these difficulties the speech you have in mind will gain from its novelty—at any rate in our own country, for the Greeks have a somewhat similar practice, though with the opposite intent.[1] To demonstrate that a law was contrary to previous legislation their method of proof was by comparison with other laws; so to show that my accusation was covered by the law dealing with the extortion of money I had to base my argument on the analogy of other laws as well. This cannot have any appeal for the ordinary man, but its interest for the professional should be proportionately greater for the lack of it for the layman. It is certainly my intention, if I agree to this reading, to invite all the legal experts.

But now think carefully whether I ought to give one at all. Set out on both sides all the arguments I have put forward, and make your decision with good reason. You are the one who will have to produce the reason: I shall have an excuse in complying with your wishes.

---

[1] P. means the Athenian γραφὴ παρανόμων.

XX

C. Plinius Calvisio Suo S.

1 Assem para et accipe auream fabulam, fabulas immo; nam me priorum nova admonuit, nec refert a 2 qua potissimum incipiam. Verania Pisonis graviter iacebat, huius dico Pisonis, quem Galba adoptavit. Ad hanc Regulus venit. Primum impudentiam hominis, qui venerit ad aegram, cuius marito inimi- 3 cissimus, ipsi invisissimus fuerat! Esto, si venit tan- tum; at ille etiam proximus toro sedit, quo die qua hora nata esset interrogavit. Ubi audiit, componit vultum intendit oculos movet labra, agitat digitos computat. Nihil. Ut diu miseram exspectatione suspendit, " Habes " inquit " climactericum tempus 4 sed evades. Quod ut tibi magis liqueat, haruspicem 5 consulam, quem sum frequenter expertus." Nec mora, sacrificium facit, adfirmat exta cum siderum significatione congruere. Illa ut in periculo credula poscit codicillos, legatum Regulo scribit. Mox in- gravescit, clamat moriens hominem nequam perfi- dum ac plus etiam quam periurum, qui sibi per 6 salutem filii peierasset. Facit hoc Regulus non minus scelerate quam frequenter, quod iram deorum, quos ipse cotidie fallit, in caput infelicis pueri detestatur.

---

[1] P. offers a "golden" story, as if he were a professional story-teller.

[2] For Regulus's conduct after the murder of L. Calpurnius Piso Licinianus, see Tacitus, *Hist.* IV. 42.

[3] *i.e.* like an astrologer.

XX

To Calvisius Rufus

Have your copper ready and hear a first-rate story,[1] or rather stories, for the new one has reminded me of others and it doesn't matter which I tell first.   Piso's widow Verania was lying seriously ill—I mean the Piso Galba adopted.   Along comes Regulus.   What impudence—to intrude on her sickness when he had been her husband's deadly enemy [2] and she hated the sight of him!   The visit alone is bad enough, but he sits down by her bed and asks her the day and hour of her birth; after which he puts on a grave look and a fixed stare, moves his lips, works his fingers, and does sums.[3]   Then   silence.   After   keeping   the   poor woman in suspense for a long time, he speaks: " You are going through a danger period, out of which you will pass.   However, to rid you of any doubts, I will consult a soothsayer with whom I have often had dealings."   Without   delay   he   then   performs   a sacrifice and declares that the entrails accord with the planetary signs.   Feeling her life in danger, Verania is ready to believe him; she asks for a codicil to be added to her will and puts Regulus down for a legacy.   Subsequently she grows worse and dies, calling aloud on the wickedness and treachery, the worse than perjury of the man who swore her a false oath on the life of his son.   This is the kind of scandalous thing Regulus is always doing, calling down the wrath of the gods (which he always manages to escape himself) on to the head of his unfortunate boy.

7 Velleius Blaesus ille locuples consularis novissima
valetudine conflictabatur: cupiebat mutare testamentum. Regulus qui speraret aliquid ex novis
tabulis, quia nuper captare eum coeperat, medicos
hortari rogare, quoquo modo spiritum homini
8 prorogarent. Postquam signatum est testamentum,
mutat personam, vertit adlocutionem isdemque
medicis: " Quousque miserum cruciatis ? quid invide-
tis bona morte, cui dare vitam non potestis ? " Moritur
Blaesus et, tamquam omnia audisset, Regulo ne
tantulum quidem.

9 Sufficiunt duae fabulae, an scholastica lege tertiam
10 poscis ? est unde fiat. Aurelia ornata femina sig-
natura testamentum sumpserat pulcherrimas tunicas.
Regulus cum venisset ad signandum, " Rogo " inquit
11 " has mihi leges." Aurelia ludere hominem putabat,
ille serio instabat; ne multa, coegit mulierem aperire
tabulas ac sibi tunicas quas erat induta legare; obse-
rvavit scribentem, inspexit an scripsisset. Et Aurelia
quidem vivit, ille tamen istud tamquam morituram
coegit. Et hic hereditates, hic legata quasi mereatur
accipit.

12 Ἀλλὰ τί διατείνομαι in ea civitate, in qua iam
pridem non minora praemia, immo maiora nequitia et
13 improbitas quam pudor et virtus habent ? Adspice
Regulum, qui ex paupere et tenui ad tantas opes per
flagitia processit, ut ipse mihi dixerit, cum consuleret

---

[1] A thesis in the schools of rhetoric was supposed to be
supported by three illustrations: see Quint. *Inst. Orat.* IV. v. 3.

Velleius Blaesus is well known as an ex-consul and a rich man. He wished to alter his will on his death-bed, and Regulus was hoping for something from the new one as he had just begun courting Blaesus. He therefore begs and implores the doctors to prolong the man's life in some way. Once the will is signed there is a change of front, and the same doctors are attacked to know how long they intend to torture the poor man and why they grudge him an easy death when they cannot give him life. Blaesus dies; he might have heard the whole story, for he leaves Regulus nothing.

Are two stories enough, or do you want another according to the rule of three? [1] There are plenty more I could tell you. The noble lady Aurelia had dressed in her best for the ceremony of signing her will. When Regulus arrived to witness her signature, he asked her to leave these clothes to him. Aurelia thought he was joking, but he pressed the point in all seriousness, and to cut a long story short, he forced her to open the will and leave him what she was wearing: he watched her writing and looked to see if she had done so. Aurelia is in fact alive today, but he forced this on her as if she were on the point of death. And this is the man who accepts estates and legacies as if they were his due.

" But why do I rouse myself " [2] over this, when I live in a country which has long offered the same (or even greater) rewards to dishonesty and wickedness as it does to honour and merit? Look at Regulus, who has risen by his evil ways from poverty and obscurity to such great wealth that he told me himself

[2] Demosthenes, *De Cor.* 142.

quam cito sestertium sescentiens impleturus esset,
invenisse se exta duplicia, quibus portendi miliens et
14 ducentiens habiturum. Et habebit, si modo ut
coepit, aliena testamenta, quod est improbissimum
genus falsi, ipsis quorum sunt illa dictaverit. Vale.

when he was trying to divine how soon he would be worth sixty million sesterces he had found a double set of entrails which were a sign that he would have twice that sum. So he will, too, if he goes on in the way he has begun, dictating wills which are not their own to the very people who are wanting to make them: the most immoral kind of fraud there is.

BOOK III

LIBER TERTIUS

I

C. Plinius Calvisio Rufo Suo S.

1 Nescio an ullum iucundius tempus exegerim, quam
quo nuper apud Spurinnam fui, adeo quidem ut
neminem magis in senectute, si modo senescere datum est, aemulari velim; nihil est enim illo vitae
2 genere distinctius. Me autem ut certus siderum
cursus ita vita hominum disposita delectat. Senum
praesertim: nam iuvenes confusa adhuc quaedam et
quasi turbata non indecent, senibus placida omnia et
ordinata conveniunt, quibus industria sera turpis
3 ambitio est. Hanc regulam Spurinna constantissime
servat; quin etiam parva haec—parva si non cotidie
fiant—ordine quodam et velut orbe circumagit.
4 Mane lectulo continetur, hora secunda calceos poscit,
ambulat milia passuum tria nec minus animum
quam corpus exercet. Si adsunt amici, honestissimi
sermones explicantur; si non, liber legitur, interdum
etiam praesentibus amicis, si tamen illi non gravantur.
5 Deinde considit, et liber rursus aut sermo libro
potior; mox vehiculum ascendit, adsumit uxorem

---

[1] The walk was round and round his *gestatio*, the drive round
his *hippodromus*.

158

BOOK III

I

To Calvisius Rufus

I can't remember ever passing the time so pleasantly as I did on my recent visit to Spurinna; and, indeed, there is no one whom I would rather take for an example in my old age, if I am spared to live so long, for no way of living is better planned than his. A well-ordered life, especially where the old are concerned, gives me the same pleasure as the fixed course of the planets. A certain amount of irregularity and excitement is not unsuitable for the young, but their elders should lead a quiet and orderly existence; their time of public activity is over, and ambition only brings them into disrepute.

This is the rule strictly observed by Spurinna, and he even maintains a due order and succession in matters which would be trivial were they not part of a daily routine. Every morning he stays in bed for an hour after dawn, then calls for his shoes and takes a three-mile walk [1] to exercise mind and body. If he has friends with him he carries on a serious conversation, if he is alone a book is read aloud, and this is sometimes done when there are friends present, so long as they do not object. Then he sits down, the book is continued, or preferably the conversation; after which he goes out in his carriage accompanied

singularis exempli vel aliquem amicorum, ut me
6 proxime. Quam pulchrum illud, quam dulce secretum! quantum ibi antiquitatis! quae facta, quos viros
audias! quibus praeceptis imbuare! quamvis ille
hoc temperamentum modestiae suae indixerit, ne
7 praecipere videatur. Peractis septem milibus passuum iterum ambulat mille, iterum residit vel se
cubiculo ac stilo reddit. Scribit enim et quidem
utraque lingua lyrica doctissima;[1] mira illis dulcedo,
mira suavitas, mira hilaritas, cuius gratiam cumulat
8 sanctitas scribentis. Ubi hora balinei nuntiata est
(est autem hieme nona, aestate octava), in sole, si
caret vento, ambulat nudus. Deinde movetur pila
vehementer et diu; nam hoc quoque exercitationis
genere pugnat cum senectute. Lotus accubat et
paulisper cibum differt; interim audit legentem re-
missius aliquid et dulcius. Per hoc omne tempus
liberum est amicis vel eadem facere vel alia si malint.
9 Adponitur cena non minus nitida quam frugi, in
argento puro et antiquo; sunt in usu et Corinthia,
quibus delectatur nec adficitur. Frequenter comoe-
dis cena distinguitur, ut voluptates quoque studiis
condiantur. Sumit aliquid de nocte et aestate;
nemini hoc longum est; tanta comitate convivium
10 trahitur. Inde illi post septimum et septuagensimum annum aurium oculorum vigor integer, inde agile

---

[1] doctissima IIγ: -ime α.

---

[1] Sunbathing (*apricatio*) is also recommended by Cicero in
De Sen. XVI. 57.

by his wife (a model to her sex) or one of his friends, a pleasure recently mine. There is a special sort of pleasure in being thus singled out and given the entry into a bygone age as he talks of great men and their deeds to give you inspiration, though modesty restrains him from any appearance of laying down the law. After a drive of seven miles he will walk another mile, then sit again or retire to his room and his writing, for he composes lyric verses of considerable learning in both Greek and Latin; they are remarkable for their wit, grace and delicacy, and their charm is enhanced by the propriety of their author. When summoned to his bath (in mid-afternoon in winter and an hour earlier in summer) he first removes his clothes and takes a walk in the sunshine [1] if there is no wind, and then throws a ball briskly for some time, this being another form of exercise whereby he keeps old age at bay. After his bath he lies down for a short rest before dinner, and listens while something light and soothing is read aloud. Meanwhile his friends are quite free to do the same as he does or not, as they prefer. Dinner is brought on in dishes of antique solid silver, a simple meal but well served; he also has Corinthian bronze for general use, which he admires though not with a collector's passion. Between the courses there is often a performance of comedy, so that the pleasures of the table have a seasoning of letters, and the meal is prolonged into the night, even in summer, without anyone finding it too long amid such pleasant company.

The result is that Spurinna has passed his seventy-seventh year, but his sight and hearing are

et vividum corpus solaque ex senectute prudentia.
11 Hanc ego vitam voto et cogitatione praesumo,
ingressurus avidissime, ut primum ratio aetatis
receptui canere permiserit. Interim mille laboribus
conteror, quorum mihi et solacium et exemplum
12 est idem Spurinna; nam ille quoque, quoad honestum
fuit, obiit officia, gessit magistratus, provincias rexit,
multoque labore hoc otium meruit. Igitur eundem
mihi cursum, eundem terminum statuo, idque iam
nunc apud te subsigno ut, si me longius evehi videris,
in ius voces ad hanc epistulam meam et quiescere
iubeas, cum inertiae crimen effugero. Vale.

II

C. Plinius Vibio Maximo Suo S.

1 Quod ipse amicis tuis obtulissem, si mihi eadem
materia suppeteret, id nunc iure videor a te meis
2 petiturus. Arrianus Maturus Altinatium est princeps; cum dico princeps, non de facultatibus loquor,
quae illi large supersunt, sed de castitate iustitia,
3 gravitate prudentia. Huius ego consilio in negotiis,
iudicio in studiis utor; nam plurimum fide, plurimum veritate, plurimum intellegentia praestat.
4 Amat me (nihil possum ardentius dicere) ut tu.
Caret ambitu; ideo se in equestri gradu tenuit, cum

---

[1] On the coast of Venetia (Altino).

unimpaired, and he is physically agile and energetic; old age has brought him nothing but wisdom. This is the sort of life I hope and pray will be mine, and I shall eagerly enter on it as soon as the thought of my years permits me to sound a retreat. Meanwhile innumerable tasks fill my time, though here again Spurinna sets me a reassuring example, for he also accepted public offices, held magistracies, and governed provinces as long as it was his duty, and thus his present retirement was earned by hard work. I have set myself the same race and goal, and I bind myself to it now with you as my witness: so, if you see me fail to stop, you can call me to account with this letter of mine and bid me retire when I can do so without being accused of laziness.

II

To Vibius Maximus

I HOPE I am justified in asking you to do the sort of favour to one of my friends which I should certainly have done for yours had I the same opportunity. Maturus Arrianus is the leading citizen of Altinum,[1] and when I say this I am not referring to his wealth, which is considerable, but to his virtue and justice, his sense of responsibility and wisdom. His is the advice I follow in business, and his the opinion I seek on literary topics, for he is a man of exceptional sincerity, integrity and understanding. He loves me as dearly as you do—I need say no more.

He is incapable of pushing himself forward, and for this reason has remained a member of the order

facile possit ascendere altissimum. Mihi tamen
5 ornandus excolendusque est. Itaque magni aestimo
dignitati eius aliquid adstruere inopinantis nescientis,
immo etiam fortasse nolentis; adstruere autem quod
6 sit splendidum nec molestum. Cuius generis quae
prima occasio tibi, conferas in eum rogo; habebis me,
habebis ipsum gratissimum debitorem. Quamvis
enim ista non adpetat, tam grate tamen excipit,
quam si concupiscat. Vale.

III

C. Plinius Corelliae Hispullae Suae S.

1   Cum patrem tuum gravissimum et sanctissimum
virum suspexerim magis an amaverim dubitem, teque
et in memoriam eius et in honorem tuum unice dili-
gam, cupiam necesse est atque etiam quantum in me
fuerit enitar, ut filius tuus avo similis exsistat; equidem malo materno, quamquam illi paternus etiam
clarus spectatusque contigerit, pater quoque et
2 patruus inlustri laude conspicui. Quibus omnibus
ita demum similis adolescet, si imbutus honestis
artibus fuerit, quas plurimum refert a quo potissi-
3 mum accipiat. Adhuc illum pueritiae ratio intra
contubernium tuum tenuit, praeceptores domi habuit, ubi est erroribus modica vel etiam nulla materia.
Iam studia eius extra limen proferenda sunt, iam

---

[1] Vibius Maximus was prefect of Egypt 103–7, and the post
sought may be there.
[2] Corellius Rufus. See I. 12. The grandson may be Corellius Pansa.

of knights, though he could easily rise to the highest rank. However, I feel it is my duty to obtain him promotion and advancement, and so I am anxious to improve his position in some way, though he neither expects nor knows of this, and may perhaps not wish it; but it must be a distinction which he will not find a burden. Please grant him something of this kind at your earliest opportunity. I shall be exceedingly grateful to you, and so will he, for, though he would not approach you for this himself, he will receive it as gratefully as if he had set his heart on it.[1]

III

To Corellia Hispulla

My love and admiration (I cannot say which comes first) for your father's [2] noble sense of duty and high principles are matched by my special affection for yourself on your own account as well as for his sake; and so I must desire your son to take after his grandfather, and will make every effort I can to ensure this. I should prefer him to resemble your own father, although on his father's side, too, fortune has granted him a grandfather who is admired and respected, and a father and uncle whose distinguished reputations are well known. He will grow up to be like them all only if he has been educated from the start on the proper lines, and thus it is most important for him to have the right teacher. Up to the present he has been too young to leave your side, and has had teachers at home where there is little or no opportunity for going astray. Now his studies must be carried

circumspiciendus rhetor Latinus, cuius scholae

4 severitas pudor in primis castitas constet. Adest
enim adulescenti nostro cum ceteris naturae fortu-
naeque dotibus eximia corporis pulchritudo, cui in
hoc lubrico aetatis non praeceptor modo sed custos

5 etiam rectorque quaerendus est. Videor ergo demon-
strare tibi posse Iulium Genitorem. Amatur a me;
iudicio tamen meo non obstat caritas hominis, quae
ex iudicio nata est. Vir est emendatus et gravis,
paulo etiam horridior et durior, ut in hac licentia

6 temporum. Quantum eloquentia valeat, pluribus
credere potes, nam dicendi facultas aperta et exposita
statim cernitur; vita hominum altos recessus magnas-
que latebras habet, cuius pro Genitore me sponsorem
accipe. Nihil ex hoc viro filius tuus audiet nisi
profuturum, nihil discet quod nescisse rectius fuerit,
nec minus saepe ab illo quam a te meque admonebi-
tur, quibus imaginibus oneretur, quae nomina et

7 quanta sustineat. Proinde faventibus dis trade
eum praeceptori, a quo mores primum mox eloquentiam discat, quae male sine moribus discitur. Vale.

---

[1] He is taken to task for intolerance in IX. 17.

farther afield, and we must look for a tutor in Latin rhetoric whose school shall combine a strict training along with good manners and, above all, moral standards; for, as our boy happens to be endowed with striking physical beauty among his natural gifts, at this dangerous time of life he needs more than a teacher. A guardian and mentor must be found.

I think then that I cannot do better than to draw your attention to Julius Genitor. The affection I have for him has not blinded my judgement, as it is in fact based on it. He is a man of serious character, quite free from faults: indeed a little too blunt and austere for the licence of our times.[1] On the subject of his eloquence you have many witnesses you may trust, for ability in speaking is obvious and readily recognized whenever it is displayed; whereas there are many deep secrets and hidden places in a man's personal life. You may rest assured that I answer for these on Genitor's behalf. Your son will hear nothing from him but what will benefit him, will learn nothing that would have been better left unknown. Genitor will remind him as often as we do of his obligations to his forbears and the great names he must carry on. So with the gods' good will you may entrust him to a teacher from whom he will learn right principles of conduct before he studies eloquence—for without principles this cannot be properly learned at all.

IV

C. PLINIUS CAECILIO MACRINO SUO S.

1 QUAMVIS et amici quos praesentes habebam, et sermones hominum factum meum comprobasse videantur, magni tamen aestimo scire quid sentias tu. 2 Nam cuius integra re consilium exquirere optassem, huius etiam peracta iudicium nosse mire concupisco. Cum publicum opus mea pecunia incohaturus in Tuscos¹ excucurrissem, accepto ut praefectus aerari commeatu, legati provinciae Baeticae, questuri de proconsulatu Caecili Classici,² advocatum me a senatu 3 petiverunt. Collegae³ optimi meique amantissimi, de communis officii necessitatibus praelocuti, excusare me et eximere temptarunt. Factum est senatus consultum perquam honorificum, ut darer provincialibus patronus si ab ipso me impetrassent. 4 Legati rursus inducti iterum me iam praesentem advocatum postulaverunt, implorantes fidem meam quam essent contra Massam Baebium experti, adlegantes patrocini foedus. Secuta est senatus

---

¹ Near Tifernum-on-Tiber (Città di Castello), 20 miles E. of Arezzo, 150 miles from Rome. See also IV. 1; X. 8.

² The case is described in III. 9.

³ Two praetorian senators were chosen by the emperor to hold office at the *aerarium Saturni* for three years. " Colleagues " must therefore include those at the *aerarium militare.*

IV

To Caecilius Macrinus

Public opinion and the friends who were with me at the time have apparently approved of my conduct, but even so I very much want to know what *you* think, for the opinion of someone whose advice I should have liked to ask before making my decision is still of great importance to me now that the matter is settled.

I had obtained leave of absence from my post in the Treasury and hurried out to my place in Tuscany[1] in order to lay the foundation stone of a temple which was to be built at my expense; at that moment the representatives of the province of Baetica (who had come to lodge a complaint against the conduct of their late governor, Caecilius Classicus[2]) applied to the Senate for my services as their counsel. My Treasury colleagues,[3] the best of men and most loyal of friends, tried to beg me off and excuse me by pleading the official duties we share. The Senate then passed the resolution—highly complimentary to me—that my services should be granted the province provided that I expressed my willingness in person. The representatives were brought in again, this time in my presence, and made their request a second time, appealing to my professional honour which they had experienced in the case against Baebius Massa,[4] and pleading that they had a claim on my patronage. There followed the open acclamation which usually

---

[4] In 93; see VII. 33. 4 ff. P.'s close relations with Baetica are mentioned in I. 7. 2, but without reference to a formal pact of *hospitium* or *patrocinium*.

clarissima adsensio, quae solet decreta praecurrere.
Tum ego "Desino" inquam, "patres conscripti,
putare me iustas excusationis causas attulisse."
5 Placuit et modestia sermonis et ratio. Compulit autem me ad hoc consilium non solum consensus senatus,
quamquam hic maxime, verum et alii quidam minores,
sed tamen numeri. Veniebat in mentem priores
nostros etiam singulorum hospitum iniurias voluntariis
accusationibus exsecutos, quo deformius arbitrabar
6 publici hospitii iura neglegere. Praeterea cum re-
cordarer, quanta pro isdem Baeticis superiore advocatione etiam pericula subissem, conservandum veteris
officii meritum novo videbatur. Est enim ita comparatum ut antiquiora beneficia subvertas, nisi illa
posterioribus cumules. Nam quamlibet saepe obli-
gati, si quid unum neges, hoc solum meminerunt
7 quod negatum est. Ducebar etiam quod decesserat
Classicus, amotumque erat quod in eiusmodi causis
solet esse tristissimum, periculum senatoris. Videbam ergo advocationi meae non minorem gratiam
quam si viveret ille propositam, invidiam nullam.
8 In summa computabam, si munere hoc iam tertio
fungerer, faciliorem mihi excusationem fore, si quis
incidisset, quem non deberem accusare. Nam cum
est omnium officiorum finis aliquis, tum optime
9 libertati venia obsequio praeparatur. Audisti con-

---

[1] Cf. III. 9. 5.

[2] The first two cases are those of Baebius Massa and Marius
Priscus.

indicates that a resolution is going to be passed; after which I begged leave to withdraw my opinion that I had given just reason for excusing myself. This was received with general approval, both for the meaning of my words and the modesty which prompted them.

I was in fact impelled to take this course not only by the unanimous feeling in the Senate, much though that influenced me, but by certain lesser considerations which could not be ignored. I recalled how our fathers needed no official direction to instigate prosecutions to avenge the wrongs of individual foreigners; which made me think it all the more disgraceful to neglect the rights of a people with whom I had ties of hospitality. Besides, when I remembered the real dangers I had faced when acting for the Baetici on an earlier occasion, I felt that I ought to maintain my credit with them for my former service by adding a new one. It is generally agreed that past benefits cease to count unless confirmed by later ones; for, if a single thing is denied people who have every reason to be grateful, the denial is all they remember.

An additional influence was the fact that Classicus was now dead,[1] which removed the most painful feature in this type of case—the downfall of a senator. I saw then that I should win the same gratitude for taking on the case as if he were alive, but without incurring ill-will. Finally I calculated that, if I discharged this duty for the third time,[2] it would be easier for me to excuse myself if later faced by a defendant whom I felt I ought not to prosecute. All duties have their limits, and permission to be

silii mei motus: superest alterutra ex parte iudicium tuum, in quo mihi aeque iucunda erit simplicitas dissentientis quam comprobantis auctoritas.   Vale.

V

C. PLINIUS BAEBIO MACRO SUO S.

1   PERGRATUM est mihi quod tam diligenter libros avunculi mei lectitas, ut habere omnes velis quaerasque
2 qui sint omnes.   Fungar indicis partibus, atque etiam quo sint ordine scripti notum tibi faciam; est enim
3 haec quoque studiosis non iniucunda cognitio.   " De iaculatione equestri unus "; hunc cum praefectus alae militaret, pari ingenio curaque composuit.   " De vita Pomponi Secundi duo "; a quo singulariter amatus hoc memoriae amici quasi debitum munus exsolvit.
4 " Bellorum Germaniae viginti "; quibus omnia quae cum Germanis gessimus bella collegit.   Incohavit cum in Germania militaret, somnio monitus: adstitit ei quiescenti Drusi Neronis effigies, qui Germaniae latissime victor ibi periit, commendabat memoriam suam orabatque ut se ab iniuria oblivionis adsereret.

---

¹ The poet and tragedian, distinguished also as legate of Upper Germany in the reign of Claudius.   See Index.
² Cited by Tacitus in *Ann.* I. 69; and Suetonius, *Cal.* 8.

freed from them is best gained by previous compliance. These then are the reasons for my decision; it remains for you to give your opinion one way or the other, bearing in mind that you will please me just as much by frankness if you disapprove as by your encouragement if I have your support.

V

To Baebius Macer

I AM delighted to hear that your close study of my uncle's books has made you wish to possess them all. Since you ask me for a complete list, I will provide a bibliography, and arrange it in chronological order, for this is the sort of information also likely to please scholars.

Throwing the Javelin from Horseback—one volume; a work of industry and talent, written when he was a junior officer in the cavalry.

The Life of Pomponius Secundus [1]—two volumes. My uncle was greatly loved by him and felt he owed this as an act of homage to his friend's memory.

The German Wars—twenty volumes, covering all the wars we have ever had with the Germans. [2] He began this during his military service in Germany, as the result of a dream; in his sleep he saw standing over him the ghost of Drusus Nero, [3] who had triumphed far and wide in Germany and died there. He committed his memory to my uncle's care, begging him to save him from the injustice of oblivion.

[3] Nero Claudius Drusus, the brother of Tiberius, died in Germany in 9 B.C.

5 " Studiosi tres," in sex volumina propter amplitudinem divisi, quibus oratorem ab incunabulis instituit
et perficit. " Dubii sermonis octo ": scripsit sub
Nerone novissimis annis, cum omne studiorum genus
paulo liberius et erectius periculosum servitus fecis-
6 set. " A fine Aufidi Bassi triginta unus." " Naturae historiarum triginta septem," opus diffusum
eruditum, nec minus varium quam ipsa natura.

7   Miraris quod tot volumina multaque in his tam
scrupulosa homo occupatus absolverit ? Magis miraberis si scieris illum aliquamdiu causas actitasse,
decessisse anno sexto et quinquagensimo, medium
tempus distentum impeditumque qua officiis maximis
8 qua amicitia principum egisse. Sed erat acre ingenium, incredibile studium, summa vigilantia.
Lucubrare Vulcanalibus incipiebat non auspicandi
causa sed studendi statim a nocte multa, hieme vero
ab hora septima vel cum tardissime octava, saepe
sexta. Erat sane somni paratissimi, non numquam
etiam inter ipsa studia instantis et deserentis.
9 Ante lucem ibat ad Vespasianum imperatorem (nam
ille quoque noctibus utebatur), inde ad delegatum sibi
officium. Reversus domum quod reliquum temporis

---

[1] Quoted by Quintilian in *Inst. Orat.* III. i. 21.

[2] His *History* is praised by Quintilian, *Inst. Orat.* X. i. 103.

[3] His sole surviving work.

[4] An *amicus principis* was a member of the Emperor's
advisory *consilium*. Cf. I. 18. 3 and note.   [5] 23 August.

[6] Evidently the Emperor's *amici* gathered for the regular
salutatio (and perhaps held a *consilium*) before dispersing to
their official duties. Those of the Elder Pliny are unknown:
the *praefectura vigilum* has been suggested (Syme, p. 61).

The Scholar—three volumes divided into six sections on account of their length, in which he trains the orator from his cradle and brings him to perfection.

Problems in Grammar[1]—eight volumes; this he wrote during Nero's last years when the slavery of the times made it dangerous to write anything at all independent or inspired.

A Continuation of the History of Aufidius Bassus[2]—thirty-one volumes.

A Natural History[3]—thirty-seven volumes, a learned and comprehensive work as full of variety as nature itself.

You may wonder how such a busy man was able to complete so many volumes, many of them involving detailed study; and wonder still more when you learn that up to a certain age he practised at the bar, that he died at the age of fifty-five, and throughout the intervening years his time was much taken up with the important offices he held and his friendship with the Emperors.[4] But he combined a penetrating intellect with amazing powers of concentration and the capacity to manage with the minimum of sleep.

From the feast of Vulcan[5] onwards he began to work by lamplight, not with any idea of making a propitious start but to give himself more time for study, and would rise half-way through the night; in winter it would often be at midnight or an hour later, and two at the latest. Admittedly he fell asleep very easily, and would often doze and wake up again during his work. Before daybreak he would visit the Emperor Vespasian[6] (who also made use of his nights) and then go to attend to his official duties. On returning home, he devoted any spare time to his

10 studiis reddebat. Post cibum saepe (quem interdiu levem et facilem veterum more sumebat) aestate si quid otii iacebat in sole, liber legebatur, adnotabat excerpebatque. Nihil enim legit quod non excerperet; dicere etiam solebat nullum esse librum tam

11 malum ut non aliqua parte prodesset. Post solem plerumque frigida lavabatur, deinde gustabat dormiebatque minimum; mox quasi alio die studebat in cenae tempus. Super hanc liber legebatur adnota-

12 batur, et quidem cursim. Memini quendam ex amicis, cum lector quaedam perperam pronuntiasset, revocasse et repeti coegisse; huic avunculum meum dixisse: "Intellexeras nempe?" Cum ille adnuisset, "Cur ergo revocabas? decem amplius

13 versus hac tua interpellatione perdidimus." Tanta erat parsimonia temporis. Surgebat aestate a cena luce, hieme intra primam noctis et tamquam aliqua lege cogente.

14 Haec inter medios labores urbisque fremitum. In secessu solum balinei tempus studiis eximebatur (cum dico balinei, de interioribus loquor; nam dum destringitur tergiturque, audiebat aliquid aut dictabat).

15 In itinere quasi solutus ceteris curis, huic uni vacabat: ad latus notarius cum libro et pugillaribus, cuius manus hieme manicis muniebantur, ut ne caeli quidem asperitas ullum studii tempus eriperet; qua

16 ex causa Romae quoque sella vehebatur. Repeto

176

work. After something to eat (his meals during the
day were light and simple in the old-fashioned way),
in summer when he was not too busy he would often
lie in the sun, and a book was read aloud while he
made notes and extracts. He made extracts of
everything he read, and always said that there was no
book so bad that some good could not be got out of it.
After his rest in the sun he generally took a cold bath,
and then ate something and had a short sleep; after
which he worked till dinner time as if he had started
on a new day. A book was read aloud during the
meal and he took rapid notes. I remember that one
of his friends told a reader to go back and repeat a
word he had mispronounced. " Couldn't you understand him ? " said my uncle. His friend admitted
that he could. " Then why make him go back ?
Your interruption has lost us at least ten lines."
To such lengths did he carry his passion for saving
time. In summer he rose from dinner while it was
still light, in winter as soon as darkness fell, as if some
law compelled him.

This was his routine in the midst of his public
duties and the bustle of the city. In the country, the
only time he took from his work was for his bath, and
by bath I mean his actual immersion, for while he
was being rubbed down and dried he had a book read
to him or dictated notes. When travelling he felt
free from other responsibilities to give every minute
to work; he kept a secretary at his side with book
and notebook, and in winter saw that his hands were
protected by long sleeves, so that even bitter weather
should not rob him of a working hour. For the same
reason, too, he used to be carried about Rome in a

me correptum ab eo, cur ambularem: "poteras"
inquit "has horas non perdere"; nam perire omne
tempus arbitrabatur, quod studiis non impenderetur.

17 Hac intentione tot ista volumina peregit electorum-
que commentarios centum sexaginta mihi reliquit,
opisthographos quidem et minutissimis scriptos; qua
ratione multiplicatur hic numerus. Referebat ipse
potuisse se, cum procuraret in Hispania, vendere
hos commentarios Larcio Licino quadringentis milibus nummum; et tunc aliquanto pauciores erant.

18 Nonne videtur tibi recordanti, quantum legerit
quantum scripserit, nec in officiis ullis nec in amicitia
principis fuisse; rursus cum audis quid studiis laboris
impenderit, nec scripsisse satis nec legisse? Quid est
enim quod non aut illae occupationes impedire aut

19 haec instantia non possit efficere? Itaque soleo
ridere cum me quidam studiosum vocant, qui si
comparer illi sum desidiosissimus. Ego autem
tantum, quem partim publica partim amicorum officia
distringunt? quis ex istis, qui tota vita litteris adsi-
dent, collatus illi non quasi somno et inertiae deditus
erubescat?

20   Extendi epistulam cum hoc solum quod requirebas
scribere destinassem, quos libros reliquisset; confido tamen haec quoque tibi non minus grata quam
ipsos libros futura, quae te non tantum ad legendos
eos verum etiam ad simile aliquid elaborandum possunt aemulationis stimulis excitare. Vale.

---

[1] The legatus iuridicus in Spain *c.* 73.

[2] It was an advocate's duty to serve his friends. Cf. Tacitus
Dial. 3. 4.

chair. I can remember how he scolded me for walking; according to him I need not have wasted those hours, for he thought any time wasted which was not devoted to work. It was this application which enabled him to finish all those volumes, and to leave me 160 notebooks of selected passages, written in a minute hand on both sides of the page, so that their number is really doubled. He used to say that when he was serving as procurator in Spain he could have sold these notebooks to Larcius Licinus[1] for 400,000 sesterces, and there were far fewer of them then.

When you consider the extent of his reading and writing I wonder if you feel that he could never have been a public official nor a friend of the Emperor, but on the other hand, now that you know of his application, that he should have achieved more? In fact his official duties put every possible obstacle in his path; and yet there was nothing which his energy could not surmount. So I cannot help smiling when anyone calls me studious, for compared with him I am the idlest of men. But am I the only one, seeing that so much of my time is taken up with official work and service to my friends?[2] Any one of your life-long devotees of literature, if put alongside my uncle, would blush to feel themselves thus enslaved to sleep and idleness.

I have let my letter run on, though I intended only to answer your question about the books left by my uncle. However, I feel sure that reading these details will give you as much pleasure as the actual books, and may even spur you on to the ambition of doing more than read them, if you can produce something similar yourself.

THE LETTERS OF PLINY

VI

C. PLINIUS ANNIO SEVERO SUO S.

1 Ex hereditate quae mihi obvenit, emi proxime
Corinthium signum, modicum quidem sed festivum
et expressum, quantum ego sapio, qui fortasse in
omni re, in hac certe perquam exiguum sapio: hoc
2 tamen signum ego quoque intellego. Est enim
nudum, nec aut vitia si qua sunt celat, aut laudes
parum ostentat. Effingit senem stantem; ossa
musculi nervi, venae rugae etiam ut spirantis ad-
parent; rari et cedentes capilli, lata frons, contracta
facies, exile collum; pendent lacerti, papillae iacent,
3 venter recessit; a tergo quoque eadem aetas ut a
tergo. Aes ipsum, quantum verus color indicat, vetus
et antiquum; talia denique omnia, ut possint arti-
4 ficum oculos tenere, delectare imperitorum. Quod
me quanquam tirunculum sollicitavit ad emendum.
Emi autem non ut haberem domi (neque enim ullum
adhuc Corinthium domi habeo), verum ut in patria
nostra celebri loco ponerem, ac potissimum in Iovis
5 templo; videtur enim dignum templo dignum deo
donum. Tu ergo, ut soles omnia quae a me tibi
iniunguntur, suscipe hanc curam, et iam nunc iube
basim fieri, ex quo voles marmore, quae nomen meum
honoresque capiat, si hos quoque putabis addendos.

---

¹ A temple served as a museum for displaying works of art;
cf. X. 8.

180

VI

To Annius Severus

Out of a sum of money I have inherited I have just bought a Corinthian bronze statue, only a small one, but an attractive and finished piece of work as far as I can judge—though in general maybe my judgement is limited, and certainly very much so here. But this is a statue that I feel even I can appreciate, for being nude it does not hide any defects it may have nor fail to reveal its merits. It represents a standing figure of an old man; the bones, muscles, sinews, and veins and even the wrinkles are clear and lifelike, the hair is sparse and receding from a broad brow, its face is lined and neck thin, and it has drooping shoulders, a flat chest, and hollow stomach. The back view, within its limits, gives the same impression of age. The bronze appears to have the true colour of a genuine antique; in fact every detail is such as to hold the attention of an artist as well as delight the amateur, and that is what persuaded me to buy it, novice though I am.

However, my intention was not to keep it in my house (I have not any Corinthian bronzes there yet) but to place it in some public position in my native town, preferably in the temple of Jupiter;[1] it is clearly a gift well worthy of a temple and a god. Will you then carry out a commission for me as you always do, and give immediate orders for a pedestal to be made? Choose what marble you like, and have it inscribed with my name and official titles if you think they should appear too. I will send you the statue

6 Ego signum ipsum, ut primum invenero aliquem qui
non gravetur, mittam tibi vel ipse (quod mavis)
adferam mecum. Destino enim, si tamen officii
7 ratio permiserit, excurrere isto.[1] Gaudes quod me
venturum esse polliceor, sed contrahes frontem, cum
adiecero " ad paucos dies ": neque enim diutius
abesse me eadem haec quae nondum exire patiuntur.
Vale.

VII

C. Plinius Caninio Rufo Suo S.

1 Modo nuntiatus est Silius Italicus in Neapolitano
2 suo inedia finisse vitam. Causa mortis valetudo.
Erat illi natus insanabilis clavus, cuius taedio ad
mortem inrevocabili constantia decucurrit usque ad
supremum diem beatus et felix, nisi quod minorem ex
liberis duobus amisit, sed maiorem melioremque
3 florentem atque etiam consularem reliquit. Laese-
rat famam suam sub Nerone (credebatur sponte ac-
cusasse), sed in Vitelli amicitia sapienter se et comiter
gesserat, ex proconsulatu Asiae gloriam reportaverat,
maculam veteris industriae laudabili otio abluerat.
4 Fuit inter principes civitatis sine potentia, sine invidia:
salutabatur colebatur, multumque in lectulo iacens
cubiculo semper, non ex fortuna frequenti,[2] doctissi-
mis sermonibus dies transigebat, cum a scribendo

---

[1] Duties at the *aerarium Saturni*. P. rarely has time to
visit Comum.
[2] Martial (XI. 48–9) says he owned one of Cicero's houses.

as soon as I can find someone who will not find it a trouble, or I will bring it myself, which you will like better, for I have it in mind to pay you a visit if my official duties permit.[1]   Your smile at this promise to come will change to a frown when I add that it will only be for a few days; the work which is still keeping me here will not let me be away for longer.

VII

To Caninius Rufus

The news has just come that Silius Italicus has starved himself to death in his house near Naples.[2] Ill-health was the reason, for he had developed an incurable tumour which wore him down until he formed the fixed resolve to escape by dying; though he had been fortunate in life and enjoyed happiness up to the end of his days, apart from the loss of the younger of his two sons.   The elder and more gifted he left well established in his career and already of consular rank.   Italicus had damaged his reputation under Nero—it was believed that he had offered his services as an informer—but he had maintained his friendship with Vitellius with tact and wisdom, won fame for his conduct as governor of Asia, and removed the stigma of his former activities by his honourable retirement.   He ranked as one of our leading citizens without exercising influence or incurring ill-will; he was waited on and sought after, and spent many hours on his couch in a room thronged with callers who had come with no thought of his rank; and so passed his days in cultured conversation whenever he

5 vacaret. Scribebat carmina maiore cura quam ingenio, non numquam iudicia hominum recitationibus
6 experiebatur. Novissime ita suadentibus annis ab
urbe secessit, seque in Campania tenuit, ac ne adventu
7 quidem novi principis inde commotus est: magna
Caesaris laus sub quo hoc liberum fuit, magna illius
8 qui hac libertate ausus est uti. Erat φιλόκαλος
usque ad emacitatis reprehensionem. Plures isdem
in locis villas possidebat, adamatisque novis priores
neglegebat. Multum ubique librorum, multum
statuarum, multum imaginum, quas non habebat
modo, verum etiam venerabatur, Vergili ante omnes,
cuius natalem religiosius quam suum celebrabat,
Neapoli maxime, ubi monimentum eius adire ut tem-
9 plum solebat. In hac tranquillitate annum quintum
et septuagensimum excessit, delicato magis corpore
quam infirmo; utque novissimus a Nerone factus est
consul, ita postremus ex omnibus, quos Nero consules
10 fecerat, decessit. Illud etiam notabile: ultimus ex
Neronianis consularibus obiit, quo consule Nero periit.
Quod me recordantem fragilitatis humanae mis-
11 eratio subit. Quid enim tam circumcisum tam breve
quam homini vita longissima? An non videtur tibi
Nero modo modo[1] fuisse? cum interim ex iis, qui sub
illo gesserant consulatum, nemo iam superest.

[1] modo modo αγ: modo β.

---

[1] Fair comment on the *Punica*, which runs to 12,200 lines.
[2] Trajan, on his arrival from Pannonia in 99; *Pan.* 22. 1.
[3] See Martial, XI. 48–9.

could spare time from his writing. He took great pains over his verses,[1] though they cannot be called inspired, and frequently submitted them to public criticism by the readings he gave. Latterly his increasing age led to his retirement from Rome; he made his home in Campania and never left it again, not even on the arrival of the new Emperor:[2] an incident which reflects great credit on the Emperor for permitting this liberty, and on Italicus for venturing to avail himself of it. He was a great connoisseur; indeed he was criticized for buying too much. He owned several houses in the same district, but lost interest in the older ones in his enthusiasm for the later. In each of them he had quantities of books, statues and portrait busts, and these were more to him than possessions—they became objects of his devotion, particularly in the case of Virgil, whose birthday he celebrated with more solemnity than his own, and at Naples especially, where he would visit Virgil's tomb as if it were a temple.[3] In this peaceful atmosphere he completed his seventy-fifth year, surrounded by attentions though not really an invalid. He was the last consul to be appointed by Nero, and the last to die of all the consuls Nero appointed; and also remarkable is the fact that not only did the last of Nero's consuls die in him but it was during his consulship that Nero perished.

The thought of this fills me with pity for human frailty; nothing is so short and fleeting as the longest of human lives. It must seem to you only the other day that Nero died, yet not one of those who held consulships in his time is alive today. I suppose I

12 Quamquam quid hoc miror? Nuper L. Piso, pater
Pisonis illius, qui a Valerio Festo per summum facinus
in Africa occisus est, dicere solebat neminem se videre
in senatu, quem consul ipse sententiam rogavisset.
13 Tam angustis terminis tantae multitudinis vivacitas
ipsa concluditur, ut mihi non venia solum dignae,
verum etiam laude videantur illae regiae lacrimae;
nam ferunt Xersen, cum immensum exercitum oculis
obisset, inlacrimasse, quod tot milibus tam brevis
14 immineret occasus. Sed tanto magis hoc, quidquid
est temporis futilis et caduci, si non datur factis (nam
horum materia in aliena manu), certe studiis pro-
feramus, et quatenus nobis denegatur diu vivere,
15 relinquamus aliquid, quo nos vixisse testemur. Scio
te stimulis non egere: me tamen tui caritas evocat,
ut currentem quoque instigem, sicut tu soles me.
Ἀγαθὴ δ᾽ ἔρις cum invicem se mutuis exhortationibus
amici ad amorem immortalitatis exacuunt. Vale.

VIII

C. Plinius Suetonio Tranquillo Suo S.

1 Facis pro cetera reverentia quam mihi praestas,
quod tam sollicite petis ut tribunatum, quem a
Neratio Marcello clarissimo viro impetravi tibi, in

---

[1] L. Calpurnius Piso, consul in 27; his son was murdered in
70 (Tacitus, *Hist.* IV. 50).

[2] The story told by Herodotus (VII. 45) and often recalled.

[3] P. regrets the loss of the freedom enjoyed by the republican
Senate; cf. III. 20. 10 ff.; IX. 2.

should not find this remarkable when only recently
Lucius Piso,[1] father of the Piso who was so criminally
done to death in Africa by Valerius Festus, used to
say that none of those he had called on to speak when
he was consul could still be seen in the Senate. So
narrow are the limits set to life, even in a large com-
munity, that it seems to me that the Persian king
should be forgiven, or even admired for his famous
tears; for it is said that after Xerxes had reviewed his
vast army, he wept to think of the end awaiting so
many thousands in so short a time.[2]

All the more reason then why we should prolong all
our passing moments, uncertain though they are, not
perhaps by action, since here the opportunity no
longer rests with us,[3] but at any rate by literary
work. Since we are denied a long life, let us leave
something to bear witness that at least we have lived.
I know you need no incentive, but my affection for
you prompts me to spur on a willing horse, as you
do for me in return. " Rivalry is good " [4] when
friends stimulate each other by mutual encouragement to desire immortal fame.

VIII

To Suetonius Tranquillus

You give proof of your high regard for me by the
delicacy with which you frame your request that I
should transfer to your relative Caesennius Silvanus

---

[4] Hesiod, *Works and Days* 24.

Caesennium Silvanum propinquum tuum transferam.
2 Mihi autem sicut iucundissimum ipsum te tribunum,
ita non minus gratum alium per te videre. Neque
enim esse congruens arbitror, quem augere honoribus cupias, huic pietatis titulis invidere, qui sunt
3 omnibus honoribus pulchriores. Video etiam, cum sit
egregium et mereri beneficia et dare, utramque te
laudem simul adsecuturum, si quod ipse meruisti alii
tribuas. Praeterea intellego mihi quoque gloriae fore,
si ex hoc tuo facto non fuerit ignotum amicos meos
non gerere tantum tribunatus posse verum etiam dare.
4 Quare ego vero honestissimae voluntati tuae pareo.
Neque enim adhuc nomen in numeros relatum est,
ideoque liberum est nobis Silvanum in locum tuum
subdere; cui cupio tam gratum esse munus tuum,
quam tibi meum est. Vale.

IX

C. Plinius Cornelio Miniciano Suo S.

1   Possum iam perscribere tibi quantum in publica
2 provinciae Baeticae causa laboris exhauserim. Nam
fuit multiplex, actaque est saepius cum magna varietate. Unde varietas, unde plures actiones? Caecilius
Classicus, homo foedus et aperte malus, proconsula-
tum in ea non minus violenter quam sordide gesserat,

---

[1] Neratius Marcellus was legate in Britain in 103.

the military tribunate which I obtained for you from
the distinguished senator Neratius Marcellus.[1] For
myself, I should have been delighted to see you as
tribune, but I shall be equally pleased if Silvanus
owes his office to you. If one has thought a man
worthy of promotion it is, I think, illogical to begrudge him the right to show his family feeling,
seeing that this does him more honour than any
official title. I see too that as the performance of
services is as laudable as the deserving of them, you
will win praise on both accounts if you give up to
someone else what you merited yourself, and I
realize that some credit will be reflected on me, too,
if as a result of your action it is known that my
friends are free either to hold the office of tribune
themselves or to give it away. Your wish is thus
excellent in every way and shall be granted. Your
name is not yet entered on the lists, so it is easy for
me to substitute that of Silvanus; and I hope that
your service will please him as much as mine pleases
you.

IX

To Cornelius Minicianus

At last I can give you a full account of all the
trouble I have had over the public action brought by
the province of Baetica, a most complicated case
which after several hearings ended in a variety of
sentences: the reasons for which you shall hear.

Caecilius Classicus had been governor of Baetica in
the same year that Marius Priscus was in Africa. His
rapacity during this time was matched by his brutality,

189

eodem anno quo in Africa Marius Priscus. Erat
3 autem Priscus ex Baetica, ex Africa Classicus. Inde
dictum Baeticorum, ut plerumque dolor etiam venus-
tos facit, non inlepidum ferebatur: " Dedi malum et
4 accepi." Sed Marium una civitas publice multique
privati reum peregerunt, in Classicum tota provincia
5 incubuit. Ille accusationem vel fortuita vel voluntaria morte praevertit. Nam fuit mors eius infamis,
ambigua tamen: ut enim credibile videbatur voluisse
exire de vita, cum defendi non posset, ita mirum
pudorem damnationis morte fugisse, quem non
6 puduisset damnanda committere. Nihilo minus
Baetica etiam in defuncti accusatione perstabat.
Provisum hoc legibus, intermissum tamen et post
longam intercapedinem tunc reductum. Addiderunt
Baetici, quod simul socios ministrosque Classici
detulerunt, nominatimque in eos inquisitionem
7 postulaverunt. Aderam Baeticis mecumque Lucceius Albinus, vir in dicendo copiosus ornatus; quem
ego cum olim mutuo diligerem, ex hac officii societate
8 amare ardentius coepi. Habet quidem gloria,[1] in
studiis praesertim, quiddam ἀκοινώνητον; nobis
tamen nullum certamen nulla contentio, cum uterque
pari iugo non pro se sed pro causa niteretur, cuius et
magnitudo et utilitas visa est postulare, ne tantum
9 oneris singulis actionibus subiremus. Verebamur ne

[1] gloria *Beroaldus*: gloriam βγ.

for he was a scoundrel who made no secret of his
evil ways. It so happened that Priscus came from
Baetica and Classicus from Africa; hence the neat
joke current among the Baetici (for exasperation
often breaks out into wit)—" I got as bad as I gave."
However, Priscus was brought to trial by a single
city and by several private individuals, whereas
Classicus was attacked by the entire province. He
forestalled the trial by his death, which might have
been accidental or self-inflicted; there was much
general suspicion but no definite proof, for, though it
seemed likely that he intended to die since he could
not defend himself, it is surprising that he should
have died to escape the shame of condemnation for
deeds which he was not ashamed to do. Nevertheless, the Baetici continued with their action after his
death. (This was legally permissible, but the practice had lapsed, and was revived on this occasion
after a long interval.) In addition to Classicus, they
extended their charges to his friends and accomplices,
demanding an individual investigation in each case.

I appeared for the Baetici, supported by Lucceius
Albinus, a fluent and elegant orator whom I have long
admired; since our association on this occasion I have
come to feel a warmer affection for him. The will to
succeed implies some reluctance to share success, and
especially where forensic oratory is concerned; but
in our case there was no rivalry nor competition. We
both put the needs of the case before personal
considerations in a combined effort, for we felt that
the importance of the issue and its outcome
demanded that we did not assume such responsibility
in a single speech from each of us. It looked as

nos dies ne vox ne latera deficerent, si tot crimina tot
reos uno velut fasce complecteremur; deinde ne
iudicum intentio multis nominibus multisque causis
non lassaretur modo verum etiam confunderetur;
mox ne gratia singulorum collata atque permixta pro
singulis quoque vires omnium acciperet; postremo ne
potentissimi vilissimo quoque quasi piaculari dato
10 alienis poenis elaberentur. Etenim tum maxime
favor et ambitio dominatur, cum sub aliqua specie
11 severitatis delitescere potest. Erat in consilio
Sertorianum illud exemplum, qui robustissimum et
infirmissimum militem iussit caudam equi —reliqua
nosti. Nam nos quoque tam numerosum agmen
reorum ita demum videbamus posse superari, si per
singulos carperetur.
12 Placuit in primis ipsum Classicum ostendere no-
centem: hic aptissimus ad socios eius et ministros
transitus erat, quia socii ministrique probari nisi illo
nocente non poterant. Ex quibus duos statim
Classico iunximus, Baebium Probum et Fabium
Hispanum, utrumque gratia, Hispanum etiam facun-
dia validum. Et circa Classicum quidem brevis et
13 expeditus labor. Sua manu reliquerat scriptum,
quid ex quaque re, quid ex quaque causa accepisset;
miserat etiam epistulas Romam ad amiculam quandam, iactantes et gloriosas, his quidem verbis: " Io
io, liber ad te venio; iam sestertium quadragiens
14 redegi parte vendita Baeticorum." Circa Hispanum
et Probum multum sudoris. Horum ante quam

---

¹ Another oft-repeated tale; see Valerius Maximus, VII.
3. 6; Horace, *Ep.* II. 1. 45; Plutarch, *Sert.* 16.

though we should run short of time and lose our breath and voice if we bundled so many accusations and defendants all together, so to speak, and then the large number of names and charges might exhaust the attention of the magistrates and possibly leave them in confusion. Moreover, the combined influence of the individuals concerned might procure for each the effect of the whole, and, finally, the influential might make scapegoats of the humble, and so escape at their expense. (Privilege and self-interest are most likely to triumph when they can be concealed behind a mask of severity.) We also had in mind the well-known example of Sertorius,[1] when he set the strongest and the weakest of his soldiers to pull off the horse's tail—you know the rest of the story—and concluded that we too could best deal with the large number of defendants if we took them one by one.

We decided that the first essential was to prove Classicus guilty; this would give us the best approach to his allies and accomplices, who could not be convicted unless he was. We coupled two of them with Classicus from the start, Baebius Probus and Fabius Hispanus, both formidable opponents through their influence, and Hispanus also for his fluent tongue. It was easy to make short work of Classicus. He had left accounts in his own hand of his receipts for every business deal and court case, and he had even sent a bragging letter to his mistress in Rome (these are his actual words): " Hurrah, hurrah, I'm coming to you a free man—I've sold up half the Baetici and raised four million! "

Over Hispanus and Probus we had to sweat. Before I dealt with the charges against them I

crimina ingrederer, necessarium credidi elaborare,
ut constaret ministerium crimen esse: quod nisi
15 fecissem, frustra ministros probassem. Neque enim
ita defendebantur, ut negarent, sed ut necessitati
veniam precarentur; esse enim se provinciales et ad
16 omne proconsulum imperium metu cogi. Solet
dicere Claudius Restitutus, qui mihi respondit, vir
exercitatus et vigilans et quamlibet subitis paratus,
numquam sibi tantum caliginis tantum perturbationis
offusum, quam cum praerepta ex extorta defensioni
suae cerneret, in quibus omnem fiduciam reponebat.
17 Consilii nostri exitus fuit: bona Classici, quae
habuisset ante provinciam, placuit senatui a reliquis separari, illa filiae haec spoliatis relinqui. Addi-
tum est, ut pecuniae quas creditoribus solverat
revocarentur. Hispanus et Probus in quinquennium
relegati; adeo grave visum est, quod initio dubita-
batur an omnino crimen esset.
18 Post paucos dies Claudium Fuscum, Classici
generum, et Stilonium Priscum, qui tribunus cohortis
sub Classico fuerat, accusavimus dispari eventu:
Prisco in biennium Italia interdictum, absolutus est
Fuscus.
19 Actione tertia commodissimum putavimus plures
congregare, ne si longius esset extracta cognitio,
satietate et taedio quodam iustitia cognoscentium
severitasque languesceret; et alioqui supererant
minores rei data opera hunc in locum reservati,

believed it was essential to establish the fact that the
carrying out of orders was a chargeable offence;
otherwise it would have been useless to prove they
had done so. Their defence was in fact not to deny
the charge, but to plead compulsion, saying that as
provincials they were terrorized into carrying out any
order of the governor. Claudius Restitutus, who
replied for the defence, is a practised speaker who is
alert and ready for anything unexpected, but he
now says that he never felt so dumbfounded and
bewildered as when he saw all the points he was most
relying on for his defence anticipated and torn out
of his grasp. The result of our policy was that
the Senate decreed that all possessions owned by
Classicus before his provincial appointment should be
set aside and given to his daughter, that the remain-
der be handed over to the people he had robbed, and,
further, that the money he had paid to his creditors
should be recalled. Hispanus and Probus were
banished for five years, so serious did their conduct
now seem, though at first it had been doubtful
whether it was indictable at all.

A few days later we charged Claudius Fuscus, the
son-in-law of Classicus, and Stilonius Priscus who had
served under him as tribune of a cohort, with varying
success: Priscus was banished from Italy for two
years, and Fuscus was acquitted.

At the third hearing we thought it best to group
several defendants together, fearing that if the trial
were prolonged too far the presiding magistrates
would be bored and tired and consequently their
strict administration of justice would begin to flag.
Moreover, there remained only people of less

excepta tamen Classici uxore, quae sicut implicita suspicionibus ita non satis convinci probationibus visa
20 est; nam Classici filia, quae et ipsa inter reos erat,
ne suspicionibus quidem haerebat. Itaque, cum ad
nomen eius in extrema actione venissem (neque
enim ut initio sic etiam in fine verendum erat, ne per
hoc totius accusationis auctoritas minueretur), honestissimum credidi non premere immerentem, idque
21 ipsum dixi et libere et varie. Nam modo legatos
interrogabam, docuissentne me aliquid quod re
probari posse confiderent; modo consilium a senatu
petebam, putaretne debere me, si quam haberem in
dicendo facultatem, in iugulum innocentis quasi
telum aliquod intendere; postremo totum locum hoc
fine conclusi: " Dicet aliquis: Iudicas ergo? Ego
vero non iudico, memini tamen me advocatum ex
iudicibus datum."
22 Hic numerosissimae causae terminus fuit quibusdam absolutis, pluribus damnatis atque etiam rele-
23 gatis, aliis in tempus aliis in perpetuum. Eodem
senatus consulto industria fides constantia nostra
plenissimo testimonio comprobata est, dignum solum-
24 que par pretium tanti laboris. Concipere animo potes
quam simus fatigati, quibus totiens agendum totiens
altercandum, tam multi testes interrogandi suble-

---

¹ A governor's wife was often implicated in a charge made
against her husband; see Martial, II. 56, and the proposal
debated in Tacitus, *Ann.* III. 33–4 that wives should remain
behind in Rome.

importance whom we had deliberately kept back until
then, apart from Classicus's wife who was strongly
suspected, though it did not look as though there was
proof enough to convict her.[1] Classicus's daughter,
who had also been included in the charge, emerged
quite free from suspicion. So when I reached her
name at the end of my speech, as there was no longer
the same danger of weakening the whole case as
there was at the beginning, I felt that the only just
course was to refrain from pressing a charge against
an innocent person: and I said so openly in many
ways. I first asked the representatives of the province if they had instructed me to make any special
charge which they were confident could be sub-
stantiated, and then I appealed to the Senate for
guidance whether I ought to direct all my powers of
oratory against an innocent woman, like a knife at
her throat. Finally, I brought the whole subject to
this conclusion. " If I am asked whether I am judging this case, my answer is No, but I cannot forget
that I should have been among the judges, had I not
been chosen to conduct the prosecution."

So ended these complicated proceedings; of the
persons involved, some were acquitted, but the
majority were convicted and banished, either for a
fixed period or for life. In its decree passing sentence, the Senate gave the fullest expression to its
appreciation of Albinus and myself, for our thorough
and scrupulous handling of the case and for our per-
severance, the only just and adequate reward for our
great labours. You can imagine how tired we are
after so much continuous speaking, debating, and
cross-examining of all the witnesses and supporting or

25 vandi refutandi. Iam illa quam ardua quam molesta,
tot reorum amicis secreto rogantibus negare, adversantibus palam obsistere! Referam unum aliquid ex
iis quae dixi. Cum mihi quidam e iudicibus ipsis pro
reo gratiosissimo reclamarent, " Non minus " inquam " hic innocens erit, si ego omnia dixero."
26 Coniectabis ex hoc quantas contentiones, quantas
etiam offensas subierimus dumtaxat ad breve tempus;
nam fides in praesentia eos quibus resistit offendit,
deinde ab illis ipsis suspicitur laudaturque. Non
27 potui magis te in rem praesentem perducere. Dices:
" Non fuit tanti; quid enim mihi cum tam longa
epistula ? " Nolito ergo identidem quaerere, quid
Romae geratur. Et tamen memento non esse
epistulam longam, quae tot dies tot cognitiones tot
28 denique reos, causasque complexa sit. Quae omnia
videor mihi non minus breviter quam diligenter
persecutus.

Temere dixi " diligenter ": succurrit quod prae-
terieram et quidem sero, sed quamquam praepostere
reddetur. Facit hoc Homerus multique illius exemplo; est alioqui perdecorum, a me tamen non ideo
29 fiet. E testibus quidam, sive iratus quod evocatus
esset invitus, sive subornatus ab aliquo reorum, ut
accusationem exarmaret, Norbanum Licinianum,
legatum et inquisitorem, reum postulavit, tamquam in
causa Castae (uxor haec Classici) praevaricaretur.

---

¹ The artistic device of *ordo praeposterus*, instead of chronological order, *e.g.* Odysseus' narrative at the court of Alcinous.
Cf. Cic. *Ep. ad Att.* 1. 16. 1: ὕστερον πρότερον, Ὁμηρικῶς.

refuting their replies; and how difficult and unpleasant it has been to have to say no to the confidential requests of the friends of the many defendants, and then to have to face their open attacks in court. I will quote one of the answers I gave when some of the magistrates were protesting on behalf of a highly influential defendant: " His innocence will not be affected if I am allowed to finish my speech." From this you can guess at the opposition and hostility we incurred, though admittedly not for long. Honesty offends those it thwarts for a time, but afterwards these are the people from whom it wins respect and approval.

I can't do more to bring you to the scene of action. You may say that it wasn't worth while and that you never expected such a long letter—then don't ask again for news of what is happening in Rome, and remember that a letter cannot really be called long when it deals with so many days and inquiries, and all the defendants involved in so many cases. I think myself that I have kept my account short and accurate—no, that was rash: I have just remembered too late something I left out, and you must have it although out of place. (This is one of Homer's devices,[1] and many writers imitate him; it can be very effective, though that was not my own intention.)

A witness who was either annoyed at being compelled to appear to give evidence, or had been suborned by one of the defendants to damage the case, charged Norbanus Licinianus (one of the representatives of Baetica who had been commissioned to collect evidence) with collusion in the case against Casta, the wife of Classicus. It is laid down by law

30 Est lege cautum ut reus ante peragatur, tunc de
praevaricatore quaeratur, videlicet quia optime ex
31 accusatione ipsa accusatoris fides aestimatur. Norbano tamen non ordo legis, non legati nomen, non
inquisitionis officium praesidio fuit; tanta conflag-
ravit invidia homo alioqui flagitiosus et Domitiani
temporibus usus ut multi, electusque tunc a provincia
ad inquirendum non tamquam bonus et fidelis, sed
tamquam Classici inimicus (erat ab illo relegatus).
32 Dari sibi diem, edi crimina postulabat; neutrum impetravit, coactus est statim respondere. Respondit,
malum pravumque ingenium hominis facit ut dubitem,
33 confidenter an constanter, certe paratissime. Ob-
iecta sunt multa, quae magis quam praevaricatio
nocuerunt; quin etiam duo consulares, Pomponius
Rufus et Libo Frugi, laeserunt eum testimonio, tamquam apud iudicem sub Domitiano Salvi Liberalis
34 accusatoribus adfuisset. Damnatus et in insulam
relegatus est. Itaque cum Castam accusarem nihil
magis pressi, quam quod accusator eius praevarica-
tionis crimine corruisset; pressi tamen frustra;
accidit enim res contraria et nova, ut accusatore prae-
35 varicationis damnato rea absolveretur. Quaeris,

---

[1] The trial of Casta must have been interrupted, against
precedent, for Norbanus to be dealt with—perhaps because of
the outcry against him.

that the trial of an accused shall be concluded before a charge of collusion with his accuser is investigated, doubtless because the honesty of the latter can best be judged from his handling of the case. However, Norbanus gained no protection from this legal provision, and none from his position as delegate nor his commission to prepare the case; he was swept away by the general indignation against his other misdemeanours and the fact that like many others he had profited by the reign of Domitian, and had in fact been chosen by his province to collect evidence on this occasion not for his honesty and reliability but for his hatred of Classicus (who had previously banished him). He asked for time and a statement of the charges against him, but both his requests were refused. He was obliged to defend himself on the spot, and did so with considerable promptitude, though the man's thoroughly bad and worthless character makes me wonder whether his reply showed courage or merely impudence. There were many other charges against him more damaging than that of collusion: indeed, two senators (the consulars Pomponius Rufus and Libo Frugi) produced the damning evidence that he had appeared in court in Domitian's time in support of the prosecution of Salvius Liberalis. He was found guilty and sentenced to banishment on an island. In charging Casta, therefore, I particularly emphasized the collusion for which her accuser had been convicted, but without success. On the contrary, the result was quite without precedent—the defendant was acquitted although her accuser was convicted of collusion with her.[1]

quid nos, dum haec aguntur? Indicavimus senatui ex Norbano didicisse nos publicam causam, rursusque debere ex integro discere, si ille praevaricator probaretur, atque ita, dum ille peragitur reus, sedimus. Postea Norbanus omnibus diebus cognitionis interfuit eandemque usque ad extremum vel constantiam vel audaciam pertulit.

36 Interrogo ipse me, an aliquid omiserim rursus, et rursus paene omisi. Summo die Salvius Liberalis reliquos legatos graviter increpuit, tamquam non omnes quos mandasset provincia reos peregissent, atque, ut est vehemens et disertus, in discrimen adduxit. Protexi viros optimos eosdemque gratissimos: mihi certe debere se praedicant, quod illum 37 turbinem evaserint. Hic erit epistulae finis, re vera finis; litteram non addam, etiamsi adhuc aliquid praeterisse me sensero. Vale.

X

C. Plinius Vestricio Spurinnae Suo et Cottiae S.

1 Composuisse me quaedam de filio vestro non dixi vobis, cum proxime apud vos fui, primum quia non ideo scripseram ut dicerem, sed ut meo amori meo dolori satisfacerem; deinde quia te, Spurinna, cum audisses recitasse me, ut mihi ipse dixisti, quid reci-

---

[1] See II. 7, for the death of Cottius. The visit was probably that described in III. 1.

You may be wondering what we were doing meanwhile. We explained to the Senate that, as it was from Norbanus that we had received our instructions on behalf of the province, if he was found guilty of collusion we must begin again with fresh ones; so while his trial was on, we remained seated. Afterwards Norbanus attended every day of the trial and kept up his courage—or impudence—to the end.

I am trying to think whether I have left anything out this time, and again I nearly did. On the last day Salvius Liberalis made a violent attack on the remaining delegates for not having brought to trial all the persons about whom their province had given them instructions, and, being a forceful and eloquent speaker, he put them in a perilous position. I undertook their defence, and found them honest men and most grateful to me; in fact they say they owe their escape from disaster entirely to me.

This is the end of this letter, really the end—I won't add another syllable even if I think of something else I have forgotten.

X

To Vestricius Spurinna and Cottia

I refrained from mentioning when I was last with you that I had written something about your son,[1] because, in the first place, I had not written it with the idea of telling you, but to give expression to my own feelings of love and grief, and then because I knew from what you had told me yourself that you, Spurinna, had heard that I had given a public reading,

2 tassem simul audisse credebam. Praeterea veritus
sum ne vos festis diebus confunderem, si in memoriam
gravissimi luctus reduxissem. Nunc quoque paulisper haesitavi, id solum, quod recitavi, mitterem
exigentibus vobis, an adicerem quae in aliud volumen
3 cogito reservare. Neque enim adfectibus meis uno
libello carissimam mihi et sanctissimam memoriam
prosequi satis est, cuius famae latius consuletur, si
4 dispensata et digesta fuerit. Verum haesitanti
mihi, omnia quae iam composui vobis exhiberem, an
adhuc aliqua differrem, simplicius et amicius visum
est omnia, praecipue cum adfirmetis intra vos futura,
5 donec placeat emittere. Quod superest, rogo ut
pari simplicitate, si qua existimabitis addenda com-
6 mutanda omittenda, indicetis mihi. Difficile est huc
usque intendere animum in dolore; difficile, sed
tamen, ut scalptorem, ut pictorem, qui filii vestri
imaginem faceret, admoneretis, quid exprimere quid
emendare deberet, ita me quoque formate regite,
qui non fragilem et caducam, sed immortalem, ut vos
putatis, effigiem conor efficere: quae hoc diuturnior
erit, quo verior melior absolutior fuerit. Valete.

and I assumed that you had also heard what its subject was. I was anxious too not to upset you during a national holiday by reviving the memory of your tragic loss.

Even now I am still in some doubt whether to send you only the passages I read, as you ask, or to add what I was intending to keep back to present on another occasion. A single composition is quite inadequate for my sentiments, if I am to do justice to the memory of one I loved and revered so much, and his fame will be more widespread if it is published abroad by degrees. But while debating whether to show you all I have written so far, or to withhold something until later, I have come to see that honesty and friendship alike constrain me to send everything; especially as you assure me that nothing shall leave your hands until I have made up my mind about publication.

One thing remains: please be equally honest about telling me if you think there are any additions, alterations, or omissions to be made. It is difficult for you to concentrate on this at a time of sorrow, I know; but, nevertheless, if a sculptor or painter were working on a portrait of your son, you would indicate to him what features to bring out or correct; and so you must give me guidance and direction as I, too, am trying to create a likeness which shall not be short-lived and ephemeral, but one you think will last for ever. It is more likely to be long-lived the more I can attain to truth and beauty and accuracy in detail.

THE LETTERS OF PLINY

XI

C. Plinius Iulio Genitori Suo S.

1 Est omnino Artemidori nostri tam benigna natura,
ut officia amicorum in maius extollat. Inde etiam
meum meritum ut vera ita supra meritum praedica-
2 tione circumfert. Equidem, cum essent philosophi
ab urbe summoti, fui apud illum in suburbano, et quo
notabilius (hoc est, periculosius) esset fui praetor.
Pecuniam etiam, qua tunc illi ampliore opus erat,
ut aes alienum exsolveret contractum ex pulcherrimis causis, mussantibus magnis quibusdam et locu-
pletibus amicis mutuatus ipse gratuitam dedi.
3 Atque haec feci, cum septem amicis meis aut occisis
aut relegatis, occisis Senecione Rustico Helvidio,
relegatis Maurico Gratilla Arria Fannia, tot circa me
iactis fulminibus quasi ambustus mihi quoque impendere idem exitium certis quibusdam notis augu-
4 rarer. Non ideo tamen eximiam gloriam meruisse
me, ut ille praedicat, credo, sed tantum effugisse
5 flagitium. Nam et C. Musonium socerum eius,
quantum licitum est per aetatem, cum admiratione
dilexi et Artemidorum ipsum iam tum, cum in Syria
tribunus militarem, arta familiaritate complexus sum,
idque primum non nullius indolis dedi specimen, quod

---

¹ The date of P.'s praetorship rests on the interpretation of
this sentence. All the evidence is set out in S-W *App*. IV.
p. 763; he concludes that there was only one expulsion in 93.

XI

To Julius Genitor

The natural generosity of our friend Artemidorus always makes him enlarge on his friends' services, and so he is spreading an account of my merits which is not untrue, but more than I deserve. It is true that, when the philosophers were expelled from Rome,[1] I went to see him in his house outside the city, and as I was praetor at that time the visit involved some risk for the attention it attracted. He was also in need of a considerable sum at the time to pay off his debts contracted in honourable causes; I raised the money and lent it to him without interest, when certain of his rich and influential friends hesitated to do so. I did this at a time when seven of my friends had been put to death or banished[2]— Senecio, Rusticus and Helvidius were dead, and Mauricus, Gratilla, Arria and Fannia were in exile— so that I stood amidst the flames of thunderbolts dropping all round me,[3] and there were certain clear indications to make me suppose a like end was awaiting me.

However, I do not believe I deserve the exaggerated reputation in these matters which Artemidorus gives me: I have not disgraced myself, but that is all. For I greatly admired his father-in-law Gaius Musonius, and loved him as much as our difference in age permitted; and when I was serving as military tribune in Syria I was on terms of close intimacy with

[2] After the death of Agricola, on 23 August 93; see Tacitus, *Agr.* 45.
[3] Cf. *Pan.* 90. 5.

virum aut sapientem aut proximum simillimumque
6 sapienti intellegere sum visus. Nam ex omnibus, qui
nunc se philosophos vocant, vix unum aut alterum
invenies tanta sinceritate, tanta veritate. Mitto,
qua patientia corporis hiemes iuxta et aestates ferat,
ut nullis laboribus cedat, ut nihil in cibo in potu
voluptatibus tribuat, ut oculos animumque contineat.
7 Sunt haec magna, sed in alio; in hoc vero minima,
si ceteris virtutibus comparentur, quibus meruit, ut a
C. Musonio ex omnibus omnium ordinum adsectatori-
8 bus gener adsumeretur. Quae mihi recordanti est
quidem iucundum, quod me cum apud alios tum apud
te tantis laudibus cumulat; vereor tamen ne modum
excedat, quem benignitas eius (illuc enim unde
9 coepi revertor) solet non tenere. Nam in hoc uno
interdum vir alioqui prudentissimus honesto quidem
sed tamen errore versatur, quod pluris amicos suos
quam sunt arbitratur. Vale.

XII

C. Plinius Catilio Severo Suo S.

1 Veniam ad cenam, sed iam nunc paciscor, sit expedita sit parca, Socraticis tantum sermonibus abundet,
2 in his quoque teneat modum. Erunt officia antelu-
cana, in quae incidere impune ne Catoni quidem
licuit, quem tamen C. Caesar ita reprehendit ut
3 laudet. Describit enim eos, quibus obvius fuerit,

---

[1] Caesar wrote an *Anti-Cato*; see Plutarch, *Caes.* 54. For
Cato's drinking, Plut. *Cat. Min.* 6.

Artemidorus himself.   In fact the first sign I showed
of having any judgement was that apparently I
appreciated a man who was a true sage, or the nearest
approach to one.   Of all those who call themselves
philosophers today, you will scarcely find one with his
sincerity and integrity.   I am saying nothing about
his physical endurance in winter and summer, how
he shrinks from no hardship and permits himself no
indulgence in food and drink, nor licence in look or
thought.   All this may be important in another
person, but for him it means little in comparison with
his other virtues; which won him the honour of being
chosen by Gaius Musonius from suitors of every rank
to be his son-in-law.

As I recall these events I am indeed happy to think
of the high tribute he pays me generally, and especially in your hearing, but at the same time I fear he
may go too far; for (to return to the point I started
from) his generosity puts no check on him.   This is
his only fault, albeit a good fault, in one otherwise so
wise: he has too high an opinion of his friends.

XII

To Catilius Severus

I will come to dinner, but I have conditions to lay
down from the start; it must be simple and informal,
rich only in Socratic conversation, though this too
must be kept within bounds; for there will be early-
morning callers to think of.   Cato himself could not
escape reproach on meeting them, though Caesar's
adverse comment is tinged with admiration.[1]   The

cum caput ebrii retexissent, erubuisse; deinde adicit:
"Putares non ab illis Catonem, sed illos a Catone
deprehensos." Potuitne plus auctoritatis tribui
Catoni, quam si ebrius quoque tam venerabilis erat?
4 Nostrae tamen cenae, ut adparatus et impendii, sic
temporis modus constet. Neque enim ii sumus quos
vituperare ne inimici quidem possint, nisi ut simul
laudent. Vale.

XIII

C. PLINIUS VOCONIO ROMANO SUO S.

1 LIBRUM, quo nuper optimo principi consul gratias
egi, misi exigenti tibi, missurus etsi non exegisses.
2 In hoc consideres velim ut pulchritudinem materiae
ita difficultatem. In ceteris enim lectorem novitas
ipsa intentum habet, in hac nota vulgata dicta sunt
omnia; quo fit ut quasi otiosus securusque lector
tantum elocutioni vacet, in qua satisfacere difficilius
3 est cum sola aestimatur. Atque utinam ordo saltem
et transitus et figurae simul spectarentur! Nam invenire praeclare, enuntiare magnifice interdum etiam
barbari solent, disponere apte, figurare varie nisi
eruditis negatum est. Nec vero adfectanda sunt
4 semper elata et excelsa. Nam ut in pictura lumen non
alia res magis quam umbra commendat, ita orationem

---

[1] On 1 September 100: later expanded and published as the
Panegyricus.

passers-by whom Cato met when drunk, blushed
when they discovered who he was, and (says Caesar)
" You would have thought they had been found out
by Cato, not Cato by them." What better tribute
to Cato's prestige than to show him still awe-inspiring
when drunk! But our dinner must have a limit, in
time as well as in preparations and expense; for we
are not the sort of people whom even our enemies
cannot blame without a word of praise.

XIII

To Voconius Romanus

I AM sending at your request the text of the speech
in which I recently expressed my thanks to our noble
Emperor for my consulship;[1] I intended to do so in
any case. I should like you to bear in mind that the
nobility of the theme brings its own difficulties. In
other speeches there is novelty, if nothing else, to
hold the attention of the reader, but here everything
is common knowledge and has been said before; consequently the reader has time and freedom to concentrate on the delivery without distractions, and if
he forms his opinion by this alone he is not easily
satisfied. I would prefer him to give equal attention
to the arrangement, the transitions and figures of
speech, for, although a powerful imagination and the
gift of forceful expression are sometimes to be found
in the uneducated, no one can display skill in arrangement and variety of figures except the trained expert.
Nor should one always be searching for the elevated
and the sublime, for a speech needs to lower as well as

5 tam summittere quam attollere decet. Sed quid ego
haec doctissimo viro? Quin potius illud: adnota,
quae putaveris corrigenda. Ita enim magis credam
cetera tibi placere, si quaedam displicuisse cognovero.
Vale.

XIV

C. Plinius Acilio Suo S.

1 Rem atrocem nec tantum epistula dignam Larcius
Macedo vir praetorius a servis suis passus est, su-
perbus alioqui dominus et saevus, et qui servisse
patrem suum parum, immo nimium meminisset.
2 Lavabatur in villa Formiana. Repente eum servi
circumsistunt. Alius fauces invadit, alius os ver-
berat, alius pectus et ventrem, atque etiam (foedum
dictu) verenda contundit; et cum exanimem puta-
rent, abiciunt in fervens pavimentum, ut experirentur
an viveret. Ille sive quia non sentiebat, sive quia se
non sentire simulabat, immobilis et extentus fidem
3 peractae mortis implevit. Tum demum quasi aestu
solutus effertur; excipiunt servi fideliores, concubinae
cum ululatu et clamore concurrunt. Ita et vocibus
excitatus et recreatus loci frigore sublatis oculis agi-
tatoque corpore vivere se (et iam tutum erat) con-

---

¹ His father must have been freed, and this would make his
sons eligible for senatorial office.
² In Latium (Mola di Gaeta).

to raise its tone: just as in a picture, light is best shown up by shadow. But there is no need for me to say this to anyone of your attainments. I ought rather to ask you to mark any alterations you think should be made, for, if I know your criticisms of some points, I shall be more ready to believe that you like the rest of the speech.

XIV

To Publius (?) Acilius

This horrible affair demands more publicity than a letter—Larcius Macedo, a senator and ex-praetor, has fallen a victim to his own slaves. Admittedly he was a cruel and overbearing master, too ready to forget that his father had been a slave, or perhaps too keenly conscious of it.[1] He was taking a bath in his house at Formiae[2] when suddenly he found himself surrounded; one slave seized him by the throat while the others struck his face and hit him in the chest and stomach and—shocking to say—in his private parts. When they thought he was dead they threw him on to the hot pavement, to make sure he was not still alive. Whether unconscious or feigning to be so, he lay there motionless, thus making them believe that he was quite dead. Only then was he carried out, as if he had fainted with the heat, and received by his slaves who had remained faithful, while his concubines ran up, screaming frantically. Roused by their cries and revived by the cooler air he opened his eyes and made some movement to show that he was alive, it being now safe to do so. The guilty slaves

4 fitetur. Diffugiunt servi; quorum magna pars
comprehensa est, ceteri requiruntur. Ipse paucis
diebus aegre focilatus non sine ultionis solacio deces-
5 sit ita vivus vindicatus, ut occisi solent. Vides
quot periculis quot contumeliis quot ludibriis simus
obnoxii; nec est quod quisquam possit esse securus,
quia sit remissus et mitis; non enim iudicio domini
sed scelere perimuntur.
6   Verum haec hactenus. Quid praeterea novi?
Quid? Nihil, alioqui subiungerem; nam et charta
adhuc superest, et dies feriatus patitur plura contexi.
Addam quod opportune de eodem Macedone succurrit. Cum in publico Romae lavaretur, notabilis
atque etiam, ut exitus docuit, ominosa res accidit.
7 Eques Romanus a servo eius, ut transitum daret,
manu leviter admonitus convertit se nec servum, a
quo erat tactus, sed ipsum Macedonem tam graviter
8 palma[1] percussit ut paene concideret. Ita balineum
illi quasi per gradus quosdam primum contumeliae
locus, deinde exitii fuit. Vale.

XV

C. Plinius Silio Proculo Suo S.

1   Petis ut libellos tuos in secessu legam examinem,
an editione sint digni; adhibes preces, adlegas exem-

---

[1] palma β: palam αγ.

---

[1] Probably all the slaves were executed.   For a similar case
of murder, see *Ep.* VIII. 14. 12 (Afranius Dexter) and Tacitus,
Ann. XIV. 42 ff. (L. Pedanius Secundus).

fled, but most of them have been arrested and a search is being made for the others. Macedo was brought back to life with difficulty, but only for a few days; at least he died with the satisfaction of having revenged himself, for he lived to see the same punishment meted out as for murder.[1] There you see the dangers, outrages and insults to which we are exposed. No master can feel safe because he is kind and considerate; for it is their brutality, not their reasoning capacity, which leads slaves to murder masters.

But let us change the subject. What news is there? None, or I would give you it, for I still have some paper, and today's holiday gives me time to continue. I will only put in a detail in connexion with Macedo which I have fortunately just remembered. He was in one of the public baths in Rome when a remarkable incident occurred which events have proved to be an omen. One of Macedo's slaves lightly touched a Roman knight to ask him to let them pass; the man turned round and struck not the slave who had touched him, but Macedo himself such a violent slap that he nearly knocked him down. So the baths have been the scene successively of insult to Macedo and then of his death.

XV

To Silius Proculus

You want me to read through some of your poems while I am away on holiday, to see if they are worth publishing, and, in begging me to spend on your work

plum: rogas enim, ut aliquid subscivi temporis studiis meis subtraham, impertiam tuis, adicis M. Tullium mira benignitate poetarum ingenia fovisse.
2 Sed ego nec rogandus sum nec hortandus; nam et poeticen ipsam religiosissime veneror et te valdissime diligo. Faciam ergo quod desideras tam dili-
3 genter quam libenter. Videor autem iam nunc posse rescribere esse opus pulchrum nec supprimendum, quantum aestimare licuit ex iis quae me praesente recitasti, si modo mihi non imposuit recitatio
4 tua; legis enim suavissime et peritissime. Confido tamen me non sic auribus duci, ut omnes aculei iudicii mei illarum delenimentis refringantur: hebetentur fortasse et paulum retundantur, evelli quidem
5 extorquerique non possunt. Igitur non temere iam nunc de universitate pronuntio, de partibus experiar legendo. Vale.

XVI

C. Plinius Nepoti Suo S.

1 Adnotasse videor facta dictaque virorum femina-
2 rumque alia clariora esse alia maiora. Confirmata est opinio mea hesterno Fanniae sermone. Neptis haec Arriae illius, quae marito et solacium mortis et exemplum fuit. Multa referebat aviae suae non minora hoc sed obscuriora; quae tibi existimo tam

---

[1] See Introduction, p. xiv and Index.

any odd moments I can spare from my own, you can cite a precedent to support your plea; Cicero, you say, was wonderfully generous about encouraging the talent of poets.

But there was no need of prayers and entreaties—I have a profound regard for poetry and the warmest affection for yourself, and so I will gladly apply myself to doing what you ask. However, I see no reason why I should not say here and now that it is a splendid work and ought not to remain unpublished, to judge from the passages I have heard you read; unless I was carried away by your style of reading, which has very great charm and skill. But I feel sure that I am not seduced by the pleasures of the ear to the extent of losing all my critical powers; my sting may perhaps be dulled and lack a little of its sharpness, but it cannot be entirely pulled out. This then is my considered opinion on the work as a whole, and I will judge the parts after I have read them.

XVI

To Maecilius Nepos

I think I have remarked that the more famous words and deeds of men and women are not necessarily their greatest. I was strengthened in this opinion by a conversation I had yesterday with Fannia,[1] granddaughter of the famous Arria who sustained and encouraged her husband by her example at the time of his death. She told me several things about her grandmother which were quite as heroic though less well known, and I think

mirabilia legenti fore, quam mihi audienti fuerunt.

3 Aegrotabat Caecina Paetus maritus eius, aegrotabat et filius, uterque mortifere, ut videbatur. Filius decessit eximia pulchritudine pari verecundia, et parentibus non minus ob alia carus quam quod filius

4 erat. Huic illa ita funus paravit, ita duxit exsequias, ut ignoraret maritus; quin immo quotiens cubiculum eius intraret, vivere filium atque etiam commodiorem esse simulabat, ac persaepe interroganti, quid ageret puer, respondebat: "Bene quievit, libenter cibum

5 sumpsit." Deinde, cum diu cohibitae lacrimae vincerent prorumperentque, egrediebatur; tunc se dolori dabat; satiata siccis oculis composito vultu

6 redibat, tamquam orbitatem foris reliquisset. Prae-clarum quidem illud eiusdem, ferrum stringere, per-fodere pectus, extrahere pugionem, porrigere marito, addere vocem immortalem ac paene divinam: "Paete, non dolet." Sed tamen ista facienti, ista dicenti, gloria et aeternitas ante oculos erant; quo maius est sine praemio aeternitatis, sine praemio gloriae, abdere lacrimas operire luctum, amissoque filio matrem adhuc agere.

7 Scribonianus arma in Illyrico contra Claudium moverat; fuerat Paetus in partibus, et occiso Scrib-

8 oniano Romam trahebatur. Erat ascensurus navem; Arria milites orabat, ut simul imponeretur. "Nempe

---

[1] See also Martial, I. 13.

[2] See Tacitus, *Hist.* I. 89; Suetonius, *Claud.* 13; Dio, LX. 15–16.

they will make the same impression on you as you read them as they did on me during their telling.

Arria's husband, Caecina Paetus, was ill, so was their son, and it was thought that neither could recover. The son died, a most beautiful boy with an unassuming manner no less remarkable, and dear to his parents for reasons beyond the fact that he was their son. Arria made all the preparations for his funeral and took her place at the ceremony without her husband knowing; in fact whenever she entered his room she pretended that their son was still alive and even rather better, and, when Paetus kept asking how the boy was, she would answer that he had had a good sleep and was willing to take some food. Then when the tears she had held back for so long could no longer be kept from breaking out, she left the room; not till then did she give way to her grief. Her weeping over, she dried her eyes, composed her face, and returned as if she had left the loss of her child outside the room. It was a glorious deed, I know, to draw a dagger, plunge it into her breast, pull it out, and hand it to her husband with the immortal, almost divine words: " It does not hurt, Paetus."[1] But on that well-known occasion she had fame and immortality before her eyes. It was surely even more heroic when she had no hope of any such reward, to stifle her tears, hide her grief, and continue to act the mother after she had lost her son.

At the time of the revolt against Claudius raised by Scribonianus [2] in Illyricum, Paetus had joined his party, and after Scribonianus's death was being brought as a prisoner to Rome. He was about to board ship when Arria begged the soldiers to take

enim " inquit " daturi estis consulari viro servolos aliquos, quorum e manu cibum capiat. a quibus vestiatur, a quibus calcietur; omnia sola praestabo."

9 Non impetravit: conduxit piscatoriam nauculam, ingensque navigium minimo secuta est. Eadem apud Claudium uxori Scriboniani, cum illa profiteretur indicium, " Ego " inquit " te audiam, cuius in gremio Scribonianus occisus est, et vivis? " Ex quo manifestum est ei consilium pulcherrimae mortis

10 non subitum fuisse. Quin etiam, cum Thrasea gener eius deprecaretur, ne mori pergeret, interque alia dixisset: " Vis ergo filiam tuam, si mihi pereundum fuerit, mori mecum? ", respondit: " Si tam diu tantaque concordia vixerit tecum quam ego cum

11 Paeto, volo." Auxerat hoc responso curam suorum; attentius custodiebatur; sensit et " Nihil agitis " inquit; " potestis enim efficere ut male moriar, ut non

12 moriar non potestis." Dum haec dicit, exsiluit cathedra adversoque parieti caput ingenti impetu impegit et corruit. Focilata " Dixeram " inquit " vobis inventuram me quamlibet duram ad mortem

13 viam, si vos facilem negassetis." Videnturne haec tibi maiora illo " Paete, non dolet," ad quod per haec perventum est? cum interim illud quidem ingens

---

[1] Her name is given as Vibia in Tacitus, *Ann.* XII. 52.

[2] The younger Arria did in fact try to die with him in 66, but was persuaded to stay alive for Fannia's sake; Tacitus, *Ann.* XVI. 34.

her with him. "This is a senator of consular rank," she insisted, "and of course you will allow him a few slaves to serve his meals, dress him and put on his shoes; all of which I can do for him myself." Her request was refused. She then hired a small fishing smack, and the great ship sailed with her following in her tiny boat.

Again, when she came before Claudius and found the wife[1] of Scribonianus volunteering to give evidence of the revolt, "Am *I* to listen to *you*," she cried, "who could go on living after Scribonianus died in your arms?" This proves that her determination to die a glorious death was not a sudden impulse. Indeed, when her son-in-law Thrasea was trying to persuade her not to carry out her resolve, in the course of his argument he asked her whether if he ever had to die she would wish her daughter to die with him.[2] "If she lives as long and happily with you," she said, "as I have with Paetus—yes." This answer increased the anxiety felt for her by her family and she was watched even more carefully. Perceiving this, "It is no good," she said. "You can make me choose an ignoble death, but you cannot make it impossible." With these words she leaped out of her chair and dashed her head against the wall opposite, so that she fell senseless from the violent blow. When she was brought round, "I told you," she said, "that I should find a hard way to die if you denied me an easy one."

Surely you think these words greater than the well-known "It does not hurt, Paetus" which was their culmination? And yet this is widely famous, while the earlier sayings are not known at all. Hence the

fama, haec nulla circumfert. Unde colligitur, quod
initio dixi, alia esse clariora alia maiora. Vale.

XVII

C. Plinius Iulio Serviano Suo S.

1 Rectene omnia, quod iam pridem epistulae tuae
cessant? an omnia recte, sed occupatus es tu? an
tu non occupatus, sed occasio scribendi vel rara
2 vel nulla? Exime hunc mihi scrupulum, cui par
esse non possum, exime autem vel data opera
tabellario misso. Ego viaticum, ego etiam prae-
3 mium dabo, nuntiet modo quod opto. Ipse valeo, si
valere est suspensum et anxium vivere, exspectantem
in horas timentemque pro capite amicissimo, quidquid accidere homini potest. Vale.

XVIII

C. Plinius Vibio[1] Severo Suo S.

1 Officium consulatus iniunxit mihi, ut rei publicae
nomine principi gratias agerem. Quod ego in
senatu cum ad rationem et loci et temporis ex more
fecissem, bono civi convenientissimum credidi eadem
2 illa spatiosius et uberius volumine amplecti, primum

---

[1] Vibio *Mommsen*: *om* αγ: Virio β.

---

[1] He was probably serving with Trajan in the Dacian war
of 101–2.
[2] The *Panegyricus* in its existing form. It has been

inference with which I began this letter, that the words and deeds which win fame are not always the greatest.

XVII

To Julius Servianus[1]

I HAVE had no letter from you for such a long time —is it because all goes well? Or is the reason that all is well but you are too busy: or, if not actually busy, have you little or no opportunity to write a letter? Please end my anxiety—I can't bear it. Do so even if you have to send a special messenger. I will pay his expenses personally and give him something for himself, as long as he brings me the news I want. I am well myself, if " well " is the right word for living in such a state of worry and suspense, expecting and fearing to hear any moment that a dear friend has met with one of the accidents which can befall mankind.

XVIII

To Vibius Severus

My acceptance of the consulship brought with it the official duty of addressing a vote of thanks to the Emperor in the name of the State. After doing so in the Senate in the usual manner befitting the place and occasion, I thought it my proper duty as a loyal citizen to give the same subject a fuller and more elaborate treatment in a written version.[2] I hoped

estimated that it would take three sessions of $1\frac{1}{2}$–2 hours to read the whole (S-W, p. 251).

ut imperatori nostro virtutes suae veris laudibus
commendarentur, deinde ut futuri principes non quasi
a magistro sed tamen sub exemplo praemonerentur,
qua potissimum via possent ad eandem gloriam niti.
3 Nam praecipere qualis esse debeat princeps, pulchrum
quidem sed onerosum ac prope superbum est; laudare vero optimum principem ac per hoc posteris
velut e specula lumen quod sequantur ostendere,
4 idem utilitatis habet adrogantiae nihil. Cepi autem
non mediocrem voluptatem, quod hunc librum cum
amicis recitare voluissem, non per codicillos, non per
libellos, sed " si commodum " et " si valde vacaret "
admoniti (numquam porro aut valde vacat Romae aut
commodum est audire recitantem), foedissimis in-
super tempestatibus per biduum convenerunt, cumque modestia mea finem recitationi facere voluisset,
5 ut adicerem tertium diem exegerunt. Mihi hunc
honorem habitum putem an studiis? studiis malo,
6 quae prope exstincta refoventur. At cui materiae
hanc sedulitatem praestiterunt? nempe quam in
senatu quoque, ubi perpeti necesse erat, gravari
tamen vel puncto temporis solebamus, eandem nunc
et qui recitare et qui audire triduo velint inveniuntur,
non quia eloquentius quam prius, sed quia liberius
7 ideoque etiam libentius scribitur. Accedet ergo
hoc quoque laudibus principis nostri, quod res antea

in the first place to encourage our Emperor in his virtues by a sincere tribute, and, secondly, to show his successors what path to follow to win the same renown, not by offering instruction but by setting his example before them. To proffer advice on an Emperor's duties might be a noble enterprise, but it would be a heavy responsibility verging on insolence, whereas to praise an excellent ruler and thereby shine a beacon on the path posterity should follow would be equally effective without appearing presumptuous.

One thing has given me a great deal of pleasure. When I had decided to give a reading of the speech to my friends, I did not invite them by note or programme, but simply asked them to come " if convenient " or if they " really had time " (though as a matter of fact no one in Rome ever finds it convenient or really has time to attend readings); the weather too was particularly bad, but nevertheless they attended two days running, and, when discretion would have put an end to the reading, they made me continue for a third day. Am I to look upon this as a tribute to myself or to the art of oratory? I hope the latter, as it is now enjoying a revival after almost dying out. And what was the subject which held their interest? A speech of thanks, which used to bore us after the first minute—even in the Senate, where we had to endure it—can now find a reader and an audience willing to listen for three days on end, not through any improvement in our standard of eloquence, but because greater freedom of speech makes writing more of a pleasure. This is yet another tribute to our Emperor: a type of speech

tam invisa quam falsa, nunc ut vera ita amabilis facta
8 est. Sed ego cum studium audientium tum iudicium
mire probavi: animadverti enim severissima quae-
9 que vel maxime satisfacere. Memini quidem me non
multis recitasse quod omnibus scripsi, nihilo minus
tamen, tamquam sit eadem omnium futura sententia.
hac severitate aurium laetor, ac sicut olim theatra
male musicos canere docuerunt, ita nunc in spem
adducor posse fieri, ut eadem theatra bene canere
10 musicos doceant. Omnes enim, qui placendi causa
scribunt, qualia placere viderint scribent. Ac mihi
quidem confido in hoc genere materiae laetioris stili
constare rationem, cum ea potius quae pressius et
adstrictius, quam illa quae hilarius et quasi exsul-
tantius scripsi, possint videri accersita et inducta.
Non ideo tamen segnius precor, ut quandoque veniat
dies (utinamque iam venerit!), quo austeris illis
severisque dulcia haec blandaque vel iusta posses-
sione decedant.
11 Habes acta mea tridui; quibus cognitis volui
tantum te voluptatis absentem et studiorum nomine
et meo capere, quantum praesens percipere potuisses.
Vale.

---

[1] See *Pan.* 2–3.

which used to be hated for its insincerity has become genuine and consequently popular today.[1] But I much admired the critical sense as well as the enthusiasm of my audience, noticing that the least elaborate passages pleased them most. I have not forgotten that only a few friends have heard me read what I have written for the general public; but even so, my delight in their keen attentiveness makes me hopeful that popular opinion will coincide with theirs. I am also encouraged to hope that we may now have an audience in the theatre which will teach the players to perform properly, instead of the audiences which produced the bad performances of the past. Every author who writes to please his public models his work on what he sees has given pleasure, and I personally am convinced that for this type of subject I did right to employ a more florid style, for a concise and terser manner is more likely to appear strained and artificial than the passages I wrote in a happier and more buoyant mood. Nevertheless, I still pray that some day the time will come—and I wish it had already—when these winning phrases, even where they are securely established, will withdraw their charms to make way for strict simplicity.

These then are my doings during the last three days. I wanted you to know them so that you could enjoy from afar the same pleasure as you would have had here, both on my account and for the cause of oratory.

THE LETTERS OF PLINY

XIX

C. Plinius Calvisio Rufo Suo S.

1 Adsumo te in consilium rei familiaris, ut soleo. Praedia agris meis vicina atque etiam inserta venalia sunt. In his me multa sollicitant, aliqua nec minora 2 deterrent. Sollicitat primum ipsa pulchritudo iungendi; deinde, quod non minus utile quam voluptuosum, posse utraque eadem opera eodem viatico invisere, sub eodem procuratore ac paene isdem actoribus habere, unam villam colere et ornare, 3 alteram tantum tueri. Inest huic computationi sumptus supellectilis, sumptus atriensium topiariorum fabrorum atque etiam venatorii instrumenti; quae plurimum refert unum in locum conferas an in diversa 4 dispergas. Contra vereor ne sit incautum, rem tam magnam isdem tempestatibus isdem casibus subdere; tutius videtur incerta fortunae possessionum varietatibus experiri. Habet etiam multum iucunditatis soli caelique mutatio, ipsaque illa pere- 5 grinatio inter sua. Iam, quod deliberationis nostrae caput est, agri sunt fertiles pingues aquosi; constant campis vineis silvis, quae materiam et ex ea reditum

---

¹ As Calvisius Rufus was a native of Comum, he would not need details of estates in the district: this account suits Tifernum.

XIX

To Calvisius Rufus

As usual, I am calling upon your expert advice on a matter of property. The estate adjoining my own [1] is for sale; the land runs in and out of mine, and, though there are many attractions tempting me to buy, there are some no less important reasons why I should not. The primary attraction is the obvious amenity if the properties were joined, and after that the practical advantage as well as the pleasure of being able to visit the two together without making more than one journey. Both could be put under the same steward and practically the same foremen, and it would be necessary to maintain and furnish one house, so long as the other was kept in repair. In this account I include the cost of furniture, household staff, landscape-gardeners, workmen, and also hunting gear; for it makes a considerable difference whether one keeps all these in one place or distributes them between several. On the other hand I am afraid it may be rash to expose a property of such a size to the same uncertainties of weather and general risks, and it might be safer to meet the hazards of fortune by having estates in different localities; and then change of place and air is very enjoyable, and so is the actual travelling between one's possessions.

But the chief point for consideration is this. The land is fertile, the soil rich and well watered, and the whole made up of fields, vineyards, and woods which produce enough to yield a steady income if

6 sicut modicum ita statum praestant. Sed haec
felicitas terrae imbecillis cultoribus fatigatur. Nam
possessor prior saepius vendidit pignora, et dum
reliqua colonorum minuit ad tempus, vires in posterum
exhausit, quarum defectione rursus reliqua creverunt.
7 Sunt ergo instruendi, eo pluris [1] quod frugi, mancipiis;
nam nec ipse usquam vinctos habeo nec ibi quisquam.
Superest ut scias quanti videantur posse emi.
Sestertio triciens, non quia non aliquando quin-
quagiens fuerint, verum et hac penuria colonorum et
communi temporis iniquitate ut reditus agrorum sic
8 etiam pretium retro abiit. Quaeris an hoc ipsum
triciens facile colligere possimus. Sum quidem
prope totus in praediis, aliquid tamen fenero, nec
molestum erit mutuari; accipiam a socru, cuius
9 arca non secus ac mea utor. Proinde hoc te non
moveat, si cetera non refragantur, quae velim quam
diligentissime examines. Nam cum in omnibus rebus
tum in disponendis facultatibus plurimum tibi et usus
et providentiae superest. Vale.

XX

C. PLINIUS MAESIO MAXIMO SUO S.

1 MEMINISTINE te saepe legisse, quantas contentiones excitarit lex tabellaria, quantumque ipsi latori

---

[1] pluris αγ: plures β.

---

[1] Cf. his uncle's view: *coli rura ab ergastulo pessimum est* (*NH*
XVIII. vi. 36). In IX. 37 P. considers solving his problems by
adopting the *mezzadria* system.
[2] Pompeia Celerina, who owned considerable properties; see
I. 4.

not a very large one. But this natural fertility is being exhausted by poor cultivation. The last owner on more than one occasion sold up the tenants' possessions, so that he temporarily reduced their arrears but weakened their resources for the future, and consequently their debts mounted up again. They will have to be set up and given a good type of slave, which will increase the expense; for nowhere do I employ chained slaves myself, and no one uses them there.[1]

It remains for you to know the estimated purchase price: three million sesterces. It used at one time to be five million, but this scarcity of tenants and the general bad times have reduced the income from the land and brought down its value. You will want to know if I can easily raise this three million. It is true that nearly all my capital is in land, but I have some investments and it will not be difficult to borrow. I can always have money from my mother-in-law,[2] whose capital I am able to use as freely as my own. So don't let this worry you if you can dispose of the other points. I hope you will give them your full attention, for as regards the administration of large sums of money, as in everything else, you have abundant experience and wisdom.

XX

To Maesius Maximus

You must often remember reading about the fierce controversy roused by the Ballot Act,[3] and the mixed

---

[3] *Lex Gabinia* 139 B.C. and *Lex Papiria* 131 B.C.

2 vel gloriae vel reprehensionis attulerit? At nunc in senatu sine ulla dissensione hoc idem ut optimum placuit: omnes comitiorum die tabellas postulaverunt.
3 Excesseramus sane manifestis illis apertisque suffragiis licentiam contionum. Non tempus loquendi, non tacendi modestia, non denique sedendi dignitas
4 custodiebatur. Magni undique dissonique clamores, procurrebant omnes cum suis candidatis, multa agmina in medio multique circuli et indecora confusio; adeo desciveramus a consuetudine parentum, apud quos omnia disposita moderata tranquilla
5 maiestatem loci pudoremque retinebant. Supersunt senes ex quibus audire soleo hunc ordinem comitiorum: citato nomine candidati silentium summum; dicebat ipse pro se; explicabat vitam suam, testes et laudatores dabat vel eum sub quo militaverat, vel eum cui quaestor fuerat, vel utrumque si poterat; addebat quosdam ex suffragatoribus; illi graviter et paucis loquebantur. Plus hoc quam preces proderat.
6 Non numquam candidatus aut natales competitoris aut annos aut etiam mores arguebat. Audiebat senatus gravitate censoria. Ita saepius digni quam
7 gratiosi praevalebant. Quae nunc immodico favore

---

¹ The assembly had been suppressed by Tiberius in A.D. 14, and the election of magistrates transferred to the Senate (Tacitus, *Ann.* I. 15. 1). The highest offices depended on the Emperor's *commendatio* which the Senate acclaimed. (But see *Pan.* 71, and note 2.)

praise and blame it brought its proposer; yet today the merits of the act have won the unanimous approval of the Senate. On the day of the recent elections everyone demanded voting-papers, for on the last occasions when we had publicly recorded our votes aloud we had certainly exceeded the disorders of the people's assemblies.[1] No regard was paid to a time-limit in speaking, to the courtesy of not interrupting, nor even the propriety of remaining seated. On all sides rose the din of opposing cries: everyone rushed forward with his candidate and crowds mingled with small groups of people in the centre of the floor in disgraceful confusion. So far had we departed from our parents' procedure, where everything was calmly conducted in a restrained and orderly manner so as to maintain the honour and dignity of the House.

There are still some of the older generation living who have often told me about their election procedure: the name of the candidate was read out and received in complete silence, after which he spoke on his own behalf, gave an account of his career and produced referees to his character, either the commanding officer under whom he had served in the army or the governor whose quaestor he had been, and both if he could. He then called upon some of the electors supporting his candidature, who said a few sober words in his favour which carried more weight than entreaties. Sometimes the candidate would raise objections to his opponent's origin, age or character, and the Senate would hear him with strict attention. The result was that merit prevailed more often than mere popularity. But now that these practices have broken down through excessive

corrupta ad tacita suffragia quasi ad remedium
decucurrerunt; quod interim plane remedium fuit
(erat enim novum et subitum), sed vereor ne proce-
8 dente tempore ex ipso remedio vitia nascantur. Est
enim periculum ne tacitis suffragiis impudentia in-
repat. Nam quoto cuique eadem honestatis cura
9 secreto quae palam? Multi famam, conscientiam
pauci verentur. Sed nimis cito de futuris: interim
beneficio tabellarum habebimus magistratus, qui
maxime fieri debuerunt. Nam ut in reciperatoriis
iudicîs, sic nos in his comitiis quasi repente adpre-
hensi sinceri iudices fuimus.

10   Haec tibi scripsi, primum ut aliquid novi scriberem,
deinde ut non numquam de re publica loquerer,
cuius materiae nobis quanto rarior quam veteribus
11 occasio, tanto minus omittenda est. Et hercule
quousque illa vulgaria? " Quid agis? ecquid commode vales? " Habeant nostrae quoque litterae
aliquid non humile nec sordidum, nec privatis rebus
12 inclusum. Sunt quidem cuncta sub unius arbitrio,
qui pro utilitate communi solus omnium curas
laboresque suscepit; quidam tamen salubri temperamento ad nos quoque velut rivi ex illo benignissimo
fonte decurrunt, quos et haurire ipsi et absentibus
amicis quasi ministrare epistulis possumus. Vale.

---

¹ A board of three or five *recuperatores,* originally used for
cases between Romans and *peregrini,* afterwards dealt sum-
marily with various types of case involving property; see II.
11.2 and note.

² The same sentiment is expressed in Tacitus, *Dial.* 41. 4,
and in *Pan.* 72. 1. See also III. vii. 14 and note.

personal influence, recourse was had to the secret ballot as a remedy, and, being a new and unaccustomed measure, for the time being it has proved successful. Yet I am afraid that as time goes on the remedy will breed its own abuses, with the risk of wanton irresponsibility finding a way in. Very few people are as scrupulously honest in secret as in public, and many are influenced by public opinion but scarcely anyone by conscience. It is too soon, though, to speak of the future; for the moment, thanks to the written vote, we are going to elect our public officials from the candidates who best deserve the honour. We have been called upon to pronounce an opinion in our elections with no more warning than is given at a summary trial,[1] and have shown ourselves uncorrupted.

I have told you this primarily to give you some genuine news, and then to be able to talk a little about political matters; a subject which gives us fewer opportunities than in the old days, so none must be missed. Besides, hasn't the time come to give up the commonplace " How are you? I hope you are well "? Our letters ought to contain something which rises above the trivialities and limitations of personal interests. Everything today, it is true, depends on the will of one man who has taken upon himself for the general good all our cares and responsibilities;[2] yet mindful of our needs he sees that streams flow down to us from his fount of generosity so that we can draw on them ourselves and dispense them by letter to our absent friends.

XXI

C. Plinius Cornelio Prisco Suo S.

1 Audio Valerium Martialem decessisse et moleste
fero. Erat homo ingeniosus acutus acer, et qui plurimum in scribendo et salis haberet et fellis, nec cando-
2 ris minus. Prosecutus eram viatico secedentem;
dederam hoc amicitiae, dederam etiam versiculis
3 quos de me composuit. Fuit moris antiqui, eos qui
vel singulorum laudes vel urbium scripserant. aut
honoribus aut pecunia ornare; nostris vero temporibus
ut alia speciosa et egregia, ita hoc in primis exolevit.
Nam postquam desîmus facere laudanda, laudari
4 quoque ineptum putamus. Quaeris, qui sint versi-
culi quibus gratiam rettuli? Remitterem te ad
ipsum volumen, nisi quosdam tenerem; tu, si placue-
5 rint hi, ceteros in libro requires. Adloquitur Musam,
mandat ut domum meam Esquilis quaerat, adeat
reverenter:

> Sed ne tempore non tuo disertam
> pulses ebria ianuam, videto.
> Totos dat tetricae dies Minervae,
> dum centum studet auribus virorum
> hoc, quod saecula posterique possint
> Arpinis quoque comparare chartis.

---

[1] Martial returned to his native Bilbilis in Spain in 98, and
lived on his property there (Martial, XII. 31) until his death,
c. 104.

[2] Martial, X. 19. He addresses a similar poem to Proculus
in I. 70.

[3] Cicero was born at Arpinum (Arpino) in Volscian Latium.

XXI

To Cornelius Priscus

I am distressed to hear that Valerius Martial is dead. He was a man of great gifts, with a mind both subtle and penetrating, and his writings are remarkable for their combination of sincerity with pungency and wit. I had made him a present of his travelling expenses when he retired from Rome,[1] in recognition of our friendship and the verses he wrote about me. It was the custom in the past to reward poets who had sung the praises of cities or individuals with gifts of office or money, but in our day this was one of the first things to fall out of fashion along with many other fine and honourable practices; for, now that we do nothing to merit a poet's tribute, it seems foolish to receive one.

You will want to know the verses which won my gratitude, and I would refer you to the book had I not some of them by heart. If you like these, you can look up the others in his published works. The poet is addressing the Muse, telling her to seek my house on the Esquiline and approach it with respect:[2]

Muse, do not knock at his learned door drunk, and at time ill-chosen;
All the hours of his working day he devotes to crabbed Minerva,
While he prepares for the Hundred Court the speeches which after ages
Judge to be worthy of taking place by those of the son of Arpinum.[3]

237

Seras tutior ibis ad lucernas:
haec hora est tua, cum furit Lyaeus,
cum regnat rosa, cum madent capilli.
Tunc me vel rigidi legant Catones.

6 Meritone eum qui haec de me scripsit et tunc dimisi
amicissime et nunc ut amicissimum defunctum esse
doleo? Dedit enim mihi quantum maximum potuit,
daturus amplius si potuisset. Tametsi quid homini
potest dari maius, quam gloria et laus et aeternitas?
At non erunt aeterna quae scripsit: non erunt fortasse, ille tamen scripsit tamquam essent futura.
Vale.

Wait till the lamps burn late and low, when Bacchus
 is ruling the revels,
Safer the night, when the brow is crowned with the
 rose and the hair drips perfume;
This is your hour, when the puritans' frown can relax
 with a smile for my verses.

Was I right then to part on such friendly terms
from the author of these verses about me? Am I
right to mourn his death now as one of my dearest
friends? He gave me of his best, and would have
given me more had he been able, though surely
nothing more can be given to man than a tribute
which will bring him fame and immortality. You
may object that his verses will not be immortal;
perhaps not, but he wrote them with that intention.

BOOK IV

LIBER QUARTUS

I

C. Plinius ⟨Calpurnio⟩[1] Fabato Prosocero Suo S.

1 Cupis post longum tempus neptem tuam meque
una videre. Gratum est utrique nostrum quod cupis,
2 mutuo mehercule. Nam invicem nos incredibili
quodam desiderio vestri tenemur, quod non ultra
differemus. Atque adeo iam sarcinulas adligamus,
festinaturi quantum itineris ratio permiserit. Erit
3 una sed brevis mora: deflectemus in Tuscos, non ut
agros remque familiarem oculis subiciamus (id enim
postponi potest), sed ut fungamur necessario officio.
4 Oppidum est praediis nostris vicinum (nomen Tiferni
Tiberini), quod me paene adhuc puerum patronum
cooptavit, tanto maiore studio quanto minore iudicio.
Adventus meos celebrat, profectionibus angitur,
5 honoribus gaudet. In hoc ego, ut referrem gratiam
(nam vinci in amore turpissimum est), templum
pecunia mea exstruxi, cuius dedicationem, cum sit
6 paratum, differre longius inreligiosum est. Erimus
ergo ibi dedicationis die, quem epulo celebrare con-

---

¹ Calpurnio *add. Barwick (coll.* V. 11).

---

¹ The first mention of P.'s third wife, Calpurnia.
² It was started about 96; cf. III. 4. 2 and X. 8.

BOOK IV

I

To Calpurnius Fabatus, his Wife's Grandfather

Your granddaughter[1] and I are touched to hear that you are anxious to see us both after so long an interval, and you can be sure that we share your feelings. I can't tell you how much we too are looking forward to paying you both a visit, and it shall not be put off any longer—indeed, we are already packing so that we can travel as fast as the route we must follow permits. One thing will delay us, but not for long: we shall have to turn off to my place in Tuscany, not to look over the land and the house I have there—this can be put off to another time—but to perform what we feel is a necessary duty. Close to my property is the town of Tifernum on Tiber which adopted me as its patron when I was scarcely more than a child—its enthusiasm outrunning its discretion. The people always celebrate my arrivals, regret my departures, and rejoice in my official titles, and so to express my gratitude (one always feels disgraced at being outdone in friendly feeling) I defrayed the cost of building a temple in the town. As this is now completed,[2] it would be sacrilegious to postpone its dedication any longer. So we shall be there for the day of the dedication, which I have decided to

stitui. Subsistemus fortasse et sequenti, sed tanto
7 magis viam ipsam corripiemus. Contingat modo te
filiamque tuam fortes invenire! nam continget hilares, si nos incolumes receperitis. Vale.

II

C. PLINIUS ATTIO CLEMENTI SUO S.

1 REGULUS filium amisit, hoc uno malo indignus,
quod nescio an malum putet. Erat puer acris ingenii sed ambigui, qui tamen posset recta sectari, si
2 patrem non referret. Hunc Regulus emancipavit,
ut heres matris exsisteret; mancipatum (ita vulgo
ex moribus hominis loquebantur) foeda et insolita
parentibus indulgentiae simulatione captabat. In-
3 credibile, sed Regulum cogita. Amissum tamen
luget insane. Habebat puer mannulos multos et
iunctos et solutos, habebat canes maiores minores-
que, habebat luscinias psittacos merulas: omnes
4 Regulus circa rogum trucidavit. Nec dolor erat ille,
sed ostentatio doloris. Convenitur ad eum mira
celebritate. Cuncti detestantur oderunt, et quasi
probent quasi diligant, cursant frequentant, utque
breviter quod sentio enuntiem, in Regulo demerendo
5 Regulum imitantur. Tenet se trans Tiberim in

244

celebrate with a public feast, and we may have to stay on for the day following, but if so we will hurry over the journey the faster.

I only hope that we shall have the pleasure of finding you and your daughter well. It will certainly be a pleasure to see your happiness if we arrive safely.

II

To Attius Clemens

Regulus has lost his son, the one misfortune he did not deserve, but doubtless no real misfortune in his eyes. The boy was sharp-witted but unreliable; still he might have proved honest if he did not take after his father. Regulus released him from parental authority so that the boy could inherit his mother's estate, but having " sold " him (so it was generally spoken of by those who knew the man's habits), he began to work on him with a disgusting show of indulgence, quite unnatural in a parent. It sounds incredible, but remember it was Regulus. Now that his son is dead he mourns with wild extravagance. The boy used to possess a number of Gallic ponies for riding and driving, also dogs of all sizes, and nightingales, parrots and blackbirds; Regulus had them all slaughtered round his pyre. That was not grief, but parade of grief. It is amazing how he is now besieged by people who all loathe and detest him, and yet flock round him in crowds as if they really loved and admired him. To put it briefly, they court Regulus by his own methods. He will not stir from his gardens beyond the Tiber, where he has covered

hortis, in quibus latissimum solum porticibus im-
mensis, ripam statuis suis occupavit, ut est in summa
avaritia sumptuosus, in summa infamia gloriosus.
6 Vexat ergo civitatem insaluberrimo tempore et,
quod vexat, solacium putat. Dicit se velle ducere
7 uxorem, hoc quoque sicut alia perverse. Audies
brevi nuptias lugentis nuptias senis; quorum alterum
immaturum alterum serum est. Unde hoc augurer
8 quaeris? Non quia adfirmat ipse, quo mendacius
nihil est, sed quia certum est Regulum esse facturum,
quidquid fieri non oportet. Vale.

III

C. Plinius Arrio Antonino Suo S.

1   Quod semel atque iterum consul fuisti similis antiquis, quod proconsul Asiae qualis ante te qualis post
te vix unus aut alter (non sinit enim me verecundia
tua dicere nemo), quod sanctitate quod auctoritate,
aetate quoque princeps civitatis, est quidem venera-
bile et pulchrum; ego tamen te vel magis in remis-
2 sionibus miror. Nam severitatem istam pari iucun-
ditate condire, summaeque gravitati tantum comi-
tatis adiungere, non minus difficile quam magnum est.
Id tu cum incredibili quadam suavitate sermonum,

---

[1] *Iliad* I. 249.

a vast area with immense colonnades and littered the
bank with his precious statues; for he is extravagant
for all his avarice, and vainglorious in spite of his
notoriety. Thus he upsets the whole city at the
worst season of the year, and finds consolation in the
nuisance he makes of himself.

He says he wants to marry again, and is as perverse
on this point as he is in everything else. You will
soon hear that the mourner is married, the old man is
wed—the one too early and the other too late. How
can I predict this? Not from anything Regulus has
said, for nothing is less likely to be true, but because
it is certain that Regulus will do whatever he should
not.

III

To Arrius Antoninus

You have twice held the consulship with the
dignity of a bygone age, and very few who have been
governors of Asia before or after your term of office
have proved your equal (your modesty forbids me to
say there has been no one). In virtue, prestige and
years you are our foremost citizen. So fine a record
cannot fail to command respect, yet for your re-
creations I personally admire you even more. To
season a gravity like yours with a pleasantry no less
remarkable, to combine such wit with your profound
wisdom is an achievement as difficult as it is splendid;
but you have been successful in the exceptional
charm of your conversation, and even more so by your
pen. When you speak the honey of Homer's Nestor [1]

3 tum vel praecipue stilo adsequeris. Nam et loquenti
tibi illa Homerici senis mella profluere et, quae scribis,
complere apes floribus et innectere videntur. Ita
certe sum adfectus ipse, cum Graeca epigrammata
4 tua, cum mimiambos proxime legerem. Quantum
ibi humanitatis venustatis, quam dulcia illa quam
amantia[1] quam arguta quam recta! Callimachum
me vel Heroden, vel si quid his melius, tenere credebam; quorum tamen neuter utrumque aut absolvit
5 aut attigit. Hominemne Romanum tam Graece
loqui? Non medius fidius ipsas Athenas tam Atticas
dixerim. Quid multa? invideo Graecis quod illorum
lingua scribere maluisti. Neque enim coniectura
eget, quid sermone patrio exprimere possis, cum hoc
insiticio et inducto tam praeclara opera perfeceris.
Vale.

IV

C. Plinius Sosio Senecioni Suo S.

1 Varisidium Nepotem valdissime diligo, virum in-
dustrium rectum disertum, quod apud me vel poten-
tissimum est. Idem C. Calvisium, contubernalem
meum amicum tuum, arta propinquitate complectitur;
2 est enim filius sororis. Hunc rogo semestri tribunatu
splendidiorem et sibi et avunculo suo facias. Obligabis Calvisium nostrum, obligabis ipsum, non minus

---

[1] amantia αγ: antiqua β.

---

[1] *i.e.* a post as *tribunus laticlavius*, the start of the senatorial
cursus. Sosius Senecio was probably legate of Upper or Lower
Moesia at this time. A-M. Guillemin (Budé ed. Vol. II, p. 10)

seems to flow from your lips, while the bees fill your
writings with sweetness from interwoven flowers.
Such were certainly my impressions when I recently
read your Greek epigrams and iambic mimes. Their
sensitivity and grace, their charm and warmth of
feeling, their wit which never wants propriety, made
me imagine I held Callimachus or Herodas in my
hands, or even some greater poet; though neither of
them excelled in both types of verse nor even
attempted them. Is such Greek possible for a
Roman? Athens herself, believe me, could not be so
Attic. In fact I envy the Greeks because you have
preferred to write in their language; for it is easy to
guess how you could express yourself in your native
idiom when you can produce such masterpieces in a
foreign and acquired tongue.

IV

To Sosius Senecio

I am exceedingly fond of Varisidius Nepos; he is
hard-working, honest, and trained in eloquence, a
quality whereby I set great store. He is a near
relative of my close friend Gaius Calvisius, who is also
a friend of yours, and is in fact his sister's son. Please
procure him the honour of a six-months' tribunate,[1]
both for his own and his uncle's sake. You will
oblige me and our friend Calvisius, and you will
oblige Nepos himself, who is as worthy of being
under obligation to you as you believe us to be. You

calls attention to the formal tone of this letter, in contrast with
the warmth of a similar request in II. 13.

3 idoneum debitorem quam nos putas. Multa beneficia in multos contulisti: ausim contendere nullum te melius, aeque bene unum aut alterum collocasse. Vale.

V

C. PLINIUS IULIO SPARSO SUO S.

1 AESCHINEN aiunt petentibus Rhodiis legisse orationem suam, deinde Demosthenis, summis utram-
2 que clamoribus. Quod tantorum virorum scriptis contigisse non miror, cum orationem meam proxime doctissimi homines hoc studio, hoc adsensu, hoc etiam labore per biduum audierint, quamvis intentionem eorum nulla hinc et inde collatio, nullum
3 quasi certamen accenderet. Nam Rhodii cum ipsis orationum virtutibus tum etiam comparationis acu-
leis excitabantur, nostra oratio sine aemulationis gratia probabatur. An merito, scies cum legeris librum, cuius amplitudo non sinit me longiore epistula
4 praeloqui. Oportet enim nos in hac certe in qua possumus breves esse, quo sit excusatius quod lib-
rum ipsum, non tamen ultra causae amplitudinem, extendimus. Vale.

---

[1] See II. 3. 10, and note.

have conferred many benefits on several people, but I venture to say that you have bestowed none more justly, and only one or two where they have been so well deserved.

V

To Julius Sparsus

There is a story that when the citizens of Rhodes asked Aeschines to read them a speech, he read first one of his own and then one of Demosthenes',[1] and both were received with loud applause. It is no surprise to me that these great men won such a success with their orations, seeing that a recent speech of my own was given a two-days' hearing by a distinguished audience and was received with the same sort of enthusiasm and attentive concentration. And yet there was no comparison to be made between speeches, nor any rivalry to rouse interest; for the Rhodians had both the respective merits of the speeches and the incentive of comparison to stimulate them, whereas my own won approval without gaining anything from competition. You will know if it was justly approved when you have read the published version—its length prevents me from introducing it to you in a longer letter. I must at least be brief where I can, in the hope of being excused for the length of the speech itself; though I don't think it is too long for the importance of the subject.

VI

C. Plinius Iulio Nasoni Suo S.

1 Tusci grandine excussi, in regione Transpadana summa abundantia, sed par vilitas nuntiatur: solum
2 mihi Laurentinum meum in reditu. Nihil quidem ibi possideo praeter tectum et hortum statimque harenas, solum tamen mihi in reditu. Ibi enim plurimum scribo, nec agrum quem non habeo sed ipsum me studiis excolo; ac iam possum tibi ut aliis in locis
3 horreum plenum, sic ibi scrinium ostendere. Igitur tu quoque, si certa et fructuosa praedia concupiscis, aliquid in hoc litore para. Vale.

VII

C. Plinius Catio Lepido Suo S.

1 Saepe tibi dico inesse vim Regulo. Mirum est quam efficiat in quod incubuit. Placuit ei lugere filium: luget ut nemo. Placuit statuas eius et imagines quam plurimas facere: hoc omnibus officinis agit, illum coloribus illum cera illum aere illum argento illum auro ebore marmore effingit.
2 Ipse vero nuper adhibito ingenti auditorio librum de vita eius recitavit; de vita pueri, recitavit tamen. Eundem in exemplaria mille transcriptum per totam

---

¹ Laurentum was a *suburbanum*, not a country estate.

VI

To Julius Naso

I HEAR that the hail has done a lot of damage to my property in Tuscany, and from beyond the Po comes the news that crops are very good but prices correspondingly low, so I have only Laurentum to bring me in anything. There I possess nothing but the house and garden and the adjoining sea-shore,[1] but still it is the only place bringing something in. For there I do most of my writing, and, instead of the land I lack, I work to cultivate myself; so that I can have a harvest in my desk to show you in place of full granaries elsewhere.

If then like me you also want a property where you can be sure of a return, you should buy one on this coast.

VII

To Catius Lepidus

I HAVE often told you about Regulus's force of character. It is amazing how he carries out whatever he sets his heart on. He made up his mind to mourn his son, so he mourns as nobody ever did; he decided to commission as many statues and portraits of the boy as he possibly could, so he sets all the workshops busy portraying him in colour, in wax, bronze, silver, gold, ivory and marble—the same boy every time. He even collected a vast audience the other day to hear him read a memoir of his son—the life of a mere boy, but nevertheless he read it, and has had countless

Italiam provinciasque dimisit. Scripsit publice, ut a decurionibus eligeretur vocalissimus aliquis ex ipsis, 3 qui legeret eum populo: factum est. Hanc ille vim, seu quo alio nomine vocanda est intentio quidquid velis optinendi, si ad potiora vertisset, quantum boni efficere potuisset! Quamquam minor vis bonis quam malis inest, ac sicut ἀμαθία μὲν θράσος, λογισμὸς δὲ ὄκνον φέρει, ita recta ingenia debilitat 4 verecundia, perversa confirmat audacia. Exemplo est Regulus. Imbecillum latus, os confusum, haesitans lingua, tardissima inventio, memoria nulla, nihil denique praeter ingenium insanum, et tamen eo impudentia ipsoque illo furore pervenit, ut orator 5 habeatur. Itaque Herennius Senecio mirifice Catonis illud de oratore in hunc e contrario vertit: " Orator est vir malus dicendi imperitus." Non mehercule Cato ipse tam bene verum oratorem quam hic 6 Regulum expressit. Habesne quo tali epistulae parem gratiam referas? Habes, si scripseris num aliquis in municipio vestro ex sodalibus meis, num etiam ipse tu hunc luctuosum Reguli librum ut circulator in foro legeris, ἐπάρας scilicet, ut ait Demosthenes, τὴν φωνὴν καὶ γεγηθὼς καὶ λαρυγγίζων. 7 Est enim tam ineptus ut risum magis possit exprimere quam gemitum: credas non de puero scriptum sed a puero. Vale.

---

[1] Thucydides, II. 40. 3.
[2] Quoted by Quintilian, *Inst. Orat.* I. prol. 9; XII. i. 1.
[3] Demosthenes, *De Corona*, 291.

copies made to distribute throughout Italy and the provinces. He has written an open letter to the town councils asking them to choose one of their number with the best voice to give a public reading of the work; and this has been done.

If he had applied to better ends this force (or whatever we are to call this determination to get one's own way), think how much good he could have done! And yet good men are less forceful than bad: " Ignorance breeds confidence, reflection leads to hesitation "[1] as the saying goes, and so diffidence is the weakness of right-thinking minds, while depravity gains strength from reckless abandon. Regulus is proof of this. He has weak lungs, indistinct articulation, and a stammer, he is slow at finding the right word and has no memory, nothing in fact but a perverted ingenuity, and yet his crazy effrontery has won him the popular reputation of being an orator. So Herennius Senecio has cleverly adapted Cato's well-known definition of an orator to fit him: " This orator is a bad man untrained in speaking."[2] Cato certainly did not define the real orator so neatly as Senecio has summed up Regulus!

Can you make me a proper return for a letter like this? You can if you will write and tell me whether any of my friends in your town—perhaps yourself— has had to read out this miserable efforts of Regulus's, shouting in public like a cheap-jack, or, to quote Demosthenes, " bawling in a loud and jubilant strain."[3] For it is so absurd that it is more likely to meet with laughter than tears; you would think it was written *by* a boy rather than about one.

VIII

C. PLINIUS MATURO ARRIANO SUO S.

1 GRATULARIS mihi quod acceperim auguratum: iure
gratularis, primum quod gravissimi principis iudicium
in minoribus etiam rebus consequi pulchrum est,
deinde quod sacerdotium ipsum cum priscum et
religiosum tum hoc quoque sacrum plane et insigne
2 est, quod non adimitur viventi. Nam alia quamquam dignitate propemodum paria ut tribuuntur
sic auferuntur; in hoc fortunae hactenus licet ut dari
3 possit. Mihi vero illud etiam gratulatione dignum
videtur, quod successi Iulio Frontino principi viro,
qui me nominationis die per hos continuos annos
inter sacerdotes nominabat, tanquam in locum suum
cooptaret; quod nunc eventus ita comprobavit, ut
4 non fortuitum videretur. Te quidem, ut scribis,
ob hoc maxime delectat auguratus meus, quod M.
Tullius augur fuit. Laetaris enim quod honoribus
5 eius insistam, quem aemulari in studiis cupio. Sed
utinam ut sacerdotium idem, ut consulatum multo
etiam iuvenior quam ille sum consecutus, ita senex
saltem ingenium eius aliqua ex parte adsequi pos-
6 sim! Sed nimirum quae sunt in manu hominum et
mihi et multis contigerunt; illud vero ut adipisci
arduum sic etiam sperare nimium est, quod dari non
nisi a dis potest. Vale.

---

[1] For his distinguished career, see Index.
[2] Cicero was consul at 43 and augur at 53; P. was consul at
39 and augur at 42 or 43, if his augurate is dated to 103.

VIII

To Maturus Arrianus

Thank you for your very proper congratulations on my appointment to the office of augur: proper because in the first place it is an honour to accept the decisions of so wise a ruler as ours even in matters less important than this, and secondly because the priesthood is an old-established religious office and has a particular sanctity in that it is held for life. There are other positions no less honourable, but they can be bestowed and taken away, whereas in this the element of chance is limited to the bestowal. I can also think of a further reason for congratulation; I have taken the place of Julius Frontinus,[1] one of our greatest citizens, who in recent years never failed to put up my name for the priesthood on nomination day, with the apparent intention of making me his successor; so that now when events have approved of his choice, my election seems more than merely fortuitous. And you, as you say in your letter, are particularly pleased to see me an augur because Cicero held the same priesthood, and are glad that I am stepping into his offices as I am so anxious to make him my model in my literary work. As I have reached the same priesthood and consulship at a much earlier age than he did,[2] I hope I may attain to something of his genius at least in later life. But whereas everything which man can bestow has fallen to my lot as it has to many another, such genius is difficult to achieve and almost too much to hope for; it can only be granted by the gods.

THE LETTERS OF PLINY

IX

C. Plinius Cornelio Urso Suo S.

1 Causam per hos dies dixit Iulius Bassus, homo laboriosus et adversis clarus. Accusatus est sub Vespasiano a privatis duobus; ad senatum remissus diu pependit, tandem absolutus vindicatusque.

2 Titum timuit ut Domitiani amicus, a Domitiano relegatus est; revocatus a Nerva sortitusque Bithyniam rediit reus, accusatus non minus acriter quam fideliter defensus. Varias sententias habuit, plures tamen

3 quasi mitiores. Egit contra eum Pomponius Rufus, vir paratus et vehemens; Rufo successit Theophanes,

4 unus ex legatis, fax accusationis et origo. Respondi ego. Nam mihi Bassus iniunxerat, totius defensionis fundamenta iacerem, dicerem de ornamentis suis quae illi et ex generis claritate et ex periculis ipsis

5 magna erant, dicerem de conspiratione delatorum quam in quaestu habebant, dicerem causas quibus factiosissimum quemque ut illum ipsum Theophanen offendisset. Eundem me voluerat occurrere crimini quo maxime premebatur. In aliis enim quamvis

---

[1] The fourth public trial in which P. took part, this time for the defence.

[2] They were legally entitled to a fourth of the condemned man's property.

IX

To Cornelius Ursus

The last few days have seen the trial of Julius Bassus,[1] a much-harassed man who is notorious for his misfortunes. During Vespasian's reign a case was brought against him by two persons on their own account which was referred to the Senate. He was then left in suspense for a long time until finally found not guilty and acquitted. He was a friend of Domitian's, and consequently nervous of Titus; and then he was banished by Domitian. Recalled by Nerva, he drew the province of Bithynia and returned from there to stand his trial, in the course of which he was violently attacked and loyally defended. The opinion of the court was divided on his sentence, but the majority took a more lenient view.

Pomponius Rufus, a ready and forceful speaker, opened the case against him and was followed by Theophanes, the representative of the province mainly responsible for sparking off the prosecution. I replied. Bassus had entrusted me with the task of laying the foundations of the whole defence, and my instructions were to refer to his official distinctions (and these because of his noble birth and hazardous career were not inconsiderable), then deal with the informers who were plotting to make a profit for themselves,[2] and finally speak of the reasons for his unpopularity with every disturber of the peace, such as Theophanes himself. He had also declared it his wish that I should meet the principal charge against him; for on the other points, which sounded more

auditu gravioribus non absolutionem modo verum
6 etiam laudem merebatur; hoc illum onerabat quod
homo simplex et incautus quaedam a provincialibus
ut amicus acceperat (nam fuerat in eadem provincia
quaestor). Haec accusatores furta ac rapinas, ipse
munera vocabat. Sed lex munera quoque accipi
7 vetat. Hic ego quid agerem, quod iter defensionis
ingrederer? Negarem? Verebar ne plane furtum
videretur, quod confiteri timerem. Praeterea rem
manifestam infitiari augentis erat crimen non diluen-
tis, praesertim cum reus ipse nihil integrum advocatis
reliquisset. Multis enim atque etiam principi dixerat, sola se munuscula dumtaxat natali suo aut Saturna-
8 libus accepisse et plerisque misisse. Veniam ergo
peterem? Iugulassem reum, quem ita deliquisse
concederem, ut servari nisi venia non posset. Tamquam recte factum tuerer? Non illi profuissem, sed
9 ipse impudens exstitissem. In hac difficultate
placuit medium quiddam tenere: videor tenuisse.
Actionem meam, ut proelia solet, nox diremit.
Egeram horis tribus et dimidia, supererat sequihora.
Nam cum e lege accusator sex horas, novem reus
accepisset, ita diviserat tempora reus inter me et eum
qui dicturus post erat, ut ego quinque horis ille

[1] *Lex Iulia Repetundarum*, 59 B.C.
[2] Measures to limit the time allowed to advocates are also referred to in Tacitus, *Dial.* 38. This is the normal provision dating from *Lex Pompeia* of 52 B.C.

260

serious, he really deserved congratulations as well as acquittal, whereas what weighed heavily against him was the fact that in all innocence he had thoughtlessly accepted certain gifts from the provincials as their friend (he had been quaestor in the same province). These his prosecutors called thefts and plunder, while he declared they were presents.

But the acceptance of presents is also forbidden by law.[1] How then was I to answer this, and what line of defence should I take? If I denied everything, I was afraid that an action which I dare not admit would be taken for an obvious theft. Besides, to deny a palpable fact was more likely to increase the gravity of the charge than to remove it, especially as the defendant had not given us a free hand at all; for he had told many people, including the Emperor himself, that he had accepted gifts, but only small ones, and only on his birthday and during the Saturnalia, and had usually sent something in return. Was I then to plead for mercy? It would be the death of my client to admit that his guilt made it impossible for anything short of mercy to save him. Should I attempt to justify his conduct? That would not help him, and would expose me to the charge of irresponsibility. Amidst these difficulties I decided to steer a middle course, and I believe I was successful.

Nightfall interrupted my speech, as it does a battle. I had spoken for three and a half hours, and still had an hour and a half, for, as the law allowed six hours to the prosecution and nine hours to the defence,[2] Bassus had divided the time between me and the speaker to follow so that I should have

10 reliquis uteretur. Mihi successus actionis silentium
finemque suadebat; temerarium est enim secundis
non esse contentum. Ad hoc verebar ne me corporis vires iterato labore desererent, quem difficilius
11 est repetere quam iungere. Erat etiam periculum
ne reliqua actio mea et frigus ut deposita et taedium
ut resumpta pateretur. Ut enim faces ignem adsidua
concussione custodiunt, dimissum aegerrime re-
parant, sic et dicentis calor et audientis intentio con-
tinuatione servatur, intercapedine et quasi remissione
12 languescit. Sed Bassus multis precibus, paene
etiam lacrimis obsecrabat, implerem meum tempus.
Parui utilitatemque eius praetuli meae. Bene cessit:
inveni ita erectos animos senatus, ita recentes, ut
priore actione incitati magis quam satiati viderentur.
13 Successit mihi Lucceius Albinus, tam apte ut orationes nostrae varietatem duarum, contextum unius
14 habuisse credantur. Respondit Herennius Pollio
instanter et graviter, deinde Theophanes rursus.
Fecit enim hoc quoque ut cetera impudentissime,
quod post duos et consulares et disertos tempus sibi et
quidem laxius vindicavit. Dixit in noctem atque
15 etiam nocte inlatis lucernis. Postero die egerunt pro
Basso Homullus et Fronto mirifice; quartum diem
probationes occuparunt.

---

[1] The Senate did not normally sit after sunset.

five hours and he the remaining four. The success of my speech made me feel that I should stop and say no more, for it is risky not to rest content when things are going well. I was also afraid that my strength would fail with a renewed effort, for it is harder to make a new start than to go straight on. There was, too, the danger that the rest of my speech would meet with a cold reception after the interruption, or seem tedious when it was resumed. A torch will stay lit if it is kept moving, but, if once the spark is lost, it is difficult to revive it again; similarly, continuity keeps up a speaker's fire and an audience's attention, but both weaken once the tension is relaxed and broken. But Bassus begged and besought me almost in tears to take my full time, and I yielded, putting his interests before my own. All went well, and I found the attention of the Senate as keen and fresh as if it had been stimulated rather than sated by my first speech.

I was followed by Lucceius Albinus, whose apt choice of phrase made it appear that we combined the variety of our separate speeches with the continuity of a single one. Herennius Pollio made a forceful and well-reasoned reply, and then Theophanes spoke again. Here, too, he showed his lack of discretion, not only in claiming time to address the court after two accomplished speakers of consular rank, but also in continuing at length; for darkness fell while he was still speaking and he went on after dark when lamps were brought in.[1] The following day Homullus and Fronto made an excellent defence of Bassus, and the fourth day was spent on examination of witnesses.

16 Censuit Baebius Macer consul designatus lege repetundarum Bassum teneri, Caepio Hispo salva
17 dignitate iudices dandos; uterque recte. " Qui fieri
potest " inquis, " cum tam diversa censuerint? "
Quia scilicet et Macro legem intuenti consentaneum
fuit damnare eum qui contra legem munera acceperat,
et Caepio cum putaret licere senatui (sicut licet)
et mitigare leges et intendere, non sine ratione
veniam dedit facto vetito quidem, non tamen inusi-
18 tato. Praevaluit sententia Caepionis, quin immo
consurgenti ei ad censendum acclamatum est, quod
solet residentibus. Ex quo potes aestimare, quanto
consensu sit exceptum, cum diceret, quod tam
19 favorabile fuit cum dicturus videretur. Sunt tamen
ut in senatu ita in civitate in duas partes hominum
iudicia divisa. Nam quibus sententia Caepionis
placuit, sententiam Macri ut rigidam duramque
reprehendunt; quibus Macri, illam alteram dissolu-
tam atque etiam incongruentem vocant; negant
enim congruens esse retinere in senatu, cui iudices
20 dederis. Fuit et tertia sententia: Valerius Paulinus
adsensus Caepioni hoc amplius censuit, referendum
de Theophane cum legationem renuntiasset. Arguebatur enim multa in accusatione fecisse, quae illa ipsa
21 lege qua Bassum accusaverat tenerentur. Sed hanc

---

[1] The Senate's judicial powers were not strictly defined by
law; see the argument at the trial of Priscus, II. 11. 4.

Then the consul-elect, Baebius Macer, proposed that Bassus should be dealt with under the law dealing with restitution of monies extorted, and Caepio Hispo that his penalty should be assessed by commission without loss of status. Both were correct, though you may wonder how this is possible when their proposals differed so widely. Well, Macer looked to the letter of the law, and so quite rightly condemned a man who had accepted gifts illegally; whereas Caepio, taking the view that the Senate has the power (as indeed it has) to reduce or increase the severity of the law,[1] had reason to excuse an action which was illegal, strictly speaking, but not without precedent. Caepio's proposal was carried; in fact on rising to speak he was greeted with the applause which is usually given when a speaker resumes his seat. You can judge then how his actual speech was received, when it was thus welcomed in anticipation. However, public opinion is no more unanimous than that of the Senate; those who approve of Caepio's proposal criticize Macer's for being too strict and severe, while others support Macer and call Caepio's suggestion lax and even illogical, saying that it is inconsistent for a man who has had a penalty assessed against him to retain his place in the Senate.

There was also a third opinion. Valerius Paulinus agreed with Caepio, but made the further proposal that the Senate should deal with Theophanes as soon as he had made his report on his commission; for it was clear that during his work for the prosecution he had committed a number of offences which came under the same law as that under which he had accused Bassus. But the consuls did not follow up

sententiam consules, quamquam maximae parti
22 senatus mire probabatur, non sunt persecuti. Paulinus tamen et iustitiae famam et constantiae tulit.
Misso senatu Bassus magna hominum frequentia,
magno clamore, magno gaudio exceptus est. Fecerat
eum favorabilem renovata discriminum vetus fama,
notumque periculis nomen, et in procero corpore
23 maesta et squalida senectus. Habebis hanc interim
epistulam ut πρόδρομον. exspectabis orationem
plenam onustamque. Exspectabis diu; neque enim
leviter et cursim, ut de re tanta retractanda est.
Vale.

X

C. PLINIUS STATIO SABINO SUO S.

1 SCRIBIS mihi Sabinam, quae nos reliquit heredes,
Modestum servum suum nusquam liberum esse
iussisse, eidem tamen sic adscripsisse legatum:
2 " Modesto quem liberum esse iussi ." Quaeris quid
sentiam. Contuli cum peritis iuris. Convenit inter
omnes nec libertatem deberi quia non sit data, nec
legatum quia servo suo dederit. Sed mihi manifestus
error videtur, ideoque puto nobis quasi scripserit
Sabina faciendum, quod ipsa scripsisse se credidit.

---

[1] But his decisions in Bithynia were rescinded; see X. 56.

266

this proposal, although it found great favour with the majority of the Senate. Paulinus at any rate won credit for making a firm stand for justice. When the court rose, Bassus was met by crowds of people clamouring to demonstrate their delight.[1] He had won public sympathy by the revival of the old story of his hazardous career, by his name, famous for his troubles in the past, and by the spectacle of his tall figure, bent with the afflictions and poverty of his old age.

This letter comes to you as a forerunner of the whole speech, which follows burdened with its details; you will have a long wait for it, as more than a superficial and cursory handling is needed for a subject of such importance.

X

To Statius Sabinus

I understand from your letter that Sabina in making us her heirs left us no instructions that her slave Modestus was to be given his freedom, but even so left him a legacy in the words: "To Modestus whom I have ordered to be set free "; and you would like to hear my view. I have consulted the legal experts, and it was their unanimous opinion that Modestus should receive neither his freedom, as it was not expressly granted, nor his legacy, as it was bequeathed to him while his status was that of a slave. But it seems to me obvious that it was a mistake on Sabina's part, and I think we ought to act as if she had set out in writing what she believed she had

3 Confido accessurum te sententiae meae, cum religiosissime soleas custodire defunctorum voluntatem,
quam bonis heredibus intellexisse pro iure est.
Neque enim minus apud nos honestas quam apud alios
4 necessitas valet. Moretur ergo in libertate sinentibus nobis, fruatur legato quasi omnia diligentissime
caverit. Cavit enim, quae heredes bene elegit.
Vale.

XI

C. PLINIUS CORNELIO MINICIANO SUO S.

1 AUDISTINE Valerium Licinianum in Sicilia profiteri?
nondum te puto audisse: est enim recens nuntius.
Praetorius hic modo[1] inter eloquentissimos causarum
actores habebatur; nunc eo decidit, ut exsul de
2 senatore, rhetor de oratore fieret. Itaque ipse in
praefatione dixit dolenter et graviter: " Quos tibi,
Fortuna, ludos facis? facis enim ex senatoribus professores, ex professoribus senatores." Cui sententiae
tantum bilis, tantum amaritudinis inest, ut mihi
3 videatur ideo professus ut hoc diceret. Idem cum
Graeco pallio amictus intrasset (carent enim togae
iure, quibus aqua et igni interdictum est), postquam
se composuit circumspexitque habitum suum,
4 " Latine " inquit " declamaturus sum." Dices tristia

---

[1] hic modo βγ: modo hic a.

---

[1] Modestus had probably been freed informally *inter amicos*.
There is a similar discussion on the spirit v. the letter of the
law in Cicero, *Brutus*, 95 ff. For P.'s view, cf. II. 16 and V. 7.
[2] Cf. Juvenal, *Sat.* VII. 197–8.

written. I am sure you will agree with me, for you are always most scrupulous about carrying out the intention of the deceased. Once understood, it should be legally binding on an honest heir, as honour puts us under an obligation as binding as necessity is for other people. Let us then allow Modestus to have his liberty and enjoy his legacy as if Sabina had taken every proper precaution. She did in fact do so by her wise choice of heirs.[1]

XI

To Cornelius Minicianus

Have you heard that Valerius Licinianus is teaching rhetoric in Sicily? The news has only just come so I doubt if it will have reached you yet. It is not long since this senator of praetorian rank was considered one of the best advocates in Rome. Now he has sunk to his present position—the senator is an exile and the orator a teacher of rhetoric.

So in his introductory lecture these melancholy words made a great impression: " O Fortune, how you sport with us! You turn senators into teachers and teachers into senators." [2] (Such rancour and bitterness makes me wonder whether he turned teacher to be able to voice it.) Then, when he had made his entry clad in a Greek cloak (those who have been ritually banished are not allowed to wear the toga), he made himself ready, looked down at his dress, and announced that he would deliver his speech in Latin.[3]

[3] *i.e.* drawing attention to the incongruity of his Greek *pallium* when speaking Latin.

et miseranda, dignum tamen illum qui haec ipsa
5 studia incesti scelere macularit. Confessus est
quidem incestum, sed incertum utrum quia verum
erat, an quia graviora metuebat si negasset. Freme-
bat enim Domitianus aestuabatque in ingenti invi-
6 dia destitutus. Nam cum Corneliam Vestalium
maximam[1] defodere vivam concupisset, ut qui in-
lustrari saeculum suum eiusmodi exemplis arbitraretur, pontificis maximi iure, seu potius immanitate
tyranni licentia domini, reliquos pontifices non in
Regiam sed in Albanam villam convocavit. Nec
minore scelere quam quod ulcisci videbatur, absentem
inauditamque damnavit incesti, cum ipse fratris
filiam incesto non polluisset solum verum etiam
7 occidisset; nam vidua abortu periit. Missi statim
pontifices qui defodiendam necandamque curarent.
Illa nunc ad Vestam, nunc ad ceteros deos manus
tendens, multa sed hoc frequentissime clamitabat:
" Me Caesar incestam putat, qua sacra faciente vicit
8 triumphavit! " Blandiens haec an inridens, ex
fiducia sui an ex contemptu principis dixerit, dubium

---

[1] Vestalium maximam αγ: Maximillam Vestalem β.

---

[1] Compare Suetonius, who believed in her guilt and refers
to two trials. *Dom.* 8. 4.
[2] The original palace of the *pontifices* and still used for their
meetings.

All this, you may say, is pitiably sad but no more than the just fate of a man who disgraced his profession by the crime of violation of a Vestal Virgin. But though Licinianus admitted this offence, it is not clear whether he did so because the charge was well founded or because he feared a worse one if he denied it. For at the time Domitian was beside himself with fury, raging at being left without witnesses when he had made up his mind to bury alive Cornelia, the chief priestess of the Vestal Virgins,[1] with the idea of making his age famous by an example of this kind. Acting on his powers as Chief Pontiff, or rather displaying a tyrant's cruelty and a despot's licence, he summoned the other priests to meet at his Alban palace instead of in the Regia,[2] and then condemned her for unchastity in absence and unheard; thereby committing a crime as great as the one he made a show of punishing. He declared her guilty of violating her vows of chastity, although he had violated his own niece[3] in an incestuous relationship and ended by causing her death, for she died as the result of an abortion during her widowhood. The priests were dispatched at once to carry out the burial and execution. Meanwhile Cornelia invoked the aid now of Vesta, now of the other gods, and amidst her many protestations was heard the frequent cry: "How can the Emperor imagine I could have broken my vows when it was I who performed the sacred rites to bring him victories and triumphs!" It is not known whether she said this in mockery or to soften the Emperor's heart, through

---

[3] Julia, daughter of Titus; see *Pan.* 52. 3; Suetonius, *Dom.* 22; Juvenal, *Sat.* II. 29-34.

9 est. Dixit donec ad supplicium, nescio an innocens,
certe tamquam innocens ducta est. Quin etiam cum
in illud subterraneum demitteretur, haesissetque
descendenti stola, vertit se ac recollegit, cumque ei
manum carnifex daret, aversata est et resiluit foedum-
que contactum quasi plane a casto puroque corpore
novissima sanctitate reiecit omnibusque numeris
pudoris πολλὴν πρόνοιαν ἔσχεν εὐσχήμων πεσεῖν.

10 Praeterea Celer eques Romanus, cui Cornelia obicie-
batur, cum in comitio virgis caederetur, in hac voce

11 perstiterat: " Quid feci? nihil feci." Ardebat ergo
Domitianus et crudelitatis et iniquitatis infamia.
Adripit Licinianum, quod in agris suis occultasset
Corneliae libertam. Ille ab iis quibus erat curae
praemonetur, si comitium et virgas pati nollet, ad
confessionem confugeret quasi ad veniam. Fecit.

12 Locutus est pro absente Herennius Senecio tale
quiddam, quale est illud: κεῖται Πάτροκλος. Ait
enim: " Ex advocato nuntius factus sum; Licinianus

13 recessit." Gratum hoc Domitiano adeo quidem ut
gaudio proderetur, diceretque: " Absolvit nos
Licinianus." Adiecit etiam non esse verecundiae
eius instandum; ipsi vero permisit, si qua posset, ex
rebus suis raperet, antequam bona publicarentur,

---

¹ Polyxena in Euripides, *Hecuba* 569. 'Carnifex' is Domitian.
² Quint. *Inst. Orat.* X. i. 49, quoting *Iliad* XVIII. 20 as a
model of brevity.

confidence in herself or out of contempt for him, but she continued to repeat it until she was led to her death. Whether she was innocent or not, she certainly appeared to be so. Moreover, when she was taken down into the famous underground chamber and her robe caught as she descended, as she turned to free it the assassin offered her his hand; but she drew away in disgust and thrust his loathsome touch from her pure and spotless person as if by a last act of chastity, and then, with due observance of the rules of modesty, she " took great care to fall in decent fashion." [1] Furthermore, when Celer, the Roman knight charged with being her accomplice, was publicly scourged, he never ceased to demand the reason and insist that he had done nothing.

Consequently Domitian was infuriated by the hatred he had incurred for his cruelty and injustice, and arrested Licinianus on the grounds of having hidden one of Cornelia's freedwomen on his estate. Licinianus was advised by those interested in him that if he wished to escape a public scourging he should have recourse to confession and beg for mercy. This he did. Herennius Senecio spoke for him in his absence, rather after the style of the well-known " Patroclus is dead."[2] " I come here as a messenger, not a defending counsel," he said; " Licinianus has withdrawn his defence." This pleased Domitian so much that he betrayed himself by his delight. " Licinianus has acquitted us! " he cried, and even went so far as to say there was no need to follow up his reasons for submission. Licinianus was accordingly granted permission to remove any of his possessions he could before they were confiscated,

14 exsiliumque molle velut praemium dedit. Ex quo
tamen postea clementia divi Nervae translatus est in
Siciliam, ubi nunc profitetur seque de fortuna prae-
fationibus vindicat.

15　Vides quam obsequenter paream tibi, qui non
solum res urbanas verum etiam peregrinas tam sedulo
scribo, ut altius repetam. Et sane putabam te, quia
tunc afuisti, nihil aliud de Liciniano audisse quam
relegatum ob incestum. Summam enim rerum
16 nuntiat fama non ordinem. Mereor ut vicissim,
quid in oppido tuo, quid in finitimis agatur (solent
enim quaedam notabilia incidere) perscribas, denique
quidquid voles dum modo non minus longa epistula
nuntia. Ego non paginas tantum sed versus etiam
syllabasque numerabo. Vale.

XII

C. Plinius Maturo Arriano Suo S.

1　Amas Egnatium Marcellinum atque etiam mihi
saepe commendas; amabis magis commendabisque,
2 si cognoveris eius recens factum. Cum in provinciam
quaestor exisset, scribamque qui sorte obtigerat ante
legitimum salarii tempus amisisset, quod acceperat
scribae daturus, intellexit et statuit subsidere apud
3 se non oportere. Itaque reversus Caesarem, deinde
Caesare auctore senatum consuluit, quid fieri de

and was given easy conditions of exile as a reward. Later, however, he was allowed to move to Sicily through the generosity of the deified Emperor Nerva, and there he is teaching today (and avenging himself on fortune in his introductions).

You see how readily I obey your orders, sending you news from abroad as well as writing about city affairs, and going into all the details; for I felt sure that as you were away at the time you would have heard nothing about Licinianus except his sentence of banishment for violating a Vestal. Gossip gives only the gist of events, not their sequence. I deserve to have a letter from you in return telling me what is happening in your town and neighbourhood—there is always something worth mentioning. In fact tell me whatever you like, only see that your letter is as long as mine. I shall count not only the pages but every line and syllable.

XII

To Maturus Arrianus

I know you are very fond of Egnatius Marcellinus, when you are always recommending him to me, and you will love and recommend him all the more when your hear what he did recently during his service abroad as quaestor. He had in his possession a sum of money intended for the salary of the secretary allotted to him who had died before the day his salary was due; and, feeling strongly that he ought not to retain this, he consulted the Emperor on his return, and with his permission the Senate, to know what was

salario vellet. Parva quaestio sed tamen quaestio.
Heredes scribae sibi, praefecti aerari populo vindica-
4 bant. Acta causa est; dixit heredum advocatus,
deinde populi, uterque percommode. Caecilius
Strabo aerario censuit inferendum, Baebius Macer
5 heredibus dandum: obtinuit Strabo. Tu lauda
Marcellinum, ut ego statim feci. Quamvis enim
abunde sufficiat illi quod est et a principe et a senatu
6 probatus, gaudebit tamen testimonio tuo. Omnes
enim, qui gloria famaque ducuntur, mirum in modum
adsensio et laus a minoribus etiam profecta delectat.
Te vero Marcellinus ita veretur ut iudicio tuo pluri-
7 mum tribuat. Accedit his quod, si cognoverit factum suum isto usque penetrasse, necesse est laudis
suae spatio et cursu et peregrinatione laetetur.
Etenim nescio quo pacto vel magis homines iuvat
gloria lata quam magna. Vale.

XIII

C. PLINIUS CORNELIO TACITO SUO S.

1   SALVUM in urbem venisse gaudeo; venisti autem,
si quando alias, nunc maxime mihi desideratus.

---

[1] P. himself had ceased to be a *praefectus aerarii* in 100 on
becoming consul. Cf. *Pan.* 92. 1. The Emperor has the final
word over the *aerarium* as well as over the *fiscus*.

[2] Either at Altinum, Arrianus's home town, or in Egypt with
Vibius Maximus (III. 2).

[3] Tacitus has not been mentioned since the trial of Priscus

to be done with it. It was a small point, but a genuine one. The secretary's heirs claimed the money for themselves and the Treasury officials [1] for the State. The case was brought to court, where the representatives of the heirs and the State spoke in turn, both very much to the point; then Baebius Macer proposed that the money should be given to the heirs and Caecilius Strabo that it should be paid into the Treasury. This latter proposal was carried, but do give Marcellinus a word of praise, as I did on the spot; for, although he is amply rewarded by having won the approval of the Emperor and the Senate, he will still be glad to have your tribute. Everyone who is influenced by thoughts of honour and reputation takes an extraordinary pleasure in words of praise and appreciation even from a lesser man than himself, and in your case Marcellinus has such a high regard for you that he sets great store by your opinion. And, besides, if he knows that the news of his action has reached as far as your ears,[2] he cannot help being delighted to think that his fame has spread so far and travelled so fast. For some reason it is widespread rather than outstanding fame which most men prefer.

XIII

To Cornelius Tacitus

I am glad to hear of your safe arrival in Rome:[3] it is always the news I want most, and particularly so

in 100, and this letter was written c. 104. It *may* refer to his return from some post abroad; but §10 implies that he is actively engaged in advocacy in Rome.

Ipse pauculis adhuc diebus in Tusculano commorabor,
2 ut opusculum quod est in manibus absolvam.   Vereor
enim ne, si hanc intentionem iam in fine laxavero,
aegre resumam.   Interim ne quid festinationi meae
pereat, quod sum praesens petiturus, hac quasi
praecursoria epistula rogo.   Sed prius accipe causas
3 rogandi [deinde ipsum quod peto].[1]   Proxime cum in
patria mea fui, venit ad me salutandum municipis
mei filius praetextatus.   Huic ego " Studes? " inquam.   Respondit: " Etiam."   " Ubi? " " Mediolani."   " Cur non hic?"   Et pater eius (erat enim
una atque etiam ipse adduxerat puerum): " Quia
4 nullos hic praeceptores habemus."   " Quare nullos?
Nam vehementer intererat vestra, qui patres estis "
(et opportune complures patres audiebant) " liberos
vestros hic potissimum discere.   Ubi enim aut iucundius morarentur quam in patria aut pudicius continerentur quam sub oculis parentum aut minore sum-
5 ptu quam domi?   Quantulum est ergo collata pecunia conducere praeceptores, quodque nunc in habita-
tiones, in viatica, in ea quae peregre emuntur (omnia autem peregre emuntur) impenditis, adicere
mercedibus?   Atque adeo ego, qui nondum liberos
habeo, paratus sum pro re publica nostra, quasi pro
filia vel parente, tertiam partem eius quod conferre
6 vobis placebit dare.   Totum etiam pollicerer, nisi

---

[1] deinde ipsum quod peto β: om. αγ.

---

[1] In Latium (Frascati). We do not know why P. is staying
in Tusculum: perhaps with a friend. It is no proof that he had

just now. I shall have to stay a few more days in Tusculum [1] to finish a small work I am busy with, for I am afraid that if I let my present concentration slacken now that I am so near the end I shall find it difficult to start again. Meanwhile, to lose no time in my impatience, here is a begging letter as a sort of forerunner to the request I intend to make in person; but you must first hear the reasons for this.

I was visiting my native town a short time ago [2] when the young son of a fellow-citizen came to pay his respects to me. "Do you go to school?" I asked. "Yes," he replied. "Where?" "In Mediolanum." [3] "Why not here?" To this the boy's father (who had brought him and was standing by) replied: "Because we have no teachers here." "Why not? Surely it is a matter of great importance to you fathers (and luckily there were several fathers listening) that your children should study here on the spot? Where can they live more happily than in their native place? Where can they be brought up more strictly than under their parents' eye or with less expense than at home? If you put your money together, what would it cost you to engage teachers? And you could add to their salaries what you now spend on lodgings, travelling-expenses, and all the things which cost money away from home—and everything is bought abroad these days. Now, as I have not yet any children of my own, I am prepared to contribute a third of whatever sum you decide to

property there; see V. 6. 45, and note. The *opusculum* means his new verses, as in IV. 14.

[2] The visit planned in IV. 1.

Milan.

timerem ne hoc munus meum quandoque ambitu
corrumperetur, ut accidere multis in locis video, in
7 quibus praeceptores publice conducuntur. Huic vitio
occurri uno remedio potest, si parentibus solis ius
conducendi relinquatur, isdemque religio recte
8 iudicandi necessitate collationis addatur. Nam qui
fortasse de alieno neglegentes, certe de suo diligentes erunt dabuntque operam, ne a me pecuniam
non nisi dignus accipiat, si accepturus et ab ipsis erit.
9 Proinde consentite conspirate maioremque animum
ex meo sumite, qui cupio esse quam plurimum, quod
debeam conferre. Nihil honestius praestare liberis
vestris, nihil gratius patriae potestis. Educentur hic
qui hic nascuntur, statimque ab infantia natale solum
amare frequentare consuescant. Atque utinam tam
claros praeceptores inducatis, ut in finitimis oppidis
studia hinc petantur, utque nunc liberi vestri aliena in
loca ita mox alieni in hunc locum confluant! ''

10   Haec putavi altius et quasi a fonte repetenda, quo
magis scires, quam gratum mihi foret si susciperes
quod iniungo. Iniungo autem et pro rei magnitudine
rogo, ut ex copia studiosorum, quae ad te ex admiratione ingenii tui convenit, circumspicias praeceptores,

---

¹ P.'s own education had probably been by private tutor, as
recommended in II. 18 and III. 3, followed by lectures in
Rome; see VI. 6. 3.

collect, as a present for our town such as I might give to a daughter or my mother. I would promise the whole amount were I not afraid that someday my gift might be abused by someone's selfish practices, as I see happen in many places where teachers' salaries are paid from public funds. There is only one remedy to meet this evil: if the appointment of teachers is left entirely to the parents, and they are conscientious about making a wise choice through their obligation to contribute to the cost. People who may be careless about another person's money are sure to be careful about their own, and they will see that only a suitable recipient shall be found for my money if he is also to have their own. So you should meet and come to some agreement; be encouraged by my generosity, for I want my own contribution to be as large as possible. You can do nothing better for your children, nothing more welcome for our town. The children born here should be brought up on their native soil, so that from their earliest years they may learn to love it and choose to stay at home. I hope that you will introduce teachers of repute, so that nearby towns will seek education here, and, instead of sending your children elsewhere as you do today, you will soon see other children flocking here to you."[1]

I thought I ought to give you a full account of this incident from the start so that you may be assured of my gratitude if you will carry out my request. I am prompted to make it by the genuine importance of the matter. From among the many students who gather round you in admiration for your abilities, will you please look for teachers for us to invite here, but

quos sollicitare possimus, sub ea tamen condicione ne
cui fidem meam obstringam. Omnia enim libera
parentibus servo: illi iudicent illi eligant, ego mihi
11 curam tantum et impendium vindico. Proinde si quis
fuerit repertus, qui ingenio suo fidat, eat illuc ea lege
ut hinc nihil aliud certum quam fiduciam suam ferat.
Vale.

XIV

C. Plinius ⟨Plinio⟩[1] Paterno Suo S.

1 Tu fortasse orationem, ut soles, et flagitas et exspec-
tas; at ego quasi ex aliqua peregrina delicataque
2 merce lusus meos tibi prodo. Accipies cum hac
epistula hendecasyllabos nostros, quibus nos in
vehiculo in balineo inter cenam oblectamus otium
3 temporis. His iocamur ludimus amamus dolemus
querimur irascimur, describimus aliquid modo pressius modo elatius, atque ipsa varietate temptamus
efficere, ut alia aliis quaedam fortasse omnibus plac-
4 eant. Ex quibus tamen si non nulla tibi petulantiora
paulo videbuntur, erit eruditionis tuae cogitare sum-
mos illos et gravissimos viros qui talia scripserunt
non modo lascivia rerum, sed ne verbis quidem nudis
abstinuisse; quae nos refugimus, non quia severiores
5 (unde enim?), sed quia timidiores sumus. Scimus
alioqui huius opusculi illam esse verissimam legem,
quam Catullus expressit:

---

[1] ⟨Plinio⟩ *Barwick* (*coll.* 1. 21), *Sherwin-White*: ⟨Decimo⟩
Mynors: om. αβγ.

282

on the understanding that I am not committed to anyone? I am leaving everything open for the parents: the decision and choice are to be theirs—all I want is to make the arrangements and pay my share. So if you find anyone who has confidence in his ability, send him there, as long as he understands that his confidence is the only certainty he brings!

XIV

To Plinius (?) Paternus

Perhaps *you* want a speech of mine as usual and are expecting one, but I have some trifles to offer instead, something choice and exotic from my store. With this letter you will receive some hendecasyllables of mine with which I amuse myself when I have time to spare in my carriage, my bath, or at dinner. Here are my jokes and witticisms, my loves, sorrows, complaints and vexations; now my style is simple, now more elevated, and I try through variety to appeal to different tastes and produce a few things to please everyone. But if some of the passages strike you as rather indelicate, your reading ought to tell you how many distinguished and serious writers in dealing with such themes neither avoided lascivious subjects nor refrained from expressing them in plain language. If I have shrunk from this, it is not because my principles are stricter than theirs (why should they be?) but because I am less courageous; and yet I know that the best rule for this kind of thing is the one in Catullus, when he says that " the

Nam castum esse decet pium poetam
ipsum, versiculos nihil necesse est,
qui tunc denique habent salem et leporem
si sunt molliculi et parum pudici.

6 Ego quanti faciam iudicium tuum, vel ex hoc potes
aestimare, quod malui omnia a te pensitari quam
electa laudari. Et sane quae sunt commodissima
7 desinunt videri, cum paria esse coeperunt. Praeterea sapiens subtilisque lector debet non diversis
conferre diversa, sed singula expendere, nec deterius
8 alio putare quod est in suo genere perfectum. Sed
quid ego plura? Nam longa praefatione vel excusare vel commendare ineptias ineptissimum est.
Unum illud praedicendum videtur, cogitare me has
meas nugas[1] ita inscribere "hendecasyllabi" qui
9 titulus sola metri lege constringitur. Proinde, sive
epigrammata sive idyllia sive eclogas sive, ut multi,
poematia seu quod aliud vocare malueris, licebit
10 voces; ego tantum hendecasyllabos praesto. A
simplicitate tua peto, quod de libello meo dicturus es
alii, mihi dicas; neque est difficile quod postulo.
Nam si hoc opusculum nostrum aut potissimum esset
aut solum fortasse posset durum videri dicere:
"Quaere quod agas"; molle et humanum est:
"Habes quod agas." Vale.

XV

C. Plinius Minicio Fundano Suo S.

1 Si quid omnino, hoc certe iudicio facio, quod
Asinium Rufum singulariter amo. Est homo eximius

[1] An allusion to Catullus, I. 1-4.

---

[1] Catullus, XVI. 5 ff.

true poet should be chaste himself, though his poetry need not be, for it must be relaxed and free from restraint if it is to have wit and charm."[1]

You can judge how much I value your opinion from the fact that I have preferred to submit the whole work to your criticism rather than pick out passages for you to admire, though admittedly these lose some of their excellence if they show signs of monotony. Moreover, an intelligent and discerning reader should not compare totally different passages, but should judge each one on its own merits, nor think one inferior to another if each is perfect of its own kind. Here I will stop, for to excuse or recommend my follies in a long preamble would be the height of folly. One thing I think I must tell you now: I intend to give these trifles of mine the title of "hendecasyllables," which refers only to the metre in which they are written. You call them what you like—epigrams, idylls, eclogues, or simply "short poems," which is the popular name, but I shall stick to my "hendecasyllables." Please be honest, and tell me now what you are likely to say about my book to someone else. It is not much to ask, for if this little work were my chief or sole effort it might possibly seem unkind to tell me to "find something else to do"; but there is nothing unkind in the gentle reminder that I "*have* something else to do."

XV

To Minicius Fundanus

If anything is proof that I do not lack judgement, it must be my special affection for Asinius Rufus.

et bonorum amantissimus.   Cur enim non me quoque
inter bonos numerem? Idem Cornelium Tacitum
(scis quem virum) arta familiaritate complexus est.
2 Proinde si utrumque nostrum probas, de Rufo quoque necesse est idem sentias, cum sit ad conectendas
amicitias vel tenacissimum vinculum morum simili-
3 tudo. Sunt ei liberi plures. Nam in hoc quoque
functus est optimi civis officio, quod fecunditate
uxoris large frui voluit, eo saeculo quo plerisque
etiam singulos filios orbitatis praemia graves faciunt.
Quibus ille despectis, avi quoque nomen adsumpsit.
Est enim avus, et quidem ex Saturio Firmo, quem
4 diliges ut ego si ut ego propius inspexeris. Haec
eo pertinent, ut scias quam copiosam, quam
numerosam domum uno beneficio sis obligaturus;
ad quod petendum voto primum, deinde bono
5 quodam omine adducimur. Optamus enim tibi
ominamurque in proximum annum consulatum: ita
nos virtutes tuae, ita iudicia principis augurari
6 volunt. Concurrit autem ut sit eodem anno quaestor
maximus ex liberis Rufi, Asinius Bassus, iuvenis
(nescio an dicam, quod me pater et sentire et dicere
cupit, adulescentis verecundia vetat) ipso patre
7 melior. Difficile est ut mihi ab absente credas
(quamquam credere soles omnia), tantum in illo
industriae probitatis eruditionis ingenii studii memoriae denique esse, quantum expertus invenies.
8 Vellem tam ferax saeculum bonis artibus haberemus,

---

¹ Minicius Fundanus was not in fact consul till 107. The
quaestors were designated before the consuls, and four out of
the twenty were chosen by the *consules ordinarii* to assist the
consuls of the year.

He is an exceptional person, the devoted admirer of every good citizen, of whom I hope I may count myself one. He is also the close friend of Cornelius Tacitus, and you know the sort of man Tacitus is. So, if you think highly of us both, you should feel the same about Rufus, since there is no stronger bond in friendship than similarity of character. He has several children, for here too he has done his duty as a good citizen, and has chosen to enjoy the blessing of a fruitful marriage at a time when the advantages of remaining childless make most people feel a single child a burden. Such advantages he has scorned, and has in fact sought the title of grandfather: and a grandfather he is, thanks to his son-in-law Saturius Firmus, whom you will appreciate as much as I do when you know him as well.

All this is to show you what a large and numerous family you can oblige by a single service, which I am led to seek through my own desires and also by my feeling of good omen for the future. I am anxious for you to hold the consulship next year, and prophesy that you will do so, for both your own merits and the Emperor's discernment surely point that way.[1] It happens that this will be the year when Asinius Bassus, Rufus's eldest son, will be quaestor, and this young man is even better than his father, though I hesitate to say what the father wants me to think and say but the son is too modest to allow. It is difficult for you to take my word (though you always trust me) for the exceptional industry and honesty, learning and ability, application and memory of a man you have not met, but you will discover all when you know him. I only wish our times were rich

ut aliquos Basso praeferre deberes: tum ego te
primus hortarer moneremque, circumferres oculos ac
9 diu pensitares, quem potissimum eligeres. Nunc
vero—sed nihil volo de amico meo adrogantius
dicere; hoc solum dico, dignum esse iuvenem quem
more maiorum in filii locum adsumas. Debent
autem sapientes viri, ut tu, tales quasi liberos a re
publica accipere, quales a natura solemus optare.
10 Decorus erit tibi consuli quaestor patre praetorio,
propinquis consularibus, quibus iudicio ipsorum,
quamquam adulescentulus adhuc, iam tamen invicem
11 ornamento est. Proinde indulge precibus meis,
obsequere consilio, et ante omnia si festinare videro
ignosce, primum quia votis suis amor plerumque
praecurrit; deinde[1] quod in ea civitate, in qua
omnia quasi ab occupantibus aguntur, quae legitimum tempus exspectant, non matura sed sera sunt;
in summa quod rerum, quas adsequi cupias, prae-
12 sumptio ipsa iucunda est. Revereatur iam te Bassus
ut consulem, tu dilige illum ut quaestorem, nos denique utriusque vestrum amantissimi laetitia duplici
13 perfruamur. Etenim cum sic te, sic Bassum diligamus, ut et illum cuiuscumque et tuum quemcumque
quaestorem in petendis honoribus omni ope labore
gratia simus iuvaturi, perquam iucundum nobis erit,
si in eundem iuvenem studium nostrum et amicitiae
meae et consulatus tui ratio contulerit, si denique

[1] quia . . . deinde β, om. αγ.

---

[1] P.'s own hopes were never realized.

enough in merit for there to be others you ought to prefer to Bassus. I should then be the first to advise you seriously to look round and take time to consider before making your choice. As things are—but I do not want to presume too far in speaking of my friend; I will only say that the young man is worthy to be treated as your son, as our forefathers did their quaestors. Wise officials like yourself should welcome these young men as children given by the State, to stand in the same position as the sons we hope nature will give us all.[1] It will befit your status as consul for you to have a quaestor whose father was a praetor and whose relatives were consuls, and one who in their opinion already does them credit in his turn even at his early age.

So grant my prayers, take my advice, but first of all forgive me if I seem to be hurrying matters. Affection usually runs ahead with its demands, and, besides, in a country where opportunities have to be seized for anything to be done, if things wait for their due season they ripen not in time, but too late; and, finally, anticipation of the object desired brings its own pleasure. Give Bassus the opportunity to wait on you as his consul, and give him your affection as your quaestor; and let me enjoy a twofold happiness in my love for you both. My regard for you and Bassus is such that I should use all my resources, energy and influence to help Bassus to be elected quaestor to any consul, and to support your quaestor whoever he might be: so it will give me great pleasure if my interests can be centred in the same young man, thanks to my double friendship and your prospective consulship; if in fact it is you who will

precibus meis tu potissimum adiutor accesseris,
cuius et suffragio senatus libentissime indulgeat et
testimonio plurimum credat. Vale.

XVI

C. Plinius Valerio Paulino Suo S.

1   Gaude meo, gaude tuo, gaude etiam publico
nomine: adhuc honor studiis durat. Proxime cum
dicturus apud centumviros essem, adeundi mihi locus
a tribunali, nisi per ipsos iudices non fuit; tanta stipa-
2 tione cetera tenebantur. Ad hoc quidam ornatus
adulescens scissis tunicis, ut in frequentia solet fieri,
sola velatus toga perstitit et quidem horis septem.
3 Nam tam diu dixi magno cum labore, maiore cum
fructu. Studeamus ergo nec desidiae nostrae prae-
tendamus alienam. Sunt qui audiant, sunt qui
legant, nos modo dignum aliquid auribus dignum
chartis elaboremus. Vale.

XVII

C. Plinius Clusinio Gallo Suo S.

1   Et admones et rogas, ut suscipiam causam Corelliae
absentis contra C. Caecilium consulem designatum.
Quod admones, gratias ago; quod rogas, queror.

---

¹ Corellia Hispulla, daughter of Corellius Rufus; see I. 12;
III. 3. The case was presumably a civil one for the Centumviral Court.

further my wishes by giving him your added support, seeing that the Senate is so ready to accept your decisions and has the highest confidence in your recommendations.

XVI

To Valerius Paulinus

Rejoice, I tell you, on my account and your own, and no less for our country; for oratory is still held in honour. When I was on my way the other day to plead before the Centumviral Court, there was no room left for me to reach my place except by way of the magistrates' bench, through their assembled ranks, as the rest of the floor was crowded. And then a young patrician who had had his clothing torn, as often happens in a crowd, stayed on clad in nothing but his toga to listen for seven hours—which was the length of the speech I made, one which cost me much effort but brought a greater reward. So we must work at our profession and not make anyone else's idleness an excuse for our own. There is no lack of readers and listeners; it is for us to produce something worth being written and heard.

XVII

To Clusinius Gallus

I have your reminder of the case Gaius Caecilius, the consul-elect, is bringing against Corellia,[1] and your request that I take charge of the defence in her absence. Thank you for the reminder, but I must

Admoneri enim debeo ut sciam, rogari non debeo ut faciam, quod mihi non facere turpissimum est. An 2 ego tueri Corelli filiam dubitem? Est quidem mihi cum isto, contra quem me advocas, non plane familia- 3 ris sed tamen amicitia. Accedit huc dignitas homi- nis atque hic ipse cui destinatus est honor, cuius nobis hoc maior agenda reverentia est, quod iam illo functi sumus. Naturale est enim ut ea, quae quis adeptus 4 est ipse, quam amplissima existimari velit. Sed mihi cogitanti adfuturum me Corelli filiae omnia ista frigida et inania videntur. Obversatur oculis ille vir quo neminem aetas nostra graviorem sanctiorem subtiliorem tulit, quem ego cum ex admiratione dili- gere coepissem, quod evenire contra solet, magis 5 admiratus sum postquam penitus inspexi. Inspexi enim penitus: nihil a me ille secretum, non ioculare 6 non serium, non triste non laetum. Adulescentulus eram, et iam mihi ab illo honor atque etiam (audebo dicere) reverentia ut aequali habebatur. Ille meus in petendis honoribus suffragator et testis, ille in inco- handis deductor et comes, ille in gerendis consiliator et rector, ille denique in omnibus officiis nostris, quamquam et imbecillus et senior, quasi iuvenis et 7 validus conspiciebatur. Quantum ille famae meae domi in publico, quantum etiam apud principem 8 adstruxit! Nam cum forte de bonis iuvenibus apud

protest against the request. I know I need to be
reminded for my own information, but I ought not
to be asked to do what would be disgraceful for me
to leave undone. How can I hesitate to defend a
daughter of Corellius? It is true that I am on friendly
though not on intimate terms with the man you ask
me to oppose; there is, moreover, his position to
consider and the office to which he has been elected,
for which I feel a special respect as I have already
held it myself, and it is natural for anyone to wish
high honour to a position he has once occupied. But
every other consideration fades into insignificance
beside the thought that it is Corellius's daughter
whom I am to defend.

I can see him now, the greatest influence, the
purest character, and the most penetrating intellect
of our age. I came to love him through my admiration, and, contrary to the general rule, when I knew
him intimately I admired him even more. For I did
know him intimately; he kept nothing hidden from
me, whether grave or gay, joy or sorrow. I was only
a young man at the time, and yet he showed me the
regard and, I will venture to say, the respect he
would have shown an equal. When I sought office
he gave me his support as sponsor, I was introduced
and attended by him when I entered upon my
duties, and had him for guide and counsellor while I
discharged them. Indeed, throughout my official
career he displayed the vigour of youth, despite his
failing health and advancing age. What a reputation he built up for me, personal and public, until
it even reached the ears of our ruler! For there
was an occasion when a discussion arose before the

Nervam imperatorem sermo incidisset, et plerique me
laudibus ferrent, paulisper se intra silentium tenuit,
quod illi plurimum auctoritatis addebat; deinde
gravitate quam noras: " Necesse est " inquit " parcius laudem Secundum, quia nihil nisi ex consilio meo
9 facit." Qua voce tribuit mihi quantum petere voto
immodicum erat, nihil me facere non sapientissime,
cum omnia ex consilio sapientissimi viri facerem.
Quin etiam moriens filiae suae (ipsa solet praedicare):
" Multos quidem amicos tibi ut longiore vita paravi,
10 praecipuos tamen Secundum et Cornutum." Quod
cum recordor, intellego mihi laborandum, ne qua
parte videar hanc de me fiduciam providentissimi
11 viri destituisse. Quare ego vero Corelliae adero
promptissime nec subire offensas recusabo; quamquam non solum veniam me verum etiam laudem
apud istum ipsum, a quo (ut ais) nova lis fortasse ut
feminae intenditur, arbitror consecuturum, si haec
eadem in actione, latius scilicet et uberius quam epistularum angustiae sinunt, vel in excusationem vel
etiam commendationem meam dixero. Vale.

---

[1] P.'s colleague at the treasury and as consul; see Index.

Emperor Nerva about the promising young men of the day and several people were singing my praises; for a time Corellius kept the silence which used to give his next words such weight, and then, in the impressive tones you will remember, " I must be moderate in my praise of Pliny," he said, " seeing that he has my advice for everything he does." In these words he paid me a tribute far beyond what I could have presumed to hope for, in implying that I did nothing which fell short of the highest wisdom, since I did everything with the advice of the wisest of men. Moreover, when he was dying he told his daughter (it is she who tells the story) that he had made many friends for her in the course of a long life, but none like Pliny and Cornutus Tertullus.[1]

I can never recall this without realizing that I must endeavour not to fail in any degree the trust placed in me by one so thoughtful for the future. So I am very ready to appear for Corellia, and will not shrink from giving offence by doing so; and yet I venture to hope for pardon and even praise from the very opponent who is bringing what you call this novel form of action (possibly because it is directed against a woman) if I have an opportunity in the course of my defence to give a fuller expression to these thoughts than is possible in the limited space of a letter, hoping thereby to win forgiveness or even approval for my conduct.

THE LETTERS OF PLINY

XVIII

C. PLINIUS ARRIO ANTONINO SUO S.

1 QUEMADMODUM magis adprobare tibi possum, quanto opere mirer epigrammata tua Graeca, quam quod quaedam Latine aemulari et exprimere temptavi? in deterius tamen. Accidit hoc primum imbecillitate ingenii mei, deinde inopia ac potius, ut Lucretius ait,
2 egestate patrii sermonis.[1] Quodsi haec, quae sunt et Latina et mea, habere tibi aliquid venustatis videbuntur, quantum putas inesse iis gratiae, quae et a te et Graece proferuntur! Vale.

XIX

C. PLINIUS CALPURNIAE HISPULLAE SUAE S.

1 CUM sis pietatis exemplum fratremque optimum et amantissimum tui pari caritate dilexeris, filiamque eius ut tuam diligas, nec tantum amitae ei adfectum verum etiam patris amissi repraesentes, non dubito maximo tibi gaudio fore cum cognoveris dignam patre
2 dignam te dignam avo evadere. Summum est acumen summa frugalitas; amat me, quod castitatis indicium est. Accedit his studium litterarum, quod ex mei caritate concepit. Meos libellos habet lecti-
3 tat ediscit etiam. Qua illa sollicitudine cum videor acturus, quanto cum egi gaudio adficitur! Disponit qui nuntient sibi quem adsensum quos clamores excitarim, quem eventum iudicî tulerim. Eadem, si

---

[1] *De Rerum Natura*, I. 832.

XVIII

To Arrius Antoninus

I HAVE been trying to make a successful Latin translation of some of your Greek epigrams; can I give you any better proof of my admiration? A change for the worse, I know, the main reason being the inadequacy of my own talent, and then the limitations, or rather what Lucretius calls " the poverty of our native tongue."[1] But if these translations—into Latin and by me—retain for you any of their charm, you can imagine the delight I take in the originals—written in Greek and by you!

XIX

To Calpurnia Hispulla

You are a model of family affection, and loved your excellent and devoted brother as dearly as he loved you; you love his daughter as if she were your own, and, by filling the place of the father she lost, you are more than an aunt to her. I know then how glad you will be to hear that she has proved herself worthy of her father, her grandfather and you. She is highly intelligent and a careful housewife, and her devotion to me is a sure indication of her virtue. In addition, this love has given her an interest in literature: she keeps copies of my works to read again and again and even learn by heart. She is so anxious when she knows that I am going to plead in court, and so happy when all is over! (She arranges to be

quando recito, in proximo discreta velo sedet, laud-
4 esque nostras avidissimis auribus excipit. Versus
quidem meos cantat etiam formatque cithara non
artifice aliquo docente, sed amore qui magister est
5 optimus. His ex causis in spem certissimam adducor,
perpetuam nobis maioremque in dies futuram esse
concordiam. Non enim aetatem meam aut corpus,
quae paulatim occidunt ac senescunt, sed gloriam
6 diligit. Nec aliud decet tuis manibus educatam, tuis
praeceptis institutam, quae nihil in contubernio tuo
viderit, nisi sanctum honestumque, quae denique
7 amare me ex tua praedicatione consueverit. Nam
cum matrem meam parentis loco vererere,[1] me a
pueritia statim formare laudare, talemque qualis
8 nunc uxori meae videor, ominari solebas. Certatim
ergo tibi gratias agimus, ego quod illam mihi, illa
quod me sibi dederis, quasi invicem elegeris. Vale.

XX

C. Plinius Novio Maximo Suo S.

1 Quid senserim de singulis tuis libris, notum tibi
ut quemque perlegeram feci; accipe nunc quid de
2 universis generaliter iudicem. Est opus pulchrum
validum acre sublime, varium elegans purum figura-

---

[1] vererere *Stangl*: verere γ: venereris β: dilexeris α.

kept informed of the sort of reception and applause I receive, and what verdict I win in the case.) If I am giving a reading she sits behind a curtain near by and greedily drinks in every word of appreciation. She has even set my verses to music and sings them, to the accompaniment of her lyre, with no musician to teach her but the best of masters, love.

All this gives me the highest reason to hope that our mutual happiness will last for ever and go on increasing day by day, for she does not love me for my present age nor my person, which must gradually grow old and decay, but for my aspirations to fame; nor would any other feelings be suitable for one brought up by your hands and trained in your precepts, who has seen only what was pure and moral in your company and learned to love me on your recommendation. For you respected my mother like a daughter, and have given me guidance and encouragement since my boyhood; you always foretold that I should become the man I am now in the eyes of my wife. And so we don't know which of us should thank you more for having given her to me and me to her as if chosen for each other.

XX

To Novius Maximus

I GAVE you my views on each section of your book as I finished reading it; now you shall have my general opinion of the work as a whole. It is a noble achievement, powerful and penetrating: its language is dignified, varied and well chosen, the style pure

tum, spatiosum etiam et cum magna tua laude diffusum, in quo tu ingenii simul dolorisque velis latissime
vectus es; et horum utrumque invicem adiumento
3 fuit. Nam dolori sublimitatem et magnificentiam
ingenium, ingenio vim et amaritudinem dolor
addidit. Vale.

XXI

C. Plinius Velio Ceriali Suo S.

1   Tristem et acerbum casum Helvidiarum sororum!
Utraque a partu, utraque filiam enixa decessit.
2 Adficior dolore, nec tamen supra modum doleo: ita
mihi luctuosum videtur, quod puellas honestissimas in
flore primo fecunditas abstulit. Angor infantium
sorte, quae sunt parentibus statim et dum nascuntur
orbatae, angor optimorum maritorum, angor etiam
3 meo nomine. Nam patrem illarum defunctum quoque perseverantissime diligo, ut actione mea librisque
testatum est; cui nunc unus ex tribus liberis superest,
domumque pluribus adminiculis paulo ante funda-
4 tam desolatus fulcit ac sustinet. Magno tamen fomento dolor meus adquiescet, si hunc saltem fortem
et incolumem, paremque illi patri illi avo fortuna
servaverit. Cuius ego pro salute pro moribus, hoc
5 sum magis anxius quod unicus factus est. Nosti in
amore mollitiam animi mei, nosti metus; quo minus
te mirari oportebit, quod plurimum timeam, de quo
plurimum spero. Vale.

---

[1] This may be the attack on Pompeius Planta referred to in
IX. 1.

[2] See VII. 30. 4 and IX. 13.

and rich in metaphor, the comprehensive scale has a breadth which will win you recognition. You were swept on by the force of genius as well as of indignation, and these have reinforced each other; genius has added dignity and grandeur to your indignation, and this in its turn has given your genius power and fury.[1]

XXI

To Velius Cerealis

THIS premature death of Helvidius's daughters is tragic—both sisters giving birth to girls and dying in labour. I am deeply distressed, and not unduly, for these were noble young women in the flower of their youth and I must mourn to see them the victims of their motherhood. I grieve too for the plight of their infants left motherless at birth, and for their excellent husbands, and I grieve no less on my own account; for my love for their father has remained constant since his death, as my defence of him and my published speeches bear witness.[2] Now only one of his three children survives, left as the sole prop and stay of a family which not so long ago had many members to support it. But if Fortune will keep him at least safe and sound, and make him as fine a man as his father and his grandfather, I can take much comfort in my sorrow. I am all the more anxious for his safety and character now that he is the last of his line. You know my nervous apprehensions for anyone I love, so you must not be surprised at my fears being worst where my hopes are highest.

THE LETTERS OF PLINY

XXII

C. PLINIUS SEMPRONIO RUFO SUO S.

1 INTERFUI principis optimi cognitioni in consilium adsumptus. Gymnicus agon apud Viennenses ex cuiusdam testamento celebratur. Hunc Trebonius Rufinus, vir egregius nobisque amicus, in duumviratu tollendum abolendumque curavit. Negabatur ex

2 auctoritate publica fecisse. Egit ipse causam non minus feliciter quam diserte. Commendabat actionem, quod tamquam homo Romanus et bonus civis in negotio suo mature et graviter loquebatur.

3 Cum sententiae perrogarentur, dixit Iunius Mauricus, quo viro nihil firmius nihil verius, non esse restituendum Viennensibus agona; adiecit " Vellem etiam

4 Romae tolli posset." Constanter, inquis, et fortiter; quidni? sed hoc a Maurico novum non est. Idem apud imperatorem Nervam non minus fortiter. Cenabat Nerva cum paucis; Veiento proximus atque etiam in sinu recumbebat: dixi omnia cum hominem

5 nominavi. Incidit sermo de Catullo Messalino, qui luminibus orbatus ingenio saevo mala caecitatis

---

¹ A judge holding a *cognitio* could invite the assistance of assessors, to form a *consilium* and give him legal advice; cf. V. 1. 5. (This is quite different from being an *amicus principis* and member of his regular advisory *consilium*, as the Elder Pliny was for Vespasian, III. 5. 18.)

² In Gallia Narbonensis (Vienne).

³ For elaborate Games at Rome, see *Pan.* 13. 5; Suetonius, *Dom.* 4. As a Greek innovation they were frowned on by Roman moralists.

XXII

To Sempronius Rufus

I have just answered a summons to act as assessor[1] to our noble Emperor during an inquiry he is holding on the gymnastic games at Vienna.[2] These used to be celebrated under the terms of some person's will until Trebonius Rufinus (a distinguished citizen and a friend of mine) became a local magistrate and took steps to have them suppressed and abolished. It was then claimed that he had no official power to do this. Rufinus spoke eloquently in his own defence and won his case; for his speech won favour by the promptitude and dignity, suitable to a true Roman and a good citizen, with which he dealt with a personal issue. When the magistrates were asked in turn for their verdict, that staunch champion of honesty, Junius Mauricus, declared that the games should not be restored at Vienna, and added that he wished they could also be abolished at Rome.[3] This showed great courage and resolution on his part, you will say, but surely this is nothing new for Mauricus. He displayed the same courage in the hearing of the Emperor Nerva. Nerva was dining with a small party where Veiento was his neighbour at table, and was even leaning on his shoulder—I need do no more than name the creature. The conversation turned on the blind Catullus Messalinus[4] whose loss of sight had increased his cruel disposition, so that he knew

---

[4] Fabricius Veiento and Catullus Messalinus were notorious *delatores*; see Tacitus, *Ann.* XIV. 50; Agr. 45: Juvenal, *Sat.* IV. 113.

addiderat: non verebatur, non erubescebat, non
miserebatur; quo saepius a Domitiano non secus ac
tela, quae et ipsa caeca et improvida feruntur, in
6 optimum quemque contorquebatur. De huius nequitia sanguinariisque sententiis in commune omnes
super cenam loquebantur, cum ipse imperator:
" Quid putamus passurum fuisse si viveret?" Et
7 Mauricus: " Nobiscum cenaret." Longius abii,
libens tamen. Placuit agona tolli, qui mores Vien-
nensium infecerat, ut noster hic omnium. Nam Vien-
nensium vitia intra ipsos residunt, nostra late vagan-
tur utque in corporibus sic in imperio gravissimus est
morbus, qui a capite diffunditur. Vale.

XXIII

C. Plinius Pomponio Basso Suo S.

1   Magnam cepi voluptatem, cum ex communibus
amicis cognovi te, ut sapientia tua dignum est, et
disponere otium et ferre, habitare amoenissime, et
nunc terra nunc mari corpus agitare, multum disputare, multum audire multum lectitare, cumque
2 plurimum scias, cotidie tamen aliquid addiscere. Ita
senescere oportet virum, qui magistratus amplissimos
gesserit, exercitus rexerit, totumque se rei publicae
3 quam diu decebat obtulerit. Nam et prima vitae

---

¹ He had been consul, *curator alimentorum*, and legate of
Galatia (ILS 6106).

neither fear, shame nor pity, and consequently was often used by Domitian to aim at honest men like a weapon which flies blindly and unthinkingly to its mark. Everyone at table was talking freely about his villainy and murderous decisions when the Emperor said: " I wonder what would have happened to him if he were alive today." " He would be dining with us," said Mauricus.

I have wandered rather far from the point, but not however unintentionally. It was decided to abolish the games at Vienna, for they had long been a corrupting influence in the town. In the same way our games at Rome spread a more general corruption, since the vices of Vienna go no farther than their town, but ours travel far and wide. The most serious diseases of the body, personal or politic, are those which spread from the head.

XXIII

To Pomponius Bassus

I was delighted to hear from our common friends that you are showing your natural wisdom in planning and spending your retirement. You live in a lovely spot, you can take exercise on the shore and in the sea, and have no lack of conversation or books to read and have read to you, so that although you know so much, every day you can add something new. This is the right way to grow old for a man who has held the highest civil offices, commanded armies, and devoted himself entirely to the service of the State as long as it was proper for him to do so.[1] It is our duty to give

tempora et media patriae, extrema nobis impertire
debemus, ut ipsae leges monent, quae maiorem annis
4 otio reddunt. Quando mihi licebit, quando per
aetatem honestum erit imitari istud pulcherrimae
quietis exemplum? quando secessus mei non desidiae
nomen sed tranquillitatis accipient? Vale.

XXIV

C. PLINIUS FABIO VALENTI SUO S.

1   PROXIME cum apud centumviros in quadruplici iudicio dixissem, subiit recordatio egisse me iuvenem
2 aeque in quadruplici. Processit animus ut solet
longius: coepi reputare quos in hoc iudicio, quos in
illo socios laboris habuissem. Solus eram qui in
utroque dixissem: tantas conversiones aut fragilitas
3 mortalitatis aut fortunae mobilitas facit. Quidam
ex iis qui tunc egerant decesserunt, exsulant alii;
huic aetas et valetudo silentium suasit, hic sponte
beatissimo otio fruitur; alius exercitum regit, illum
4 civilibus officiis principis amicitia exemit. Circa
nos ipsos quam multa mutata sunt! Studiis proces-
simus, studiis periclitati sumus, rursusque processi-
5 mus: profuerunt nobis bonorum amicitiae, bonorum
obfuerunt iterumque prosunt. Si computes annos, exi-
6 guum tempus, si vices rerum, aevum putes; quod

---

[1] *i.e.* a member of the Emperor's *consilium*; see IV. 22, and
note.   [2] See III. 11; *Pan.* 95. 3.

up our youth and manhood to our country, but our last years are our own: this the law itself suggests in permitting the old to retire. I wonder when this will be permitted me—when shall I reach the honourable age which will allow me to follow your example of a graceful retirement, when my withdrawal will not be termed laziness but rather a desire for peace?

XXIV

To Fabius Valens

The other day, when I had just finished addressing a joint session of the four panels of the Centumviral Court, I remembered a speech which I had made as a young man in the same court. As usual my thoughts travelled on, and I began to reckon up the people with whom I had worked on the present occasion and the earlier one. I was the only person present who had spoken in both cases; such are the changes due to mortal frailty or the fickleness of fortune. Some of those who had spoken then are dead, others are in exile: age and ill-health has silenced one man, another has chosen to enjoy the blessings of retirement, another holds a military command, and another has given up his career to become the Emperor's personal friend.[1] In my own case I have known many changes. My profession brought me advancement, then danger, then advancement again; I was helped by my friendship with honest men, then injured by it, and now am helped again.[2] If you add up the years it would not seem very long, but it would be a lifetime if you count the changes of fortune.

307

potest esse documento nihil desperare, nulli rei
fidere, cum videamus tot varietates tam volubili
7 orbe circumagi. Mihi autem familiare est omnes
cogitationes meas tecum communicare, isdemque te
vel praeceptis vel exemplis monere, quibus ipse me
moneo; quae ratio huius epistulae fuit. Vale.

XXV

C. Plinius Maesio Maximo Suo S.

1 Scripseram tibi verendum esse, ne ex tacitis suffragiis vitium aliquod exsisteret. Factum est.
Proximis comitiis in quibusdam tabellis multa iocu-
laria atque etiam foeda dictu, in una vero pro candidatorum nominibus suffragatorum nomina inventa
2 sunt. Excanduit senatus magnoque clamore ei qui
scripsisset iratum principem est comprecatus. Ille
tamen fefellit et latuit, fortasse etiam inter indig-
3 nantes fuit. Quid hunc putamus domi facere, qui in
tanta re tam serio tempore tam scurriliter ludat, qui
denique omnino in senatu dicax et urbanus et bellus
4 est? Tantum licentiae pravis ingeniis adicit illa
fiducia: "quis enim sciet?" Poposcit tabellas,[1]
stilum accepit, demisit caput, neminem veretur, se
5 contemnit. Inde ista ludibria scaena et pulpito
digna. Quo te vertas? quae remedia conquiras?

---

[1] tabellas βγ: tabellam α, *Stout.*

[1] III. 20.

This should be a warning never to lose heart and to be sure of nothing, when we see so many fluctuations of fortune following each other in rapid succession.

It is a habit of mine to share my thoughts with you and to set out for your guidance the rules and examples which shape my own conduct. That was the purpose of this letter.

XXV

To Maesius Maximus

I told you in my last letter[1] that there was a risk of the secret ballot's leading to abuses, and this has already happened. At the recent election some of the voting-papers were found to have jokes and obscenities scribbled on them, and on one the names of the candidates were replaced by those of their sponsors. This incensed the Senate and members clamoured for the wrath of the Emperor to be visited on the culprit; but he kept quiet and undetected—he may even have joined in the general indignation. If this man can play such ribald tricks in an important matter on a serious occasion, and thinks the Senate is the place where he can pass for a nimble wit and a fine fellow, what are we to suppose his personal conduct can be? This is the confidence unprincipled characters derive from the assurance that "no one will know." This man could ask for a voting-paper, take a pen, and bend his head to write, with neither fear of anyone nor any self-respect. The result was that ribaldry fit for nothing but the vulgar stage. Where is one to turn in

Ubique vitia remediis fortiora. Ἀλλὰ ταῦτα τῷ ὑπὲρ ἡμᾶς μελήσει, cui multum cotidie vigiliarum, multum laboris adicit haec nostra iners et tamen effrenata petulantia. Vale.

XXVI

C. PLINIUS MAECILIO[1] NEPOTI SUO S.

1   PETIS ut libellos meos, quos studiosissime comparasti, recognoscendos emendandosque curem. Faciam. Quid enim suscipere libentius debeo, te praesertim
2 exigente? Nam cum vir gravissimus doctissimus disertissimus, super haec occupatissimus, maximae provinciae praefuturus, tanti putes scripta nostra circumferre tecum, quanto opere mihi providendum est, ne te haec pars sarcinarum tamquam supervacua
3 offendat! Adnitar ergo, primum ut comites istos quam commodissimos habeas, deinde ut reversus invenias, quos istis addere velis. Neque enim mediocriter me ad nova opera tu lector hortaris. Vale.

XXVII

C. PLINIUS POMPEIO FALCONI SUO S.

1   TERTIUS dies est quod audivi recitantem Sentium Augurinum cum summa mea voluptate, immo etiam

---

[1] Maecilio *om.* αγ (*in hac ep. deest* β); Metilio Nepoti *Mommsen.*

---

[1] Plato, *Phaedo* 95b.
[2] Maecilius Nepos had perhaps acquired copies on the fine parchment recommended by Martial, I. 2, and wished to be sure the scribes had made no mistakes. His province is un-

search of a remedy? Everywhere the disease has gone too far to be cured. " But this will concern the power above us "[1] whose daily task of vigilance is greatly increased by the futile impudence in our midst which we cannot control.

XXVI

To Maecilius Nepos

You want me to re-read and correct the copies of my speeches which you have assembled with such care.[2] Of course I will, for there is nothing which I ought to do so gladly, especially at your request. When a man of your judgement, scholarship, and eloquence (and moreover as busy as yourself and the future governor of an important province) thinks my writings worth carrying around with him, I should surely do my utmost to see that this item of luggage is not a useless encumbrance. My first care then shall be to make your present travelling companions as congenial as possible; and my second to provide you with more which you may like to add to them on your return. The fact that you are one of my readers is no small encouragement to new work.

XXVII

To Pompeius Falco

For the last three days I have been present at a reading given by Sentius Augurinus which gave me great pleasure and filled me with admiration for his

known, unless he is to be identified with P. Metilius Sabinus Nepos (as Syme, p. 647, who suggests Pannonia).

admiratione. Poematia adpellat. Multa tenuiter multa sublimiter, multa venuste multa tenere, mul-
2 ta dulciter multa cum bile. Aliquot annis puto nihil generis eiusdem absolutius scriptum, nisi forte me fallit aut amor eius aut quod ipsum me laudibus vexit.
3 Nam lemma sibi sumpsit, quod ego interdum versibus ludo. Atque adeo iudicii mei te iudicem faciam, si mihi ex hoc ipso lemmate secundus versus occurrerit; nam ceteros teneo et iam explicui.

4   Canto carmina versibus minutis,
      his olim quibus et meus Catullus
      et Calvus veteresque. Sed quid ad me?
      Unus Plinius est mihi priores:
      mavolt versiculos foro relicto
      et quaerit quod amet, putatque amari.[1]
      I nunc, quisquis amas, amare noli.
      Ille o Plinius, ille quot[2] Catones!

5 Vides quam acuta omnia quam apta quam expressa. Ad hunc gustum totum librum repromitto, quem tibi ut primum publicaverit exhibebo. Interim ama iuvenem et temporibus nostris gratulare pro ingenio tali, quod ille moribus adornat. Vivit cum Spurinna,
6 vivit cum Antonino, quorum alteri adfinis, utrique contubernalis est. Possis ex hoc facere coniecturam, quam sit emendatus adulescens, qui a gravissimis senibus sic amatur. Est enim illud verissimum:

$$\gamma\iota\nu\acute{\omega}\sigma\kappa\omega\nu \ \acute{o}\tau\iota$$
$$\tau o\iota o\hat{v}\tau\acute{o}s \ \acute{\epsilon}\sigma\tau\iota\nu, \ o\acute{\iota}\sigma\pi\epsilon\rho \ \H{\eta}\delta\epsilon\tau\alpha\iota \ \sigma\upsilon\nu\acute{\omega}\nu.$$

Vale.

---

[1] amari γ: amare αβ.   [2] quot *Barth*: quod αβγ.

works. He calls them "short poems." Many are
simple, many in the grand style: many are full of
delicate charm and express either tender feeling or
indignation. It is many years, I think, since anything of this kind has attained such perfection, unless
my judgement is affected by my feeling for Augurinus or the fact that he has paid me a tribute in taking
my occasional attempts at versifying as a theme.
You may be judge of my opinion if I can remember
the second line of this: I have all the others clear in
my mind.

My verse is light and tender, as Catullus long ago,
But what care I for poets past, when I my Pliny know?
Outside the courts in mutual love and song he makes
  his name;
You lovers and you statesmen, to Pliny yield your
  fame![1]

This will give you an idea of the wit and polished
perfection of his style, and I can promise you that it
is a true foretaste of the whole book. As soon as it is
published I will send it to you. Meanwhile, give
the young poet your affection, and congratulate our
age on having produced such talent allied to fine
character. He spends much time with Spurinna and
Antoninus, being related to one and the close friend
of both, and from this you may estimate the merit of
a young man who has thus won the affection of his
elders and superiors in judgement. Nothing is more
true than that " you may know a man by the company
he keeps."[2]

---

[1] The free translation reflects the banality of the original.
[2] Euripides, *Frag.* 812 N^2.

XXVIII

C. Plinius Vibio Severo Suo S.

1 Herennius Severus vir doctissimus magni aestimat
in bibliotheca sua ponere imagines municipum tuorum Corneli Nepotis et Titi Cati petitque, si sunt
istic, ut esse credibile est, exscribendas pingendasque
2 delegem. Quam curam tibi potissimum iniungo,
primum quia desideriis meis amicissime obsequeris,
deinde quia tibi studiorum summa reverentia, summus amor studiosorum, postremo quod patriam tuam
omnesque, qui nomen eius auxerunt, ut patriam ipsam
3 veneraris et diligis. Peto autem, ut pictorem quam
diligentissimum adsumas. Nam cum est arduum
similitudinem effingere ex vero, tum longe difficillima
est imitationis imitatio; a qua rogo ut artificem quem
elegeris ne in melius quidem sinas aberrare. Vale.

XXIX

C. Plinius Romatio Firmo Suo S.

1 Heia tu! cum proxime res agentur, quoquo modo
ad iudicandum veni: nihil est quod in dextram aurem
fiducia mei dormias. Non impune cessatur. Ecce
2 Licinius Nepos praetor! Acer et fortis et praetor,
multam dixit etiam senatori. Egit ille in senatu

---

[1] Nepos the historian and Catius an Epicurean philosopher,
both of Insubrian Gaul; the town may be Milan.

XXVIII

To Vibius Severus

THE well-known scholar Herennius Severus is very anxious to hang in his library portraits of your fellow-townsmen, Cornelius Nepos and Titus Catius,[1] and asks me to have the originals copied in colour if, as seems likely, they are in your possession. I am passing on his request to you rather than anyone else for three reasons: your usual kindness in falling in with my wishes, your deep admiration for literature and warm feeling for its students, and your affectionate regard for your native place and similarly for all who have made its name famous. All I ask is that you find as accurate a painter as you can, for it is hard enough to make a likeness from life, but a portrait from a portrait is by far the most difficult of all. Please do not let the artist you choose depart from the original even to improve on it.

XXIX

To Romatius Firmus[2]

Now then, you really must come along somehow to take your place on the bench next time the court is sitting—you can't rely on me to let you sleep soundly; if you default, you will suffer. Along comes our stern praetor Licinius Nepos: bold man, he has just fined a senator! The culprit made his

---

[2] Of Comum; see I. 19. Now *decurio* and member of the *decuriae iudicum*.

causam suam, egit autem sic ut deprecaretur.
Remissa est multa, sed timuit, sed rogavit, sed opus
3 venia fuit. Dices: "Non omnes praetores tam
severi." Falleris; nam vel instituere vel reducere
eiusmodi exemplum non nisi severi, institutum re-
ductumve exercere etiam lenissimi possunt. Vale.

XXX

C. Plinius Licinio Surae Suo S.

1 Attuli tibi ex patria mea pro munusculo quaestion-
2 em altissima ista eruditione dignissimam. Fons
oritur in monte, per saxa decurrit, excipitur cenatiun-
cula manu facta; ibi paulum retentus in Larium
lacum decidit. Huius mira natura: ter in die
statis auctibus ac diminutionibus crescit decrescit-
3 que. Cernitur id palam et cum summa voluptate
deprenditur.[1] Iuxta recumbis et vesceris, atque
etiam ex ipso fonte (nam est frigidissimus) potas;
interim ille certis dimensisque momentis vel sub-
4 trahitur vel adsurgit. Anulum seu quid aliud ponis
in sicco, adluitur sensim ac novissime operitur,
detegitur rursus paulatimque deseritur. Si diutius
5 observes, utrumque iterum ac tertio videas. Spirit-
usne aliquis occultior os fontis et fauces modo laxat
modo includit, prout inlatus occurrit aut decessit ex-
6 pulsus? quod in ampullis ceterisque generis eiusdem

---

[1] deprenditur *poscunt numeri*; deprehend- αβγ.

---

[1] Licinius Nepos is active again in V. 4.
[2] The famous general; see Index.
[3] See Pliny, *NH* II. 232. The spring can still be seen in
the grounds of the Villa Pliniana at Torno on Lake Como.

defence before the Senate, but he had to plead for pardon.   He was let off the fine, but he had a fright; he had need of mercy and had to beg for it.   You may say that all praetors are not so strict, but you are wrong there.   It may take a strict one to establish or revive such a precedent, but once that is done the mildest of men can act on it.[1]

XXX

To Licinius Sura[2]

I have brought you a small present from my native place—a problem fully worthy of your great learning. There is a spring which has its source in a mountain and then runs down over the rocks to a small artificial grotto, where it is caught and held for a time; then it flows down into Lake Como.[3]   This is its remarkable feature : three times a day it fills and empties with a regular increase and decrease of water, and this can be seen quite clearly and is a great pleasure to watch.   You settle yourself close by for a meal and also a drink from the ice-cold water of the spring; meanwhile it ebbs and flows at regular intervals. Put a ring or anything else on the margin where it is dry, and the waters gently creep over it until it is covered, then reveal it again as they gradually recede.   If you watch long enough you can see the process repeated a second and third time.

Is there some hidden current of air which opens and closes the vent and outlet of the spring, possibly by blocking the way on entry and leaving it free when forced out?   We see this happen in the case of

videmus accidere, quibus non hians nec statim patens
exitus. Nam illa quoque, quamquam prona atque
vergentia, per quasdam obluctantis animae moras
crebris quasi singultibus sistunt quod effundunt.
7 An, quae oceano natura, fonti quoque, quaque
ille ratione aut impellitur aut resorbetur, hac modicus
8 hic umor vicibus alternis supprimitur egeritur? An
ut flumina, quae in mare deferuntur, adversantibus
ventis obvioque aestu retorquentur, ita est aliquid
9 quod huius fontis excursum repercutiat? An laten-
tibus venis certa mensura, quae dum colligit quod
exhauserat, minor rivus et pigrior; cum collegit,
10 agilior maiorque profertur? An nescio quod libra-
mentum abditum et caecum, quod cum exinanitum
est, suscitat et elicit fontem; cum repletum, moratur
11 et strangulat? Scrutare tu causas (potes enim), quae
tantum miraculum efficiunt: mihi abunde est, si
satis expressi quod efficitur. Vale.

---

¹ This is nearest to the correct explanation; the spring works
on the siphon principle.

bottles and similar vessels with narrow restricted necks, which, though tilted downwards, pour out their contents in jerks with a repeated gulping sound as if checked by the opposing inrush of air. Or is the spring substantially the same as the sea, so that its lesser volume of water is alternately driven back and forth by the same laws which govern the ebb and flow of the tide? Or is there something to drive back the outflow of the spring in the same way as rivers flowing into the sea are turned back if they meet an opposing force of wind and tide? Or is there a fixed supply of water in a hidden channel, so that the stream diminishes and flows slowly while water accumulates after it has emptied, but flows faster and increases when the supply is sufficient?[1] Or is there some force of water hidden out of sight which sets the spring in motion when it has drained away, but checks and cuts off the flow when it has filled up? It is for you to investigate the cause of this remarkable phenomenon, as you have the ability. I have done more than enough if I have managed to describe clearly what happens.

BOOK V

LIBER QUINTUS

I

C. PLINIUS ANNIO SEVERO SUO S.

1 LEGATUM mihi obvenit modicum sed amplissimo gratius. Cur amplissimo gratius? Pomponia Galla exheredato filio Asudio Curiano heredem reliquerat me, dederat coheredes Sertorium Severum praetorium virum aliosque splendidos equites Romanos.
2 Curianus orabat, ut sibi donarem portionem meam seque praeiudicio iuvarem; eandem tacita conven-
3 tione salvam mihi pollicebatur. Respondebam non convenire moribus meis aliud palam aliud agere secreto; praeterea non esse satis honestum donare et locupleti et orbo; in summa non profuturum ei si donassem, profuturum si cessissem, esse autem me paratum cedere si inique exheredatum mihi liqueret.
4 Ad hoc ille: " Rogo cognoscas." Cunctatus paulum " Faciam " inquam; " neque enim video cur ipse me minorem putem, quam tibi videor. Sed iam nunc memento non defuturam mihi constantiam, si ita fides duxerit, secundum matrem tuam pronuntiandi."
5 " Ut voles " ait; " voles enim quod aequissimum."

---

[1] Such action would be generally taken as an indication that the will was unjust.

BOOK V

I

To Annius Severus

I have just come in for a legacy: not a large one, but more welcome than a substantial sum for reasons which I will explain. The donor, Asudius Curianus, had previously been disinherited by his mother, Pomponia Galla, who had then divided her estate between myself, the senator and ex-praetor Sertorius Severus, and several distinguished Roman knights. Curianus had begged me to present him with my share and help him by setting a precedent,[1] on the tacit understanding that he should eventually restore the capital untouched. I replied that it was not my nature to do one thing in public and another in private, nor did I think it honest to make a present of money to a rich and childless man; in short, that I could do him no good by giving him my share, but he would benefit if I waived my claim to it. This I was willing to do only if I was satisfied that he had been unfairly disinherited. He then asked me to hold an inquiry, and after some hesitation I agreed, remarking that as he apparently thought me capable of doing so I saw no reason not to share his opinion, but reminding him that I should not hesitate to pronounce judgement in favour of his mother if that was my honest opinion. He told me to act as I thought

Adhibui in consilium duos quos tunc civitas nostra spectatissimos habuit, Corellium et Frontinum. His 6 circumdatus in cubiculo meo sedi. Dixit Curianus quae pro se putabat. Respondi paucis ego (neque enim aderat alius, qui defunctae pudorem tueretur), deinde secessi, et ex consilii sententia " Videtur " inquam, " Curiane, mater tua iustas habuisse causas irascendi tibi."

Post hoc ille cum ceteris subscripsit centumvirale 7 iudicium, non subscripsit mecum. Adpetebat iudicii dies; coheredes mei componere et transigere cupiebant non diffidentia causae, sed metu temporum. Verebantur quod videbant multis accidisse, ne ex 8 centumvirali iudicio capitis rei exirent. Et erant quidam in illis, quibus obici et Gratillae amicitia et 9 Rustici posset. Rogant me ut cum Curiano loquar. Convenimus in aedem Concordiae. Ibi ego " Si mater " inquam " te ex parte quarta scripsisset heredem, num queri posses? Quid si heredem quidem instituisset ex asse, sed legatis ita exhausisset ut non amplius apud te quam quarta remaneret? Igitur sufficere tibi debet, si exheredatus a matre quartam partem ab heredibus eius accipias, quam 10 tamen ego augebo. Scis te non subscripsisse mecum, et iam biennium transisse omniaque me usu cepisse.

---

[1] Cf. III. 11. 3. This dates the episode to the last years of Domitian.

fit, as that was sure to be fair. I then invited the support of the two most respected citizens of the day, Corellius and Frontinus, and took my seat between them in my room. Curianus put forward his best arguments, and I made a brief reply myself, for there was no one else present to defend the honour of the deceased. Then after withdrawing for consultation I told him our joint decision: namely that we found his mother had a just reason for her displeasure with him.

Subsequently he served a notice on the other heirs, though not on me, of a charge to be brought before the Centumviral Court. As the day fixed for the case approached, my co-heirs were anxious to compromise and settle out of court, not out of any lack of confidence in their cause, but through distrust of the times; they feared the fate they had seen overtake many another—that they might leave the Centumviral Court with a criminal case against them. Some of them, too, could be made to suffer for their friendship with Gratilla and Rusticus.[1] They therefore asked me to speak to Curianus, and I met him in the temple of Concord. There I put this question: " Would you have any cause for complaint if your mother had left you the statutory fourth part of her estate,[2] or if you were made her sole heir, but with so many legacies to be paid out that your share was reduced to a fourth? Then you should be satisfied if you are given a fourth share by your mother's heirs, after being disinherited yourself. However, I will add something to it myself. You must realize that

[2] By the *Lex Falcidia* of 40 B.C. the heir-at-law was entitled to a minimum fourth of an estate.

THE LETTERS OF PLINY

Sed ut te coheredes mei tractabiliorem experiantur, utque tibi nihil abstulerit reverentia mei, offero pro mea parte tantundem." Tuli fructum non con-
11 scientiae modo verum etiam famae. Ille ergo Curianus legatum mihi reliquit et factum meum, nisi forte blandior mihi antiquum, notabili honore signavit.

12 Haec tibi scripsi, quia de omnibus quae me vel delectant vel angunt, non aliter tecum quam mecum loqui soleo; deinde quod durum existimabam, te amantissimum mei fraudare voluptate quam ipse
13 capiebam. Neque enim sum tam sapiens ut nihil mea intersit, an iis quae honeste fecisse me credo, testificatio quaedam et quasi praemium accedat. Vale.

II

C. PLINIUS CALPURNIO FLACCO SUO S.

1 ACCEPI pulcherrimos turdos, cum quibus parem calculum ponere nec urbis copiis ex Laurentino nec
2 maris tam turbidis tempestatibus possum. Recipies ergo epistulas steriles et simpliciter gratas,[1] ac ne illam quidem sollertiam Diomedis in permutando munere imitantes. Sed, quae facilitas tua, hoc magis dabis veniam, quod se non mereri fatentur. Vale.

---

[1] gratas *Mynors* [1]: ingratas Mβγ *Mynors* [2].

---

[1] *Iliad* VI. 235. Diomedes exchanged his bronze armour with Glaucus for a gold set.

you have brought no action against me, and the two years have elapsed which establish my claim. But to make you more willing to negotiate with the other heirs and prevent your losing anything by showing me special consideration, I am prepared to give you a sum equivalent to my share.''

I have had my reward in reputation as well as a good conscience, for it is this Curianus who has left me a legacy and paid this notable tribute to my conduct—conduct which (unless I flatter myself) was in the best tradition. I have told you this tale since I always talk about all my joys and sorrows as freely to you as I would to myself, and then because I thought it cruel to deny my best friend a pleasure which I was enjoying. Nor am I enough of a philosopher to remain quite indifferent whether what I believe to be a good deed of mine is to win some just reward.

II

To Calpurnius Flaccus

Thank you for the fine fieldfares, but being at Laurentum I can't match them with anything from town, nor can I send you any fish as long as the weather is so bad. So all you will get is a letter which comes empty-handed, nothing but simple thanks without any of Diomedes' ingenuity in exchanging gifts.[1] However, I know you are kind enough to be all the readier to excuse where an excuse is admittedly undeserved.

THE LETTERS OF PLINY

III

C. Plinius Titio Aristoni Suo S.

1 Cum plurima officia tua mihi grata et iucunda sunt,
tum vel maxime quod me celandum non putasti, fuisse
apud te de versiculis meis multum copiosumque
sermonem, eumque diversitate iudiciorum longius
processisse, exstitisse etiam quosdam, qui scripta
quidem ipsa non improbarent, me tamen amice
simpliciterque reprehenderent, quod haec scriberem
2 recitaremque. Quibus ego, ut augeam meam cul-
pam, ita respondeo: facio non numquam versiculos
severos parum, facio; nam et comoedias audio et
specto mimos et lyricos lego et Sotadicos[1] intellego;
aliquando praeterea rideo iocor ludo, utque omnia
innoxiae remissionis genera breviter amplectar, homo
3 sum. Nec vero moleste fero hanc esse de moribus meis existimationem, ut qui nesciunt talia doctis-
simos gravissimos sanctissimos homines scriptitasse,
4 me scribere mirentur. Ab illis autem quibus notum
est, quos quantosque auctores sequar, facile impetrari
posse confido, ut errare me sed cum illis sinant,
quorum non seria modo verum etiam lusus expri-
5 mere laudabile est. An ego verear (neminem viven-
tium, ne quam in speciem adulationis incidam, nomi-
nabo), sed ego verear ne me non satis deceat, quod
decuit M. Tullium, C. Calvum, Asinium Pollionem,

---

[1] Sotadicos *Catanaeus*: Socraticos *Mβγ*.

---

[1] This type of licentious verse (called after the Alexandrian
iambic poet) was notorious. See Quintilian, *Inst. Orat.* I.
viii. 6.   [2] Terence, *Heaut. Tim.* 77.

III

To Titius Aristo

I HAVE many welcome acts of kindness to thank you for, but you do me a real service by thinking I ought to know that my verses have been the subject of much discussion at your house, a discussion which was prolonged because of difference of opinion. There were some people, you say, who had no criticism to make of the actual poems, but thought I deserved their censure—in a frank and friendly way—for composing and reading them in public. My answer to these critics will probably aggravate the offence. I admit that I do often write verse which is far from serious, for I also listen to comedy, watch farces, read lyric poetry, and appreciate Sotadic[1] verse; there are besides times when I laugh, make jokes, and enjoy my fun, in fact I can sum up all these innocent relaxations in a word " I am human."[2] I am not complaining if my character is valued so highly that some people express surprise at my writing on such themes, if they are themselves unaware that the same thing has often been done by serious scholars of blameless reputation. But I am sure that those who realize what famous authors have set me an example can easily be persuaded to let me go astray, so long as I am in their company; for it is an honour to imitate their lighter as well as their more serious work. I am not citing a living author, lest I seem exaggerated in my praises, but surely I need not be afraid that this practice is unsuitable for me, when it was perfectly proper in the case of Cicero, C. Calvus, Asinius Pollio,

M. Messalam, Q. Hortensium, M. Brutum, L. Sullam, Q. Catulum, Q. Scaevolam, Servium Sulpicium, Varronem, Torquatum, immo Torquatos, C. Memmium, Lentulum Gaetulicum, Annaeum Senecam[1] et proxime Verginium Rufum et, si non sufficiunt exempla privata, divum Iulium, divum Augus-

6 tum, divum Nervam, Tiberium Caesarem? Neronem enim transeo, quamvis sciam non corrumpi in deterius quae aliquando etiam a malis, sed honesta manere quae saepius a bonis fiunt. Inter quos vel praecipue numerandus est P. Vergilius, Cornelius Nepos et prius Accius Enniusque. Non quidem hi senatores,

7 sed sanctitas morum non distat ordinibus. Recito tamen, quod illi an fecerint nescio. Etiam: sed illi iudicio suo poterant esse contenti, mihi modestior constantia est quam ut satis absolutum putem, quod

8 a me probetur. Itaque has recitandi causas sequor, primum quod ipse qui recitat aliquanto acrius scriptis suis auditorum reverentia intendit; deinde quod de quibus dubitat, quasi ex consilii sententia statuit.

9 Multa etiam a multis admonetur, et si non admoneatur, quid quisque sentiat perspicit ex vultu oculis nutu manu murmure silentio; quae satis apertis

10 notis iudicium ab humanitate discernunt. Atque adeo si cui forte eorum qui interfuerunt curae fuerit eadem illa legere, intelleget me quaedam aut com-

---

[1] Senecam βγ: Senecam Lucanum Mθ.

---

[1] P. must mean the consul of 65 B.C. and his son, L. Manlius Torquatus, the subject of Catullus's marriage ode (LXI).

M. Messala, Q. Hortensius, M. Brutus, L. Sulla, Q. Catulus, Q. Scaevola, Servius Sulpicius, Varro, Torquatus (in fact several Torquati),[1] C. Memmius, Lentulus Gaetulicus, and Annaeus Seneca, and also Verginius Rufus in our own times. If these individuals are not enough, I can quote the deified Julius Caesar and the deified Emperors Augustus and Nerva and Tiberius Caesar. I except Nero, though I know what is the occasional practice of the vicious is not corrupted thereby, but retains its integrity through being the usual practice of the virtuous. In the latter class Virgil, Cornelius Nepos, and, before their date, Accius and Ennius must rank high: it is true they were not senators, but moral integrity knows no class distinctions.

However, it can be said that I give readings of my work without knowing if these authors did. So I do; but they could rest content with their own judgement, whereas I am too diffident to feel confident that I have done everything I can to what has only my own approval. I have therefore two reasons for reading in public; the reader is made more keenly critical of his own work if he stands in some awe of his audience, and he has a kind of panel of experts to confirm his decision on any doubtful point. He receives suggestions from different members, and, failing this, he can infer their various opinions from their expressions, glances, nods, applause, murmurs and silence, signs which make clear the distinction between their critical judgement and polite assent. And then if any of the company is interested in reading what he has heard, he will realize that I shall have made certain alterations or omissions which may

mutasse aut praeterisse, fortasse etiam ex suo iudicio,
11 quamvis ipse nihil dixerit mihi. Atque haec ita dis-
puto quasi populum in auditorium, non in cubiculum
amicos advocarim, quos plures habere multis gloriosum, reprehensioni nemini fuit. Vale.

IV

C. Plinius Iulio Valeriano Suo S.

1 Res parva, sed initium non parvae. Vir praetorius
Sollers a senatu petît, ut sibi instituere nundinas in
agris suis permitteretur. Contra dixerunt legati
Vicetinorum; adfuit Tuscilius Nominatus. Dilata
2 causa est. Alio senatu Vicetini sine advocato intraverunt, dixerunt se deceptos, lapsine verbo, an quia ita
sentiebant. Interrogati a Nepote praetore, quem
docuissent, responderunt quem prius. Interrogati an
tunc gratis adfuisset,[1] responderunt sex milibus nummum; an rursus aliquid dedissent, dixerunt mille
denarios. Nepos postulavit ut Nominatus induc-
3 eretur. Hactenus illo die. Sed quantum auguror
longius res procedet. Nam pleraque tacta[2] tantum
et omnino commota latissime serpunt. Erexi aures

---

[1] adfuisset *Beroaldus*: adfuissent βγ.
[2] tacta. *Scheffer*: tacita *M*β: iacta γ: tacita tantummodo
commota *Stout*.

---

[1] Claudius similarly asked permission of the consuls;
Suetonius, *Claud*. 12. 2.
[2] In Venetia (Vicenza).
[3] Licinius Nepos; see IV. 29.
[4] A-M. Guillemin refers this metaphor to the frequency of
collapsing buildings in Rome.

perhaps accord with his opinion, although he never actually expressed it to me. But now I am arguing this point as if I invited the general public to a lecture hall instead of having my friends in my own room—though if I have many friends to invite this has been a source of pride to many people and a reproach to none.

IV

To Julius Valerianus

THIS is a small matter, but likely to go far. A praetorian senator named Sollers asked the Senate for permission to hold a weekly market on his property.[1] This was opposed by representatives of the town of Vicetia,[2] with Tuscilius Nominatus acting on their behalf, and the case was adjourned until a subsequent meeting of the Senate. The Vicetians then appeared without anyone to plead for them and said they had been cheated—whether a verbal slip on their part or their genuine opinion I don't know. Asked by the praetor Nepos[3] whom they had instructed to act for them, they replied, " The same as before." To the question whether he had taken on the case without a fee, they said that they had given him 6,000 sesterces. Had they paid him a second fee? Yes, another 4,000. Nepos then issued a summons to Nominatus to appear before the court. This was as far as the matter went that day, but I can see that it will not end there, for often a mere touch is enough to set things moving with far-reaching consequences.[4]

4 tuas. Quam diu nunc oportet, quam blande roges,
ut reliqua cognoscas! si tamen non ante ob haec ipsa
veneris Romam, spectatorque malueris esse quam
lector. Vale.

V

C. Plinius Novio Maximo Suo S.

1 Nuntiatum mihi C. Fannium decessisse; qui nuntius me gravi dolore confudit, primum quod amavi
hominem elegantem disertum, deinde quod iudicio
eius uti solebam. Erat enim acutus natura, usu
2 exercitatus, veritate promptissimus. Angit me
super ista casus ipsius: decessit veteri testamento,
omisit quos maxime diligebat, prosecutus est quibus
offensior erat. Sed hoc utcumque tolerabile; gravius
illud, quod pulcherrimum opus imperfectum reliquit.
3 Quamvis enim agendis causis distringeretur, scribebat tamen exitus occisorum aut relegatorum a Nerone
et iam tres libros absolverat subtiles et diligentes et
Latinos atque inter sermonem historiamque medios,
ac tanto magis reliquos perficere cupiebat, quanto
4 frequentius hi lectitabantur. Mihi autem videtur
acerba semper et immatura mors eorum, qui im-

---

[1] Cf. Titinius Capito, who also admires Nero's victims and
writes their lives in verse, I. 17.

That has made you prick up your ears, but now you will have to beg me nicely for a long time before you hear the rest of the story—unless you come to Rome first to find it out, and see things for yourself as a change from reading about them.

V

To Novius Maximus

I HAVE just heard that Gaius Fannius is dead, news which has upset me very much. Not only did I love and admire his good taste and learning, but I could always rely on his judgement; for his natural intelligence had been trained by experience and he was always ready with an accurate opinion. It distresses me, too, that he had the misfortune to die without making a new will, when the old one leaves out some of his dearest friends and benefits people who had become his enemies.

This is hard but not unbearable; much more serious is the fact that he has left his finest work unfinished. Although his career at the bar took up most of his time, he was bringing out a history of the various fates of the people put to death or banished by Nero.[1] His accuracy in research and pure Latin style (which was midway between the discursive and historical) were evident in the three volumes he had already finished and he was all the more anxious to complete the series when he saw how eagerly the first books were read by a large public. Death always seems to me cruel and untimely when it comes to those who are engaged on some immortal work, for when people

mortale aliquid parant. Nam qui voluptatibus dediti
quasi in diem vivunt, vivendi causas cotidie finiunt;
qui vero posteros cogitant, et memoriam sui operibus
extendunt, his nulla mors non repentina est, ut quae
5 semper incohatum aliquid abrumpat. Gaius quidem
Fannius, quod accidit, multo ante praesensit. Visus
est sibi per nocturnam quietem iacere in lectulo suo
compositus in habitum studentis, habere ante se
scrinium (ita solebat); mox imaginatus est venisse
Neronem, in toro resedisse, prompsisse primum librum
quem de sceleribus eius ediderat, eumque ad extremum revolvisse; idem in secundo ac tertio fecisse,
6 tunc abisse. Expavit et sic interpretatus est, tamquam idem futurus esset scribendi finis, qui fuisset illi
7 legendi: et fuit idem. Quod me recordantem miseratio subit, quantum vigiliarum quantum laboris
exhauserit frustra. Occursant animo mea mortalitas
mea scripta. Nec dubito te quoque eadem cogitatione terreri, pro istis quae inter manus habes.
8 Proinde, dum suppetit vita, enitamur ut mors quam
paucissima quae abolere possit inveniat. Vale.

VI

C. Plinius Domitio Apollinari Suo S.

1 Amavi curam et sollicitudinem tuam, quod cum
audisses me aestate Tuscos meos petiturum, ne face-
2 rem suasisti, dum putas insalubres. Est sane gravis
et pestilens ora Tuscorum, quae per litus extenditur;

abandon themselves to pleasure and live from day to
day, their reasons for living are finished as each day
comes to an end; but for those who think of posterity
and seek to be remembered in their works, death is
always sudden as it always cuts short some unfinished
project. Fannius had in fact had a premonition long
ago of what has now happened. He dreamed in his
sleep one night that he was lying on his couch, dressed
and ready for work, and with his desk in front of him,
just as usual; then he fancied that Nero appeared,
sat down on the end of the bed, took up the first
volume Fannius had published about his crimes, and
read it through to the end; then he did the same to
the second and third volumes, after which he departed. Fannius was horrified, and inferred that his
writing would end at the point where Nero stopped
reading; and so it did. When I remember this, I am
filled with pity for all the wakeful hours he spent and
the trouble he took, all in vain; and I think of my
own mortality and what I have written. Doubtless
the same thought makes you equally fearful for the
work you have in hand, so while life lasts we must see
there shall be as little as possible for death to destroy.

VI

To Domitius Apollinaris

I am touched by your kind concern when you try to
dissuade me from my intention of staying in Tuscany
in summer. You think the place is unhealthy, but
while it is perfectly true that the Tuscan strip of sea-
coast is relaxing and dangerous to the health, my

sed hi procul a mari recesserunt, quin etiam Appen-
3 nino saluberrimo montium subiacent. Atque adeo
ut omnem pro me metum ponas, accipe temperiem
caeli regionis situm villae amoenitatem, quae et tibi
auditu et mihi relatu iucunda erunt.

4   Caelum est hieme frigidum et gelidum; myrtos
oleas quaeque alia adsiduo tepore[1] laetantur, asper-
natur ac respuit; laurum tamen patitur atque etiam
nitidissimam profert, interdum sed non saepius quam
5 sub urbe nostra necat. Aestatis mira clementia:
semper aer spiritu aliquo movetur, frequentius
6 tamen auras quam ventos habet. Hinc senes multi:
videas avos proavosque iam iuvenum, audias fabulas
veteres sermonesque maiorum, cumque veneris illo
7 putes alio te saeculo natum. Regionis forma pulcherrima. Imaginare amphitheatrum aliquod immensum, et quale sola rerum natura possit effingere.
Lata et diffusa planities montibus cingitur, montes
summa sui parte procera nemora et antiqua habent.
8 Frequens ibi et varia venatio. Inde caeduae silvae
cum ipso monte descendunt. Has inter pingues
terrenique colles (neque enim facile usquam saxum
etiam si quaeratur occurrit) planissimis campis

---

[1] tepore *M* (*sicut et Catanaeus*): tempore βγ.

---

[1] A large villa a few miles N. of Città di Castello (at Campo
di Santa Fiora) has been identified as P.'s by tiles stamped

property is some distance away from the sea, and is in fact at the very foot of the Apennines, which are considered the healthiest of mountains. So to rid you of all your fears on my account, let me tell you about the climate, the countryside, and the lovely situation of my house, which will be a pleasure alike for me to tell and you to hear.[1]

The climate in winter is cold and frosty, and so quite impossible for myrtles and olives and any other trees which will only flourish in a continuous mild temperature, but the laurel can grow and does very well; it is sometimes killed off by the cold, but not oftener than in the neighbourhood of Rome. The summer is wonderfully temperate, for there is always some movement of the air, more often a breeze than a real wind. Hence the number of elderly people living there—you can see the grandfathers and great-grandfathers of people who have reached their own manhood, and hear old stories and tales of the past, so that a visit here is like a return to another age.

The countryside is very beautiful. Picture to yourself a vast amphitheatre such as could only be a work of nature; the great spreading plain is ringed round by mountains, their summits crowned by ancient woods of tall trees, where there is a good deal of mixed hunting to be had.[2] Down the mountain slopes are timber woods interspersed with small hills of soil so rich that there is scarcely a rocky outcrop to be found; these hills are fully as fertile as the level plain

with his initials; it is in fact just over the border of Tuscany, in Umbria.

[2] Such as P. enjoys in I. 6.

fertilitate non cedunt, opimamque messem serius
9 tantum, sed non minus percoquunt. Sub his per
latus omne vineae porriguntur, unamque faciem longe
lateque contexunt; quarum a fine imoque quasi mar-
10 gine arbusta nascuntur. Prata inde campique,
campi quos non nisi ingentes boves et fortissima
aratra perfringunt: tantis glaebis tenacissimum
solum cum primum prosecatur adsurgit, ut nono
11 demum sulco perdometur. Prata florida et gemmea
trifolium aliasque herbas teneras semper et molles et
quasi novas alunt. Cuncta enim perennibus rivis
nutriuntur; sed ubi aquae plurimum, palus nulla,
quia devexa terra, quidquid liquoris accepit nec
12 absorbuit, effundit in Tiberim. Medios ille agros
secat navium patiens omnesque fruges devehit in
urbem, hieme dumtaxat et vere; aestate summit-
titur immensique fluminis nomen arenti alveo deserit,
13 autumno resumit. Magnam capies voluptatem, si
hunc regionis situm ex monte prospexeris. Neque
enim terras tibi sed formam aliquam ad eximiam
pulchritudinem pictam videberis cernere: ea varietate, ea descriptione, quocumque inciderint oculi,
reficientur.
14 Villa in colle imo sita prospicit quasi ex summo: ita
leviter et sensim clivo fallente consurgit, ut cum
ascendere te non putes, sentias ascendisse. A tergo
Appenninum, sed longius habet; accipit ab hoc auras

---

[1] Rome is 150 miles away, which seems a long way for trans-
port; but elsewhere P. refers to Tifernum as *oppidum*, so it is
unlikely to be the *urbs* mentioned here.

and yield quite as rich a harvest, though it ripens rather later in the season. Below them the vineyards spreading down every slope weave their uniform pattern far and wide, their lower limit bordered by a plantation of trees. Then come the meadows and cornfields, where the land can be broken up only by heavy oxen and the strongest ploughs, for the soil is so stiff that it is thrown up in great clods at the first ploughing and is not thoroughly broken until it has been gone over nine times. The meadows are bright with flowers, covered with trefoil and other delicate plants which always seem soft and fresh, for everything is fed by streams which never run dry; though the ground is not marshy where the water collects, because of its downward slope, so that any surplus water it cannot absorb is drained off into the river Tiber flowing through the fields. The river is navigable, so that all produce is conveyed to Rome[1] by boat, but only in winter and spring—in summer its level falls and its dry bed has to give up its claim to the title of a great river until the following autumn. It is a great pleasure to look down on the countryside from the mountain, for the view seems to be a painted scene of unusual beauty rather than a real landscape, and the harmony to be found in this variety refreshes the eye wherever it turns.

My house is on the lower slopes of a hill but commands as good a view as if it were higher up, for the ground rises so gradually that the slope is imperceptible, and you find yourself at the top without noticing the climb. Behind it is the Apennine range, though some way off, so that even on a still and cloudless day there is a breeze from the mountains, but one

quamlibet sereno et placido die, non tamen acres et
15 immodicas, sed spatio ipso lassas et infractas.   Magna
sui parte meridiem spectat aestivumque solem ab
hora sexta, hibernum aliquanto maturius quasi
invitat, in porticum latam et pro modo longam.[1]
Multa in hac membra, atrium etiam ex more veterum.
16 Ante porticum xystus in plurimas species distinctus
concisusque buxo; demissus inde pronusque pulvinus,
cui bestiarum effigies invicem adversas buxus in-
scripsit; acanthus in plano, mollis et paene dixerim
17 liquidus.   Ambit hunc ambulatio pressis varieque
tonsis viridibus inclusa; ab his gestatio in modum
circi, quae buxum multiformem humilesque et reten-
tas manu arbusculas circumit. Omnia maceria
muniuntur: hanc gradata buxus operit et subtrahit.
18 Pratum inde non minus natura quam superiora illa
arte visendum; campi deinde porro multaque alia
19 prata et arbusta.   A capite porticus triclinium excurrit; valvis xystum desinentem et protinus pratum
multumque ruris videt, fenestris hac latus xysti et
quod prosilit villae, hac adiacentis hippodromi nemus
20 comasque prospectat. Contra mediam fere porticum diaeta paulum recedit, cingit areolam, quae
quattuor platanis inumbratur.   Inter has marmoreo

---

[1] pro modo longam βγ: prominulam M.

which has had its force broken by the distance so that it is never cutting nor boisterous. It faces mainly south, and so from midday onwards in summer (a little earlier in winter) it seems to invite the sun into the colonnade. This is broad, and long in proportion, with several rooms opening out of it as well as the old-fashioned type of entrance hall.

In front of the colonnade is a terrace laid out with box hedges clipped into different shapes, from which a bank slopes down, also with figures of animals cut out of box facing each other on either side. On the level below there is a bed of acanthus so soft one could say it looks like water. All round is a path hedged by bushes which are trained and cut into different shapes, and then a drive, oval like a race-course, inside which are various box figures and clipped dwarf shrubs. The whole garden is enclosed by a dry-stone wall which is hidden from sight by a box hedge planted in tiers; outside is a meadow, as well worth seeing for its natural beauty as the formal garden I have described; then fields and many more meadows and woods.

From the end of the colonnade projects a dining-room: through its folding doors it looks on to the end of the terrace, the adjacent meadow, and the stretch of open country beyond, while from its windows on one side can be seen part of the terrace and the projecting wing of the house, on the other the tree-tops in the enclosure of the adjoining riding-ground. Almost opposite the middle of the colonnade is a suite of rooms set slightly back and round a small court shaded by four plane trees. In the centre a fountain plays in a marble basin, watering the plane

labro aqua exundat circumiectasque platanos et
21 subiecta platanis leni aspergine fovet. Est in hac
diaeta dormitorium cubiculum quod diem clamorem
sonum excludit, iunctaque ei [1] cotidiana amicorumque
cenatio: areolam illam, porticus alam [2] eademque
22 omnia quae porticus adspicit. Est et aliud cubiculum
a proxima platano viride et umbrosum, marmore
excultum podio tenus, nec cedit gratiae marmoris
ramos insidentesque ramis aves imitata pictura.
23 Fonticulus in hoc, in fonte crater; circa sipunculi
plures miscent iucundissimum murmur. In cornu
porticus amplissimum cubiculum triclinio occurrit;
aliis fenestris xystum, aliis despicit pratum, sed ante
piscinam, quae fenestris servit ac subiacet, strepitu
24 visuque iucunda; nam ex edito desiliens aqua suscepta marmore albescit. Idem cubiculum hieme
25 tepidissimum, quia plurimo sole perfunditur. Cohaeret hypocauston et, si dies nubilus, immisso vapore
solis vicem supplet. Inde apodyterium balinei laxum
et hilare excipit cella frigidaria, in qua baptisterium
amplum atque opacum. Si natare latius aut tepidius
velis, in area piscina est, in proximo puteus, ex quo
26 possis rursus adstringi, si paeniteat teporis. Frigi-
dariae cellae conectitur media, cui sol benignissime
praesto est; caldariae magis, prominet enim. In hac
tres descensiones, duae in sole, tertia a sole longius,
27 a luce non longius. Apodyterio superpositum est

---

[1] ei β: et Mγ.

[2] porticus alam *Ios. Martin*: -cum aliam *M*: -cus alia β: *om. γ.*

344

trees round it and the ground beneath them with its light spray. In this suite is a bedroom which no daylight, voice, nor sound can penetrate, and next to it an informal dining-room where I entertain my personal friends; it looks on to the small courtyard, a wing of the colonnade, and the view from the colonnade. There is also another bedroom, green and shady from the nearest plane tree, which has walls decorated with marble up to the ceiling and a fresco (which is no less attractive) of birds perched on the branches of trees. Here is a small fountain with a bowl surrounded by tiny jets which together make a lovely murmuring sound. At the corner of the colonnade is a large bedroom facing the dining-room; some windows look out on to the terrace, others on to the meadow, while just below the windows in front is an ornamental pool, a pleasure both to see and to hear, with its water falling from a height and foaming white when it strikes the marble. This room is very warm in winter since it is bathed in sunshine, and on a cloudy day hot steam from the adjacent furnace-room serves instead. Then you pass through a large and cheerful dressing-room, belonging to the bath, to the cooling-room, which contains a good-sized shady swimming-bath. If you want more space to swim or warmer water, there is a pool in the courtyard and a well near it to tone you up with cold water when you have had enough of the warm. Next to the cooling-room is a temperate one which enjoys the sun's kindly warmth, though not as much as the hot room which is built out in a bay. This contains three plunging-baths, two full in the sun and one in the shade, though still in the light. Over the dressing-room is

sphaeristerium, quod plura genera exercitationis
pluresque circulos capit. Non procul a balineo scalae,
quae in cryptoporticum ferunt prius ad diaetas tres.
Harum alia areolae illi, in qua platani quattuor, alia
prato, alia vineis imminet diversasque caeli partes ut

28 prospectus habet. In summa cryptoporticu cubiculum ex ipsa cryptoporticu excisum, quod hippodromum vineas montes intuetur. Iungitur cubiculum obvium soli, maxime hiberno. Hinc oritur
diaeta, quae villae hippodromum adnectit. Haec
facies, hic usus a fronte.

29 A latere aestiva cryptoporticus in edito posita, quae
non adspicere vineas sed tangere videtur. In media
triclinium saluberrimum adflatum ex Appenninis
vallibus recipit; post latissimis fenestris vineas,
valvis aeque vineas sed per cryptoporticum quasi

30 admittit. A latere triclinii quod fenestris caret,
scalae convivio utilia secretiore ambitu suggerunt.
In fine cubiculum, cui non minus iucundum prospectum cryptoporticus ipsa quam vineae praebent.
Subest cryptoporticus subterraneae similis; aestate
incluso frigore riget contentaque aere suo nec desi-

31 derat auras nec admittit. Post utramque cryptoporticum, unde triclinium desinit, incipit porticus
ante medium diem hiberna, inclinato die aestiva.
Hac adeuntur diaetae duae, quarum in altera cubi-

built the ball court, and this is large enough for
several sets of players to take different kinds of
exercise. Not far from the bath is a staircase leading
to three suites of rooms and then to a covered arcade.
One looks on to the small court with the four plane
trees, another on to the meadow, and the third faces
the vineyard and has an uninterrupted view across
the sky. The head of the arcade is divided off as a
bedroom, from which can be seen the riding-
ground, the vineyard, and the mountains. Next
to it is another room which has plenty of sun,
especially in winter, and then comes a suite which
connects the riding-ground with the house. That
is the appearance and lay-out of the front of the
house.

Down the side is a covered arcade for summer use
which is built on higher ground and seems not to look
down on but be actually touching the vineyard below;
half-way along is a dining-room which receives the
fresh breezes blowing down the Apennine valleys.
Its broad windows at the back look on to the vineyard, and so do its folding doors, but through the
arcade between, and along the side where there are
no windows, there is a private staircase which is
used for serving at dinner parties. At the far end is
a bedroom with a view of the arcade as pleasant as
that of the vineyard. Underneath runs a semi-
underground arcade which never loses its icy temperature in summer and is airy enough not to need
to admit the outside air. Next to both these
arcades begins an open one where the dining-room
ends, which is cool before noon but hot during the
later part of the day. It leads to two suites, one

cula quattuor, altera tria ut circumit sol aut sole
utuntur aut umbra.

32   Hanc dispositionem amoenitatemque tectorum
longe longeque praecedit hippodromus. Medius
patescit statimque intrantium oculis totus offertur,
platanis circumitur; illae hedera vestiuntur utque
summae suis ita imae alienis frondibus virent.
Hedera truncum et ramos pererrat vicinasque platanos transitu suo copulat. Has buxus interiacet;
exteriores buxos circumvenit laurus, umbraeque
33 platanorum suam confert. Rectus hic hippodromi
limes in extrema parte hemicyclio frangitur mutatque
faciem: cupressis ambitur et tegitur, densiore umbra
opacior nigriorque; interioribus circulis (sunt enim
34 plures) purissimum diem recipit. Inde etiam rosas
effert, umbrarumque frigus non ingrato sole distinguit.
Finito vario illo multiplicique curvamine recto limiti
redditur nec huic uni, nam viae plures intercedentibus
35 buxis dividuntur. Alibi pratulum, alibi ipsa buxus
intervenit in formas mille descripta, litteras interdum,
quae modo nomen domini dicunt modo artificis:
alternis metulae surgunt, alternis inserta sunt poma,
et in opere urbanissimo subita velut inlati ruris imitatio. Medium spatium brevioribus utrimque plat-
36 anis adornatur. Post has acanthus hinc inde lubricus
et flexuosus, deinde plures figurae pluraque nomina.

348

of four and the other of three bedrooms, which are alternately sunny or shady as the sun moves round.

The design and beauty of the buildings are greatly surpassed by the riding-ground. The centre is quite open so that the whole extent of the course can be seen as one enters. It is planted round with ivy-clad plane trees, green with their own leaves above, and below with the ivy which climbs over trunk and branch and links tree to tree as it spreads across them. Box shrubs grow between the plane trees, and outside there is a ring of laurel bushes which add their shade to that of the planes. Here the straight part of the course ends, curves round in a semicircle, and changes its appearance, becoming darker and more densely shaded by the cypress trees planted round to shelter it, whereas the inner circuits—for there are several—are in open sunshine; roses grow there and the cool shadow alternates with the pleasant warmth of the sun. At the end of the winding alleys of the rounded end of the course you return to the straight path, or rather paths, for there are several separated by intervening box hedges. Between the grass lawns here and there are box shrubs clipped into innumerable shapes, some being letters which spell the gardener's name or his master's; small obelisks of box alternate with fruit trees, and then suddenly in the midst of this ornamental scene is what looks like a piece of rural country planted there. The open space in the middle is set off by low plane trees planted on each side; farther off are acanthuses with their flexible glossy leaves, then more box figures and names.

349

In capite stibadium candido marmore vite protegitur;
vitem quattuor columellae Carystiae subeunt. Ex
stibadio aqua velut expressa cubantium pondere
sipunculis effluit, cavato lapide suscipitur, gracili
marmore continetur atque ita occulte temperatur, ut
37 impleat nec redundet. Gustatorium graviorque
cena margini imponitur, levior nauculorum et avium
figuris innatans circumit. Contra fons egerit aquam
et recipit; nam expulsa in altum in se cadit iunctisque hiatibus et absorbetur et tollitur. E regione
stibadii adversum cubiculum tantum stibadio reddit
38 ornatus, quantum accipit ab illo. Marmore splendet,
valvis in viridia prominet et exit, alia viridia superiori-
bus inferioribusque fenestris suspicit despicitque.
Mox zothecula refugit quasi in cubiculum idem
atque aliud. Lectus hic et undique fenestrae, et
39 tamen lumen obscurum umbra premente. Nam
laetissima vitis per omne tectum in culmen nititur et
ascendit. Non secus ibi quam in nemore iaceas,
imbrem tantum tamquam in nemore non sentias.
40 Hic quoque fons nascitur simulque subducitur. Sunt
locis pluribus disposita sedilia e marmore, quae
ambulatione fessos ut cubiculum ipsum iuvant.
Fonticuli sedilibus adiacent; per totum hippodromum inducti[1] strepunt rivi, et qua manus duxit

---

[1] inducti γ: inductis fistulis *F*: dulces *M*.

At the upper end of the course is a curved dining-seat of white marble, shaded by a vine trained over four slender pillars of Carystian marble. Water gushes out through pipes from under the seat as if pressed out by the weight of people sitting there, is caught in a stone cistern and then held in a finely-worked marble basin which is regulated by a hidden device so as to remain full without overflowing. The preliminaries and main dishes for dinner are placed on the edge of the basin, while the lighter ones float about in vessels shaped like birds or little boats. A fountain opposite plays and catches its water, throwing it high in the air so that it falls back into the basin, where it is played again at once through a jet connected with the inlet. Facing the seat is a bedroom which contributes as much beauty to the scene as it gains from its position. It is built of shining white marble, extended by folding doors which open straight out into greenery; its upper and lower windows all look out into more greenery above and below. A small alcove which is part of the room but separated from it contains a bed, and although it has windows in all its walls, the light inside is dimmed by the dense shade of a flourishing vine which climbs over the whole building up to the roof. There you can lie and imagine you are in a wood, but without the risk of rain. Here too a fountain rises and disappears underground, while here and there are marble chairs which anyone tired with walking appreciates as much as the building itself. By every chair is a tiny fountain, and throughout the riding-ground can be heard the sound of the streams directed into it, the flow of which can be controlled by hand to water one part of

sequuntur: his nunc illa viridia, nunc haec, interdum simul omnia lavantur.

41 Vitassem iam dudum ne viderer argutior, nisi proposuissem omnes angulos tecum epistula circum- ire. Neque enim verebar ne laboriosum esset legenti tibi, quod visenti non fuisset, praesertim cum inter- quiescere, si liberet, depositaque epistula quasi residere saepius posses. Praeterea indulsi amori meo; amo enim, quae maxima ex parte ipse incohavi

42 aut incohata percolui. In summa (cur enim non aperiam tibi vel iudicium meum vel errorem?) primum ego officium scriptoris existimo, titulum suum legat atque identidem interroget se quid coeperit scribere, sciatque si materiae immoratur non esse longum, longissimum si aliquid accersit atque attra-

43 hit. Vides quot versibus Homerus, quot Vergilius arma hic Aeneae Achillis ille describat; brevis tamen uterque est quia facit quod instituit. Vides ut Aratus minutissima etiam sidera consectetur et colligat; modum tamen servat. Non enim excursus

44 hic eius, sed opus ipsum est. Similiter nos ut " parva magnis," cum totam villam oculis tuis subicere cona- mur, si nihil inductum et quasi devium loquimur, non epistula quae describit sed villa quae describitur magna est.

352

the garden or another or sometimes the whole at once.

I should have been trying long ago not to say too much, had I not suggested that this letter should take you into every corner of the place. I don't imagine you will find it tiresome to read about a spot which could hardly tire you on a visit, especially as you have more opportunities if you want an occasional rest, and can take a seat, so to speak, by putting down the letter. Besides, I have been indulging the love I have for all the places I have largely laid out myself or where I have perfected an earlier design. In short (for why should I not state my opinion, right or wrong?) I think a writer's first duty is to read his title, to keep on asking himself what he set out to say, and to realize that he will not say too much if he sticks to his theme, though he certainly will if he brings in extraneous matter. You know the number of lines Homer and Virgil devote to their descriptions of the arms of Achilles and Aeneas:[1] yet neither passage seems long because both poets are carrying out their original intention. You see too how Aratus traces and tabulates the smallest stars,[2] but because this is his main subject and not a digression his work does not lack proportion. It is the same with me, if I may " compare small things with great." [3] I am trying to set my entire house before your eyes, so, if I introduce nothing irrelevant, it is the house I describe which is extensive, not the letter describing it.

---

[1] *Iliad* XVIII. 475 ff. and *Aeneid* VIII. 620 ff.

[2] In his astronomical poem, *Phaenomena*.

[3] Virgil, *Georgics* IV. 176.

Verum illuc unde coepi, ne secundum legem meam iure reprendar, si longior fuero in hoc in quod excessi. 45 Habes causas cur ego Tuscos meos Tusculanis Tiburtinis Praenestinisque praeponam. Nam super illa quae rettuli, altius ibi otium et pinguius eoque securius: nulla necessitas togae, nemo accersitor ex proximo, placida omnia et quiescentia, quod ipsum salubritati regionis ut purius caelum, ut aer liquidior 46 accedit. Ibi animo, ibi corpore maxime valeo. Nam studiis animum, venatu corpus exerceo. Mei quoque nusquam salubrius degunt; usque adhuc certe neminem ex iis quos eduxeram mecum, (venia sit dicto) ibi amisi. Di modo in posterum hoc mihi gaudium, hanc gloriam loco servent! Vale.

VII

C. PLINIUS CALVISIO RUFO SUO S.

1 NEC heredem institui nec praecipere posse rem publicam constat; Saturninus autem, qui nos reliquit heredes, quadrantem rei publicae nostrae, deinde pro quadrante praeceptionem quadringentorum milium dedit. Hoc si ius adspicias inritum, si defuncti

---

[1] In Latium (Frascati, Tivoli, Palestrina). These are fashionable places for a country seat; P. does not own property there himself.

[2] A town was still legally *persona incerta* and so incapable of inheriting, though Nerva had relaxed the law and there had been exceptions in the past: *e.g.* Massilia in 25 (Tac. *Ann.* IV.

But to return to my starting-point—for I shall justly be censured under my own law if I pursue this digression further—these are my reasons for preferring my home in Tuscany to one in Tusculum, Tibur, or Praeneste.[1] And I can add another reason: I can enjoy a profounder peace there, more comfort, and fewer cares; I need never wear a formal toga and there are no neighbours to disturb me; everywhere there is peace and quiet, which adds as much to the healthiness of the place as the clear sky and pure air. There I enjoy the best of health, both mental and physical, for I keep my mind in training with work and my body with hunting. My servants too are healthier here than anywhere else; up to the present I have not lost a single one of those I brought here with me—may I be forgiven for saying so, and may the gods continue to make this the pride of the place and a joy to me.

VII

To Calvisius Rufus

It is well known that a corporation cannot be made heir to an estate nor receive a preliminary legacy,[2] but Saturninus, who has made me his heir, left a fourth part of his estate to our native town of Comum, and later changed this to a preliminary legacy of 400,000 sesterces. This is null and void from the legal point of view, but clearly valid if one looks to

43). *Praeceptio* was a form devised to enable a testator to leave a specific object to an heir, as normally an inheritance was divided between heirs on a cost evaluation.

2 voluntatem ratum et firmum est. Mihi autem defuncti voluntas (vereor quam in partem iuris consulti quod sum dicturus accipiant) antiquior iure est, utique in eo quod ad communem patriam voluit per-
3 venire. An cui de meo sestertium sedecies contuli, huic quadringentorum milium paulo amplius tertiam partem ex adventicio denegem? Scio te quoque a iudicio meo non abhorrere, cum eandem rem publicam
4 ut civis optimus diligas. Velim ergo, cum proxime decuriones contrahentur, quid sit iuris indices, parce tamen et modeste; deinde subiungas nos quadringenta milia offerre, sicut praeceperit Saturninus. Illius hoc munus, illius liberalitas; nostrum tantum
5 obsequium vocetur. Haec ego scribere publice supersedi. primum quod memineram pro necessitudine amicitiae nostrae, pro facultate prudentiae tuae et debere te et posse perinde meis ac tuis partibus fungi; deinde quia verebar ne modum, quem tibi in sermone custodire facile est, tenuisse in epistula non viderer.
6 Nam sermonem vultus gestus vox ipsa moderatur, epistula omnibus commendationibus destituta malignitati interpretantium exponitur. Vale.

VIII

C. Plinius Titinio Capitoni Suo S.

1 Suades ut historiam scribam, et suades non solus: multi hoc me saepe monuerunt et ego volo, non quia

---

¹ For P.'s benefactions to Comum, see Index, under his name; for his view of equity compare II. 16 and IV. 10.

the intention of the deceased. I shudder to think how the legal experts will receive what I am going to say, but this intention carries more weight with me than the law, at any rate as regards the sum Saturninus intended to come to our native town.[1] I have given 1,600,000 sesterces to the town out of my own money, so surely I ought not to grudge it this 400,000, little more than a third of my unexpected inheritance. I am sure you will share my opinion, for you love our birthplace as a loyal citizen should. So next time the town Council meets, I should be grateful if you would make a statement, quite simply and shortly, on the legal question; then add that I am making this offer of 400,000 sesterces in accordance with Saturninus's instructions. The gift and the generosity are his—I can only be said to comply with his wishes.

I have refrained from writing officially to the Council for two reasons: I remembered that our close friendship obliges you to act for me as you would for yourself, just as your wise judgement enables you to do so, and I was afraid that a letter might seem lacking in the restraint which you will have no difficulty in keeping in a speech. There the tone is set by the expression, gestures and voice of the speaker, whereas a letter lacks such recommendations and is liable to wilful misinterpretation.

VIII

To TITINIUS CAPITO

YOUR suggestion that I should write history has often been made, for a good many people have given

commode facturum esse confidam (id enim temere
credas nisi expertus), sed quia mihi pulchrum in
primis videtur non pati occidere, quibus aeternitas
debeatur, aliorumque famam cum sua extendere.

2 Me autem nihil aeque ac diuturnitatis amor et cupido
sollicitat, res homine dignissima, eo praesertim qui
nullius sibi conscius culpae posteritatis memoriam

3 non reformidet. Itaque diebus ac noctibus cogito,
si " qua me quoque possim tollere humo "; id enim
voto meo sufficit, illud supra votum " victorque virum
volitare per ora "; " quamquam o—": sed hoc satis
est, quod prope sola historia polliceri videtur.

4 Orationi enim et carmini parva gratia, nisi eloquentia
est summa: historia quoquo modo scripta delectat.
Sunt enim homines natura curiosi, et quamlibet
nuda rerum cognitione capiuntur, ut qui sermunculis
etiam fabellisque ducantur. Me vero ad hoc studium

5 impellit domesticum quoque exemplum. Avunculus
meus idemque per adoptionem pater historias et
quidem religiosissime scripsit. Invenio autem apud
sapientes honestissimum esse maiorum vestigia
sequi, si modo recto itinere praecesserint. Cur ergo

6 cunctor? Egi magnas et graves causas. Has,
etiamsi mihi tenuis ex iis spes, destino retractare, ne
tantus ille labor meus, nisi hoc quod reliquum est

7 studii addidero, mecum pariter intercidat. Nam si

Virgil, *Georgics* III. 8–9, an echo of Ennius's epitaph.
[2] *Aeneid*, V. 195.   [3] See his bibliography in III. 5.

me the same advice. I like the idea: not that I feel
at all sure of being successful—it would be rash in an
amateur—but because the saving of those who
deserve immortality from sinking into oblivion, and
spreading the fame of others along with one's own,
seem to me a particularly splendid achievement.
Nothing attracts me so much as that love and longing
for a lasting name, man's worthiest aspiration,
especially in one who is aware that there is nothing in
him to blame and so has no fear if he is to be remembered by posterity. So day and night I wonder if
" I too may rise from earth "; that would answer my
prayer, for " to hover in triumph on the lips of man "[1]
is too much to hope. " Yet O if I could——"[2] but
I must rest content with what history alone seems
able to guarantee. Oratory and poetry win small
favour unless they reach the highest standard of
eloquence, but history cannot fail to give pleasure
however it is presented. Humanity is naturally in-
quisitive, and so factual information, plain and unadorned, has its attraction for anyone who can enjoy
small talk and anecdote.

In my case family precedent is an additional
incentive to work of this kind. My uncle, who was
also my father by adoption, was a historian of scrupulous accuracy,[3] and I find in the philosophers that it is
an excellent thing to follow in the footsteps of one's
forbears, provided that they trod an honest path.
Why then do I delay? I have acted in certain important and complicated cases, and I intend to revise my
speeches (without building too many hopes on them)
so that all the work I put into them will not perish
with me for want of this last attention. For, if one

359

rationem posteritatis habeas, quidquid non est peractum, pro non incohato est. Dices: " Potes simul
et rescribere actiones et componere historiam."
Utinam! sed utrumque tam magnum est, ut abunde
8 sit alterum efficere. Unodevicensimo aetatis anno
dicere in foro coepi, et nunc demum quid praestare
debeat orator, adhuc tamen per caliginem video.
9 Quid si huic oneri novum accesserit? Habet quidem
oratio et historia multa communia, sed plura diversa
in his ipsis, quae communia videntur. Narrat illa
narrat haec, sed aliter: huic pleraque humilia et
sordida et ex medio petita, illi omnia recondita splen-
10 dida excelsa conveniunt; hanc saepius ossa musculi
nervi, illam tori quidam et quasi iubae decent; haec
vel maxime vi amaritudine instantia, illa tractu et
suavitate atque etiam dulcedine placet; postremo alia
11 verba alius sonus alia constructio. Nam plurimum
refert, ut Thucydides ait, κτῆμα sit an ἀγώνισμα;
quorum alterum oratio, alterum historia est. His ex
causis non adducor ut duo dissimilia et hoc ipso diversa, quo[1] maxima, confundam misceamque, ne tanta
quasi colluvione turbatus ibi faciam quod hic debeo;
ideoque interim veniam, ut ne a meis verbis recedam,
12 advocandi peto. Tu tamen iam nunc cogita quae

[1] quo M: quod γ.

---

[1] Quintilian draws the same distinction: history lies midway between oratory and poetry (*Inst. Orat.* X. i. 31 ff.).

looks to posterity, anything left unfinished might as well not have been begun. You will tell me that I can rewrite my speeches and write history at the same time. I wish I could, but both are such great undertakings that it will be more than enough to carry out one. I was eighteen when I began my career at the bar, and it is only now, and still only dimly, that I begin to realize the true qualities of the orator. What would happen if I shouldered a new burden in addition to the old? It is true that oratory and history have much in common, but they differ in many of the points where they seem alike. Both employ narrative, but with a difference: oratory deals largely with the humble and trivial incidents of everyday life, history is concerned with profound truths and the glory of great deeds. The bare bones of narrative and a nervous energy often distinguish the one, a fullness and a certain freedom of style the other. Oratory succeeds by its vigour and severity of attack, history by the ease and grace with which it develops its theme. Finally, they differ in vocabulary, rhythm and period-structure,[1] for, as Thucydides says,[2] there is all the difference between a " lasting possession " and a " prize essay ": the former is history, the latter oratory. For these reasons I am not inclined to blend and mix two dissimilar subjects which are fundamentally opposed in the very quality to which each owes its prominence, lest I am swept away in the resultant confusion and treat one in the manner proper to the other. And so, to keep to my own language, for the time being I apply for an adjournment.

[2] Thucydides, 1. 22, in a rather different sense.

potissimum tempora adgrediar. Vetera et scripta
aliis? Parata inquisitio, sed onerosa collatio. In-
13 tacta et nova? Graves offensae levis gratia. Nam
praeter id, quod in tantis vitiis hominum plura cul-
panda sunt quam laudanda, tum si laudaveris parcus,
si culpaveris nimius fuisse dicaris, quamvis illud
14 plenissime, hoc restrictissime feceris. Sed haec me
non retardant; est enim mihi pro fide satis animi:
illud peto praesternas ad quod hortaris, eligasque
materiam, ne mihi iam scribere parato alia rursus
cunctationis et morae iusta ratio nascatur. Vale.

IX

C. Plinius Sempronio Rufo Suo S.

1 Descenderam in basilicam Iuliam, auditurus
quibus proxima comperendinatione respondere debe-
2 bam. Sedebant iudices, decemviri venerant, obversabantur advocati, silentium longum; tandem a
praetore nuntius. Dimittuntur centumviri, eximitur
dies me gaudente, qui numquam ita paratus sum ut
3 non mora laeter. Causa dilationis Nepos praetor, qui
legibus quaerit. Proposuerat breve edictum, ad-

---

[1] Cf. IX. 27 and Tacitus, *Ann*, IV. 33 and *Hist*. I. I. P.
seems to imply that Tacitus had not yet written on the Flavian
period in the *Histories*.

[2] The *decemviri stlitibus iudicandis* had presided over the
four panels of the Centumviral Court since the time of Augustus
(Suetonius, *Aug*. 36).

You however, can, be considering now what period of history I am to treat. Is it to be ancient history which has had its historians? The material is there, but it will be a great labour to assemble it. Or shall it be recent times which no one has handled? I shall receive small thanks and give serious offence,[1] for beside the fact that there is much more to censure than to praise in the serious vices of the present day, such praise as one gives, however generous, is considered grudging, and however restrained one's blame it is said to be excessive. But I have enough courage of my convictions not to be deterred by such considerations. All I ask of you is to prepare the way for what you want me to do and to choose me a subject; or another good reason for delay and hesitation may arise when I am ready to start at last.

IX

To SEMPRONIUS RUFUS

I HAD gone down to the Basilica Julia to listen to the speeches in a case where I had to appear for the defence at the next hearing. The court was seated, the presiding magistrates[2] had arrived and counsel on both sides were coming and going; then there was a long silence, broken at last by a message from the praetor. The court adjourned and the case was suspended, much to my delight, for I am never so well prepared as not to be glad of a delay. The reason for this one was a short edict published by the praetor Nepos, who is dealing with the case, in which he warned both prosecution and defence that he would

monebat accusatores, admonebat reos exsecuturum se
4 quae senatus consulto continerentur. Suberat edicto
senatus consultum: hoc omnes qui quid negotii
haberent iurare prius quam agerent iubebantur, nihil
se ob advocationem cuiquam dedisse promisisse
cavisse. His enim verbis ac mille praeterea et
venire advocationes et emi vetabantur; peractis
tamen negotiis permittebatur pecuniam dumtaxat
5 decem milium dare. Hoc facto Nepotis commotus
praetor qui centumviralibus praesidet, deliberaturus
an sequeretur exemplum, inopinatum nobis otium
6 dedit. Interim tota civitate Nepotis edictum carpi-
tur laudatur. Multi: " Invenimus, qui curva cor-
rigeret! Quid? ante hunc praetores non fuerunt?
quis autem hic est, qui emendet publicos mores?'
Alii contra: "Rectissime fecit; initurus magistratum
iura cognovit, senatus consulta legit, reprimit foe-
dissimas pactiones, rem pulcherrimam turpissime
7 venire non patitur." Tales ubique sermones, qui
tamen alterutram in partem ex eventu praevale-
bunt. Est omnino iniquum, sed usu receptum, quod
honesta consilia vel turpia, prout male aut prospere
cedunt, ita vel probantur vel reprehenduntur. Inde
plerumque eadem facta modo diligentiae modo
vanitatis, modo libertatis modo furoris nomen acci-
piunt. Vale.

---

[1] The *praetor hastarius* who exercised general supervision
over the court. Nepos may be primarily concerned with
criminal cases, but evidently interested in the workings of the
civil courts.

strictly enforce all the provisions of the senatorial decree appended to the edict: " All persons bringing cases before the court are hereby required to state on oath before their case is heard that they have neither paid, promised, nor guaranteed any sum to any person for his legal assistance." By these words, and a great many more, the buying and selling of counsels' services were expressly forbidden; but permission was given, after a case was settled, for clients to give their counsel a sum not exceeding 10,000 sesterces. This action of Nepos's had raised doubts in the mind of the president of the Centum-viral Court,[1] and, in order to consider whether to follow his example, he gave us our unexpected holiday.

Meanwhile the edict is the subject of praise or criticism throughout the city. Many people are saying that " We have found someone to set the crooked straight, but were there no praetors before him? Who is he to correct public morals?" The other party says that Nepos has done well; he has learnt the law before taking up office, reads the Senate's decrees, puts a check on disgraceful bargaining, and will not allow a noble profession to sell its services in this scandalous way. So everyone talks, but events will have to show which view will prevail. Right and wrong intentions are praised and blamed only in so far as their results are good or bad—that is the generally accepted practice, though it is none the less unfair. Hence it generally happens that the self-same actions are variously ascribed to zeal, conceit, independence, or folly.

THE LETTERS OF PLINY

X

C. Plinius Suetonio Tranquillo Suo S.

1 Libera tandem hendecasyllaborum meorum fidem,
qui scripta tua communibus amicis spoponderunt.
Adpellantur cotidie, efflagitantur, ac iam periculum
est ne cogantur ad exhibendum formulam accipere.
2 Sum et ipse in edendo haesitator, tu tamen meam
quoque cunctationem tarditatemque vicisti.
Proinde aut rumpe iam moras aut cave ne eosdem istos
libellos, quos tibi hendecasyllabi nostri blanditiis
elicere non possunt, convicio scazontes extorqueant.
3 Perfectum opus absolutumque est, nec iam splendes-
cit lima sed atteritur. Patere me videre titulum
tuum, patere audire describi legi venire volumina
Tranquilli mei. Aequum est nos in amore tam mutuo
eandem percipere ex te voluptatem, qua tu per-
frueris ex nobis. Vale.

XI

C. Plinius Calpurnio Fabato Prosocero Suo S.

1 Recepi litteras tuas ex quibus cognovi speciosissi-
mam te porticum sub tuo filiique tui nomine dedicasse,
sequenti die in portarum ornatum pecuniam promisisse, ut initium novae liberalitatis esset consum-
2 matio prioris. Gaudeo primum tua gloria, cuius ad

---

¹ This book might be the projected *De viris illustribus* or a
lost volume of verse.

X

To Suetonius Tranquillus

Do please release my hendecasyllables from their promise—they were guarantors to our friends for the appearance of your work,[1] and every day brings in some new request and demand; so they now run the risk of being served with a writ to produce it. I know I am very slow to publish my own work, but *you* outdo even my doubts and hesitations. So bestir yourself, or else beware lest I drag those books out of you by the fury of my scazons,[2] since my hendecasyllables failed to entice them with honeyed words! The work is already finished and perfect; revision will not give it further polish but only dull its freshness. Please let me see your name published and hear that my friend's books are being copied, read and sold. In view of our warm friendship, it is only fair that you should let me have the same pleasure from you as you enjoy in me.

XI

To Calpurnius Fabatus, his Wife's Grandfather

Thank you for your letter telling me about your dedication of a handsome public colonnade in your own name and that of your son, followed on the next day by your promise of a sum of money for the decoration of the doors, thus making your second act of generosity the consummation of the first. I am glad

[2] The scazon was regularly used for invective. Quintilian makes the same joke (*ad Tryphonem* 1.).

me pars aliqua pro necessitudine nostra redundat;
deinde quod memoriam soceri mei pulcherrimis
operibus video proferri; postremo quod patria nostra
florescit, quam mihi a quocumque excoli iucundum,
3 a te vero laetissimum est. Quod superest, deos
precor ut animum istum tibi, animo isti tempus
quam longissimum tribuant. Nam liquet mihi
futurum ut peracto quod proxime promisisti, incohes
aliud. Nescit enim semel incitata liberalitas stare,
cuius pulchritudinem usus ipse commendat. Vale.

XII

C. PLINIUS TERENTIO SCAURO SUO S.

1 RECITATURUS oratiunculam quam publicare cogito,
advocavi aliquos ut vererer, paucos ut verum audirem.
Nam mihi duplex ratio recitandi, una ut sollicitudine
intendar, altera ut admonear, si quid forte me ut
2 meum fallit. Tuli quod petebam: inveni qui mihi
copiam consilii sui facerent, ipse praeterea quaedam
emendanda adnotavi. Emendavi librum, quem misi
3 tibi. Materiam ex titulo cognosces, cetera liber
explicabit, quem iam nunc oportet ita consuescere,
4 ut sine praefatione intellegatur. Tu velim quid de

of this, primarily on account of your own reputation,
from which I have some reflected glory through my
connexion with you; I am glad too to see my father-
in-law's memory perpetuated in such a fine monument, and, finally, the enrichment of our native place
is a source of pleasure to me whoever it is who honours
her, but especially so when that person is you.

It remains for me to pray that the gods will
continue to grant you this generous spirit and as
many years as possible in which to employ it, for I am
sure that once you have carried out your recent
undertaking you will begin on another: generosity
cannot stand still when once set in motion, and its
beauty shines out the more it is exercised.

XII

To Terentius Scaurus

I invited some friends to hear me read a short
speech which I am thinking of publishing, just
enough of an audience to make me nervous, but not
a large one, as I wanted to hear the truth. I have
in fact a double motive for these readings, hoping
to gain both a stimulus by my anxiety to succeed and
criticism where any faults have escaped my notice
through being my own. Here I succeeded, and found
people to give me the benefit of their advice; I also
noticed for myself some corrections to be made, and,
now that these are done, I am sending you the result.
The title will tell you the subject and the text will
explain everything else, for it ought to be familiar
enough by now to be intelligible without any

universo, quid de partibus sentias, scribas mihi.   Ero enim vel cautior in continendo vel constantior in edendo, si huc vel illuc auctoritas tua accesserit. Vale.

XIII

C. Plinius Iulio Valeriano Suo S.

1   Et tu rogas et ego promisi si rogasses, scripturum me tibi quem habuisset eventum postulatio Nepotis circa Tuscilium Nominatum.   Inductus est Nominatus; egit ipse pro se nullo accusante.   Nam legati Vicetinorum non modo non presserunt eum verum 2 etiam sublevaverunt.   Summa defensionis, non fidem sibi in advocatione sed constantiam defuisse; descendisse ut acturum, atque etiam in curia visum, deinde sermonibus amicorum perterritum recessisse; monitum enim ne desiderio senatoris, non iam quasi de nundinis sed quasi de gratia fama dignitate certantis, tam pertinaciter praesertim in senatu repugnaret, alioqui maiorem invidiam quam proxime passurus. 3 Erat sane prius, a paucis tamen, acclamatum exeunti. Subiunxit preces multumque lacrimarum; quin etiam tota actione homo in dicendo exercitatus

---

[1] See V. 4.
[2] Bellicius Sollers; cf. V. 4. 1.

introduction. I should be grateful for your written opinion on the speech as a whole and in detail, for I shall be the more careful to withhold it or determined to publish, whichever way you pronounce judgement.

XIII

To Julius Valerianus

I have just had your request for the result of the summons issued by Nepos to Tuscilius Nominatus,[1] which I promised I would let you know if you asked for it.

Nominatus came before the court and made his own defence. No one brought any charge, for the representatives of Vicetia did not press theirs—they were in fact now ready to defend him. His line of defence was that it was his courage not his sense of duty which had failed him when he came to make his speech. He had arrived with good intentions and had even been seen in the Senate, but then he had been alarmed by talking to his friends and had left the court. They had advised him not to be too persistent in opposing the wishes of a senator[2] (and especially in the Senate) who was no longer fighting the case on account of the proposed market, but because his influence, reputation and position were at stake; otherwise Nominatus would make himself more unpopular than on the last occasion. (He had in fact received some applause as he went out, but not from many people.) He went on to weep and beg for leniency, and indeed, throughout his speech, he was careful to give the impression that

operam dedit, ut deprecari magis (id enim et favor-
4 abilius et tutius) quam defendi videretur.   Absolutus
est sententia designati consulis Afrani Dextri, cuius
haec summa: melius quidem Nominatum fuisse facturum, si causam Vicetinorum eodem animo quo susceperat pertulisset; quia tamen in hoc genus culpae
non fraude incidisset, nihilque dignum animadversione
admisisse convinceretur, liberandum, ita ut Vicetinis
5 quod acceperat redderet.   Adsenserunt omnes praeter
Fabium [1] Aprum.   Is interdicendum ei advocationi-
bus in quinquennium censuit, et quamvis neminem
auctoritate traxisset, constanter in sententia mansit;
quin etiam Dextrum, qui primus diversum censuerat,
prolata lege de senatu habendo iurare coegit e re
6 publica esse quod censuisset.   Cui quamquam legiti-
mae postulationi a quibusdam reclamatum est; exprobrare enim censenti ambitionem videbatur.   Sed
prius quam sententiae dicerentur, Nigrinus tribunus
plebis recitavit libellum disertum et gravem, quo
questus est venire advocationes, venire etiam prae-
varicationes, in lites coiri, et gloriae loco poni ex
7 spoliis civium magnos et statos reditus.   Recitavit
capita legum, admonuit senatus consultorum, in fine
dixit petendum ab optimo principe, ut quia leges,
quia senatus consulta contemnerentur, ipse tantis
8 vitiis mederetur.   Pauci dies, et liber principis

---

[1] Fabium (Flavium *a*) Aprum is *Ma*: lacrumis γ.

---

[1] The Augustan law of 9 B.C. Cf. VIII. 14. 19.
[2] An oath which could regularly be exacted in times of crisis. See Livy, XXX. 40. 12; Tacitus, *Ann.* IV. 31.
[3] C. Avidius Nigrinus (ii); see Index.

he was not defending his conduct but appealing for mercy; as a practised speaker he knew that this was safer and more likely to win favour.

He was acquitted on a proposal of the consul-elect, Afranius Dexter, to the effect that though Nominatus would have done better to complete the case for the Vicetians in the same spirit as he had undertaken it, his negligence was without fraudulent intent and no punishable offence could be proved against him. He should then be discharged on condition that he returned his fee to the Vicetians. Everyone agreed except Fabius Aper, who proposed that Nominatus should be forbidden to conduct a case for five years, and he stuck stoutly to his opinion although he could not persuade anyone to support him. He even quoted the statute on senatorial procedure,[1] and insisted that Dexter (who had been the first to put forward the contrary motion) should state on oath that his proposal was in the interests of the State.[2] His demand was in order, but it met with a good deal of protest, as it appeared to be accusing Dexter of corrupt practice. But before a vote could be taken, Nigrinus,[3] the tribune of the people, read out a well-phrased statement of great importance. In this he complained that counsel sold their services, faked lawsuits for money, settled them by collusion, and made a boast of the large regular incomes to be made by robbery of their fellow-citizens. He quoted the relevant paragraphs of the law, reminded the Senate of its decrees, and ended by saying that our noble Emperor should be asked to remedy these serious evils himself, since the law and the Senate's decrees were fallen into contempt. After a few days the

severus et tamen moderatus: leges ipsum; est in publicis actis. Quam me iuvat, quod in causis agendis non modo pactione dono munere verum etiam
9 xeniis semper abstinui! Oportet quidem, quae sunt inhonesta, non quasi inlicita sed quasi pudenda vitare; iucundum tamen si prohiberi publice videas, quod numquam tibi ipse permiseris. Erit fortasse, immo non dubie, huius propositi mei et minor laus et obscurior fama, cum omnes ex necessitate facient
10 quod ego sponte faciebam. Interim fruor voluptate, cum alii divinum me, alii meis rapinis meae avaritiae occursum per ludum ac iocum dictitant. Vale.

XIV

C. PLINIUS PONTIO ALLIFANO SUO S.

1 SECESSERAM in municipium, cum mihi nuntiatum est Cornutum Tertullum accepisse Aemiliae viae curam.
2 Exprimere non possum, quanto sim gaudio adfectus, et ipsius et meo nomine: ipsius quod, sit licet (sicut est) ab omni ambitione longe remotus, debet tamen ei iucundus honor esse ultro datus, meo quod aliquanto magis me delectat mandatum mihi officium, postquam
3 par Cornuto datum video. Neque enim augeri dignitate quam aequari bonis gratius. Cornuto autem quid melius, quid sanctius, quid in omni genere

---

[1] The *acta diurna*; cf. VII. 33. 3.
[2] The *Via Aemilia* led to N. Italy, Milan and Como.
[3] As *curator alvei Tiberis et riparum et cloacarum urbis.* See Appendix A. 1. (S. 230).

Emperor issued a decree, which was firm but moderate in tone. It is published in the official records,[1] so you can read it.

How glad I am that I have always kept clear of any contracts, presents, remunerations, or even small gifts for my conduct of cases! It is true that one ought to shun dishonesty as a shameful thing, not because it is illegal; but, even so, it is a pleasure to find an official ban on a practice one would never have permitted oneself. Perhaps I shall lose some of the credit and reputation I won from my resolve—in fact I am sure to do so, when everyone is compelled to behave as I did of my own free will—but meanwhile I am enjoying my friends' teasing, when they hail me as a prophet or pretend that this measure is directed against my own robberies and greed.

XIV

To Pontius Allifanus

I HAD left Rome for a visit to my native town when news reached me that Cornutus Tertullus had accepted the office of Curator of the Aemilian Road.[2] Words cannot express my delight, for both our sakes; for although he is known to be far removed from any feelings of ambition, the unsolicited offer of this post cannot fail to give him pleasure, and I am better pleased with the duties assigned to me [3] now that I see Cornutus in a similar position. To be in the same rank as a good citizen is as welcome as a promotion. And is there anyone who can equal Cornutus in merit and integrity, anyone who is a more perfect example

375

laudis ad exemplar antiquitatis expressius? quod
mihi cognitum est non fama, qua alioqui optima et
meritissima fruitur, sed longis magnisque experi-
4 mentis. Una diligimus, una dileximus omnes fere
quos aetas nostra in utroque sexu aemulandos tulit;
quae societas amicitiarum artissima nos familiaritate
5 coniunxit. Accessit vinculum necessitudinis publicae; idem enim mihi, ut scis, collega quasi voto
petitus in praefectura aerarii fuit, fuit et in consulatu.
Tum ego qui vir et quantus esset altissime inspexi,
cum sequerer ut magistrum, ut parentem vererer,
quod non tam aetatis maturitate quam vitae mere-
6 batur. His ex causis ut illi sic mihi gratulor, nec
privatim magis quam publice, quod tandem homines
non ad pericula ut prius verum ad honores virtute
perveniunt.
7 In infinitum epistulam extendam, si gaudio meo
indulgeam. Praevertor ad ea, quae me agentem hic
8 nuntius deprehendit. Eram cum prosocero meo,
eram cum amita uxoris, eram cum amicis diu desi-
deratis, circumibam agellos, audiebam multum rusticarum querellarum, rationes legebam invitus et cursim (aliis enim chartis, aliis sum litteris initiatus),
9 coeperam etiam itineri me praeparare. Nam inclu-
dor angustiis commeatus, eoque ipso, quod delegatum Cornuto audio officium, mei admoneor. Cupio
te quoque sub idem tempus Campania tua remittat,
ne quis cum in urbem rediero, contubernio nostro
dies pereat. Vale.

---

¹ See *Pan.* 91. 1. Tertullus was about seventeen years older
than P.

of the ancient virtues in every way? His character is
known to me not from the splendid reputation he so
justly deserves, but from the close personal experience of many years. Together we have admired and
still admire almost every man or woman who is an
example to our generation, and this association has
been a close bond of intimacy between us. Another
link was forged in our public relations; as you know,
Cornutus was my colleague as a Treasury official and
as consul,[1] as if in answer to my prayers. It was then
that I knew him to the full for the great man he is;
I followed him as my teacher and honoured him as a
parent as he deserved, for his was the ripe wisdom not
of years but of experience. For these reasons I congratulate myself no less than him, for public as well
as personal considerations. Now at last men's merits
bring them official recognition instead of the dangers
of the past.

I could let my letter run on indefinitely to give free
expression to my joy, but I must turn to what I was
doing when the news reached me. I was staying
with my wife's grandfather and aunt, meeting friends
I had long wished to see; I was going the round of my
few acres, hearing the peasants' many complaints and
looking over the accounts—unwillingly and super-
ficially I must admit, for I am devoted to literary
documents of a very different order. I had also begun
to make preparations for my return, for I am restricted
by the shortness of my leave, especially now that the
news of Cornutus's duties is a reminder of my own.
I trust that your Campania will let you return about
the same time, so that I shall not lose a day of your
company once I am back in Rome.

THE LETTERS OF PLINY

XV

C. Plinius Arrio Antonino Suo S.

1 Cum versus tuos aemulor, tum maxime quam sint
boni experior. Ut enim pictores pulchram absolu-
tamque faciem raro nisi in peius effingunt, ita ego ab
2 hoc archetypo labor et decido. Quo magis hortor,
ut quam plurima proferas, quae imitari omnes con-
cupiscant, nemo aut paucissimi possint. Vale.

XVI

C. Plinius Aefulano Marcellino Suo S.

1 Tristissimus haec tibi scribo, Fundani nostri filia
minore defuncta. Qua puella nihil umquam festivius
amabilius, nec modo longiore vita sed prope immortali-
2 tate dignius vidi. Nondum annos xiiii [1] impleverat,
et iam illi anilis prudentia, matronalis gravitas erat
et tamen suavitas puellaris cum virginali verecundia.
3 Ut illa patris cervicibus inhaerebat! ut nos amicos
paternos et amanter et modeste complectebatur! ut
nutrices, ut paedagogos, ut praeceptores pro suo
quemque officio diligebat! quam studiose, quam in-
tellegenter lectitabat! ut parce custoditeque lude-
bat! Qua illa temperantia, qua patientia, qua etiam
4 constantia novissimam valetudinem tulit! Medicis

[1] xiiii *Mγ*: xiii *ILS* 1030.

[1] C. Minicius Fundanus. See IV. 15 and Index.

378

XV

To Arrius Antoninus

It is only when I try to imitate your verse that I fully realize its excellence, for my halting efforts fall short of the original just as an artist's copy can never be more than a poor version of a wholly beautiful face. That is why I urge you all the more to produce as much as possible for all of us to try to emulate even though none or very few will be successful.

XVI

To Aefulanus Marcellinus

I am writing to you in great distress: our friend Fundanus[1] has lost his younger daughter. I never saw a girl so gay and lovable, so deserving of a longer life or even a life to last for ever. She had not yet reached the age of fourteen,[2] and yet she combined the wisdom of age and dignity of womanhood with the sweetness and modesty of youth and innocence. She would cling to her father's neck, and embrace us, his friends, with modest affection; she loved her nurses, her attendants and her teachers, each one for the service given her; she applied herself intelligently to her books and was moderate and restrained in her play. She bore her last illness with patient resignation and, indeed, with courage; she obeyed

[2] Minicia Marcella. Her age is given in ILS 1030 as 12 years 11 months and 7 days.

obsequebatur, sororem patrem adhortabatur ipsamque se destitutam corporis viribus vigore animi sus-
5 tinebat.   Duravit hic illi usque ad extremum, nec aut
spatio valetudinis aut metu mortis infractus est, quo
plures gravioresque nobis causas relinqueret et
6 desiderii et doloris.   O triste plane acerbumque funus!
o morte ipsa mortis tempus indignius! iam destinata
erat egregio iuveni, iam electus nuptiarum dies, iam
nos vocati.   Quod gaudium quo maerore mutatum
7 est!   Non possum exprimere verbis quantum animo
vulnus acceperim, cum audivi Fundanum ipsum, ut
multa luctuosa dolor invenit, praecipientem, quod
in vestes margarita gemmas fuerat erogaturus, hoc
8 in tus et unguenta et odores impenderetur.   Est
quidem ille eruditus et sapiens, ut qui se ab ineunte
aetate altioribus studiis artibusque dediderit; sed
nunc omnia, quae audiit saepe quae dixit, asper-
natur expulsisque virtutibus aliis pietatis est totus.
9 Ignosces, laudabis etiam, si cogitaveris quid amiserit.
Amisit enim filiam, quae non minus mores eius quam
os vultumque referebat, totumque patrem mira simili-
10 tudine exscripserat.   Proinde si quas ad eum de
dolore tam iusto litteras mittes, memento adhibere
solacium non quasi castigatorium et nimis forte, sed
molle et humanum.   Quod ut facilius admittat,
11 multum faciet medii temporis spatium.   Ut enim
crudum adhuc vulnus medentium manus reformidat,
deinde patitur atque ultro requirit, sic recens animi

her doctors' orders, cheered her sister and father, and by sheer force of will carried on after her physical strength had failed her. This will-power remained with her to the end, and neither the length of her illness nor fear of death could break it. So she has left us all the more sad reasons for lamenting our loss. Hers is a truly tragic and untimely end—death itself was not so cruel as the moment of its coming. She was already engaged to marry a distinguished young man, the day for the wedding was fixed, and we had received our invitations. Such joy, and now such sorrow! No words can express my grief when I heard Fundanus giving his own orders (for one heart-rending detail leads to another) for the money he had intended for clothing, pearls and jewels to be spent on incense, ointment and spices. He is indeed a cultivated man and a philosopher who has devoted himself from youth to higher thought and the arts, but at the moment he rejects everything he has so often heard and professed himself: he has cast off all his other virtues and is wholly absorbed by his love for his child. You will forgive and even admire him if you think of what he has lost—a daughter who resembled him in character no less than in face and expression, and was her father's living image in a wonderful way.

If then you write anything to him in his very natural sorrow, be careful not to offer any crude form of consolation which might suggest reproof; be gentle and sympathetic. Passage of time will make him readier to accept this: a raw wound shrinks from a healing hand but later permits and even seeks help, and so the mind rejects and repels any consolation

THE LETTERS OF PLINY

dolor consolationes reicit ac refugit, mox desidera et clementer admotis adquiescit. Vale.

XVII

C. PLINIUS VESTRICIO SPURINNAE SUO S.

1 Scio quanto opere bonis artibus faveas, quantum gaudium capias, si nobiles iuvenes dignum aliquid maioribus suis faciant. Quo festinantius nuntio tibi 2 fuisse me hodie in auditorio Calpurni Pisonis. Recitabat κατασστερισμῶν[1] eruditam sane luculentamque materiam. Scripta elegis erat fluentibus et teneris et enodibus, sublimibus etiam, ut poposcit locus. Apte enim et varie nunc attollebatur, nunc residebat; excelsa depressis, exilia plenis, severis iucunda muta- 3 bat, omnia ingenio pari. Commendabat haec voce suavissima, vocem verecundia: multum sanguinis, multum sollicitudinis in ore, magna ornamenta recitantis. Etenim nescio quo pacto magis in studiis 4 homines timor quam fiducia decet. Ne plura (quamquam libet plura, quo sunt pulchriora de iuvene, rariora de nobili), recitatione finita multum ac diu exosculatus adulescentem, qui est acerrimus stimulus monendi, laudibus incitavi, pergeret qua coepisset, lumenque quod sibi maiores sui praetulissent, 5 posteris ipse praeferret. Gratulatus sum optimae

---

[1] ΚΑΤΑCΤΕΡΙCΜΩΝ *Ma*: tacte pigmon *γ*.

---

[1] Contrast the austere admonitions of Servius Sulpicius to Cicero on the death of Tullia (*ad Fam.* IV. 5).

in its first pangs of grief, then feels the need of comfort and is calmed if this is kindly offered.[1]

XVII

To Vestricius Spurinna

I know your interest in the liberal arts and your pleasure when any of our young men of good family do anything worthy of their ancestry, so I am hastening to give you my news. Today I was among the audience to which Calpurnius Piso read his poem on the *Legends of the Stars*, a scholarly subject and a splendid theme, written in flowing elegiac couplets whose delicate flexibility could rise to grandeur when required. He showed an appropriate versatility in raising or lowering his tone, and the same talent whether he descended from the heights to a lower level, rose to complexity from simplicity, or moved between a lighter and more serious approach to his subject. His unusually pleasant voice was a further asset, and gained much itself from his modesty, his blushes, and anxious expression, which always add charm to a reading—for some reason shyness suits an author better than confidence. To cut short my story (though I should like to say more, as these qualities are so becoming in the young and rare in the upper classes), after the recital I gave him a warm and prolonged embrace, and urged him by my congratulations (the most stimulating kind of encouragement) to complete the task he had begun and pass on to posterity the torch his ancestors had handed to him. I also congratulated his excellent mother and

matri, gratulatus et fratri, qui ex auditorio illo non
minorem pietatis gloriam quam ille alter eloquentiae
retulit: tam notabiliter pro fratre recitante primum
metus eius, mox gaudium eminuit.

6 Di faciant ut talia tibi saepius nuntiem! Faveo
enim saeculo ne sit sterile et effetum, mireque cupio
ne nobiles nostri nihil in domibus suis pulchrum nisi
imagines habeant; quae nunc mihi hos adulescentes
tacitae laudare adhortari, et quod amborum gloriae
satis magnum est, agnoscere videntur. Vale.

XVIII

C. Plinius Calpurnio Macro Suo S.

1 Bene est mihi quia tibi bene est. Habes uxorem
tecum, habes filium; frueris mari fontibus viridibus
agro villa amoenissima. Neque enim dubito esse
amoenissimam, in qua se composuerat homo felicior,
2 ante quam felicissimus fieret. Ego in Tuscis et
venor et studeo, quae interdum alternis, interdum
simul facio; nec tamen adhuc possum pronuntiare,
utrum sit difficilius capere aliquid an scribere.
Vale.

---

[1] For *nobilitas*, see *Pan.* 69. 5 and note.
[2] The Emperor Nerva; or possibly the dictator Sulla, who
was called Felix.

his brother who, as a member of the audience, won as much credit for his brotherly affection as Piso did for his eloquent reading, for the concern he showed during the recital and his delight afterwards were most striking.

I pray the gods to give me more news like this to send you; for I believe in this generation, and am anxious for it not to prove barren and outworn. Still less do I want our noble families[1] to have no distinction in their homes other than family portraits; though these, I think, must now be silently congratulating and encouraging these two young men and doing them both the great honour of acknowledging them as descendants.

XVIII

To Calpurnius Macer

All is well with me since it is with you. You have your wife and son with you, and all the pleasures of the sea, streams, woods and fields are yours, along with your lovely house; which I know must be lovely, when it was the retreat of the man[2] who was so fortunate before he rose to the supreme good fortune. I am in my home in Tuscany, hunting and studying, either in turn or both at once, but I'm not yet ready to pronounce judgement on which I find harder to do—catch something or write it.

THE LETTERS OF PLINY

XIX

C. Plinius Valerio Paulino Suo S.

1 Video quam molliter tuos habeas; quo simplicius
2 tibi confitebor, qua indulgentia meos tractem. Est
mihi semper in animo et Homericum illud πατὴρ δ᾽ ὣς
ἤπιος ἦεν et hoc nostrum " pater familiae." Quod si
essem natura asperior et durior, frangeret me tamen
infirmitas liberti mei Zosimi, cui tanto maior humanitas exhibenda est, quanto nunc illa magis eget.
3 Homo probus officiosus litteratus; et ars quidem
eius et quasi inscriptio comoedus, in qua plurimum
facit. Nam pronuntiat acriter sapienter apte decenter etiam; utitur et cithara perite, ultra quam
comoedo necesse est. Idem tam commode orationes
et historias et carmina legit, ut hoc solum didi-
4 cisse videatur. Haec tibi sedulo exposui, quo magis
scires, quam multa unus mihi et quam iucunda
ministeria praestaret. Accedit longa iam caritas
5 hominis, quam ipsa pericula auxerunt. Est enim ita
natura comparatum, ut nihil aeque amorem incitet et
accendat quam carendi metus; quem ego pro hoc
6 non semel patior. Nam ante aliquot annos, dum
intente instanterque pronuntiat, sanguinem reiecit
atque ob hoc in Aegyptum missus a me post longam
peregrinationem confirmatus redît nuper; deinde
dum per continuos dies nimis imperat voci, veteris in-

---

¹ *Odyssey* II. 47.

XIX

To Valerius Paulinus

I HAVE noticed your kindness to your household, so will frankly confess my indulgence to mine. I always have in mind the phrase of Homer's: " he was gentle as a father,"[1] and also our own " father of the household "; but, even if I were harsh and unfeeling by nature, my heart would be softened by the illness of my freedman Zosimus, whose claim to sympathy is all the stronger now that he needs it so much. He is an honest fellow, obliging and educated, marked out by his talent for comedy, where he has great success. His delivery is clear and intelligent, his acting correct and balanced, and he plays the lyre well, better than an actor need do. He also reads speeches, history and poetry so well that it might be his sole accomplishment. I have told you all this in detail so that you may better realize all the pleasant services I receive from Zosimus which no one else can give me. I have moreover long felt for him an affection which has increased with the dangers he has come through; for it seems a law of nature for nothing to excite and intensify love so much as the fear of losing its object, and this has happened to me more than once in his case.

Some years ago he was exerting himself during a passionate performance when he began to spit blood. I then sent him to Egypt, and after a long stay there he recently returned with his health restored. Now after demanding too much of his voice for several days on end he has had a slight return of his cough

firmitatis tussicula admonitus rursus sanguinem red-
7 didit. Qua ex causa destinavi eum mittere in praedia
tua, quae Foro Iulii possides. Audivi enim te saepe
referentem esse ibi et aera salubrem et lac eiusmodi
8 curationibus accommodatissimum. Rogo ergo scribas
tuis, ut illi villa, ut domus pateat, offerant etiam sump-
9 tibus eius, si quid opus erit. Erit autem opus modico;
est enim tam parcus et continens, ut non solum
delicias verum etiam necessitates valetudinis frugalitate restringat. Ego proficiscenti tantum viatici
dabo, quantum sufficiat eunti in tua. Vale.

XX

C. Plinius Cornelio Urso Suo S.

1   Iterum Bithyni: breve tempus a Iulio Basso, et
Rufum Varenum proconsulem detulerunt, Varenum
quem nuper adversus Bassum advocatum et postula-
rant et acceperant. Inducti in senatum inquisitionem
2 postulaverunt. Varenus petit ut sibi quoque defensionis causa evocare testes liceret; recusantibus
Bithynis cognitio suscepta est. Egi pro Vareno non
3 sine eventu; nam bene an male liber indicabit. In
actionibus enim utramque in partem fortuna domina-

---

[1] In Gallia Narbonensis (Fréjus).
[2] See IV. 9. This case and that of Bassus gave P. valuable
inside information on Bithynian affairs.
[3] This right was not normally granted the defence. See

as a reminder of the old trouble, and once again has brought up blood. So I think the thing to do is to send him to your place at Forum Julii,[1] for I have often heard you say that the air is healthy there and the milk excellent for treating this kind of case Please write to your people and ask them to receive him on the estate and in your home, and to meet the expenses of anything he may need. This will not be much, for he is abstemious and moderate in his habits to the point of frugally denying himself not only delicacies but even essentials for his health. I will see myself that he has sufficient money for his journey to you when he sets out.

XX

To Cornelius Ursus

The Bithynians again! It is no time since their case against Julius Bassus,[2] but they have brought another one against the governor Rufus Varenus—the Varenus they had previously demanded and accepted to conduct their case against Bassus. Summoned before the Senate, they applied for time to collect evidence. Then Varenus also requested the right himself to call witnesses from the province in his defence.[3] The Bithynians objected, so the case was heard at once. I appeared for Varenus, not without success: whether my speech was good or bad will be seen when it is published. In a speech as delivered chance is the dominant factor either way, for much

Quintilian, *Inst. Orat.* V. vii. 9. The Bithynians demand the shorter process of a summary trial.

tur: multum commendationis et detrahit et adfert
memoria vox gestus tempus ipsum, postremo vel
amor vel odium rei; liber offensis, liber gratia, liber
4 et secundis casibus et adversis caret. Respondit
mihi Fonteius Magnus, unus ex Bithynis, plurimis
verbis paucissimis rebus. Est plerisque Graecorum,
ut illi, pro copia volubilitas: tam longas tamque
frigidas perihodos uno spiritu quasi torrente contor-
5 quent. Itaque Iulius Candidus non invenuste solet
dicere, aliud esse eloquentiam aliud loquentiam.
Nam eloquentia vix uni aut alteri, immo (si M.
Antonio credimus) nemini, haec vero, quam Candidus
loquentiam adpellat, multis atque etiam impudentis-
6 simo cuique maxime contigit. Postero die dixit pro
Vareno Homullus callide acriter culte, contra Nigrinus
presse graviter ornate. Censuit Acilius Rufus consul
designatus inquisitionem Bithynis dandam, postula-
7 tionem Vareni silentio praeterît. Haec forma negandi
fuit. Cornelius Priscus consularis et accusatoribus
quae petebant et reo tribuit, vicitque numero.
Impetravimus rem nec lege comprehensam nec satis
usitatam, iustam tamen. Quare iustam, non sum
epistula exsecuturus, ut desideres actionem. Nam si
verum est Homericum illud:

> τὴν γὰρ ἀοιδὴν μᾶλλον ἐπικλείουσ᾽ ἄνθρωποι,
> ἥ τις ἀκουόντεσσι νεωτάτη ἀμφιπέληται,

providendum est mihi, ne gratiam novitatis et florem,

---

[1] Compare Theophanes, another voluble Greek, in IV. 9. 14.
[2] *Odyssey* I. 351–2.

can be gained or lost by the speaker's memory, voice and gestures, the occasion and the good or bad impression made by the defendant; whereas the written speech is quite free from influence one way or the other, and owes nothing to chance, whether lucky or not. I was opposed by one of the Bithynians, Fonteius Magnus, whose words were many and arguments few, for, like most Greeks, he mistakes volubility for fullness of expression; they all pour out a torrent of long monotonous periods without taking breath.[1] Hence Julius Candidus's frequent witty remark that eloquence and loquacity are two different things. Scarcely anyone has the gift of eloquence—or no one if we are to believe Marcus Antonius—but what Candidus calls loquacity is common to many people and the special gift of every impudent rascal.

The following day Homullus defended Varenus with considerable subtlety, spirit and elegance, and Nigrinus made a concise, impressive and well-phrased speech in reply. The consul elect, Acilius Rufus, then moved that the Bithynians should be given permission to collect their evidence, but he passed over Varenus's application in silence, which was tantamount to a refusal. The consular Cornelius Priscus proposed to grant the petitions of both parties, and his motion was carried by a majority. So we won our point, not one mentioned in law or covered by precedent, but none the less just. Why it was I shall not say by letter, for I want you to ask for the speech. If Homer is right, and " Men praise most the song which rings newest in their ears "[2] I must be careful not to talk too much, or my letter will

quae oratiunculam illam vel maxime commendat,
epistulae loquacitate praecerpam. Vale.

XXI

C. Plinius Pompeio Saturnino Suo S.

1 Varie me adfecerunt litterae tuae; nam partim
laeta partim tristia continebant: laeta quod te in
urbe teneri nuntiabant (" nollem " inquis; sed ego
volo), praeterea quod recitaturum statim ut venissem
2 pollicebantur; ago gratias quod exspector. Triste
illud, quod Iulius Valens graviter iacet; quamquam
ne hoc quidem triste, si illius utilitatibus aestimetur,
cuius interest quam maturissime inexplicabili morbo
3 liberari. Illud plane non triste solum verum etiam
luctuosum, quod Iulius Avitus decessit dum ex
quaestura redit, decessit in nave, procul a fratre
4 amantissimo, procul a matre a sororibus (nihil ista ad
mortuum pertinent, sed pertinuerunt cum moreretur,
pertinent ad hos qui supersunt); iam quod in flore
primo tantae indolis iuvenis exstinctus est summa
5 consecuturus, si virtutes eius maturuissent. Quo ille
studiorum amore flagrabat! quantum legit, quantum
etiam scripsit! quae nunc omnia cum ipso sine fructu
6 posteritatis abierunt. Sed quid ego indulgeo dolori?
cui si frenos remittas, nulla materia non maxima est.
Finem epistulae faciam, ut facere possim etiam lacrimis quas epistula expressit. Vale.

nip in the bud the bloom of novelty which is my little speech's chief attraction.

XXI

To Pompeius Saturninus

I RECEIVED your letter with mixed feelings, for it was a mixture of good and bad news. It is good news that you are kept in Rome (against your will, you will say, but it is not against mine) and that you intend to give a reading as soon as I arrive. Thank you for waiting for me. It was sad, however, to hear that Julius Valens is lying seriously ill—though perhaps not so sad if one considers what a blessing it would be for him to be released as quickly as possible from an incurable disease. But it is more than sad, it is tragic that Julius Avitus should have died, and died at sea on his way home from the province where he had been quaestor, far from his loving brother, his mother and his sisters. All this cannot affect him now that he is dead, but must have done while he was dying; and it affects those he leaves behind, as does the thought that a young man of such promise has died in early youth when he might have attained the highest honours had his gifts been allowed to mature. Think of his ardent love of literature and all he read and wrote: all of which has now died with him, leaving nothing for posterity. But I must not give way to my grief, for once it is uncontrolled, every reason for it becomes a serious one. I will end this letter, so that I can also check the tears it has brought to my eyes.

BOOK VI

LIBER SEXTUS

I

C. Plinius Tironi Suo S.

1 Qvamdiu ego trans Padum tu in Piceno, minus te
requirebam; postquam ego in urbe tu adhuc in
Piceno, multo magis, seu quod ipsa loca in quibus esse
una solemus acrius me tui commonent, seu quod desiderium absentium nihil perinde ac vicinitas acuit,
quoque propius accesseris ad spem fruendi, hoc im-
2 patientius careas. Quidquid in causa, eripe me huic
tormento. Veni, aut ego illuc unde inconsulte pro-
peravi revertar, vel ob hoc solum, ut experiar an
mihi, cum sine me Romae coeperis esse, similes his
epistulas mittas. Vale.

II

C. Plinius Arriano Suo S.

1 Soleo non numquam in iudiciis quaerere M. Regu-
2 lum; nolo enim dicere desiderare. Cur ergo quaero?
Habebat studiis honorem, timebat pallebat scribebat, quamvis non posset ediscere. Illud ipsum, quod

---

[1] N.E. of the Apennines, the region round Ancona, where
Tiro probably had property.

BOOK VI

I

To Calestrius Tiro

As long as I was staying north of the Po and you were in Picenum[1] I did not notice your absence so much, but now that I am back in Rome again and you are still away, I feel it much more. Perhaps I think of you more in the places where we are usually together, or else it is that we never miss our absent friends so keenly as when they are not far away; the nearer you are to enjoying their company, the less you are able to be patient without it. Whatever the cause, do take me out of my misery and come, or I shall return to the place I foolishly left in a hurry, with no other purpose than to see if you will write me letters like this when you find yourself in Rome without me.

II

To Maturus Arrianus

I often find myself missing Marcus Regulus in court, though I don't mean I want him back again. Why then should I miss him? He was a person who really valued oratory. He used to be pale with anxiety, would write out his speeches though he could never learn them by heart, paint round one of his eyes

oculum modo dextrum modo sinistrum circumlinebat
(dextrum si a petitore, alterum si a possessore esset
acturus), quod candidum splenium in hoc aut in
illud supercilium transferebat, quod semper haruspices
consulebat de actionis eventu, a nimia [1] superstitione
sed tamen et a magno studiorum honore veniebat.

3 Iam illa perquam iucunda una dicentibus, quod libera
tempora petebat, quod audituros corrogabat. Quid
enim iucundius quam sub alterius invidia quamdiu
velis, et in alieno auditorio quasi deprehensum commode dicere?

4 Sed utcumque se habent ista, bene fecit Regulus
quod est mortuus: melius, si ante. Nunc enim sane
poterat sine malo publico vivere, sub eo principe sub
quo nocere non poterat. Ideo fas est non numquam
5 eum quaerere. Nam, postquam obiit ille, increbruit
passim et invaluit consuetudo binas vel singulas
clepsydras, interdum etiam dimidias et dandi et
petendi. Nam et qui dicunt, egisse malunt quam
agere, et qui audiunt, finire quam iudicare. Tanta
neglegentia tanta desidia, tanta denique inreverentia
6 studiorum periculorumque est. An nos sapientiores
maioribus nostris, nos legibus ipsis iustiores, quae tot
horas tot dies tot comperendinationes largiuntur?
Hebetes illi et supra modum tardi; nos apertius
dicimus, celerius intellegimus, religiosius iudicamus,

---

[1] a nimia *M corr.*: animi *Mγ Stout.*

---

[1] There were three water-clocks to the Roman hour, varying
in size according to its length. In private cases the time
allotted to speeches was arranged with the presiding judge.

(the right if he was appearing for the plaintiff and the left for the defendant), change a white patch over from one eyebrow to the other, and never fail to consult the soothsayers on the result of his case. This may have been gross superstition on his part, but it did show respect for his profession. Besides, two of his habits were very pleasant for anyone acting with him; he used to gather an audience by invitation and apply for unlimited time to speak, and nothing could be more enjoyable than to find yourself addressing someone else's audience on his responsibility, and to go on at your ease for as long as you liked.

All the same, Regulus did well to die, and would have done better to die sooner; though today he could certainly have been alive without being a public nuisance, now that we have an Emperor who would prevent him from doing harm. So there is now no reason why we should not miss him at times, especially as since his death the custom of applying for and granting two water-clocks[1] or one (or even half of one) has gained ground and is generally accepted. Counsel would rather get their speeches over than go on speaking, and judges care more about finishing a case than passing judgement: such is the widespread indifference, idleness, and general disrespect for oratory and its attendant risks. Are we wiser than our forbears and juster than the very laws which assign us so many hours, days, and adjournments?[2] Perhaps our predecessors were stupid and unduly slow, and we are clearer speakers, quicker thinkers, and more scrupulous judges than they were,

[2] The compulsory interval of at least a day between the *actio prima* and *actio secunda* of a criminal trial.

quia paucioribus clepsydris praecipitamus causas
7 quam diebus explicari solebant. O Regule, qui
ambitione ab omnibus obtinebas quod fidei paucissimi
praestant! Equidem quotiens iudico, quod vel
saepius facio quam dico, quantum quis plurimum post-
8 ulat aquae do. Etenim temerarium existimo divin-
are quam spatiosa sit causa inaudita, tempusque
negotio finire cuius modum ignores, praesertim cum
primam religioni suae iudex patientiam debeat, quae
pars magna iustitiae est. At quaedam supervacua
dicuntur. Etiam: sed satius est et haec dici quam
9 non dici necessaria. Praeterea, an sint supervacua,
nisi cum audieris scire non possis. Sed de his melius
coram ut de pluribus vitiis civitatis. Nam tu quoque
amore communium soles emendari cupere quae iam
corrigere difficile est.
10 Nunc respiciamus domos nostras. Ecquid omnia
in tua recte? in mea novi nihil. Mihi autem et
gratiora sunt bona quod perseverant, et leviora in-
commoda quod adsuevi. Vale.

III

C. Plinius Vero Suo S.

1 Gratias ago, quod agellum quem nutrici meae
donaveram colendum suscepisti. Erat, cum donarem, centum milium nummum; postea decrescente
reditu etiam pretium minuit, quod nunc te curante

when we hurry through our cases in fewer hours than the days they spent on developing their case. To think that Regulus's self-interest won from every judge a concession which few today will grant to honest intentions!

Personally, whenever I am hearing a case (which I do more often than I conduct one) I allow all the time anyone asks for, thinking it rash to predict the length of anything still unheard and to set a time-limit to a trial before its extent is known, especially when one of the first duties of a magistrate with scruples is patience—an important element in justice itself. You will protest that a good deal is said which is irrelevant. That may be, but it is better than leaving out essentials, and it is impossible to judge what is irrelevant without first hearing it.

But I can really discuss these and other public abuses better when we meet; you too have the general interest at heart and are anxious for reform even where it has become difficult to put things right. To turn to domestic affairs—is all well with you? I have no news, but I'm increasingly grateful for my blessings while they last, and I notice my troubles less now that I am used to them.

III

To Verus

Thank you for taking over the working of the small farm I gave my nurse. At the time I gave it to her it was worth 100,000 sesterces, but since then it has done badly and depreciated in value. It will recover

2 reparabit. Tu modo memineris commendari tibi
a me non arbores et terram, quamquam haec quoque,
sed munusculum meum, quod esse quam fructuosis-
simum non illius magis interest quae accepit, quam
mea qui dedi. Vale.

IV

C. Plinius Calpurniae Suae S.

1 Numquam sum magis de occupationibus meis questus, quae me non sunt passae aut proficiscentem te
valetudinis causa in Campaniam prosequi aut profec-
2 tam e vestigio subsequi. Nunc enim praecipue simul
esse cupiebam, ut oculis meis crederem quid viribus
quid corpusculo adparares, ecquid denique secessus
voluptates regionisque abundantiam inoffensa trans-
3 mitteres. Equidem etiam fortem te non sine cura
desiderarem; est enim suspensum et anxium de eo
quem ardentissime diligas interdum nihil scire.
4 Nunc vero me cum absentiae tum infirmitatis tuae
ratio incerta et varia sollicitudine exterret. Vereor
omnia, imaginor omnia, quaeque natura metuentium
est, ea maxime mihi quae maxime abominor fingo.
5 Quo impensius rogo, ut timori meo cottidie singulis
vel etiam binis epistulis consulas. Ero enim securior
dum lego, statimque timebo cum legero. Vale.

---

¹ P. may still be *curator alvei Tiberis* and is also busy in
court.

now that it is in your hands, but do remember that I have entrusted to you more than vines and land, though these of course are included. I am thinking of my little gift, for it means as much to me, the donor, as it does to my nurse that the farm shall prove as profitable as you can make it.

IV

To his Wife Calpurnia

Never have I complained so much about my public duties as I do now.[1] They would not let me come with you to Campania in search of better health, and they still prevent me from following hard on your heels. This is a time when I particularly want to be with you, to see with my own eyes whether you are gaining in strength and weight, and if the pleasures of your holiday and the luxuries of the district are doing you no harm. Indeed, I should worry when you are away even if you were well, for there are always anxious moments without news of anyone one loves dearly, and, as things are, I have the thought of your health as well as your absence to alarm me with fluctuating doubts and fears. I am full of forebodings of every imaginable disaster, and like all nervous people dwell most on what I pray fervently will not happen. So do please think of my anxiety and write to me once or even twice a day—I shall worry less while I am reading your letters, but my fears will return as soon as I have finished them.

THE LETTERS OF PLINY

V

C. Plinius Urso Suo S.

1 Scripseram tenuisse Varenum, ut sibi evocare testes liceret; quod pluribus aequum, quibusdam iniquum et quidem pertinaciter visum, maxime Licinio Nepoti, qui sequenti senatu, cum de rebus aliis referretur, de proximo senatus consulto disseruit 2 finitamque causam retractavit. Addidit etiam petendum a consulibus ut referrent sub exemplo legis ambitus de lege repetundarum, an placeret in futurum ad eam legem adici, ut sicut accusatoribus inquirendi testibusque denuntiandi potestas ex ea 3 lege esset, ita reis quoque fieret. Fuerunt quibus haec eius oratio ut sera et intempestiva et praepostera displiceret, quae omisso contra dicendi tempore 4 castigaret peractum, cui potuisset occurrere. Iuventius quidem Celsus praetor tamquam emendatorem senatus et multis et vehementer increpuit. Respondit Nepos rursusque Celsus; neuter contumeliis 5 temperavit. Nolo referre quae dici ab ipsis moleste tuli. Quo magis quosdam e numero nostro impro-

---

¹ V. 20.

V

To Cornelius Ursus

I TOLD you in my last letter[1] that Varenus obtained permission to call witnesses in his defence from his province. The majority approved of this, but some people (notably Licinius Nepos) held that it was illegal, and clung stubbornly to their opinion. At the next meeting of the Senate, although there was other business under discussion, Nepos brought up the motion passed at the last meeting and reopened a case that had been settled. He went on to declare that the consuls should be asked to raise the whole question of the law of restitution of money extorted and to determine whether, following the procedure of the law of bribery, a clause should not henceforward be added to give the defendant the same powers to prepare his case and to compel the attendance of witnesses as the law allows the plaintiff. Some members found fault with this speech as being too late, ill-timed and misplaced. Nepos, they said, had let the right moment go by for raising objections, and had withheld his censure until the affair was finally settled, though he could have opposed it before. In fact the praetor, Juventius Celsus, attacked him violently and at length for setting himself up as a reformer of the Senate. Nepos replied, and Celsus spoke again, neither of them refraining from abuse.

I have no wish to repeat words which I found distasteful to hear, and still less do I approve of certain of our senators who ran to and fro between

bavi, qui modo ad Celsum modo ad Nepotem, prout
hic vel ille diceret, cupiditate audiendi cursitabant, et
nunc quasi stimularent et accenderent, nunc quasi
reconciliarent ac recomponerent, frequentius singulis,
ambobus interdum propitium Caesarem ut in ludicro
6 aliquo precabantur. Mihi quidem illud etiam pera-
cerbum fuit, quod sunt alter alteri quid pararent
indicati. Nam et Celsus Nepoti ex libello respondit
7 et Celso Nepos ex pugillaribus. Tanta loquacitas
amicorum, ut homines iurgaturi id ipsum invicem
scierint, tamquam convenisset. Vale.

VI

C. PLINIUS FUNDANO SUO S.

1 Si quando, nunc praecipue cuperem esse te Romae,
et sis rogo. Opus est mihi voti laboris sollicitudinis
socio. Petit honores Iulius Naso; petit cum multis,
cum bonis, quos ut gloriosum sic est difficile superare.
2 Pendeo ergo et exerceor spe, adficior metu et me consularem esse non sentio; nam rursus mihi videor
3 omnium quae decucurri candidatus. Meretur hanc
curam longa mei caritate. Est mihi cum illo non
sane paterna amicitia (neque enim esse potuit per
meam aetatem); solebat tamen vixdum adulescen-
tulo mihi pater eius cum magna laude monstrari.
406

Celsus and Nepos (according to which one was speaking) in their eagerness to hear every word. They seemed now to be spurring them on to fresh fury, then to be trying to appease them and restore order, as they called on the Emperor usually to favour one party or another but sometimes both. The whole scene might have been a public show. Another thing which disgusted me very much was the fact that each was informed of the other's intentions; Celsus addressed Nepos from a written speech and Nepos replied from his notes, for their friends had gossiped so much that they knew each other's arguments as if it had all been arranged beforehand.

VI

To Minicius Fundanus

If ever I wished you were in Rome, it is now. Please come, for I need someone to share my prayers, efforts and anxiety. Julius Naso is a candidate for office, along with several other likely young men, so victory over his rivals will be difficult though it will be a real triumph if he succeeds. I am on tenterhooks, torn between hope and fear, and I can't realize that I have already been a consul—I feel as though I am putting up again for all the offices I have ever held.

I owe this to Naso in return for his long-standing regard for me, and am bound to him by ties of friendship; and, though difference in age made it impossible for me to be a friend of his father, when I was a young man his father was pointed out for me to

Erat non studiorum tantum verum etiam studiosorum amantissimus, ac prope cotidie ad audiendos,
quos tunc ego frequentabam, Quintilianum Niceten
Sacerdotem ventitabat, vir alioqui clarus et gravis
4 et qui prodesse filio memoria sui debeat. Sed multi
nunc in senatu quibus ignotus ille, multi quibus
notus, sed non nisi viventes reverentur. Quo magis
huic, omissa gloria patris in qua magnum ornamentum
gratia infirma, ipsi enitendum ipsi elaborandum est.
5 Quod quidem semper, quasi provideret hoc tempus,
sedulo fecit: paravit amicos, quos paraverat coluit,
me certe, ut primum sibi iudicare permisit, ad amorem
6 imitationemque delegit. Dicenti mihi sollicitus
adsistit, adsidet recitanti; primis etiam et cum
maxime nascentibus opusculis meis interest, nunc
solus ante cum fratre, cuius nuper amissi ego susci-
7 pere partes, ego vicem debeo implere. Doleo enim
et illum immatura morte indignissime raptum, et
hunc optimi fratris adiumento destitutum solisque
8 amicis relictum. Quibus ex causis exigo ut venias,
et suffragio meo tuum iungas. Permultum interest
mea te ostentare, tecum circumire. Ea est auctoritas
tua, ut putem me efficacius tecum etiam meos amicos
9 rogaturum. Abrumpe si qua te retinent: hoc tempus meum, hoc fides, hoc etiam dignitas postulat.
Suscepi candidatum, et suscepisse me notum est;

---

[1] The author of the *Institutio Oratoria*.
[2] A teacher of rhetoric from Smyrna.
[3] Probably the Julius Avitus whose death is mentioned in
V. 21.

admire. He was indeed a true lover of learning and
its students, and would come every day to hear
Quintilian[1] and Nicetes Sacerdos[2] whose lectures I
was then attending. A man of his character and
distinction should benefit his son by the reputation
he leaves behind him, but there are many people in
the Senate today who never knew him, many too
who knew him but pay regard to none but the living.
Consequently, Naso cannot rely on his father's
fame—he may take great pride in it but it has little
influential value—and must try all the more to get on
by his own efforts. This indeed he has always been
careful to do, as if he foresaw this occasion; he has
made friends and cultivated their friendship, and, in
my own case, he singled me out for his friend and
model as soon as he felt he could trust his own judgement. He is at my side, full of concern, when I plead
in court or give a reading; he is there to take an
interest the moment my trifling works see the light,
and is there alone since he lost the brother[3] who
came with him and whose place I must now try to fill.
I mourn the cruel death which has taken him from us
so young, and I grieve, too, for Naso, who has lost
such a brother's support and has no one left him but
his friends.

This is what makes me insist that you come and
add your vote to mine. It means so much to me to be
able to show you off and take you canvassing with
me; knowing your influence, I think I shall meet with
a better response even from my friends if I have your
support. Break off whatever is keeping you—my
situation, honour, and official position all demand
this. Everyone knows I have backed a candidate,

ego ambio, ego periclitor; in summa, si datur Nasoni
quod petit, illius honor, si negatur, mea repulsa est.
Vale.

VII

C. PLINIUS CALPURNIAE SUAE S.

1 SCRIBIS te absentia mea non mediocriter adfici
unumque habere solacium, quod pro me libellos meos
2 teneas, saepe etiam in vestigio meo colloces.   Gratum
est quod nos requiris,[1] gratum quod his fomentis
adquiescis; invicem ego epistulas tuas lectito
3 atque identidem in manus quasi novas sumo.   Sed
eo magis ad desiderium tui accendor: nam cuius litterae tantum habent suavitatis, huius sermonibus
quantum dulcedinis inest! Tu tamen quam frequentissime scribe, licet hoc ita me delectet ut
torqueat. Vale.

VIII

C. PLINIUS PRISCO SUO S.

1 ATILIUM Crescentem et nosti et amas.   Quis enim
illum spectatior paulo aut non novit aut non amat?
2 Hunc ego non ut multi, sed artissime diligo.   Oppida
nostra unius diei itinere dirimuntur; ipsi amare
invicem, qui est flagrantissimus amor, adulescentuli

---

[1] requiris *Catanaeus*: requires *M*.

and it is I who am canvassing and running the risks; in fact, if Naso wins his election the credit is his, but if he fails the defeat is mine.

VII

To his Wife Calpurnia

You say that you are feeling my absence very much, and your only comfort when I am not there is to hold my writings in your hand and often put them in my place by your side. I like to think that you miss me and find relief in this sort of consolation. I, too, am always reading your letters, and returning to them again and again as if they were new to me—but this only fans the fire of my longing for you. If your letters are so dear to me, you can imagine how I delight in your company; do write as often as you can, although you give me pleasure mingled with pain.

VIII

To Neratius (?) Priscus[1]

You know and love Atilius Crescens—is there anyone at all distinguished who does not? But I am more than one of his many acquaintances, I am his close friend. Our home towns are only a day's journey apart,[2] we become friends as boys when

---

[1] Not precisely identified. Compare the views of Syme (*Tacitus*, p. 224) and Sherwin-White (*Letters*, p. 363).
[2] About 30 miles, between Milan and Comum. (In II. 17. 2. an easy half-day's journey is 17 miles.)

coepimus. Mansit hoc postea, nec refrixit iudicio
sed invaluit. Sciunt qui alterutrum nostrum fami-
liarius intuentur. Nam et ille amicitiam meam
latissima praedicatione circumfert, et ego prae me
fero, quantae sit mihi curae modestia quies securitas
3 eius. Quin etiam, cum insolentiam cuiusdam tribunatum plebis inituri vereretur, idque indicasset mihi,
respondi: οὔ τις ἐμεῦ ζῶντος. Quorsus haec? ut
4 scias non posse Atilium me incolumi iniuriam accipere.
Iterum dices " quorsus haec? " Debuit ei pecuniam
Valerius Varus. Huius est heres Maximus noster,
5 quem et ipse amo, sed coniunctius tu. Rogo ergo,
exigo etiam pro iure amicitiae, cures ut Atilio meo
salva sit non sors modo verum etiam usura plurium
annorum. Homo est alieni abstinentissimus sui
diligens; nullis quaestibus sustinetur, nullus illi nisi
6 ex frugalitate reditus. Nam studia, quibus plurimum
praestat, ad voluptatem tantum et gloriam exercet.
Gravis est ei vel minima iactura; quam ⟨quam⟩¹
7 reparare quod amiseris gravius. Exime hunc illi,
exime hunc mihi scrupulum: sine me suavitate eius,
sine leporibus perfrui. Neque enim possum tristem
videre, cuius hilaritas me tristem esse non patitur.
8 In summa nosti facetias hominis; quas velim attendas, ne in bilem et amaritudinem vertat iniuria.
Quam vim habeat offensus, crede ei quam in amore
habet. Non feret magnum et liberum ingenium

¹ quamquam *Brakman*: quam *M*: et quia γ (quia *a*, *Stout*).

---

¹ *Iliad* I. 88.

feelings are warmest, and later judgement has not cooled our affection but strengthened it, as anyone who knows either of us at all intimately is aware. Atilius boasts widely of his friendship with me, and I make no secret of my concern for his honour, security, and peace of mind. In fact when he told me he was nervous about the insolent attitude of one of the tribunes-elect, like Achilles I replied that no one should harm him " while I live." [1] All this goes to show that Atilius cannot be wronged without my being concerned, but you may still wonder what I am leading up to. Well, Valerius Varus has died owing him some money. Varus's heir is our friend Maximus, and, as you are more intimate with him than I am, I beg, or rather insist, in the name of our friendship, that you will see that Atilius recovers not only his principal intact, but also the accumulated interest of several years. He is a man who never covets other people's possessions and is careful of his own, and he has no investments to support him, and no income but what he saves out of his frugal way of life; for though he makes such a success of his studies, he pursues them only for pleasure and the reputation they bring him. The slightest loss is serious for him, though it can be worse if one has to recover after a set-back. Do rid him and me of the worry, and let me still enjoy his charm and wit. I can't bear to see him in distress, when his natural gaiety never lets me be sad. In fact you know his witticisms: please do not let injustice turn them to bitterness and gall. The warmth of his affection should convince you of his passion if offended, and his bold spirit of independence will not submit to loss

9 cum contumelia damnum. Verum, ut ferat ille, ego meum damnum meam contumeliam iudicabo, sed non tamquam pro mea (hoc est, gravius) irascar. Quamquam quid denuntiationibus et quasi minis ago? Quin potius, ut coeperam, rogo oro des operam, ne ille se (quod valdissime vereor) a me, ego me neglectum a te putem. Dabis autem, si hoc perinde curae est tibi quam illud mihi. Vale.

IX

C. PLINIUS TACITO SUO S.

1 COMMENDAS mihi Iulium Nasonem candidatum. Nasonem mihi? quid si me ipsum? Fero tamen et ignosco. Eundem enim commendassem tibi, si te Romae morante ipse afuissem. Habet hoc sollicitudo, 2 quod omnia necessaria putat. Tu tamen censeo alios roges; ego precum tuarum minister adiutor particeps ero. Vale.

X

C. PLINIUS ALBINO SUO S.

1 CUM venissem in socrus meae villam Alsiensem,[1] quae aliquamdiu Rufi Vergini fuit, ipse mihi locus optimi illius et maximi viri desiderium non sine

---

[1] A coastal town of Etruria, and a convenient stopping-place for P. on his way to Centum Cellae (VI. 31).

coupled with insult. But if he did, I should count the loss and insult my own, but be far angrier than I should for myself.

But this is no time for threats and intimidations—I will end as I began, and beg and pray you to make every effort; then Atilius will not feel that I am doing nothing for him, as I very much fear he will, nor shall I feel the same about you. I am sure you will do this if you care as much for my feelings as I do for his.

IX

To Cornelius Tacitus

So you recommend Julius Naso as a candidate for office. Naso to me? It might be me to myself! Never mind, I will forgive you. I should have done the same myself, had I been away and you still in Rome: anxiety has a way of thinking nothing superfluous. My advice is that you go away and canvass someone else, then I will help and support you and add my plea to yours.

X

To Lucceius Albinus

I HAVE been visiting my mother-in-law at Alsium,[1] staying in the house which for a time belonged to Verginius Rufus.[2] The mere sight of the place revived all my grief and longing for that great and noble man.

[2] See II. l. He died in 97, so this letter is firmly dated to 106–7.

dolore renovavit. Hunc enim colere secessum atque
etiam senectutis suae nidulum vocare consueverat.
2 Quocumque me contulissem, illum animus illum
oculi requirebant. Libuit etiam monimentum eius
3 videre, et vidisse paenituit. Est enim adhuc imperfectum, nec difficultas operis in causa, modici ac
potius exigui, sed inertia eius cui cura mandata est.
Subit indignatio cum miseratione, post decimum
mortis annum reliquias neglectumque cinerem sine
titulo sine nomine iacere, cuius memoria orbem ter-
4 rarum gloria pervagetur. At ille mandaverat
caveratque, ut divinum illud et immortale factum
versibus inscriberetur:

> Hic situs est Rufus, pulso qui Vindice quondam
> imperium adseruit non sibi sed patriae.

5 Tam rara in amicitiis fides, tam parata oblivio mortu-
orum, ut ipsi nobis debeamus etiam conditoria ex-
6 struere omniaque heredum officia praesumere. Nam
cui non est verendum, quod videmus accidisse
Verginio? cuius iniuriam ut indigniorem, sic etiam
notiorem ipsius claritas facit. Vale.

XI

C. Plinius Maximo Suo S.

1 O diem laetum! Adhibitus in consilium a prae-
fecto urbis audivi ex diverso agentes summae spei
summae indolis iuvenes, Fuscum Salinatorem et

---

[1] The revolt of Julius Vindex, *legatus p.p.* of Gallia Lugdu-
nensis, was put down by Verginius Rufus at the battle of
Vesontio in 68. See Tacitus, *Hist.* I. 8: *Ep.* II. 1. 2. and note.

This was where he lived in retirement, calling it the nest of his old age; and wherever I went I realized how I missed the sight of him there. I had also an urge to see his tomb, but then I was sorry I had seen it. It is still unfinished, not through any difficulty of construction (it is on a modest, even a humble scale) but because the man in charge of it takes no interest. I was filled with indignation and pity to think that nine years after Verginius's death his remaining ashes should still lie neglected without a name or inscription, although his glorious memory travels over the whole world. And yet he had made proper provision for recording in verse the immortal deed whereby his name lives for ever:

Here lies Rufus, who once defeated Vindex[1] and
    set free the imperial power
Not for himself, but for his country.

Loyalty in friendship is so rare and the dead so easily forgotten that we ought to set up our own monuments and anticipate all the duties of our heirs. Which of us has no reason to fear the fate of Verginius? His fame only makes the wrong done to him all the more conspicuous for being undeserved.

XI

To Maximus

This has been a happy day for me. I was called upon by the City Prefect to act as assessor, and heard two young men of outstanding ability and promise plead opposite each other. They were Fuscus

Ummidium Quadratum, egregium par nec modo
temporibus nostris sed litteris ipsis ornamento fu-
2 turum. Mira utrique probitas, constantia salva,
decorus habitus, os Latinum, vox virilis, tenax
memoria, magnum ingenium, iudicium aequale;
quae singula mihi voluptati fuerunt, atque inter haec
illud, quod et ipsi me ut rectorem, ut magistrum
intuebantur, et iis [1] qui audiebant me aemulari, meis
3 instare vestigiis videbantur. O diem (repetam
enim) laetum notandumque mihi candidissimo cal-
culo! Quid enim aut publice laetius quam clarissi-
mos iuvenes nomen et famam ex studiis petere, aut
mihi optatius quam me ad recta tendentibus quasi
4 exemplar esse propositum? Quod gaudium ut perpetuo capiam deos oro; ab isdem teste te peto, ut
omnes qui me imitari tanti putabunt meliores esse
quam me velint. Vale.

XII

C. PLINIUS FABATO PROSOCERO SUO S.

1 Tu vero non debes suspensa manu commendare
mihi quos tuendos putas. Nam et te decet multis
prodesse et me suscipere quidquid ad curam tuam
2 pertinet. Itaque Bittio [2] Prisco quantum plurimum
potuero praestabo, praesertim in harena mea, hoc est

---

[1] iis] his *M*: ii *a*: *om. γ*.   [2] Bittio *a*: Bettio *Mγ*.

---

[1] See Index for their subsequent careers.
[2] Literally, " a day to be marked by the whitest of stones ";

Salinator and Ummidius Quadratus,[1] a remarkable pair who are likely to prove an ornament not only to the present age but to literature itself. Both combined exceptional honesty with strength of character; their appearance was pleasant, their accent pure, and their voices fully developed, and they both had excellent memories and discretion to match their ability. All this delighted me, as did the fact that they looked to me as their guide and teacher, and gave their hearers the impression that they sought to follow in my footsteps. So it was a happy day, as I said before—a real red-letter day.[2] What could be happier for our country than for two such distinguished young men to make their name and reputation in eloquence? What more could I desire than to be chosen to lead them on the right road? I pray the gods that I shall always be so happy, and you can bear me witness that I pray heaven all who think me worth imitating may wish to be better men than I.

XII

To Calpurnius Fabatus,
his Wife's Grandfather

You are the last person who should hesitate to bring to my notice anyone you think needs assistance, for, if helping many is your proper concern, taking on any case you have at heart is mine. So I will do all I can for Bittius Priscus; especially in my own sphere of action, the Centumviral Court. You bid

a Thracian custom according to the elder Pliny (N.H. VII. 40–41, § 131).

3 apud centumviros. Epistularum, quas mihi ut ais
" aperto pectore " scripsisti, oblivisci me iubes; at
ego nullarum libentius memini. Ex illis enim vel
praecipue sentio, quanto opere me diligas, cum sic
4 exegeris mecum, ut solebas cum tuo filio. Nec dis-
simulo hoc mihi iucundiores eas fuisse, quod habebam
bonam causam, cum summo studio curassem quod
5 tu curari volebas. Proinde etiam atque etiam rogo,
ut mihi semper eadem simplicitate, quotiens cessare
videbor (" videbor " dico, numquam enim cessabo),
convicium facias, quod et ego intellegam a summo
amore proficisci, et tu non meruisse me gaudeas.
Vale.

XIII

C. Plinius Urso Suo S.

1 Umquamne vidisti quemquam tam laboriosum et
exercitum quam Varenum meum? cui quod summa
contentione impetraverat defendendum et quasi
2 rursus petendum fuit. Bithyni senatus consultum
apud consules carpere ac labefactare sunt ausi,
atque etiam absenti principi criminari; ab illo ad
senatum remissi non destiterunt. Egit Claudius
Capito inreverenter magis quam constanter, ut qui
3 senatus consultum apud senatum accusaret. Respondit Catius Fronto [1] graviter et firme. Senatus

---

[1] Catius Fronto *M*: Fronto Catius *γ*.

---

[1] See V. 20; VI. 5.
[2] Trajan was engaged in the 2nd Dacian War, 105–6.

me forget the letters which you call outspoken, but there are none I like better to remember. They make me realize as never before how you love me, when you make the same demands on me as you used to on your own son. I admit my pleasure was increased by knowing that I had a good case: I had already done my best to carry out your request. I do beg you then most earnestly to reprove me with the same frankness whenever I seem to fail in my duty (I say " seem " because I shall never really fail). I shall understand that true love prompts your reproaches, and you may be glad to find that I did not deserve them.

XIII

To Cornelius Ursus

Have you ever seen anyone so tried and harassed as my friend Varenus?[1] He won his concession after a hard fight, and now he has had to defend it and practically apply for it all over again. The Bithynians have had the audacity to approach the consuls, impugn the Senate's decision and try to have it reversed, and they have even dared to address a complaint to the Emperor, who is not in Rome.[2] He has referred them back to the Senate, but their attacks have not ceased. Claudius Capito spoke on their behalf, not out of principle so much as with a certain irresponsibility which led him to attack a decree in front of the Senate which had passed it. Catius Fronto made an impressive and convincing reply. The Senate behaved admirably, for even the

421

ipse mirificus; nam illi quoque qui prius negarant
Vareno quae petebat, eadem danda postquam erant
4 data censuerunt; singulos enim integra re dis-
sentire fas esse, peracta quod pluribus placuisset
5 cunctis tuendum. Acilius tantum Rufus et cum eo
septem an octo, septem immo, in priore sententia
perseverarunt. Erant in hac paucitate non nulli,
quorum temporaria gravitas vel potius gravitatis
6 imitatio ridebatur. Tu tamen aestima, quantum nos
in ipsa pugna certaminis maneat, cuius quasi prae-
lusio atque praecursio has contentiones excitavit.
Vale.

XIV

C. Plinius Maurico Suo S.

1 Sollicitas me in Formianum. Veniam ea condicione, ne quid contra commodum tuum facias; qua
pactione invicem mihi caveo. Neque enim mare et
litus, sed te otium libertatem sequor: alioqui satius
2 est in urbe remanere. Oportet enim omnia aut ad
alienum arbitrium aut ad suum facere. Mei certe
stomachi haec natura est, ut nihil nisi totum et
merum velit. Vale.

XV

C. Plinius Romano Suo S.

1 Mirificae rei non interfuisti; ne ego quidem, sed
me recens fabula excepit. Passennus[1] Paulus,

---

[1] Passennus *Haupt*: Passen(n)ius *My*.

---

[1] See V. 20. 6, where as consul-elect he ignores Varenus's
request to be allowed to call witnesses.
[2] On the coast of Latium(Mola di Gaeta).

members who had previously refused Varenus's application were in favour of granting it now that the proposal had been carried, on the grounds that though individuals were at liberty to dissent while a matter was still under discussion, once it had been settled the whole assembly should abide by the will of the majority. Only Acilius Rufus[1] and seven or eight others (seven to be precise) held to their previous opinion; and several of this small minority raised a laugh for their temporary conscience, or rather their affectation of one. But you can guess what a struggle awaits us when the real battle begins, if this kind of preliminary skirmishing has made feeling run so high.

XIV

To Junius Mauricus

I accept your invitation to stay with you at Formiae[2] on the understanding that you don't put yourself out in any way—and I will keep to these terms myself. It is not the sea and shore which attract me, but the peace and freedom I shall enjoy in your company; otherwise I might just as well stay in town. Every man has to choose between pleasing others and pleasing himself, and I personally have no taste for half-measures.

XV

To Voconius Romanus

You have missed an extraordinary scene, and so did I, though the tale has reached me almost at once.

splendidus eques Romanus et in primis eruditus,
scribit elegos. Gentilicium hoc illi: est enim municeps Properti atque etiam inter maiores suos Pro-
2 pertium numerat. Is cum recitaret, ita coepit dicere:
" Prisce, iubes ...". Ad hoc Iavolenus Priscus
(aderat enim ut Paulo amicissimus): " Ego vero non
3 iubeo." Cogita qui risus hominum, qui ioci. Est
omnino Priscus dubiae sanitatis, interest tamen
officiis, adhibetur consiliis atque etiam ius civile
publice respondet: quo magis quod tunc fecit et
4 ridiculum et notabile fuit. Interim Paulo aliena
deliratio aliquantum frigoris attulit. Tam sollicite
recitaturis providendum est, non solum ut sint ipsi
sani verum etiam ut sanos adhibeant. Vale.

XVI

C. PLINIUS TACITO SUO S.

1 PETIS ut tibi avunculi mei exitum scribam, quo
verius tradere posteris possis. Gratias ago; nam
video morti eius si celebretur a te immortalem gloriam
2 esse propositam. Quamvis enim pulcherrimarum
clade terrarum, ut populi ut urbes memorabili casu,

---

¹ Asisium in Umbria (Assisi).
² As Javolenus Priscus was a distinguished jurist and mili-
tary legate (see Index), this outburst is more likely to indicate
boredom and impatience.
³ It is not clear whether P. means that Priscus was called

Passennus Paulus, a distinguished Roman knight and a scholar of repute, writes elegiac verse. This runs in his family, for he comes from the same town[1] as Propertius and considers him one of his ancestors. Paulus was giving a public reading and began by saying " You bid me, Priscus——" at which Javolenus Priscus,[2] who was present as a great friend of Paulus, exclaimed " Indeed I don't! " You can imagine the laughter and witticisms which greeted this remark. It is true that Priscus is somewhat eccentric, but he takes part in public functions, is called on for advice,[3] and is also one of the official experts on civil law; which makes his behaviour on this occasion all the more remarkable and absurd. Meanwhile Paulus has someone else's folly to blame for a chilly reception, and this shows how anyone giving a reading must beware of eccentricity either in himself or in the audience he invites.

XVI

To Cornelius Tacitus

Thank you for asking me to send you a description of my uncle's death so that you can leave an accurate account of it for posterity;[4] I know that immortal fame awaits him if his death is recorded by you. It is true that he perished in a catastrophe which destroyed the loveliest regions of the earth, a fate shared by

on as a legal expert in special cases or was a member of Trajan's regular *consilium*.

[4] Presumably in the lost second half of the Histories, planned to cover the reigns of Titus and Domitian. The eruption took place in 79. See F. A. Sullivan S. J., *Class. Phil.* LXIII. 3. p. 196.

quasi semper victurus occiderit, quamvis ipse plurima
opera et mansura condiderit, multum tamen perpe-
tuitati eius scriptorum tuorum aeternitas addet.
3 Equidem beatos puto, quibus deorum munere datum
est aut facere scribenda aut scribere legenda, beatis-
simos vero quibus utrumque. Horum in numero
avunculus meus et suis libris et tuis erit. Quo libentius suscipio, deposco etiam quod iniungis.

4 Erat Miseni classemque imperio praesens regebat.
Nonum kal. Septembres hora fere septima mater
mea indicat ei adparere nubem inusitata et magnitu-
5 dine et specie. Usus ille sole, mox frigida, gustaverat
iacens studebatque; poscit soleas, ascendit locum
ex quo maxime miraculum illud conspici poterat.
Nubes—incertum procul intuentibus ex quo monte
(Vesuvium fuisse postea cognitum est)—oriebatur,
cuius similitudinem et formam non alia magis arbor
6 quam pinus expresserit. Nam longissimo velut
trunco elata in altum quibusdam ramis diffundebatur,
credo quia recenti spiritu evecta, dein senescente eo
destituta aut etiam pondere suo victa in latitudinem
vanescebat, candida interdum, interdum sordida et
7 maculosa prout terram cineremve sustulerat. Mag-

---

[1] The northern arm of the Bay of Naples (Capo Miseno).
[2] P. means the umbrella pine of the Mediterranean.

whole cities and their people, and one so memorable
that it is likely to make his name live for ever: and
he himself wrote a number of books of lasting value:
but you write for all time and can still do much to
perpetuate his memory. The fortunate man, in my
opinion, is he to whom the gods have granted the
power either to do something which is worth recording or to write what is worth reading, and most
fortunate of all is the man who can do both. Such a
man was my uncle, as his own books and yours will
prove. So you set me a task I would choose for
myself, and I am more than willing to start on it.

My uncle was stationed at Misenum,[1] in active
command of the fleet. On 24 August, in the early
afternoon, my mother drew his attention to a cloud
of unusual size and appearance. He had been out in
the sun, had taken a cold bath, and lunched while
lying down, and was then working at his books. He
called for his shoes and climbed up to a place which
would give him the best view of the phenomenon. It
was not clear at that distance from which mountain
the cloud was rising (it was afterwards known to be
Vesuvius); its general appearance can best be
expressed as being like a pine[2] rather than any other
tree, for it rose to a great height on a sort of trunk
and then split off into branches, I imagine because it
was thrust upwards by the first blast and then left
unsupported as the pressure subsided, or else it was
borne down by its own weight so that it spread out
and gradually dispersed. Sometimes it looked white,
sometimes blotched and dirty, according to the amount
of soil and ashes it carried with it. My uncle's
scholarly acumen saw at once that it was important

num propiusque noscendum ut eruditissimo viro
visum. Iubet liburnicam aptari; mihi si venire una
vellem facit copiam; respondi studere me malle, et
8 forte ipse quod scriberem dederat. Egrediebatur
domo; accipit codicillos Rectinae Tasci [1] imminenti
periculo exterritae (nam villa eius subiacebat, nec
ulla nisi navibus fuga): ut se tanto discrimini eriperet
9 orabat. Vertit ille consilium et quod studioso animo
incohaverat obit maximo. Deducit quadriremes,
ascendit ipse non Rectinae modo sed multis (erat
enim frequens amoenitas orae) laturus auxilium.
10 Properat illuc unde alii fugiunt, rectumque cursum
recta gubernacula in periculum tenet adeo solutus
metu, ut omnes illius mali motus omnes figuras
ut deprenderat oculis dictaret enotaretque.

11 Iam navibus cinis incidebat, quo propius acceder-
ent, calidior et densior; iam pumices etiam nigrique
et ambusti et fracti igne lapides; iam vadum subitum ruinaque montis litora obstantia. Cunctatus
paulum an retro flecteret, mox gubernatori ut ita
faceret monenti " Fortes " inquit " fortuna iuvat:
12 Pomponianum pete." Stabiis erat diremptus sinu
medio (nam sensim circumactis curvatisque litoribus

---

[1] recti netasci *M*: recti necasci *γ*: Rectinae Nasci *a*.

---

[1] Terence, *Phormio* 203.
[2] Stabiae was four miles S. of Pompeii.

enough for a closer inspection, and he ordered a fast boat to be made ready, telling me I could come with him if I wished. I replied that I preferred to go on with my studies, and as it happened he had himself given me some writing to do.

As he was leaving the house he was handed a message from Rectina, wife of Tascius, whose house was at the foot of the mountain, so that escape was impossible except by boat. She was terrified by the danger threatening her and implored him to rescue her from her fate. He changed his plans, and what he had begun in a spirit of inquiry he completed as a hero. He gave orders for the warships to be launched and went on board himself with the intention of bringing help to many more people besides Rectina, for this lovely stretch of coast was thickly populated. He hurried to the place which everyone else was hastily leaving, steering his course straight for the danger zone. He was entirely fearless, describing each new movement and phase of the portent to be noted down exactly as he observed them. Ashes were already falling, hotter and thicker as the ships drew near, followed by bits of pumice and blackened stones, charred and cracked by the flames: then suddenly they were in shallow water, and the shore was blocked by the debris from the mountain. For a moment my uncle wondered whether to turn back, but when the helmsman advised this he refused, telling him that Fortune stood by the courageous [1] and they must make for Pomponianus at Stabiae. [2] He was cut off there by the breadth of the bay (for the shore gradually curves round a basin filled by the sea) so that he was not as yet in danger, though it was

mare infunditur); ibi quamquam nondum periculo
adpropinquante, conspicuo tamen et cum cresceret
proximo, sarcinas contulerat in naves, certus fugae si
contrarius ventus resedisset. Quo tunc avunculus
meus secundissimo invectus, complecitur trepidantem
consolatur hortatur, utque timorem eius sua securitate
leniret, deferri in balineum iubet; lotus accubat
cenat, aut hilaris aut (quod aeque magnum) similis
13 hilari. Interim e Vesuvio monte pluribus locis
latissimae flammae altaque incendia relucebant,
quorum fulgor et claritas tenebris noctis excitabatur.
Ille agrestium trepidatione ignes relictos desertasque
villas per solitudinem ardere in remedium formidinis
dictitabat. Tum se quieti dedit et quievit verissimo
quidem somno; nam meatus animae, qui illi propter
amplitudinem corporis gravior et sonantior erat, ab
14 iis qui limini obversabantur audiebatur. Sed area ex
qua diaeta adibatur ita iam cinere mixtisque pumici-
bus oppleta surrexerat, ut si longior in cubiculo mora,
exitus negaretur. Excitatus procedit, seque Pom-
15 poniano ceterisque qui pervigilaverant reddit. In
commune consultant, intra tecta subsistant an in
aperto vagentur. Nam crebris vastisque tremoribus
tecta nutabant, et quasi emota sedibus suis nunc huc
16 nunc illuc abire aut referri videbantur. Sub dio

---

[1] Hence the many bodies found in the excavations at Pompeii.

clear that this would come nearer as it spread. Pomponianus had therefore already put his belongings on board ship, intending to escape if the contrary wind fell. This wind was of course full in my uncle's favour, and he was able to bring his ship in. He embraced his terrified friend, cheered and encouraged him, and thinking he could calm his fears by showing his own composure, gave orders that he was to be carried to the bathroom. After his bath he lay down and dined; he was quite cheerful, or at any rate he pretended he was, which was no less courageous.

Meanwhile on Mount Vesuvius broad sheets of fire and leaping flames blazed at several points, their bright glare emphasized by the darkness of night. My uncle tried to allay the fears of his companions by repeatedly declaring that these were nothing but bonfires left by the peasants in their terror, or else empty houses on fire in the districts they had abandoned. Then he went to rest and certainly slept, for as he was a stout man his breathing was rather loud and heavy and could be heard by people coming and going outside his door. By this time the courtyard giving access to his room was full of ashes mixed with pumice-stones, so that its level had risen, and if he had stayed in the room any longer he would never have got out.[1] He was wakened, came out and joined Pomponianus and the rest of the household who had sat up all night. They debated whether to stay indoors or take their chance in the open, for the buildings were now shaking with violent shocks, and seemed to be swaying to and fro as if they were torn from their foundations. Outside on the other hand, there was the

431

rursus quamquam levium exesorumque pumicum
casus metuebatur, quod tamen periculorum collatio
elegit; et apud illum quidem ratio rationem, apud
alios timorem timor vicit. Cervicalia capitibus im-
posita linteis constringunt; id munimentum adversus
17 incidentia fuit. Iam dies alibi, illic nox omnibus
noctibus nigrior densiorque; quam tamen faces
multae variaque lumina solvebant. Placuit egredi in
litus, et ex proximo adspicere, ecquid iam mare ad-
mitteret; quod adhuc vastum et adversum permane-
18 bat. Ibi super abiectum linteum recubans semel
atque iterum frigidam aquam poposcit hausitque.
Deinde flammae flammarumque praenuntius odor
sulpuris[1] alios in fugam vertunt, excitant illum.
19 Innitens servolis[2] duobus adsurrexit et statim conci-
dit, ut ego colligo, crassiore caligine spiritu obstructo,
clausoque stomacho qui illi natura invalidus et angus-
20 tus et frequenter aestuans erat. Ubi dies redditus
(is ab eo quem novissime viderat tertius), corpus in-
ventum integrum inlaesum opertumque ut fuerat
indutus: habitus corporis quiescenti quam defuncto
similior.
21 Interim Miseni ego et mater—sed nihil ad historiam, nec tu aliud quam de exitu eius scire voluisti.
22 Finem ergo faciam. Unum adiciam, omnia me quibus
interfueram quaeque statim, cum maxime vera
memorantur, audieram, persecutum. Tu potissima

---

[1] sulpuris *M*: sulphuri sed γ: sulpuris et alios *Guillemin*.
[2] innitens servolis *M*: innixus servis γ.

danger of falling pumice-stones, even though these were light and porous; however, after comparing the risks they chose the latter. In my uncle's case one reason outweighed the other, but for the others it was a choice of fears. As a protection against falling objects they put pillows on their heads tied down with cloths.

Elsewhere there was daylight by this time, but they were still in darkness, blacker and denser than any night that ever was, which they relieved by lighting torches and various kinds of lamp. My uncle decided to go down to the shore and investigate on the spot the possibility of any escape by sea, but he found the waves still wild and dangerous. A sheet was spread on the ground for him to lie down, and he repeatedly asked for cold water to drink. Then the flames and smell of sulphur which gave warning of the approaching fire drove the others to take flight and roused him to stand up. He stood leaning on two slaves and then suddenly collapsed, I imagine because the dense fumes choked his breathing by blocking his windpipe which was constitutionally weak and narrow and often inflamed. When daylight returned on the 26th—two days after the last day he had seen—his body was found intact and uninjured, still fully clothed and looking more like sleep than death.

Meanwhile my mother and I were at Misenum, but this is not of any historic interest, and you only wanted to hear about my uncle's death. I will say no more, except to add that I have described in detail every incident which I either witnessed myself or heard about immediately after the event, when reports were most likely to be accurate. It is for

excerpes; aliud est enim epistulam aliud historiam,
aliud amico aliud omnibus scribere. Vale.

XVII

C. Plinius Restituto Suo S.

1 Indignatiunculam, quam in cuiusdam amici auditorio cepi, non possum mihi temperare quo minus
apud te, quia non contigit coram, per epistulam
2 effundam. Recitabatur liber absolutissimus. Hunc
duo aut tres, ut sibi et paucis videntur, diserti surdis
mutisque similes audiebant. Non labra diduxerunt,
non moverunt manum, non denique adsurrexerunt
3 saltem lassitudine sedendi. Quae tanta gravitas?
quae tanta sapientia? quae immo pigritia adro-
gantia sinisteritas ac potius amentia, in hoc totum
diem impendere ut offendas, ut inimicum relinquas
ad quem tamquam amicissimum veneris? Disertior
4 ipse es? Tanto magis ne invideris; nam qui invidet
minor est. Denique sive plus sive minus sive idem
praestas, lauda vel inferiorem vel superiorem vel
parem: superiorem quia nisi laudandus ille non potes
ipse laudari, inferiorem aut parem quia pertinet ad
tuam gloriam quam maximum videri, quem praecedis
5 vel exaequas. Equidem omnes qui aliquid in studiis
faciunt venerari etiam mirarique soleo; est enim res
difficilis ardua fastidiosa, et quae eos a quibus con-

434

you to select what best suits your purpose, for there is a great difference between a letter to a friend and history written for all to read.

XVII

To Claudius Restitutus

I HAVE come away from a reading given by a friend of mine feeling really rather put out, so that I simply must pour out the whole story to you by letter, seeing that there is no chance of doing so in person. The work being read was highly finished in every way, but two or three clever speakers—or so they seemed to themselves and a few others—listened to it like deaf mutes. They never opened their lips, stirred a hand, nor even rose to their feet if only as a change from sitting still. What is the point of all this dignity and learning, or rather this laziness and conceit, this want of tact or even good sense, which makes you spend a whole day giving offence and leaving an enemy in the man you came to hear as your dearest friend? Are you a better speaker than he is? All the more reason not to grudge him his success, for jealousy is a sign of inferiority. In fact, whether your own performance is better or worse or on a par with his, you should show your appreciation; for if your superior does not meet with applause neither will you, and it is in your own interests that anyone you equal or surpass should be well received.

Personally I always respect and admire anyone who achieves something in literature, for she is an uncertain mistress, coy and hard to please, apt to

temnitur invicem contemnat. Nisi forte aliud iudicas
tu. Quamquam quis uno te reverentior huius operis,
6 quis[1] benignior aestimator? Qua ratione ductus
tibi potissimum indignationem meam prodidi, quem
habere socium maxime poteram. Vale.

XVIII

C. Plinius Sabino Suo S.

1 Rogas ut agam Firmanorum publicam causam;
quod ego quamquam plurimis occupationibus disten-
tus adnitar. Cupio enim et ornatissimam coloniam
advocationis officio, et te gratissimo tibi munere
2 obstringere. Nam cum familiaritatem nostram, ut
soles praedicare, ad praesidium ornamentumque
tibi sumpseris, nihil est quod negare debeam, praesertim pro patria petenti. Quid enim precibus aut
3 honestius piis aut efficacius amantis? Proinde
Firmanis tuis ac iam potius nostris obliga fidem
meam; quos labore et studio meo dignos cum splen-
dor ipsorum tum hoc maxime pollicetur, quod credibile est optimos esse inter quos tu talis exstiteris.
Vale.

XIX

C. Plinius Nepoti Suo S.

1 Scis tu accessisse pretium agris, praecipue subur-
banis? Causa subitae caritatis res multis agitata

---

[1] quis *Laetus*: qui γ (*deest M*).

---

[1] In Picenum (Fermo).

despise those who despise her. Perhaps you think
otherwise, though there is no more serious and
appreciative critic of this subject than yourself.
That is why I have chosen you rather than anyone
else to hear about my indignation: you are most
likely to share it.

XVIII

To Statius Sabinus

I will do my best to take on the case for Firmum,[1]
as you ask me, although I have a great deal of
business on my hands; I am glad to oblige such a distinguished town by my professional services, and you
too by a favour which will please you so much. You
are always saying that you sought my friendship for
the help and distinction I bring you, so there is
nothing I should deny you, especially when your
request is made on behalf of your native town. No
petition is so honourable as a loyal citizen's, none
so effective as a friend's. You can pledge my word
then to your people of Firmum, or rather *our* people;
their excellent reputation is a sufficient guarantee
that they are worthy of my care and attention, added
to the fact that there is likely to be nothing but good
in the people who can claim a citizen like you.

XIX

To Maecilius Nepos

Have you heard that the price of land has gone up,
particularly in the neighbourhood of Rome? The

437

sermonibus. Proximis comitiis honestissimas voces
senatus expressit: "Candidati ne conviventur, ne
2 mittant munera, ne pecunias deponant." Ex quibus
duo priora tam aperte quam immodice fiebant; hoc
tertium, quamquam occultaretur, pro comperto habe-
3 bantur. Homullus deinde noster vigilanter usus
hoc consensu senatus sententiae loco postulavit,
ut consules desiderium universorum notum principi
facerent, peterentque sicut aliis vitiis huic quoque
4 providentia sua occurreret. Occurrit; nam sumptus
candidatorum, foedos illos et infames, ambitus lege
restrinxit; eosdem patrimonii tertiam partem conferre iussit in ea quae solo continerentur, deforme
arbitratus (et erat) honorem petituros urbem Italiam-
que non pro patria sed pro hospitio aut stabulo quasi
5 peregrinantes habere. Concursant ergo candidati;
certatim quidquid venale audiunt emptitant, quoque
6 sint plura venalia efficiunt. Proinde si paenitet te
Italicorum praediorum, hoc vendendi tempus tam
hercule quam in provinciis comparandi, dum idem
candidati illic vendunt ut hic emant. Vale.

XX

C. PLINIUS TACITO SUO S.

1   Ais te adductum litteris quas exigenti tibi de morte
avunculi mei scripsi, cupere cognoscere, quos ego

---

¹ Trajan's enactment was renewed by Marcus Aurelius, who
reduced the necessary investment to a quarter. Cf. SHA,
Marcus, 11. 8.

reason for the sudden increase in price has given rise
to a good deal of discussion. At the last election, the
Senate expressed the very proper opinion that " Candidates should be prohibited from providing dinners,
distributing presents, and depositing money with
agents." The first two practices were employed
without restraint or concealment, and the third was
done secretly but was well known to all. When the
debate reached our friend Homullus, he was quick to
take advantage of the agreement in the Senate; he
asked that the consuls should inform the Emperor of
this unanimous feeling and petition him to take
thought, as on previous occasions, to find means to
remedy this evil. This the Emperor has done, by
applying the law against bribery to force candidates
to limit their scandalously gross expenditure; and he
has also compelled them to invest a third of their
capital in real estate,[1] thinking it unseemly (as indeed
it was) that candidates for office should treat Rome
and Italy not as their native country, but as a mere
inn or lodging house for them on their visits. Consequently candidates are rushing about, struggling
to buy up anything they hear is for sale, and thus
bringing more into the market. So if you are tired
of your Italian estates, now is the time, believe me,
for selling out and buying in the provinces—the same
candidates are selling there to be able to buy here.

XX

To Cornelius Tacitus

So the letter which you asked me to write on my
uncle's death has made you eager to hear about the

Miseni relictus (id enim ingressus abruperam) non solum metus verum etiam casus pertulerim. " Quamquam animus meminisse horret, . . . incipiam."

2 Profecto avunculo ipse reliquum tempus studiis (ideo enim remanseram) impendi; mox balineum 3 cena somnus inquietus et brevis. Praecesserat per multos dies tremor terrae, minus formidolosus quia Campaniae solitus; illa vero nocte ita invaluit, ut non 4 moveri omnia sed verti crederentur. Inrupit cubiculum meum mater; surgebam invicem, si quiesceret excitaturus. Resedimus in area domus, quae mare a 5 tectis modico spatio dividebat. Dubito, constantiam vocare an imprudentiam debeam (agebam enim duodevicensimum annum): posco librum Titi Livi, et quasi per otium lego atque etiam ut coeperam excerpo. Ecce amicus avunculi qui nuper ad eum ex Hispania venerat, ut me et matrem sedentes, me vero etiam legentem videt, illius patientiam securitatem meam corripit. Nihilo segnius ego intentus in librum.

6 Iam hora diei prima, et adhuc dubius et quasi languidus dies. Iam quassatis circumiacentibus tectis, quamquam in aperto loco, angusto tamen, magnus et 7 certus ruinae metus. Tum demum excedere oppido visum; sequitur vulgus attonitum, quodque in pavore simile prudentiae, alienum consilium suo

---

[1] *Aeneid* II. 12.
[2] 25 August.

terrors and also the hazards I had to face when left at Misenum, for I broke off at the beginning of this part of my story. "Though my mind shrinks from remembering . . . I will begin." [1]

After my uncle's departure I spent the rest of the day with my books, as this was my reason for staying behind. Then I took a bath, dined, and then dozed fitfully for a while. For several days past there had been earth tremors which were not particularly alarming because they are frequent in Campania: but that night the shocks were so violent that everything felt as if it were not only shaken but overturned. My mother hurried into my room and found me already getting up to wake her if she were still asleep. We sat down in the forecourt of the house, between the buildings and the sea close by. I don't know whether I should call this courage or folly on my part (I was only seventeen at the time) but I called for a volume of Livy and went on reading as if I had nothing else to do. I even went on with the extracts I had been making. Up came a friend of my uncle's who had just come from Spain to join him. When he saw us sitting there and me actually reading, he scolded us both—me for my foolhardiness and my mother for allowing it. Nevertheless, I remained absorbed in my book.

By now it was dawn,[2] but the light was still dim and faint. The buildings round us were already tottering, and the open space we were in was too small for us not to be in real and imminent danger if the house collapsed. This finally decided us to leave the town. We were followed by a panic-stricken mob of people wanting to act on someone else's decision in preference

praefert, ingentique agmine abeuntes premit et im-
8 pellit. Egressi tecta consistimus. Multa ibi mir-
anda, multas formidines patimur. Nam vehicula
quae produci iusseramus, quamquam in planissimo
campo, in contrarias partes agebantur, ac ne lapidibus
9 quidem fulta in eodem vestigio quiescebant. Praeterea mare in se resorberi et tremore terrae quasi
repelli videbamus. Certe processerat litus, multaque
animalia maris siccis harenis detinebat. Ab altero
latere nubes atra et horrenda, ignei spiritus tortis
vibratisque discursibus rupta, in longas flammarum
figuras dehiscebat; fulguribus illae et similes et
10 maiores erant. Tum vero idem ille ex Hispania
amicus acrius et instantius " Si frater " inquit " tuus,
tuus avunculus vivit, vult esse vos salvos; si periit,
superstites voluit. Proinde quid cessatis evadere ? "
Respondimus non commissuros nos ut de salute illius
11 incerti nostrae consuleremus. Non moratus ultra
proripit se effusoque cursu periculo aufertur. Nec
multo post illa nubes descendere in terras, operire
maria; cinxerat Capreas et absconderat, Miseni quod
12 procurrit abstulerat. Tum mater orare hortari iubere, quoquo modo fugerem; posse enim iuvenem,
se et annis et corpore gravem bene morituram, si

to their own (an element in fear which is like prudence), who hurried us on our way by pressing hard behind in a dense crowd. Once beyond the buildings we stopped, and there we had some extraordinary experiences which thoroughly alarmed us. The carriages we had ordered to be brought out began to run in different directions though the ground was quite level, and would not remain stationary even when wedged with stones. We also saw the sea sucked away and apparently forced back by the earthquake: at any rate it receded from the shore so that quantities of sea creatures were left stranded on dry sand. On the landward side a fearful black cloud was rent by forked and quivering bursts of flame, and parted to reveal great tongues of fire, like flashes of lightning magnified in size.

At this point my uncle's friend from Spain spoke up still more urgently: " If your brother, if your uncle is still alive, he will want you both to be saved; if he is dead, he would want you to survive him—so why put off your escape ?" We replied that we would not think of considering our own safety as long as we were uncertain of his. Without waiting any longer, our friend rushed off and hurried out of danger as fast as he could.

Soon afterwards the cloud sank down to earth and covered the sea; it had already blotted out Capri and hidden the promontory of Misenum from sight. Then my mother implored, entreated, and commanded me to escape as best I could—a young man might escape, whereas she was old and slow and could die in peace as long as she had not been the cause of my death too. I told her I refused to save myself

443

mihi causa mortis non fuisset. Ego contra salvum
me nisi una non futurum; dein manum eius amplexus
addere gradum cogo. Paret aegre incusatque se,
quod me moretur.

13 Iam cinis, adhuc tamen rarus. Respicio: densa
caligo tergis imminebat, quae nos torrentis modo in-
fusa terrae sequebatur. "Deflectamus" inquam
"dum videmus, ne in via strati comitantium turba
14 in tenebris obteramur." Vix consideramus, et nox
non qualis inlunis aut nubila, sed qualis in locis clausis
lumine exstincto. Audires ululatus feminarum, in-
fantum quiritatus, clamores virorum; alii parentes
alii liberos alii coniuges vocibus requirebant, vocibus
noscitabant; hi suum casum, illi suorum misera-
bantur; erant qui metu mortis mortem precarentur;
15 multi ad deos manus tollere, plures nusquam iam deos
ullos aeternamque illam et novissimam noctem mun-
do interpretabantur. Nec defuerunt qui fictis men-
titisque terroribus vera pericula augerent. Aderant
qui Miseni illud ruisse illud ardere falso sed credenti-
16 bus nuntiabant. Paulum reluxit, quod non dies
nobis, sed adventantis ignis indicium videbatur. Et
ignis quidem longius substitit; tenebrae rursus cinis
rursus, multus et gravis. Hunc identidem adsur-
gentes excutiebamus; operti alioqui atque etiam
17 oblisi pondere essemus. Possem gloriari non gemitum mihi, non vocem parum fortem in tantis periculis excidisse, nisi me cum omnibus, omnia mecum

444

without her, and grasping her hand forced her to quicken her pace. She gave in reluctantly, blaming herself for delaying me. Ashes were already falling, not as yet very thickly. I looked round: a dense black cloud was coming up behind us, spreading over the earth like a flood. "Let us leave the road while we can still see," I said, "or we shall be knocked down and trampled underfoot in the dark by the crowd behind." We had scarcely sat down to rest when darkness fell, not the dark of a moonless or cloudy night, but as if the lamp had been put out in a closed room. You could hear the shrieks of women, the wailing of infants, and the shouting of men; some were calling their parents, others their children or their wives, trying to recognize them by their voices. People bewailed their own fate or that of their relatives, and there were some who prayed for death in their terror of dying. Many besought the aid of the gods, but still more imagined there were no gods left and that the universe was plunged into eternal darkness for evermore. There were people, too, who added to the real perils by inventing fictitious dangers: some reported that part of Misenum had collapsed or another part was on fire, and though their tales were false they found others to believe them. A gleam of light returned, but we took this to be a warning of the approaching flames rather than daylight. However, the flames remained some distance off; then darkness came on once more and ashes began to fall again, this time in heavy showers. We rose from time to time and shook them off, otherwise we should have been buried and crushed beneath their weight. I could boast that not a groan or cry of fear escaped

perire, misero magno tamen mortalitatis solacio credidissem.

18 Tandem illa caligo tenuata quasi in fumum nebulamve discessit; mox dies verus; sol etiam effulsit, luridus tamen qualis esse cum deficit solet. Occursabant trepidantibus adhuc oculis mutata omnia

19 altoque cinere tamquam nive obducta. Regressi Misenum curatis utcumque corporibus suspensam dubiamque noctem spe ac metu exegimus. Metus praevalebat; nam et tremor terrae perseverabat, et plerique lymphati terrificis vaticinationibus et sua

20 et aliena mala ludificabantur. Nobis tamen ne tunc quidem, quamquam et expertis periculum et exspectantibus, abeundi consilium, donec de avunculo nuntius.

Haec nequaquam historia digna non scripturus leges et tibi scilicet qui requisisti imputabis, si digna ne epistula quidem videbuntur. Vale.

XXI

C. PLINIUS CANINIO SUO S.

1 SUM ex iis qui mirer antiquos, non tamen (ut quidam) temporum nostrorum ingenia despicio. Neque enim quasi lassa et effeta natura nihil iam laudabile

---

[1] 25–6 August.
[2] A common idea in antiquity. Cf. Lucretius, II. 1150 ff.

me in these perils, had I not derived some poor
consolation in my mortal lot from the belief that the
whole world was dying with me and I with it.

At last the darkness thinned and dispersed into
smoke or cloud; then there was genuine daylight,
and the sun actually shone out, but yellowish as it is
during an eclipse. We were terrified to see everything changed, buried deep in ashes like snowdrifts.
We returned to Misenum where we attended to our
physical needs as best we could, and then spent an
anxious night[1] alternating between hope and fear.
Fear predominated, for the earthquakes went on,
and several hysterical individuals made their own
and other people's calamities seem ludicrous in
comparison with their frightful predictions. But
even then, in spite of the dangers we had been
through and were still expecting, my mother and I
had still no intention of leaving until we had news
of my uncle.

Of course these details are not important enough
for history, and you will read them without any idea
of recording them; if they seem scarcely worth
even putting in a letter, you have only yourself to
blame for asking for them.

XXI

To Caninius Rufus

I am an admirer of the ancients, but, not like some
people, so as to despise the talent of our own times.
It is not true that the world is too tired and exhausted
to be able to produce anything worth praising:[2] on

2 parit. Atque adeo nuper audivi Vergilium Romanum
paucis legentem comoediam ad exemplar veteris
comoediae scriptam, tam bene ut esse quandoque
3 possit exemplar. Nescio an noris hominem, quamquam nosse debes; est enim probitate morum, ingenii elegantia, operum varietate monstrabilis.
4 Scripsit mimiambos tenuiter argute venuste, atque
in hoc genere eloquentissime; nullum est enim genus
quod absolutum non possit eloquentissimum dici.
Scripsit comoedias Menandrum aliosque aetatis
eiusdem aemulatus; licet has inter Plautinas Teren-
5 tianasque numeres. Nunc primum se in vetere co-
moedia, sed non tamquam inciperet ostendit. Non
illi vis, non granditas, non subtilitas, non amaritudo,
non dulcedo, non lepos defuit; ornavit virtutes, in-
sectatus est vitia; fictis nominibus decenter, veris
6 usus est apte. Circa me tantum benignitate nimia
modum excessit, nisi quod tamen poetis mentiri
7 licet. In summa extorquebo ei librum legendum-
que, immo ediscendum mittam tibi; neque enim
dubito futurum, ut non deponas si semel sumpseris.
Vale.

XXII

C. Plinius Tironi Suo S.

1 Magna res acta est omnium qui sunt provinciis prae-
futuri, magna omnium qui se simpliciter credunt

448

the contrary, I have just heard Vergilius Romanus reading to a small audience a comedy which was so skilfully modelled on the lines of the Old Comedy that one day it may serve as a model itself. I don't know whether you know the man, but you certainly ought to. He is remarkable for his moral integrity, his intellectual refinement, and his versatility as an author. His iambic mimes are subtle, witty and altogether delightful, in the best style for their type—for there is no type which cannot command the best style if this achieves perfection. He has also written comedies in imitation of Menander and his contemporaries which can be classed with those of Plautus and Terence. This was his first appearance in Old Comedy, though it did not seem like a first attempt. He lacked neither vigour, grandeur, nor subtlety of style, pungency, charm, nor humour; he praised virtue and attacked vice, introduced fictitious names when suitable and made appropriate use of real ones. Only in my own case did his excess of kind feeling lead him to exaggerate, but, after all, poets are not obliged to keep to the truth.

In fact I will get the book out of him and send it to you to read, or rather to learn by heart, for I am quite sure that once you have laid hands on it you will never be able to put it down.

XXII

To Calestrius Tiro

An important case has just been heard which is of interest to all future provincial governors and to

2 amicis. Lustricius Bruttianus cum Montanium Atticinum comitem suum in multis flagitiis deprehendisset, Caesari scripsit. Atticinus flagitiis addidit, ut quem deceperat accusaret. Recepta cognitio est; fui in consilio. Egit uterque pro se, egit autem carptim et κατὰ κεφάλαιον, quo genere veritas statim
3 ostenditur. Protulit Bruttianus testamentum suum, quod Atticini manu scriptum esse dicebat; hoc enim et arcana familiaritas et querendi de eo, quem sic
4 amasset, necessitas indicabatur. Enumeravit crimina foeda manifesta; quae ille cum diluere non posset, ita regessit, ut dum defenditur turpis, dum accusat sceleratus probaretur. Corrupto enim scribae servo interceperat commentarios intercideratque, ac per summum nefas utebatur adversus amicum crimine
5 suo. Fecit pulcherrime Caesar: non enim de Bruttiano, sed statim de Atticino perrogavit. Damnatus et in insulam relegatus; Bruttiano iustissimum integritatis testimonium redditum, quem
6 quidem etiam constantiae gloria secuta est. Nam defensus expeditissime accusavit vehementer, nec
7 minus acer quam bonus et sincerus adparuit. Quod

---

[1] To Trajan, home from Dacia in 106.

[2] The practice introduced by Nero (Suetonius, *Nero* 15) which dispensed with long orations.

[3] Baetica, a province assigned to a praetorian senator. See VII. 16.

anyone who trusts his friends without reserve. Lustricius Bruttianus had detected his colleague, Montanius Atticinus, in a number of criminal offences and had sent a report to the Emperor. Atticinus then added to his misdeeds by bringing a case against the man he had deceived. The trial came on, and I acted as assessor.[1] Each side conducted his own case, dealing with the main items one by one, which is the quickest way at arriving at the truth.[2] Bruttianus produced his will, which he said was written in the hand of Atticinus, as a proof both of the confidence he had placed in their relationship and of the necessity which constrained him to complain about a man who had been so dear to him. He cited a number of shocking charges, all clearly proved; being unable to refute them, Atticinus retorted with counter-charges, but merely proved himself a rogue in his defence and a scoundrel by his accusations. He had bribed a slave belonging to Bruttianus's secretary, had intercepted certain papers and falsified some of them, and, worst of all, had directed a charge intended for himself against his friend.

The Emperor dealt with him admirably, asking for an immediate verdict not on Bruttianus but on Atticinus, who was found guilty and banished to an island. Bruttianus received a well-deserved tribute to his honesty, and has also won a reputation for determination, for he finished his defence as quickly as he could and then pressed his charges vigorously; thus proving his spirit as well as his honour and good faith.

I have described this case to you as a warning, now you have been allotted your province,[3] to rely chiefly

tibi scripsi, ut te sortitum provinciam praemonerem,
plurimum tibi credas, nec cuiquam satis fidas, deinde
scias si quis forte te (quod abominor) fallat, paratam
ultionem. Qua tamen ne sit opus, etiam atque etiam
8 attende; neque enim tam iucundum est vindicari
quam decipi miserum. Vale.

XXIII

C. PLINIUS TRIARIO SUO S.

1 IMPENSE petis ut agam causam pertinentem ad
curam tuam, pulchram alioqui et famosam. Faciam,
sed non gratis. " Qui fieri potest " inquis " ut non
gratis tu? " Potest:[1] exigam enim mercedem
2 honestiorem gratuito patrocinio. Peto atque etiam
paciscor ut simul agat Cremutius Ruso. Solitum
hoc mihi et iam in pluribus claris adulescentibus
factitatum; nam mire concupisco bonos iuvenes
3 ostendere foro, adsignare famae. Quod si cui,
praestare Rusoni meo debeo, vel propter natales
ipsius vel propter eximiam mei caritatem; quem
magni aestimo in isdem iudiciis, ex isdem etiam parti-
4 bus conspici audiri. Obliga me, obliga ante quam
dicat; nam cum dixerit gratias ages. Spondeo
sollicitudini tuae, spei meae, magnitudini causae
suffecturum. Est indolis optimae brevi producturus

---

[1] tu? potest R. Agricola: tu potes Mγ Stout.

---

[1] P. never took fees; cf. V. 13. 8–9.

on yourself and trust no one very far. I want you to know, too, that if by any chance anyone does deceive you (though I pray that no one will) there is punishment awaiting him. But be always on your guard so that it shall not be necessary, for the satisfaction of obtaining redress is no compensation for the misery of being deceived.

XXIII

To Triarius

As you are so anxious for me to appear in a case in which you are interested (a good cause, you say, which will add to my reputation), I will do so, but not for nothing. " Impossible," you will say, " for *you* to want a fee! "[1] But it *is* possible, and the fee I am exacting does me more credit than offering my services for nothing. I have a request, or rather a stipulation to make: that Cremutius Ruso shall act with me. This is my usual way of treating young men of distinction, for I take a special pleasure in introducing promising young people to the courts and setting them on the path to fame. My friend Ruso should have my help before anyone, for he comes of a good family and has a marked regard for me, and I think it important for him to be seen and heard in the same case and acting on the same side as myself. Please do me this favour, and do it before you hear him speak; you will thank me for it afterwards. The case is important and you will be anxious, but I promise you he will come up to expectations. He is a highly talented young man and will soon be

5 alios, si interim provectus fuerit a nobis. Neque
enim cuiquam tam clarum statim ingenium ut possit
emergere, nisi illi materia occasio, fautor etiam com-
mendatorque contingat. Vale.

XXIV

C. Plinius Macro Suo S.

1 QUAM multum interest quid a quoque fiat! Eadem
enim facta claritate vel obscuritate facientium aut
tolluntur altissime aut humillime deprimuntur.
2 Navigabam per Larium nostrum, cum senior amicus
ostendit mihi villam, atque etiam cubiculum quod in
lacum prominet: " Ex hoc " inquit " aliquando muni-
3 ceps nostra cum marito se praecipitavit." Causam
requisivi. Maritus ex diutino morbo circa velanda
corporis ulceribus putrescebat; uxor inspiceret exe-
git; neque enim quemquam fidelius indicaturum,
4 possetne sanari. Vidit desperavit hortata est ut
moreretur, comesque ipsa mortis, dux immo et exemplum et necessitas fuit; nam se cum marito ligavit
5 abiecitque in lacum. Quod factum ne mihi quidem,
qui municeps, nisi proxime auditum est, non quia
minus illo clarissimo Arriae facto, sed quia minor
ipsa. Vale.

---

[1] This suggests that Macer came from P.'s native district,
if not from Comum itself.

bringing others forward if in the meantime he has his introduction from us. No one can make a start, however outstanding his abilities, if he lacks scope and opportunity and a patron to support him.

XXIV

To Calpurnius Macer

How often we judge actions by the people who perform them! The selfsame deeds are lauded to the skies or allowed to sink into oblivion simply because the persons concerned are well known or not.

I was sailing on our[1] Lake Como with an elderly friend when he pointed out a house with a bedroom built out over the lake. " From there," he said, " a woman of our town once threw herself with her husband." I asked why. The husband had long been suffering from ulcers in the private parts, and his wife insisted on seeing them, promising that no one would give him a more candid opinion whether the disease was curable. She saw that there was no hope and urged him to take his life; she went with him, even led him to his death herself, and forced him to follow her example by roping herself to him and jumping into the lake. Yet even I, who come from the same town, never heard of this until the other day—not because it was less heroic than Arria's famous deed,[2] but because the woman was less well known.

[2] For the elder Arria, see III. 16.

THE LETTERS OF PLINY

XXV

C. Plinius Hispano Suo S.

1 Scribis Robustum, splendidum equitem Romanum,
cum Atilio Scauro amico meo Ocriculum usque commune iter peregisse, deinde nusquam comparuisse;
petis ut Scaurus veniat nosque, si potest, in aliqua
2 inquisitionis vestigia inducat. Veniet; vereor ne
frustra. Suspicor enim tale nescio quid Robusto
accidisse quale aliquando Metilio Crispo municipi
3 meo. Huic ego ordinem impetraveram atque etiam
proficiscenti quadraginta milia nummum ad in-
struendum se ornandumque donaveram, nec postea
aut epistulas eius aut aliquem de exitu nuntium
4 accepi. Interceptusne sit a suis an cum suis dubium:
certe non ipse, non quisquam ex servis eius adparuit,
5 ut ne Robusti quidem. Experiamur tamen, accer-
samus Scaurum; demus hoc tuis, demus optimi
adulescentis honestissimis precibus, qui pietate mira
mira etiam sagacitate patrem quaerit. Di faveant
ut sic inveniat ipsum, quemadmodum iam cum quo
fuisset invenit! Vale.

XXVI

C. Plinius Serviano Suo S.

1 Gaudeo et gratulor, quod Fusco Salinatori filiam
tuam destinasti. Domus patricia, pater honestissi-

---

[1] Baebius Hispanus may be the *praefectus vigilum.*
[2] In Umbria, on the Via Flaminia (Ocricoli).
[3] The young man described in VI. 11.

XXV

To Baebius Hispanus[1]

You say that the distinguished Roman knight Robustus travelled as far as Ocriculum[2] with my friend Atilius Scaurus, and then completely vanished, and you want Scaurus to come and see if he can put us on the scent. He shall come, though I fear it may be no use. I suspect something has happened to Robustus of the same sort as once befell my fellow-townsman Metilius Crispus. I had obtained his promotion to the rank of centurion and had given him 40,000 sesterces for his outfit and equipment when he set out, but I never had a letter from him afterwards, nor any news of his death. Whether he was killed by his slaves or along with them, no one knows: at any rate, neither Crispus nor any of them were seen again, any more than the slaves of Robustus. But let us try, and send for Scaurus—this much we can do in answer to your request and the very proper entreaties of the worthy young man who is showing intelligence as well as devotion to his father in the way he is organizing the search. I pray that with the gods' help he will be as successful in finding his father as he was in discovering the man who travelled with him.

XXVI

To Julius Servianus

I am glad to hear that your daughter is to marry Fuscus Salinator,[3] and must congratulate you on your

mus, mater pari laude; ipse studiosus litteratus etiam
disertus, puer simplicitate comitate iuvenis senex
2 gravitate. Neque enim amore decipior. Amo quidem effuse (ita officiis ita reverentia meruit), iudico
tamen, et quidem tanto acrius quanto magis amo;
tibique ut qui exploraverim spondeo, habiturum te
generum quo melior fingi ne voto quidem potuit.
3 Superest ut avum te quam maturissime similium sui
faciat. Quam felix tempus illud, quo mihi liberos illius
nepotes tuos, ut meos vel liberos vel nepotes, ex
vestro sinu sumere et quasi pari iure tenere continget! Vale.

XXVII

C. Plinius Severo Suo S.

1 Rogas ut cogitem, quid designatus consul in honorem principis censeas. Facilis inventio, non facilis
electio; est enim ex virtutibus eius larga materia.
Scribam tamen vel (quod malo) coram indicabo, si
prius haesitationem meam ostendero. Dubito num
2 idem tibi suadere quod mihi debeam. Designatus
ego consul omni hac, etsi non adulatione, specie
tamen adulationis abstinui, non tamquam liber et
constans, sed tamquam intellegens principis nostri,

choice. He belongs to one of our noble families and his father and mother are both highly respected; while he himself is scholarly, well read, and something of an orator, and he combines a childlike frankness and youthful charm with mature judgement. Nor am I blinded by affection—I love him as dearly as his merits and regard for me deserve, but I have kept my critical powers: in fact they are sharpened by my love for him. I can assure you (knowing him as I do) that he will be a son-in-law who will prove better than your fondest hopes could wish. It only remains for him to give you grandchildren like himself as soon as possible. It will be a happy day for me when I can take his children, who are also your grandchildren, from your arms as if it were my right and they were my own.

XXVII

To Vettenius Severus

You ask me to consider what tribute you should pay the Emperor in your speech as consul-elect. His virtues provide abundant material, so that it is easy enough to think of subjects but not so easy to choose between them. However, I will write and send you my opinion, or preferably give it you when we meet; but I must first explain my hesitation. I am wondering whether I ought to advise you to do as I did when I was consul-elect. I made a point of avoiding anything which looked like flattery, even if not intended as such, acting not on any principle of independence but on my knowledge of our Emperor.

cuius videbam hanc esse praecipuam laudem, si nihil
3 quasi ex necessitate decernerem. Recordabar etiam
plurimos honores pessimo cuique delatos, a quibus
hic optimus separari non alio magis poterat, quam
diversitate censendi; quod ipsum non dissimulatione
et silentio praeterii, ne forte non iudicium illud meum
4 sed oblivio videretur. Hoc tunc ego; sed non omnibus eadem placent, ne [1] conveniunt quidem. Praeterea faciendi aliquid non faciendive ratio cum
hominum ipsorum tum rerum etiam ac temporum
5 condicione mutatur. Nam recentia opera maximi
principis praebent facultatem, nova **magna** vera
censendi. Quibus ex causis, ut supra scripsi, dubito
an idem nunc tibi quod tunc mihi suadeam. Illud
non dubito, debuisse me in parte consilii tui ponere,
quid ipse fecissem. Vale.

XXVIII

C. Plinius Pontio Suo S.

1 Scio quae tibi causa fuerit impedimento, quominus
praecurrere adventum meum in Campaniam posses.
Sed quamquam absens totus huc migrasti: tantum
mihi copiarum qua urbanarum qua rusticarum nomine
tuo oblatum est, quas omnes improbe, accepi tamen.

---

[1] ne *Gesner*: nec *Mγ*.

---

[1] Not, of course, that of the delivery of the *Panegyricus* (as
P. is still *designatus*), but perhaps that of the appeal to Trajan
to accept a fourth consulship (*Pan.* 78).

[2] The conquest of Dacia was completed in 106.

I realized that the highest praise I could offer him was to show that I said nothing because it was expected of me. I also had in mind the many tributes paid to the worst of his predecessors, and I felt that nothing could distinguish our noble Emperor from them so well as a different type of speech. I made no attempt to conceal my intention and did not pass over it without mention, for I did not want him to think it forgetfulness on my part rather than a deliberate decision.

This was the line I took on that occasion,[1] but the same method does not appeal to everyone nor indeed is it always suitable, and our reasons for doing or not doing anything depend on changes in human affairs as well as times and situations. In fact, the recent achievements[2] of our great ruler give you an opportunity to say something original which shall be true and worth saying. Hence my doubts, as I said above, whether I should advise you to act as I did in my time. One thing I don't doubt—I could not have given you any advice without telling you what I did myself.

XXVIII

To Pontius Allifanus

I know what has kept you from being here to welcome my arrival in Campania, but though absent in person you might have been here with all you possess, to judge by the quantities of town and country delicacies I have been offered in your name. I must own I was shameless enough to accept everything.

461

2 Nam me tui ut ita facerem rogabant, et verebar ne et
mihi et illis irascereris, si non fecissem. In posterum
nisi adhibueritis modum ego adhibebo; et iam tuis
denuntiavi, si rursus tam multa attulissent, omnia
3 relaturos. Dices oportere me tuis rebus ut meis uti.
Etiam: sed perinde illis ac meis parco. Vale.

XXIX

C. Plinius Quadrato Suo S.

1 Avidius Quietus, qui me unice dilexit et (quo non
minus gaudeo) probavit, ut multa alia Thraseae (fuit
enim familiaris) ita hoc saepe referebat, praecipere
solitum suscipiendas esse causas aut amicorum aut
destitutas aut ad exemplum pertinentes. Cur ami-
2 corum, non eget interpretatione. Cur destitutas?
quod in illis maxime et constantia agentis et
humanitas cerneretur. Cur pertinentes ad exemplum? quia plurimum referret, bonum an malum
3 induceretur. Ad haec ego genera causarum am-
bitiose fortasse, addam tamen claras et inlustres.
Aequum est enim[1] agere non numquam gloriae
et famae, id est suam causam. Hos terminos,
quia me consuluisti, dignitati ac verecundiae
4 tuae statuo. Nec me praeterit usum et esse et

---

[1] est enim *M*: enim est *γ*.

---

[1] Thrasea Paetus: see Index.

Your servants begged me to do so and I was afraid you would be angry with us all if I refused. In future I shall have to set bounds to your hospitality myself if you will not, and I have already warned your people that if they bring so much another time they will have to take it all back again. You may say that all you have is mine to use: yes, but that means it is also mine to use in moderation.

XXIX

To Ummidius Quadratus

Avidius Quietus, whose good opinion of me I valued as much as his warm affection, had been a friend of Thrasea's[1] and used to tell me many of his sayings. A common one he often quoted was that there were three kinds of case which we should undertake: our friends', those which no one else would take on, and those which establish a precedent. No explanation is needed to show why we should help our friends; we should undertake the second type, he said, as the best means of showing our generosity and strength of mind, and the third because nothing is so important as establishing the right precedent. To these I will add a fourth type of case, though it may seem presumption on my part: cases which bring fame and recognition, for there is no reason why a speaker should not sometimes act for his honour and reputation's sake, and so plead his own case. These then (as you ask my opinion) are the limits I would lay down for a person of your high standing and discretion.

haberi optimum dicendi magistrum; video etiam
multos parvo ingenio litteris nullis, ut bene agerent
5 agendo consecutos. Sed et illud, quod vel Pollionis
vel tamquam Pollionis accepi, verissimum experior:
" Commode agendo factum est ut saepe agerem,
saepe agendo ut minus commode," quia scilicet ad-
siduitate nimia facilitas magis quam facultas, nec
6 fiducia sed temeritas paratur. Nec vero Isocrati quo
minus haberetur summus orator offecit, quod in-
firmitate vocis mollitia frontis ne in publico diceret
impediebatur. Proinde multum lege scribe meditare,
ut possis cum voles dicere: dices cum velle debebis.
7 Hoc fere temperamentum ipse servavi; non numquam necessitati quae pars rationis est parui.
Egi enim quasdam a senatu iussus, quo tamen in
numero fuerunt ex illa Thraseae divisione, hoc est ad
8 exemplum pertinentes. Adfui Baeticis contra Baebium Massam: quaesitum est, an danda esset inquisitio; data est. Adfui rursus isdem querentibus
de Caecilio Classico: quaesitum est, an provinciales
ut socios ministrosque proconsulis plecti oporteret;
9 poenas luerunt. Accusavi Marium Priscum, qui lege
repetundarum damnatus utebatur clementia legis,

---

[1] Cf. Corellius Rufus in I. 12. 3, for whom the supremacy of
reason took the place of necessity.
[2] In 93; see III. 4. 4 and VII. 33.
[3] In 101; see III. 4 and 9.　　　[4] In 99–100; see II. 11.

I am quite well aware that practice is generally held to be the best teacher of public speaking, and rightly so; I see plenty of people with small talent and no education who have acquired the art of speaking well simply by speaking, but at the same time I have found by experience that this saying (which I am told is Pollio's, or at any rate is attributed to him) comes nearest the truth: " By pleading well I came to plead often, but this in turn led me to plead less well." In fact excessive application is more likely to produce facility and foolhardiness than fluency and confidence. His shyness and weak voice prevented Isocrates from speaking in public: nevertheless he was judged to be an orator of the first rank. So read, write, and make all the preparations you can; you will then be able to speak when you wish and when duty calls you.

This was my own guiding principle on the whole, though there were times when I had to yield to necessity, which is one aspect of reason.[1] I undertook certain cases at the bidding of the Senate, but some of these come under Thrasea's heading as establishing a precedent. I appeared for the people of Baetica against Baebius Massa,[2] when the question arose whether time should be granted them in which to collect evidence: it was granted. I acted for them again when they brought a charge against Caecilius Classicus;[3] this time the question was whether provincials should be penalized for being the governor's allies and accomplices: they were punished. I appeared for the prosecution when Marius Priscus[4] was found guilty of taking bribes and tried to profit from the leniency of the law dealing

cuius severitatem immanitate criminum excesserat;
10 relegatus est. Tuitus sum Iulium Bassum, ut in-
custoditum nimis et incautum, ita minime malum;
11 iudicibus acceptis in senatu remansit. Dixi proxime
pro Vareno postulante, ut sibi invicem evocare testes
liceret; impetratum est. In posterum opto ut ea
potissimum iubear, quae me deceat vel sponte fecisse.
Vale.

XXX

C. Plinius Fabato Prosocero Suo S.

1 Debemus mehercule natales tuos perinde ac nostros
celebrare, cum laetitia nostrorum ex tuis pendeat,
cuius diligentia et cura hic hilares istic securi sumus.
2 Villa Camilliana, quam in Campania possides, est
quidem vetustate vexata; et tamen, quae sunt pre-
tiosiora, aut integra manent aut levissime laesa sunt.
3 Attendimus ergo, ut quam saluberrime reficiantur.
Ego videor habere multos amicos, sed huius generis,
cuius et tu quaeris et res exigit, prope neminem.
4 Sunt enim omnes togati et urbani; rusticorum autem
praediorum administratio poscit durum aliquem et
agrestem, cui nec labor ille gravis nec cura sordida
5 nec tristis solitudo videatur. Tu de Rufo honestis-

---

[1] In 102–3; see IV. 9.
[2] In 106–7; see V. 20, and VI. 5 and 13.

with such cases, although the charges against him
were too serious to be covered by the maximum
penalty it allowed: he was banished. I defended
Julius Bassus[1] on the ground that he had acted
foolishly and without proper caution, but with no
criminal intent: he was allowed to have his penalty
assessed by special court and retained his place in the
Senate. I spoke recently on behalf of Varenus[2]
when he applied for permission to call witnesses from
his province for his defence: his request was granted.
As for the future, I hope I shall be required to take up
cases only when I might suitably have done so un-
bidden.

XXX

To Calpurnius Fabatus, his Wife's Grandfather

I am bound indeed to celebrate your birthday like
my own, when my enjoyment of life depends on you;
for thanks to your careful management I can be
happy here and have no worries about things at
Comum.

Your Villa Camilla in Campania is certainly suffering from its age, but the more valuable parts of the
building are still intact or else only very slightly
damaged, so I will have it restored as reasonably as
I can. Among my many friends I seem to have
practically no one of the type you want for this post—
they are all thorough townsfolk, whereas the management of country estates needs a stalwart countryman
who will neither find the work too hard or beneath
him, nor the lonely life depressing. You are quite

sime cogitas; fuit enim filio tuo familiaris. Quid tamen nobis ibi praestare possit ignoro, velle plurimum credo. Vale.

XXXI

C. Plinius Corneliano Suo S.

1 Evocatus in consilium a Caesare nostro ad Centum Cellas (hoc loco nomen), magnam cepi voluptatem.
2 Quid enim iucundius quam principis iustitiam gravitatem comitatem in secessu quoque ubi maxime recluduntur inspicere? Fuerunt variae cognitiones et quae virtutes iudicis per plures species experirentur.
3 Dixit causam Claudius Aristion[1] princeps Ephesiorum, homo munificus et innoxie popularis; inde invidia et a dissimillimis delator immissus, itaque absolutus vindicatusque est.
4 Sequenti die audita est Gallitta adulterii rea. Nupta haec tribuno militum honores petituro, et suam et mariti dignitatem centurionis amore maculaverat. Maritus legato consulari, ille Caesari
5 scripserat. Caesar excussis probationibus centur-

---

[1] Aristion γ: Ariston M.

---

[1] On the coast of Etruria (now Cività Vecchia); its importance later was due to Trajan's artificial harbour.
[2] Probably, like St. Paul, he had exercised his right as a Roman citizen to appeal to Caesar.
[3] The husband and wife are of senatorial rank, the centurion

right to consider Rufus, as he was your son's friend
—I don't know quite what he can do for us there, but
I am sure he intends to do his best.

XXXI

To Cornelianus

I was delighted to be summoned by the Emperor
to act as his assessor at Centum Cellae[1] (as this place
is called). Nothing could give me more pleasure
than to have first-hand experience of our ruler's
justice and wisdom and also to see his lighter moods,
in the sort of country environment where these
qualities are easily revealed. There were several
different types of case which tested his judicial powers
in various ways. The first one was that of Claudius
Ariston, the leading citizen of Ephesus,[2] popular for
his generosity and politically harmless; but he had
roused the envy of people of a vastly different character who had suborned an informer against him. He
was accordingly cleared of the charge and acquitted.

The case heard on the following day was that of
Gallitta, charged with adultery. She was the wife
of a military tribune who was just about to stand for
civil office, and had brought disgrace on her own and
her husband's position by an affair with a centurion.
Her husband had reported it to the governor, and he
had informed the Emperor.[3] After sifting the evidence the Emperor cashiered the centurion and

is not, and this may be why the consular legate preferred not
to deal with the case himself. Later on Trajan implies that it
could have gone to the Senate.

ionem exauctoravit atque etiam relegavit. Supererat crimini, quod nisi duorum esse non poterat, reliqua pars ultionis; sed maritum non sine aliqua repre-
hensione patientiae amor uxoris retardabat, quam
quidem etiam post delatum adulterium domi habue-
6 rat quasi contentus aemulum removisse. Admonitus
ut perageret accusationem, peregit invitus. Sed
illam damnari etiam invito accusatore necesse erat:
damnata et Iuliae legis poenis relicta est. Caesar et
nomen centurionis et commemorationem disciplinae
militaris sententiae adiecit, ne omnes eius modi
causas revocare ad se videretur.

7 Tertio die inducta cognitio est multis sermonibus et
vario rumore iactata, Iuli Tironis codicilli, quos ex
parte veros esse constabat, ex parte falsi dicebantur.
8 Substituebantur crimini Sempronius Senecio eques
Romanus et Eurythmus Caesaris libertus et procurator. Heredes, cum Caesar esset in Dacia,[1] com-
muniter epistula scripta, petierant ut susciperet
9 cognitionem. Susceperat; reversus diem dederat, et
cum ex heredibus quidam quasi reverentia Eurythmi
omitterent accusationem, pulcherrime dixerat: " Nec
ille Polyclitus est nec ego Nero." Indulserat tamen
petentibus dilationem, cuius tempore exacto con-

---

[1] Dacia *Laetus*: dacta γ: patia *M*.

---

[1] The law required the injured husband both to divorce and
to prosecute his wife within 60 days.
[2] Under the *lex Iulia de adulteriis* a woman forfeited half her
dowry and a third of her property, and was banished to an
island.

banished him. There still remained the second half of the sentence, for the charge could only have been made against two persons; but here the husband held back out of affection for his wife and was censured for condoning her conduct.[1] Even after he had reported his wife's adultery he had kept her in his house, apparently satisfied once he had got rid of his rival. When summoned to complete his accusation he did so with reluctance, but it was essential that the woman should be convicted, however unwilling her accuser. She was duly found guilty and sentenced under the Julian law.[2] In pronouncing judgement the Emperor mentioned the name of the centurion and made a statement on military discipline, for he did not wish all cases of this kind to be referred to him.

On the third day began an inquiry into Julius Tiro's will, a case which had given rise to a good deal of discussion and conflicting rumours. Some of the additional clauses to the will were agreed to be genuine; the rest were said to be forged. The persons charged were a Roman knight, Sempronius Senecio, and Eurythmus, one of the Emperor's freedmen and procurators. The heirs had written a joint letter to the Emperor while he was in Dacia, begging him to conduct the inquiry. He had agreed to do so, and had fixed a day for the trial on his return. Then he found that some of the heirs were reluctant to appear against Eurythmus and intended to drop the case, but he had very properly declared that "He is not Polyclitus[3] nor am I Nero." He had however agreed to an adjournment, and took his seat to hear the case

---

[3] Nero's notorious freedman.

10 sederat auditurus. A parte heredum intraverunt
duo omnino; postulaverunt, omnes heredes agere
cogerentur, cum detulissent omnes, aut sibi quoque
11 desistere permitteretur. Locutus est Caesar summa
gravitate summa moderatione, cumque advocatus
Senecionis et Eurythmi dixisset suspicionibus relinqui
reos, nisi audirentur, " Non curo " inquit " an isti
12 suspicionibus relinquantur, ego relinquor." Dein
conversus ad nos: " Ἐπιστήσατε quid facere debeamus; isti enim queri volunt quod sibi licuerit non
accusari."[1] Tum ex consilii sententia iussit denun-
tiari heredibus omnibus, aut agerent aut singuli
adprobarent causas non agendi; alioqui se vel de
calumnia pronuntiaturum.

13 Vides quam honesti, quam severi dies; quos iucun-
dissimae remissiones sequebantur. Adhibebamur
cotidie cenae; erat modica, si principem cogitares.
Interdum acroamata audiebamus, interdum iucun-
14 dissimis sermonibus nox ducebatur. Summo die
abeuntibus nobis (tam diligens in Caesare humanitas)
xenia sunt missa. Sed mihi ut gravitas cognitio-
num, consilii honor, suavitas simplicitasque convictus,
15 ita locus ipse periucundus fuit. Villa pulcherrima
cingitur viridissimis agris, imminet litori, cuius in
sinu fit cum maxime portus. Huius sinistrum brach-

---

[1] accusari *Guillemin*: accusare *Mγ Stout*.

---

[1] Cf. the description by Rutilius Namatianus, *De reditu*, I.
239–45.

now that the time-limit had expired. Only two of the heirs came to court, and they asked that either all the heirs should be compelled to appear, as all were responsible for the prosecution, or that they should themselves be allowed to drop the case. The Emperor's reply was restrained and impressive, but, when the counsel for Senecio and Eurythmus said that his clients were left under suspicion if they were not given a hearing, " I am not concerned so much with their position," he said, " as with the fact I am left under suspicion myself." Then he turned to us. " Consider what we ought to do. These people want to complain about being let off the charge against them." Acting on our advice he then gave orders that all the heirs were to be summoned to carry on the case or else to give adequate reasons individually for dropping it: otherwise he would declare them guilty even of instituting false charges.

As you see, our days were well spent on serious matters, but we enjoyed our relaxations in the evenings. The Emperor invited us to dinner every day, a simple affair if you consider his position. Sometimes we were entertained by recitations, or else the night was prolonged by pleasant conversation, and, on our last day, with his usual thoughtful generosity, he sent us all parting gifts. I took great pleasure in the importance of the cases, the honour of being an assessor, and the charm and informality of our social life, and I was no less delighted in the place itself. The house is really beautiful: it is surrounded by green fields and faces the sea-shore, where a natural bay is being converted at this moment into a harbour.[1] The left arm has already been reinforced by a solid

ium firmissimo opere munitum est, dextrum elabora-
16 tur. In ore portus insula adsurgit, quae inlatum
vento mare obiacens frangat, tutumque ab utroque
latere decursum navibus praestet. Adsurgit autem
arte visenda: ingentia saxa latissima navis provehit
contra; haec[1] alia super alia deiecta ipso pondere
manent ac sensim quodam velut aggere construuntur.
17 Eminet iam et adparet saxeum dorsum impactosque
fluctus in immensum elidit et tollit; vastus illic
fragor canumque circa mare. Saxis deinde pilae
adicientur quae procedente tempore enatam insulam
imitentur. Habebit hic portus, et iam habet nomen
auctoris, eritque vel maxime salutaris; nam per
longissimum spatium litus importuosum hoc recep-
taculo utetur. Vale.

XXXII

C. Plinius Quintiliano Suo S.

1 Quamvis et ipse sis continentissimus, et filiam tuam
ita institueris ut decebat tuam filiam, Tutili neptem,
cum tamen sit nuptura honestissimo viro Nonio
Celeri, cui ratio civilium officiorum necessitatem
quandam nitoris imponit, debet secundum condicionem mariti ⟨uti⟩[2] veste comitatu, quibus non quidem
2 augetur dignitas, ornatur tamen et instruitur.[3] Te

---

[1] provehit; contra haec *Stout*: provehit oneraria *Guillemin*.
[2] uti *add. Mommsen*, augeri *post* comitatu θ: *om. M*γ, Stout.
[3] et instruitur *M*θ: instrui γ, *Stout*.

---

[1] This is not confirmed elsewhere.
[2] Not the famous Quintilian, who was dead by this time.

mole and the right is in process of construction. At the entrance to the harbour an island is rising out of the water to act as a breakwater when the wind blows inland, and so give a safe passage to ships entering from either side. Its construction is well worth seeing. Huge stones are brought by large barges and thrown out one on top of another facing the harbour; their weight keeps them in position and the pile gradually rises in a sort of rampart. A hump of rocks can already be seen sticking up, which breaks the waves beating against it and tosses them high into the air with a resounding crash, so that the sea all round is white with foam. Later on piers will be built on the stone foundation, and as time goes on it will look like a natural island. The harbour will be called after its maker,[1] and is in fact already known by his name; and it will save countless lives by providing a haven on this long stretch of harbourless coast.

XXXII

To Quintilianus [2]

I know your own tastes are of the simplest and that you have brought up your daughter as befits a daughter of yours and a grandchild of Tutilius; but as she is to marry so distinguished a person as Nonius Celer, whose public duties oblige him to keep up a certain amount of style, she ought to be provided with clothes and attendants in keeping with her husband's position. These things cannot increase her worth, but can give it the proper setting it needs. I know

porro animo beatissimum, modicum facultatibus scio.
Itaque partem oneris tui mihi vindico, et tamquam
parens alter puellae nostrae confero quinquaginta
milia nummum plus collaturus, nisi a verecundia tua
sola mediocritate munusculi impetrari posse con-
fiderem, ne recusares.   Vale.

XXXIII

C. Plinius Romano Suo S.

1   " Tollite cuncta " inquit " coeptosque auferte
labores! "   Seu scribis aliquid seu legis, tolli auferri
iube et accipe orationem meam ut illa arma divinam
(num superbius potui?), re vera ut inter meas pul-
2 chram; nam mihi satis est certare mecum.   Est
haec pro Attia Viriola, et dignitate personae et exempli raritate et iudicii magnitudine insignis.   Nam
femina splendide nata, nupta praetorio viro, exhere-
data ab octogenario patre intra undecim dies quam
illi novercam amore captus induxerat, quadruplici
3 iudicio bona paterna repetebat.   Sedebant centum
et octoginta iudices (tot enim quattuor consiliis
colliguntur), ingens utrimque advocatio et numerosa
subsellia, praeterea densa circumstantium corona
4 latissimum iudicium multiplici circulo ambibat.   Ad

---

[1] *Aeneid* VIII. 439.

too that you are rich in intellectual gifts but that your means are limited, so I want to share your burden and play the part of a second father to our daughter. I am therefore settling 50,000 sesterces on her, and would offer more were I not sure that it is only the trifling nature of the gift which will prevail on your sense of delicacy to accept it.

XXXIII

To Voconius Romanus

" Away with everything," he said, " and put aside whatever you have begun! " [1] You may be reading something or writing—have it cleared away and take up my speech; like Vulcan's arms, it is divine. Could conceit go farther? But, seriously, compared with my other speeches it is very fine, and I am quite content to rival myself. It was delivered on behalf of Attia Viriola, and its interest lies not only in the position of the person concerned but also in the rarity of this type of case and the size of the court which heard it. Here was a woman of high birth, the wife of a praetorian senator, disinherited by her eighty-year-old father ten days after he had fallen in love and brought home a stepmother for his daughter, and now suing for her patrimony in the united Centumviral Court. One hundred and eighty judges were sitting, the total for the four panels acting together; both parties were fully represented and had a large number of seats filled with their supporters, and a close-packed ring of onlookers, several rows deep, lined the walls of the courtroom. The bench was

hoc stipatum tribunal, atque etiam ex superiore
basilicae parte qua feminae qua viri et audiendi
(quod difficile) et (quod facile) visendi studio immine-
bant. Magna exspectatio patrum, magna filiarum,
5 magna etiam novercarum. Secutus est varius
eventus; nam duobus consiliis vicimus, totidem victi
sumus. Notabilis prorsus et mira eadem in causa,
isdem iudicibus, isdem advocatis, eodem tempore
6 tanta diversitas. Accidit casu, quod non casus
videretur: victa est noverca, ipsa heres ex parte
sexta, victus Suburanus,[1] qui exheredatus a patre
singulari impudentia alieni patris bona vindicabat,
non ausus sui petere.

7   Haec tibi exposui, primum ut ex epistula scires,
quae ex oratione non poteras, deinde (nam detegam
artes) ut orationem libentius legeres, si non legere
tibi sed interesse iudicio videreris; quam, sit licet
magna, non despero gratiam brevissimae impetratu-
8 ram. Nam et copia rerum et arguta divisione et
narratiunculis pluribus et eloquendi varietate re-
novatur. Sunt multa (non auderem nisi tibi dicere)
9 elata, multa pugnacia, multa subtilia. Intervenit
enim acribus illis et erectis frequens necessitas com-
putandi ac paene calculos tabulamque poscendi, ut
repente in privati iudicii formam centumvirale
10 vertatur. Dedimus vela indignationi, dedimus irae,

---

[1] Suburanus *Catanaeus*: Suberinus *Mθ Stout*: Subberimus
(*vel* Suberrimus) γ.

also crowded, and even the galleries were full of men and women leaning over in their eagerness to see and also to hear, though hearing was rather more difficult. Fathers, daughters and stepmothers all anxiously awaited the verdict. This proved not to be united, for two divisions voted for us and two against. Such divergence of opinion was particularly surprising in a single case, conducted by the same counsel before the same judges at the same hearing. By pure chance, though it might have been thought otherwise, the stepmother, who had been left a sixth of the estate, lost her case, and so did Suburanus, who had the extraordinary impudence to claim someone else's patrimony when he had been disherited by his own father and dare not sue for his own.

I have told you this first so that this letter shall explain anything you cannot understand from the speech, and also (for I don't conceal my guile) because I thought you would be more willing to read the speech if you imagined yourself not reading but present at the actual trial. It is long, but I feel sure it will be as popular as a short one, for the interest is kept up by the lively arrangement of the abundant material, the frequent use of short anecdotes, and the variety of oratorical style. Much of it is in the grand manner and full of fire (I wouldn't dare say this to anyone else) but there are long sections in a plainer style, where I was often obliged to introduce calculations into the midst of my impassioned and lofty arguments, and practically demand counters and a board for reckoning, as if my chancery case had been transformed into a private one. I gave full play to my feelings of wrath and indignation, and steered my

dedimus dolori, et in amplissima causa quasi magno
11 mari pluribus ventis sumus vecti. In summa solent
quidam ex contubernalibus nostris existimare hanc
orationem (iterum dicam) ut inter meas ὑπὲρ Κτησι-
φῶντος esse: an vere, tu facillime iudicabis, qui tam
memoriter tenes omnes, ut conferre cum hac dum
hanc legis possis. Vale.

XXXIV

C. PLINIUS MAXIMO SUO S.

1 RECTE fecisti quod gladiatorium munus Veronensi-
bus nostris promisisti, a quibus olim amaris suspiceris
ornaris. Inde etiam uxorem carissimam tibi et
probatissimam habuisti, cuius memoriae aut opus
aliquod aut spectaculum atque hoc potissimum, quod
2 maxime funeri, debebatur. Praeterea tanto consensu rogabaris, ut negare non constans, sed durum
videretur. Illud quoque egregie, quod tam facilis
tam liberalis in edendo fuisti; nam per haec etiam
3 magnus animus ostenditur Vellem Africanae, quas
coemeras plurimas, ad praefinitum diem occurrissent:
sed licet cessaverint illae tempestate detentae, tu
tamen meruisti ut acceptum tibi fieret, quod quo
minus exhiberes, non per te stetit. Vale.

---

[1] Demosthenes' most celebrated speech.

course on the open sea through this vastly important case with the wind full in my favour. In fact—for the second time—some of my friends think that in comparison with my other speeches, this one is my "*De Corona.*"[1] Whether this is so or not, you can easily judge. You have all my speeches by heart, so you only have to read the one I am sending now to be able to make your comparison.

XXXIV

To VALERIUS (?) MAXIMUS

You did well to put on a show of gladiators for our people of Verona, who have long shown their affection and admiration for you and have voted you many honours. Verona was also the home town of the excellent wife you loved so dearly, whose memory you owe some public building or show, and this kind of spectacle is particularly suitable for a funeral tribute. Moreover, the request came from so many people that a refusal would have been judged churlish rather than strong-minded on your part. You have also done admirably in giving the show so readily and on such a lavish scale, for this indicates a true spirit of generosity.

I am sorry the African panthers you had bought in such quantities did not turn up on the appointed day, but you deserve the credit although the weather prevented their arriving in time: it was not your fault that you could not show them.

BOOK VII

LIBER SEPTIMUS

I

C. Plinius Gemino Suo S.

1 Terret me haec tua tam pertinax valetudo, et quamquam te temperantissimum noverim, vereor tamen
2 ne quid illi etiam in mores tuos liceat. Proinde
moneo patienter resistas: hoc laudabile hoc salutare.
3 Admittit humana natura quod suadeo. Ipse certe
sic agere sanus cum meis soleo: " Spero quidem, si
forte in adversam valetudinem incidero, nihil me
desideraturum vel pudore vel paenitentia dignum;
si tamen superaverit morbus, denuntio ne quid mihi
detis, nisi permittentibus medicis, sciatisque si
dederitis ita vindicaturum, ut solent alii quae negan-
4 tur." Quin etiam cum perustus ardentissima febre,
tandem remissus unctusque, acciperem a medico
potionem, porrexi manum utque tangeret dixi, ad-
5 motumque iam labris poculum reddidi. Postea cum
vicensimo valetudinis die balineo praepararer, mus-
santesque medicos repente vidissem, causam requisivi. Responderunt posse me tuto lavari, non tamen
6 omnino sine aliqua suspicione. " Quid " inquam

---

[1] Pliny was seriously ill about 97. See X. 5; 8. 3; 11.

BOOK VII

I

To Rosianus Geminus

This persistent ill-health of yours is alarming, and, although I know that your self-control is generally excellent, I am afraid that your character may be affected. I can only advise you to be patient and endure; there is hope of recovery as well as merit in this, and what I am asking is not beyond human capacity. At any rate I personally, when in good health, have often spoken like this to my household: " I hope that if I chance to fall ill, I shall not ask for anything which would be a reason for subsequent shame and regret, but, if illness gets the upper hand, I warn you now not to give me anything without the doctors' permission, or else I shall punish you as anyone else would for refusing." I was indeed once suffering from a raging fever:[1] at last it began to abate, I was oiled and massaged and was just taking a drink from the doctor when I held out my hand and asked him to feel my pulse, refusing the cup which had been put to my lips. Later on, when I had been ill nearly three weeks, I was being prepared for a bath, but suddenly noticed the doctors whispering and asked the reason why. They replied that probably it was quite safe for me to take a bath, but they felt a little doubtful about it. "Then is it necessary?"

" necesse est? " atque ita spe balinei, cui iam vide-
bar inferri, placide leniterque dimissa, ad abstinen-
tiam rursus, non secus ac modo ad balineum, animum
7 vultumque composui.   Quae tibi scripsi, primum ut te
non sine exemplo monerem, deinde ut in posterum
ipse ad eandem temperantiam adstringerer, cum me
hac epistula quasi pignore obligavissem.   Vale.

II

C. Plinius Iusto Suo S.

1   Quemadmodum congruit, ut simul et adfirmes te
adsiduis occupationibus impediri, et scripta nostra
desideres, quae vix ab otiosis impetrare aliquid peri-
2 turi temporis possunt?   Patiar ergo aestatem inquie-
tam vobis exercitamque transcurrere, et hieme demum, cum credibile erit noctibus saltem vacare te
posse, quaeram quid potissimum ex nugis meis tibi
3 exhibeam.   Interim abunde est si epistulae non sunt
molestae; sunt autem et ideo breviores erunt.   Vale.

III

C. Plinius Praesenti Suo S.

1   Tantane perseverantia tu modo in Lucania, modo
in Campania?   " Ipse enim " inquis " Lucanus, uxor

---

[1] This suggests an army command c. 106, perhaps Upper
Moesia (Syme, *JRS*, XLIX, 28 ff.).

I asked, and so without protest quietly gave up hope
of the bath which in my imagination I was already
entering, and resigned myself again to do without it
with the same inward and outward composure as
when I was in a state of anticipation.

My initial reason for telling you this was to have an
example to illustrate my advice, but I can also use
this letter as a kind of pledge to bind me to practise
the same self-control in future.

II

To Fabius (?) Justus

I don't see how you can say in the same breath
that your time is taken up by incessant public duties
and ask to see my speeches! I have difficulty enough
when people have plenty of time in persuading them
to give up a moment of their wasted hours. I will
let you finish the summer, which I know is always a
busy and trying time for you,[1] and then in winter,
when your nights at least are likely to be free, I will
look through my efforts for something to send.
Meanwhile I am more than satisfied if my letters are
not a nuisance; but I expect they are and will make
them shorter in future.

III

To Bruttius Praesens

How much longer will you persist in dividing your
time between Lucania and Campania? I know you

2 Campana." Iusta causa longioris absentiae, non
perpetuae tamen. Quin ergo aliquando in urbem
redis? ubi dignitas honor amicitiae tam superiores
quam minores. Quousque regnabis? quousque
vigilabis cum voles, dormies quamdiu voles? quousque calcei nusquam, toga feriata, liber totus dies?

3 Tempus est te revisere molestias nostras, vel ob hoc
solum ne voluptates istae satietate languescant.
Saluta paulisper, quo sit tibi iucundius salutari;

4 terere in hac turba, ut te solitudo delectet. Sed quid
imprudens quem evocare conor retardo? Fortasse
enim his ipsis admoneris, ut te magis ac magis otio
involvas; quod ego non abrumpi sed intermitti volo.

5 Ut enim, si cenam tibi facerem, dulcibus cibis acres
acutosque miscerem, ut obtusus illis et oblitus stomachus his excitaretur, ita nunc hortor ut iucundissimum genus vitae non nullis interdum quasi acoribus
condias. Vale.

IV

C. PLINIUS PONTIO SUO S.

1 AIS legisse te hendecasyllabos meos; requiris
etiam quemadmodum coeperim scribere, homo ut

---

[1] This fits in with the career of Praesens in an inscription
from N. Africa (S. 193). He was praetor by about 104 but
consul much later, 118 or 119, though a legionary legate in
114 and legate of Cilicia in 117.

say that Lucania is your native district and Campania
your wife's, but that can only justify a prolonged
absence, not a perpetual one. Are you ever coming
back to Rome,[1] back to your honours and official
duties, your influential friendships, and your clients'
attentions? How much longer will you be your own
master, stay up when you feel inclined, and sleep as
long as you like? How long will your shoes go un-
worn and your toga stay on holiday, while all your
day is your own? It is time you renewed acquaintance with our vexations, if only to prevent your
pleasures diminishing through sheer surfeit. Come
and pay your respects to us for a while so as to be
better pleased to receive other peoples', and rub
shoulders in the crowd here in order to appreciate
your solitude the more.

But it is silly of me to risk discouraging the very
person I am trying to persuade; my arguments may
well induce you to sink deeper and deeper into
retirement, though I am not asking you to give it up,
only to interrupt it. If I were giving you a dinner,
I should alternate the sweet dishes with piquant
savouries to stimulate your palate when dulled and
cloyed by too much sweetness; and so I am asking
you now to season your pleasant way of living with
something a little more stimulating.

IV

To Pontius Allifanus

You say that you have read my hendecasyllables,
and you want to know how a serious man like me

tibi videor severus, ut ipse fateor non ineptus.
2 Numquam a poetice (altius enim repetam) alienus
fui; quin etiam quattuordecim natus annos Graecam
tragoediam scripsi. " Qualem? " inquis. Nescio;
3 tragoedia vocabatur. Mox, cum e militia rediens in
Icaria insula ventis detinerer, Latinos elegos in illud
ipsum mare ipsamque insulam feci. Expertus sum
me aliquando et heroo, hendecasyllabis nunc primum,
quorum hic natalis haec causa est. Legebantur in
Laurentino mihi libri Asini Galli de comparatione
patris et Ciceronis. Incidit epigramma Ciceronis
4 in Tironem suum. Dein cum meridie (erat enim
aestas) dormiturus me recepissem, nec obreperet
somnus, coepi reputare maximos oratores hoc studii
genus et in oblectationibus habuisse et in laude
5 posuisse. Intendi animum contraque opinionem
meam post longam desuetudinem perquam exiguo
temporis momento id ipsum, quod me ad scribendum
sollicitaverat, his versibus exaravi:

6 Cum libros Galli legerem, quibus ille parenti
ausus de Cicerone dare est[1] palmamque decusque,
lascivum inveni lusum Ciceronis et illo
spectandum ingenio, quo seria condidit et quo
humanis salibus multo varioque lepore
magnorum ostendit mentes gaudere virorum.
Nam queritur quod fraude mala frustratus amantem
paucula cenato sibi debita savia Tiro
tempore nocturno subtraxerit. His ego lectis

---

[1] dare est *Casaubon*: dare *a*: daret *Mγ*.

---

[1] In the Aegean, between Delos and Samos (now Nicaria).
He was returning from Syria via Corinth.

came to write them; and I am not frivolous, I admit. To start at the beginning, I was always interested in poetry and wrote a Greek tragedy at the age of fourteen. What it was like I can't say—anyway, I called it a tragedy. Later on I was weatherbound in the island of Icaria[1] while on my way home from military service, and wrote some Latin elegiacs with the sea and island for theme. I have also occasionally tried my hand at epic verse, but this is my first attempt at hendecasyllables. This is how they came into being. While I was staying in my house at Laurentum I had Asinius Gallus's works read aloud to me, in which he draws a comparison between his father and Cicero and quotes an epigram of Cicero's on his favourite Tiro. Then, when I had retired for my siesta (it was summer) and was unable to sleep, I began to reflect upon the fact that all the greatest orators had amused themselves with this kind of writing and had seen merit in doing so. I set my mind to it, and, to my surprise, in spite of being long out of practice, I had soon expressed the very thought which had inspired me to write. This was the result:

Reading the works of Gallus, where he ventures
To hand the palm of glory to his father,
I found that Cicero could unbend his talent
To play with polished wit on lighter theme.
He showed how well the minds of mighty men
Enjoyed the pleasure of much varied charms:
Tiro, he says, defrauds and cheats his lover;
Kisses—not many—promised for a dinner
Are afterwards denied when night-time comes.

THE LETTERS OF PLINY

" cur post haec " inquam " nostros celamus amores
nullumque in medium timidi damus atque fatemur
Tironisque dolos, Tironis nosse fugaces
blanditias et furta novas addentia flammas ? "

7 Transii ad elegos; hos quoque non minus celeriter
explicui, addidi alios facilitate corruptus. Deinde in
8 urbem reversus sodalibus legi; probaverunt. Inde
plura metra si quid otii, ac maxime in itinere temptavi. Postremo placuit exemplo multorum unum
separatim hendecasyllaborum volumen absolvere,
9 nec paenitet. Legitur describitur cantatur etiam,
et a Graecis quoque, quos Latine huius libelli amor
10 docuit, nunc cithara nunc lyra personatur. Sed
quid ego tam gloriose ? Quamquam poetis furere
concessum est. Et tamen non de meo sed de
aliorum iudicio loquor; qui sive iudicant sive errant,
me delectat.[1] Unum precor, ut posteri quoque aut
errent similiter aut iudicent. Vale.

V

C. Plinius Calpurniae Suae S.

1 INCREDIBILE est quanto desiderio tui tenear. In
causa amor primum, deinde quod non consuevimus
abesse. Inde est quod magnam noctium partem in
imagine tua vigil exigo; inde quod interdiu, quibus
horis te visere solebam, ad diaetam tuam ipsi me,

---

[1] delectat *M*: delectant *γ*.

---

[1] These verses are not, of course, in hendecasyllables, but in
hexameters. The implied relationship between Cicero and his
freedman Tiro is not certain.

Why then conceal my blushes, fear to publish
My Tiro's wiles and coy endearing favours
Whereby he heaps the fuel on my passion?[1]

Next I tried some elegiac verses, which I finished
just as quickly, and finding them so easy I was
tempted to add more. Afterwards, when I returned
to Rome, I read them to my friends, who were appreciative. Then I made attempts in various other
metres whenever I had time, especially when travelling. Finally I decided to do as many authors have
done and complete a separate volume of hendecasyllables; and I have never regretted this. My verses
are read and copied, they are even sung, and set to
the cithara or lyre by Greeks who have learned Latin
out of liking for my little book. But I must not boast
(though poets are allowed to talk wildly!), even if it
is not my own opinion I am quoting but other people's
—which pleases me whether right or wrong. I only
pray that posterity will be right or wrong in the same
way.

V

To his Wife Calpurnia

You cannot believe how much I miss you. I love
you so much, and we are not used to separations. So
I stay awake most of the night thinking of you, and
by day I find my feet carrying me (a true word,
carrying) to your room at the times I usually visited

ut verissime dicitur, pedes ducunt; quod denique aeger et maestus ac similis excluso a vacuo limine recedo. Unum tempus his tormentis caret, quo in
2 foro et amicorum litibus conteror. Aestima tu, quae vita mea sit, cui requies in labore, in miseria curisque solacium. Vale.

VI

C. PLINIUS MACRINO SUO S.

1 RARA et notabilis res Vareno contigit, sit licet adhuc dubia. Bithyni accusationem eius ut temere incohatam omisisse narrantur. " Narrantur " dico? Adest provinciae legatus, attulit decretum concilii ad Caesarem, attulit ad multos principes viros, attulit
2 etiam ad nos Vareni advocatos. Perstat tamen idem ille Magnus; quin etiam Nigrinum optimum virum pertinacissime exercet. Per hunc a consulibus postulabat, ut Varenus exhibere rationes cogeretur.
3 Adsistebam Vareno iam tantum ut amicus et tacere decreveram. Nihil enim tam contrarium quam si advocatus a senatu datus defenderem ut reum, cui
4 opus esset ne reus videretur. Cum tamen finita postulatione Nigrini consules ad me oculos rettulissent, " Scietis " inquam " constare nobis silentii nostri rationem, cum veros legatos provinciae audieri-

---

[1] See V. 20, and VI. 5 and 13.
[2] *i.e.* a second deputation from Bithynia.
[3] Fonteius Magnus, V. 20. 4, and Avidius Nigrinus, V. 20. 6.

you; then finding it empty I depart, as sick and sorrowful as a lover locked out. The only time I am free from this misery is when I am in court and wearing myself out with my friends' lawsuits. You can judge then what a life I am leading, when I find my rest in work and distraction in troubles and anxiety.

VI

To Caecilius Macrinus

A most extraordinary thing has happened to Varenus,[1] though it is not yet definitely settled. The Bithynians are reported to have dropped their case against him, as an ill-advised venture. I say "reported," but the representative of the province is here[2] with his Council's decree, copies of which he has presented to the Emperor, to a large number of prominent citizens, and to us, as acting for Varenus. However, Magnus[3] is being as obstinate as ever and keeps on harassing that excellent man Nigrinus,[3] through whom he has approached the consuls with a demand for Varenus to be compelled to produce his accounts.

At this stage I was standing by Varenus in a friendly capacity only and decided to say nothing, for it could only have done him harm if the counsel given him by the Senate began by defending him as if he were on trial when the essential thing was to show that he was not on trial at all. But when Nigrinus had made his request and the consuls turned to me, I said that they would see that I had good reason for my silence as soon as they had heard the true

tis." Contra Nigrinus: " Ad quem missi sunt? '
Ego: " Ad me quoque: habeo decretum provinciae."
5 Rursus ille: " Potest tibi liquere." Ad hoc ego:
" Si tibi ex diverso liquet, potest et mihi quod est
6 melius liquere." Tum legatus Polyaenus causas
abolitae accusationis exposuit, postulavitque ne
cognitioni Caesaris praeiudicium fieret. Respondit
Magnus iterumque Polyaenus. Ipse raro et breviter interlocutus multum me intra silentium tenui.
7 Accepi enim non minus interdum oratorium esse
tacere quam dicere.

Atque adeo repeto me quibusdam capitis reis vel
magis silentio quam oratione accuratissima profuisse.
8 Mater amisso filio (quid enim prohibet, quamquam
alia ratio scribendae epistulae fuerit, de studiis disputare?) libertos eius eosdemque coheredes suos falsi
et veneficii reos detulerat ad principem, iudicemque
9 impetraverat Iulium Servianum. Defenderam reos
ingenti quidem coetu; erat enim causa notissima,
praeterea utrimque ingenia clarissima. Finem cognitioni quaestio imposuit, quae secundum reos dedit.
10 Postea mater adiit principem, adfirmavit se novas
probationes invenisse. Praeceptum est Suburano, ut
vacaret finitam causam retractanti, si quid novi

---

[1] The Latin is obscure and the legal situation complex.
Evidently Servianus had been told to hold an inquiry (*cognitio*)
into the question of procedure, as the law did not permit
accusations of more than one person. He appears to have
allowed a dispensation, and the case then went to the regular
praetor's court (*quaestio*). (See S-W, pp. 409-10.)

[2] Attius Suburanus. See Index.

representatives of the province. "To whom have they been sent?" countered Nigrinus. "To me, among others," I replied: "I have the Council's decree." "You may have your own information," he said. "If you have yours," I retorted, "surely I may have mine—of a better sort." Then Polyaenus, the Bithynian spokesman, explained their reasons for dropping the prosecution and asked that no decision should be taken before the Emperor held an inquiry. Magnus replied to this, and Polyaenus spoke again. I threw in a few words now and then, but kept silent most of the time, for I have learned that there are occasions when silence is as effective a form of oratory as eloquence.

I can indeed remember certain criminal cases when I did my clients more good by saying nothing than I could have done by the most elaborate speech. For example (there is nothing to stop me from discussing my professional activities, though I had another purpose in writing this letter), a mother who had lost her son charged his freedmen, who were heirs to the estate with her, of poisoning their master and forging his will. She had brought her case before the Emperor and been granted Julius Servianus to judge it. I had defended the accused men before a large assembly, for the case was celebrated and there were distinguished personalities engaged on both sides. The inquiry was stopped after the court had decided in favour of the defendants.[1] Subsequently the mother approached the Emperor with a declaration that she had discovered fresh evidence. Suburanus[2] was instructed to find time for the case again, if she could produce any new material. The mother

11 adferret. Aderat matri Iulius Africanus, nepos illius oratoris, quo audito Passienus Crispus dixit: " Bene mehercule, bene; sed quo tam bene? " Huius nepos, iuvenis ingeniosus sed non[1] parum callidus, cum multa dixisset adsignatumque tempus implesset, " Rogo " inquit, " Suburane, permittas mihi 12 unum verbum adicere." Tum ego, cum omnes me ut diu responsurum intuerentur," Respondissem " inquam " si unum illud verbum Africanus adiecisset, 13 in quo non dubito omnia nova fuisse." Non facile me repeto tantum adsensum agendo consecutum, quantum tunc non agendo.

Similiter nunc et probatum et exceptum est, quod 14 pro Vareno hactenus [non] tacui.[2] Consules, ut Polyaenus postulabat, omnia integra principi servaverunt; cuius cognitionem suspensus exspecto. Nam dies ille nobis pro Vareno aut securitatem et otium dabit aut intermissum laborem renovata sollicitudine iniunget. Vale.

VII

C. PLINIUS SATURNINO SUO S.

ET proxime Prisco nostro et rursus, quia ita iussisti, gratias egi. Libentissime quidem: est enim mihi periucundum, quod viri optimi mihique amicissimi adeo cohaesistis, ut invicem vos obligari putetis.

---

[1] sed *My*: et *θ*: non *My*: del. *R. Agricola, Guillemin.*
[2] tacui *R. Agricola*: non tacui *My, Stout.*

was represented by Julius Africanus, the grandson of the famous orator about whom Passienus Crispus said after hearing him speak, " Fine, by Jove, fine; but *why* so fine ? " His grandson, an able young man but a bit too sharp, had said a good deal and come to the end of his time-limit, but then asked Suburanus for permission to add " just one more word." My turn came, and everyone was looking to me for a lengthy reply. " I should have spoken in reply," I said, " if Africanus had added his ' one more word,' for this, I am sure, would have contained all the fresh evidence." I can scarcely remember ever winning such applause for a speech as I did on that occasion for not making one.

The same sort of reception and applause has greeted my policy of saying nothing for Varenus. The consuls have granted Polyaenus's request and left the whole question open for the Emperor to decide. I am anxiously awaiting the result of the inquiry; for that day will determine whether we are to have some peace and respite from worry on Varenus's account or to renew our efforts with fresh anxiety.

VII

To Pompeius Saturninus

I THANKED our friend Priscus only the other day, but I was very glad to do so again at your bidding. It is a great pleasure to me that splendid men like yourselves, both friends of mine, should be so devoted and conscious of your mutual attachment. Priscus also

2 Nam ille quoque praecipuam se voluptatem ex amicitia tua capere profitetur, certatque tecum honestissimo certamine mutuae caritatis, quam ipsum tempus augebit. Te negotiis distineri ob hoc moleste
fero, quod deservire studiis non potes. Si tamen
alteram litem per iudicem, alteram (ut ais) ipse finieris,
incipies primum istic otio frui, deinde satiatus ad nos
reverti. Vale.

VIII

C. Plinius Prisco Suo S.

1 Exprimere non possum. quam iucundum sit mihi
quod Saturninus noster summas tibi apud me gratias
2 aliis super alias epistulis agit. Perge ut coepisti,
virumque optimum quam familiarissime dilige,
magnam voluptatem ex amicitia eius percepturus nec
3 ad breve tempus. Nam cum omnibus virtutibus
abundat, tum hac praecipue, quod habet maximam in
amore constantiam. Vale.

IX

C. Plinius Fusco Suo S.

1 Quaeris quemadmodum in secessu, quo iam diu
2 frueris, putem te studere oportere. Utile in primis,
et multi praecipiunt, vel ex Graeco in Latinum vel
ex Latino vertere in Graecum. Quo genere exerci-

declares that nothing gives him greater happiness than his friendship with you and vies with you in this best of rivalries, a reciprocated affection which will increase as time goes on.

I am sorry to hear that you are immersed in business, as it keeps you from your own work, but if you can settle one case by arbitration and the other, as you say, by your own efforts, you will begin to enjoy your leisure where you are; and then can return to us when you are tired of it.

VIII

To Neratius (?) Priscus

Words cannot express my pleasure on receiving letter after letter from our friend Saturninus, in which he expresses his warmest thanks to you. Go on as you have begun, love this splendid man as much as you can; his friendship will prove a source of long and lasting happiness for he is endowed with all the virtues, not least the gift of unfailing loyalty in his affections.

IX

To Fuscus Salinator

You ask me what course of study I think you should follow during your present prolonged holiday. The most useful thing, which is always being suggested, is to translate Greek into Latin and Latin into Greek. This kind of exercise develops in one a precision and richness of vocabulary, a wide range of metaphor

tationis proprietas splendorque verborum, copia
figurarum, vis explicandi, praeterea imitatione
optimorum similia inveniendi facultas paratur; simul
quae legentem fefellissent, transferentem fugere non
3 possunt. Intellegentia ex hoc et iudicium adquiritur.
Nihil offuerit quae legeris hactenus, ut rem argu-
mentumque teneas, quasi aemulum scribere lectisque
conferre, ac sedulo pensitare, quid tu quid ille commodius. Magna gratulatio si non nulla tu, magnus
pudor si cuncta ille melius. Licebit interdum et notis-
4 sima eligere et certare cum electis. Audax haec,
non tamen improba, quia secreta contentio: quamquam multos videmus eius modi certamina sibi cum
multa laude sumpsisse, quosque subsequi satis habe-
5 bant, dum non desperant, antecessisse. Poteris et
quae dixeris post oblivionem retractare, multa retinere plura transire, alia interscribere alia rescribere.
6 Laboriosum istud et taedio plenum, sed difficultate
ipsa fructuosum, recalescere ex integro et resumere
impetum fractum omissumque, postremo nova velut
membra peracto corpori intexere nec tamen priora
7 turbare. Scio nunc tibi esse praecipuum studium
orandi; sed non ideo semper pugnacem hunc et
quasi bellatorium stilum suaserim. Ut enim terrae

and power of exposition, and, moreover, imitation of the best models leads to a like aptitude for original composition. At the same time, any point which might have been overlooked by a reader cannot escape the eye of a translator. All this cultivates perception and critical sense.

When you have read a passage sufficiently to remember the subject-matter and line of thought, there is no harm in your trying to compete with it; then compare your efforts with the original and consider carefully where your version is better or worse. You may well congratulate yourself if yours is sometimes better and feel much ashamed if the other is always superior to yours. You may also sometimes choose a passage you know well and try to improve on it. This is a daring attempt, but does not presume too far when it is made in private; and yet we see many people entering this type of contest with great credit to themselves and, by not lacking confidence, outstripping the authors whom they intended only to follow. You can also revise the speeches you have put aside, retaining much of the original, but leaving out still more and making other additions and alterations. This I know you will think a tedious labour, but its very difficulty makes it profitable to rekindle your fire and recover your enthusiasm after its force is spent; to graft new limbs, in fact, on a finished trunk without disturbing the balance of the original.

I know that your chief interest at the present time is forensic oratory, but that is not a reason for advising you to limit yourself to this provocative and somewhat pugnacious style. The soil is refreshed when

variis mutatisque seminibus, ita ingenia nostra nunc
8 hac nunc illa meditatione recoluntur. Volo interdum aliquem ex historia locum adprendas, volo epistulam diligentius scribas. Nam saepe in oratione
quoque non historica modo sed prope poetica de-
scriptionum necessitas incidit, et pressus sermo
9 purusque ex epistulis petitur. Fas est et carmine re-
mitti, non dico continuo et longo (id enim perfici nisi
in otio non potest), sed hoc arguto et brevi, quod apte
quantas libet occupationes curasque distinguit.
10 Lusus vocantur; sed hi lusus non minorem interdum
gloriam quam seria consequuntur. Atque adeo (cur
enim te ad versus non versibus adhorter?)

11   ut laus est cerae, mollis cedensque sequatur
     si doctos digitos iussaque fiat opus
   et nunc informet Martem castamve Minervam,
     nunc Venerem effingat, nunc Veneris puerum;
   utque sacri fontes non sola incendia sistunt,
     saepe etiam flores vernaque prata iuvant,
   sic hominum ingenium flecti ducique per artes
     non rigidas docta mobilitate decet.

12 Itaque summi oratores, summi etiam viri sic se aut
exercebant aut delectabant, immo delectabant exer-
13 cebantque. Nam mirum est ut his opusculis animus
intendatur remittatur. Recipiunt enim amores odia
iras misericordiam urbanitatem, omnia denique quae
14 in vita atque etiam in foro causisque versantur. Inest

sown with successive changes of seed, and so are our minds if cultivated by different subjects. I should like you sometimes to take a passage of historical narrative or turn your attention to letter-writing, for often even in a speech the subject calls for a narrative or even a poetic style of description; and letters develop brevity and simplicity of style. It is permissible, too, to seek relaxation in writing poetry, by which I mean not a long continuous poem (which can only be finished if one has plenty of leisure), but one of those short, polished sets of verses which make a break in your duties and responsibilities, however pressing. This is called light verse, but it sometimes brings its authors as much fame as serious work. In fact (for why shouldn't I versify to encourage you to take to verse?)

> The beauty of wax is its power to yield
>   To the fingers' skilful touch;
> Thus taught, it can shape the god of War,
>   Chaste Wisdom or Love or her son.
> The sacred springs can quench a flame,
>   Or gladden the flowers and fields;
> So the mind of man, through the gentle arts
>   Is taught the wisdom of change.

The greatest orators, and the greatest men, too, used to train or amuse themselves in this way—or rather, to combine their training with amusement, for it is remarkable how the mind is both stimulated and relaxed by these trifles. They comprise our loves and hatreds, our indignation, compassion and wit, in fact every phase of life and every detail of our public and professional activities. They also offer

his quoque eadem quae aliis carminibus utilitas,
quod metri necessitate devincti soluta oratione
laetamur, et quod facilius esse comparatio ostendit,
libentius scribimus.

15 Habes plura etiam fortasse quam requirebas;
unum tamen omisi. Non enim dixi quae legenda
arbitrarer: quamquam dixi, cum dicerem quae
scribenda. Tu memineris sui cuiusque generis
auctores diligenter eligere. Aiunt enim multum
16 legendum esse, non multa. Qui sint hi adeo notum
probatumque est, ut demonstratione non egeat; et
alioqui tam immodice epistulam extendi, ut dum tibi
quemadmodum studere debeas suadeo, studendi
tempus abstulerim. Quin ergo pugillares resumis,
et aliquid ex his vel istud ipsum quod coeperas scribis?
Vale.

X

C. Plinius Macrino Suo S.

1 Quia ipse, cum prima cognovi, iungere extrema
quasi avulsa cupio, te quoque existimo velle de
Vareno et Bithynis reliqua cognoscere. Acta causa
2 hinc a Polyaeno, inde a Magno. Finitis actionibus
Caesar "Neutra" inquit "pars de mora queretur; erit
3 mihi curae explorare provinciae voluntatem." Multum interim Varenus tulit. Etenim quam dubium
est an merito accusetur, qui an omnino accusetur

the same advantage as other forms of poetry; when we have been bound by the restrictions of metre, we delight in the freedom of prose and gladly return to what comparison has shown to be the easier style.

Perhaps this is more than you wanted, but there is one more thing. I have said nothing about what I think you should read, though this was implied when I was telling you what to write. Remember to make a careful selection from representative authors in each subject, for the saying is that a man should be deeply, not widely, read. These authors are too well known and approved to need further indication; and, besides, I have let this letter run on so far that I am robbing you of time for work with all my advice on planning it. Back then to your books and writing— either something on the lines I suggest, or what you have already started.

X

To Caecilius Macrinus

If I have heard the beginning of a story I always want to pick up the thread and add the conclusion, so I expect you, too, would like to hear the end of the affair between Varenus and the Bithynians. Polyaenus spoke on one side and Magnus on the other. The Emperor listened to both speeches and then declared that neither party should have cause to complain of delay; he would undertake to find out the wishes of the province. Meanwhile Varenus has gained much, for the justice of the charge against him is all the more doubtful when it is still uncertain

incertum est! Superest ne rursus provinciae quod
damnasse dicitur placeat, agatque paenitentiam
paenitentiae suae. Vale.

XI

C. Plinius Fabato Prosocero Suo S.

1 Miraris quod Hermes libertus meus hereditarios
agros, quos ego iusseram proscribi, non exspectata
auctione pro meo quincunce ex septingentis milibus
Corelliae addixerit. Adicis hos nongentis milibus
posse venire, ac tanto magis quaeris, an quod
2 gessit ratum servem. Ego vero servo: quibus ex
causis, accipe. Cupio enim et tibi probatum et
coheredibus meis excusatum esse, quod me ab illis
3 maiore officio iubente secerno. Corelliam cum summa reverentia diligo, primum ut sororem Corelli
Rufi, cuius mihi memoria sacrosancta est, deinde ut
4 matri meae familiarissimam. Sunt mihi et cum
marito eius Minicio Iusto, optimo viro, vetera iura;
fuerunt et cum filio maxima, adeo quidem ut prae-
5 tore me ludis meis praesederit. Haec, cum proxime
istic fui, indicavit mihi cupere se aliquid circa Larium
nostrum possidere. Ego illi ex praediis meis quod
vellet et quanti vellet obtuli exceptis maternis pater-
nisque; his enim cedere ne Corelliae quidem pos-

---

¹ See Letter 6. Nothing more is heard of this case, and the
prosecution is evidently dropped.

² The basis on which inheritance-tax was collected. See
note to Letter 14.

³ See I. 12 and Index.

⁴ There is no other reference to these games.

if he is being charged at all. We can only hope that the province will not decide again in favour of what it was reported to have rejected, nor think better of its change of heart.[1]

XI

To CALPURNIUS FABATUS, HIS WIFE'S GRANDFATHER

You are surprised to hear that my freedman Hermes has sold to Corellia, without waiting for the public auction,[2] the land which I inherited and ordered to be put up for sale, valuing my five-twelfths of the estate at 700,000 sesterces. It might have fetched 900,000 you say, and this makes you wonder all the more whether I shall confirm what he has done. Yes, I do; and here are my reasons, for I am anxious to have your approval and my fellow-heirs' forgiveness if I disassociate myself from them in obedience to a higher claim.

I have the greatest respect and affection for Corellia, first as the sister of Corellius Rufus,[3] whose memory I always hold sacred, and then as my mother's dearest friend. Then I have old ties of friendship with her excellent husband Minicius Justus, as I did with her son, who presided over the games held during my praetorship.[4] During my last visit to you, when Corellia told me that she would like to own some property on the shores of our Lake Como, it was I who offered her any one of my estates she liked, at her own price, with the exception of what I inherited from my parents; for those I could not give up even to her. Consequently, when I

6 sum. Igitur cum obvenisset mihi hereditas in qua
praedia ista, scripsi ei venalia futura. Has epistulas
Hermes tulit exigentique, ut statim portionem meam
sibi addiceret, paruit. Vides quam ratum habere
debeam, quod libertus meus meis moribus gessit.

7 Superest ut coheredes aequo animo ferant separatim
me vendidisse, quod mihi licuit omnino non vendere.

8 Nec vero coguntur imitari meum exemplum: non
enim illis eadem cum Corellia iura. Possunt ergo
intueri utilitatem suam, pro qua mihi fuit amicitia.
Vale.

XII

C. PLINIUS MINICIO SUO S.

1 LIBELLUM formatum a me, sicut exegeras, quo amicus tuus, immo noster (quid enim non commune
nobis?), si res posceret uteretur, misi tibi ideo tardius
ne tempus emendandi eum, id est disperdendi,
2 haberes. Habebis tamen, an emendandi nescio,
utique disperdendi. Ὑμεῖς γὰρ οἱ εὔζηλοι optima
3 quaeque detrahitis. Quod si feceris, boni consulam.
Postea enim illis ex aliqua occasione ut meis utar, et
beneficio fastidi tui ipse laudabor, ut in eo quod ad-
notatum invenies et suprascripto aliter explicitum.
4 Nam cum suspicarer futurum, ut tibi tumidius videretur, quoniam est sonantius et elatius, non alienum
existimavi, ne te torqueres, addere statim pressius

---

[1] Εὔζηλοι refers to the Atticists, just as κακόζηλοι is used
by Quintilian (*Inst. Orat.* VIII. iii. 55 ff.) to define the expo-
nents of the Asiatic style.

inherited this property, which included the land you
refer to, I wrote and told her it was for sale. Hermes
took her the letter, and when she asked him to transfer my share to her at once, he did so.

I am bound then, as you see, to confirm an action
of my own freedman which was in accordance with
my own wishes. The only thing now is for my
fellow-heirs not to be annoyed with me for having
allowed a separate sale of what I need not have sold
at all. There is no necessity for them to follow my
example, for they have not the same ties with
Corellia; so they are permitted to consider their own
interests, though friendship took priority over mine.

XII

To Minicius Fundanus

Here is the short speech which you asked me to
write, for your friend (or rather for our friend, as we
have everything in common) to use if he needs it. I
have sent it at the last minute, to leave you no time
to correct, which means to spoil it. Doubtless
though you *will* find time—for spoiling certainly, for
correcting I can't say: you purists[1] cut out all the
best passages! But I shan't care if you do, for I can
pass the result off as my own some day, and take the
credit for your fastidiousness, as I do for the passages
you will find marked with an alternative version
written between the lines. For I suspected that you
would find its sonority and grandeur rather too pom-
pous, so I thought it would be best to put you out of
your misery by adding something shorter and plainer

quiddam et exilius, uel potius humilius et peius,
5 vestro tamen iudicio rectius. Cur enim non usque-
quaque tenuitatem vestram insequar et exagitem?
Haec ut inter istas occupationes aliquid aliquando
6 rideres, illud serio: vide ut mihi viaticum reddas,
quod impendi data opera cursore dimisso. Ne tu,
cum hoc legeris, non partes libelli, sed totum libellum improbabis, negabisque ullius pretii esse, cuius
pretium reposcaris. Vale.

XIII

C. Plinius Feroci Suo S.

1 Eadem epistula et non studere te et studere significat. Aenigmata loquor? Ita plane, donec distinc-
2 tius quod sentio enuntiem. Negat enim te studere,
sed est tam polita quam nisi a studente non potest
scribi; aut es tu super omnes beatus, si talia per
desidiam et otium perficis. Vale.

XIV

C. Plinius Corelliae Suae S.

1 Tu quidem honestissime, quod tam impense et
rogas et exigis, ut accipi iubeam a te pretium agrorum non ex septingentis milibus, quanti illos a liberto

512

straight away—a meaner, inferior version, in fact, though you may think it an improvement. (Here's my chance to make a real attack on your ultra-refinement.) So far I have been trying to raise a smile from you in the midst of your responsibilities, but this is serious: be sure to refund my expenses for taking the trouble to send this by special messenger. Now you have read this request you will condemn the whole speech out of hand and not just the details, being unwilling to admit it is worth anything when you are asked to pay for it.

XIII

To Julius Ferox

THE same letter of yours tells me that you are doing no work and yet you are working. I speak in riddles, you protest; so I do, until I make my meaning clear. You say you are not working, but your letter is so well phrased that it could only have been written by someone who worked at it; or else you are luckier than the rest of us in being able to produce work of such finish in your idle moments.

XIV

To Corellia

IT is very generous of you to insist so warmly that I should give orders for the price you are to pay for my land to be raised from the 700,000 sesterces agreed by my freedman to 900,000, the real value on which

meo, sed ex nongentis, quanti a publicanis partem
2 vicensimam emisti. Invicem ego et rogo et exigo,
ut non solum quid te verum etiam quid me deceat
adspicias, patiarisque me in hoc uno tibi eodem
animo repugnare, quo in omnibus obsequi soleo.
Vale.

XV

C. Plinius Saturnino Suo S.

1 Requiris quid agam. Quae nosti: distringor
officio, amicis deservio, studeo interdum, quod non
interdum sed solum semperque facere, non audeo
2 dicere rectius, certe beatius erat. Te omnia alia
quam quae velis agere moleste ferrem, nisi ea quae
agis essent honestissima. Nam et rei publicae suae
negotia curare et disceptare inter amicos laude dig-
3 nissimum est. Prisci nostri contubernium iucundum
tibi futurum sciebam. Noveram simplicitatem eius,
noveram comitatem; eundem esse (quod minus
noram) gratissimum experior, cum tam iucunde
officiorum nostrorum meminisse eum scribas. Vale.

XVI

C. Plinius Fabato Prosocero Suo S.

1 Calestrium Tironem familiarissime diligo et
privatis mihi et publicis necessitudinibus implicitum.

---

¹ See VII. 11 and *Pan.* 40 for the *vicesima hereditatum*. The
treasury through the publicani collected the tax by selling a
twentieth part of the property. On this basis the value of P.'s
$\frac{5}{12}$ share should be 900,000, but Corellia had only paid him
700,000.

you have had to pay the five-per-cent inheritance tax.[1] But I must insist in my turn that you consider what is the right course for me, as well as for you, and allow me to oppose you on this one point in the same spirit in which I usually comply with all your wishes.

XV

To Pompeius Saturninus

You want my news, but there is nothing new to tell; I am involved in public duties, active on behalf of my friends,[2] and occasionally doing some work of my own. If I could describe the work as exclusive and continuous I should certainly be happier, though I would not like to say my time would be better spent. As for your news, I should be sorry to hear that your activities are the opposite of what you would choose were you not so honourably employed; for managing the affairs of one's city merits our highest praise no less than settling disputes between friends.

I felt sure that you would enjoy the company of our friend Priscus.[3] I know what a frank and charming person he is, but I had yet to learn how grateful he could be: if, as you say in your letter, he has such happy memories of my services.

XVI

To Calpurnius Fabatus, his Wife's Grandfather

Calestrius Tiro is one of my dearest friends, and we have been closely associated in both personal

---

[2] *i.e.* his work on the Tiber Conservancy Board and in court.
[3] See VII. 7 and 8.

2 Simul militavimus, simul quaestores Caesaris fuimus.
Ille me in tribunatu liberorum iure praecessit, ego
illum in praetura sum consecutus, cum mihi Caesar
annum remisisset. Ego in villas eius saepe secessi,
3 ille in domo mea saepe convaluit. Hic nunc pro
consule provinciam Baeticam per Ticinum est petit-
4 urus. Spero, immo confido facile me impetraturum,
ex itinere deflectat ad te, si voles vindicta liberare,
quos proxime inter amicos manumisisti. Nihil est
quod verearis ne sit hoc illi molestum, cui orbem ter-
5 rarum circumire non erit longum mea causa. Proinde
nimiam istam verecundiam pone, teque quid velis
consule. Illi tam iucundum quod ego, quam mihi
quod tu iubes. Vale.

XVII

C. PLINIUS CELERI SUO S.

1 SUA cuique ratio recitandi; mihi quod saepe iam
dixi, ut si quid me fugit (ut certe fugit) admonear.
2 Quo magis miror, quod scribis fuisse quosdam qui
reprehenderent quod orationes omnino recitarem;

---

[1] *Quaestores Augusti* were assigned to the Emperor to convey
his wishes to the Senate.

[2] The most likely date for Pliny's and Tiro's praetorship is
93. See S-W, Appendix IV, p. 763, for all the available
evidence. P. then forged ahead, while Tiro had an unexplained
interval of about 14 years before he was praetorian proconsul
of Baetica.

and official relations. We did our military service together and were both quaestors serving the Emperor.[1] He held the office of tribune before me, through the privilege granted to fathers of children, but I caught him up in the praetorship when the Emperor gave me a year's remission.[2] I have often visited him in his country houses, and he has often spent times of convalescence in my home.

He is now setting out for Baetica as governor of the province, and will pass through Ticinum.[3] I hope, in fact I am sure, that I can easily persuade him to leave his direct route to pay you a visit, if you really intend to liberate formally the slaves you recently pronounced free before your friends.[4] You need not fear that this will be a trouble to a man who would not find a journey round the world too far on my behalf. So be rid of your usual diffidence and consult your own inclinations. He will be as pleased to do my bidding as I am to do yours.

XVII

To Caecilius (?) Celer

EVERYONE has his own reasons for reading his work aloud; my own, as I have often said, is to be told of the slips I know I am sure to have made. So I am all the more surprised to read in your letter that there were people who criticized me for giving any reading of my speeches at all: unless they think that this is

[3] In Gallia Cisalpina, on the Via Aemilia (Pavia).
[4] If they were informally freed by *manumissio inter amicos* they remained *Latini Iuniani* without full freedman status. See X. 104–5.

3 nisi vero has solas non putant emendandas. A quibus
libenter requisierim, cur concedant (si concedunt
tamen) historiam debere recitari, quae non ostenta-
tioni sed fidei veritatique componitur; cur tragoediam, quae non auditorium sed scaenam et actores;
cur lyrica, quae non lectorem sed chorum et lyram
poscunt. At horum recitatio usu iam recepta est.
4 Num ergo culpandus est ille qui coepit? Quamquam
orationes quoque et nostri quidam et Graeci lecti-
5 taverunt. Supervacuum tamen est recitare quae
dixeris. Etiam, si eadem omnia, si isdem omnibus,
si statim recites; si vero multa inseras multa com-
mutes, si quosdam novos quosdam eosdem sed post
tempus adsumas, cur minus probabilis sit causa
recitandi quae dixeris quam edendi? Sed difficile est
6 ut oratio dum recitatur satisfaciat. Iam hoc ad
laborem recitantis pertinet, non ad rationem non
7 recitandi. Nec vero ego dum recito laudari, sed dum
legor cupio. Itaque nullum emendandi genus omitto.
Ac primum quae scripsi mecum ipse pertracto;
deinde duobus aut tribus lego; mox aliis trado ad-
notanda, notasque eorum, si dubito, cum uno rursus
aut altero pensito; novissime pluribus recito, ac si
8 quid mihi credis tunc acerrime emendo; nam tanto
diligentius quanto sollicitius intendo. Optime autem
518

the only kind of writing which never needs correction. I should like to ask them why they allow (if they do allow) readings of history, whose authors aim at truth and accuracy rather than at displaying their talents, and tragedy, which needs a stage and actors rather than a lecture-room, and lyric poetry, which calls for a chorus and a lyre instead of a reader. They say that such readings are an established custom. Then is their originator to be blamed? Besides, there have been readings of speeches before, by some of our own orators as well as by the Greeks.

" But it is unnecessary to read a speech already delivered." It would be if the audience and the speech were exactly the same, and you read the speech immediately after delivery; but if you make many additions and alterations, if you invite new people along with those who heard you before, and after a certain interval, why should it be less suitable to read a speech than to publish it? " It is difficult for a reading of a speech to be satisfactory." That depends on the efforts of the reader and is no reason for not reading at all. Personally, I do not seek praise for my speech when it is read aloud, but when the text can be read after publication, and consequently I employ every possible method of correction. First of all, I go through my work myself; next, I read it to two or three friends and send it to others for comment. If I have any doubts about their criticisms, I go over them again with one or two people, and finally I read the work to a larger audience; and that is the moment, believe me, when I make my severest corrections, for my anxiety makes me concentrate all the more carefully. Respect for

reverentia pudor metus iudicant, idque adeo sic
habe: Nonne si locuturus es cum aliquo quamlibet
docto, uno tamen, minus commoveris quam si cum
9 multis vel indoctis? Nonne cum surgis ad agendum,
tunc maxime tibi ipse diffidis, tunc commutata non
dico plurima sed omnia cupis? utique si latior scaena
et corona diffusior; nam illos quoque sordidos pulla-
10 tosque reveremur. Nonne si prima quaeque im-
probari putas, debilitaris et concidis? Opinor, quia
in numero ipso est quoddam magnum collatumque
consilium, quibusque singulis iudicii parum, omnibus
11 plurimum. Itaque Pomponius Secundus (hic scriptor
tragoediarum), si quid forte familiarior amicus tollendum, ipse retinendum arbitraretur, dicere solebat: " Ad populum provoco," atque ita ex populi vel
silentio vel adsensu aut suam aut amici sententiam
12 sequebatur. Tantum ille populo dabat; recte an
secus, nihil ad me. Ego enim non populum advocare
sed certos electosque soleo, quos intuear quibus credam, quos denique et tamquam singulos observem
13 et tamquam non singulos timeam. Nam, quod M.
Cicero de stilo, ego de metu sentio: timor est, timor
emendator asperrimus. Hoc ipsum quod nos reci-
taturos cogitamus emendat; quod auditorium ingredi-
mur emendat; quod pallemus horrescimus circum-

---

[1] In *De Oratore*, I. 150: *stilus optimus et praestantissimus dicendi effector ac magister.*

an audience, modesty and anxiety are the best
critics. Look at it in this way: if you are going to
talk to a single individual, however well informed,
won't you be less nervous than you are before large
numbers who may be quite ignorant? When you
rise to plead in court, isn't that the moment when you
have least confidence in yourself, when you wish you
could alter most of your speech or indeed the whole?
Especially if the scene is imposing and the assembly
large, for even the sight of dirty working clothes can
be intimidating. If you feel that your opening
words are badly received, don't you falter and break
down? I imagine it is because there is some sort of
sound collective wisdom in mere numbers, so that,
though individual judgements may be poor, when
combined they carry weight. Thus it was that
Pomponius Secundus, the author of tragedies, if one
of his close friends happened to think that some
passage should be deleted when he wished to keep
it, used to say that he " appealed to the people ":
and according to the people's silence or applause he
would act on his own judgement or that of his friend.
Such was his faith in public opinion, whether rightly
or wrongly it is not for me to say. For I do not
invite the general public, but a select and limited
audience of persons whom I admire and trust, whom
I observe individually and fear as a whole; seeing
that I apply to fear what Cicero said about the
practice of writing.[1] Fear is the sternest corrective
—the prospect of giving a reading, our entry into
the lecture-room, our white faces, our trembling, and
our nervous glances, all prompt us to correct our
work.

14 spicimus emendat. Proinde non paenitet me con-
suetudinis meae quam utilissimam experior, adeoque
non deterreor sermunculis istorum, ut ultro te rogem
15 monstres aliquid quod his addam. Nihil enim curae
meae satis est. Cogito quam sit magnum dare
aliquid in manus hominum, nec persuadere mihi possum non et cum multis et saepe tractandum, quod
placere et semper et omnibus cupias. Vale.

XVIII

C. PLINIUS CANINIO SUO S.

1 DELIBERAS mecum quemadmodum pecunia, quam
municipibus nostris in epulum obtulisti, post te quoque salva sit. Honesta consultatio, non expedita
sententia. Numeres rei publicae summam: verendum est ne dilabatur. Des agros: ut publici negle-
2 gentur. Equidem nihil commodius invenio, quam
quod ipse feci. Nam pro quingentis milibus nummum, quae in alimenta ingenuorum ingenuarumque
promiseram, agrum ex meis longe pluris actori publico mancipavi; eundem vectigali imposito recepi,
3 tricena milia annua daturus. Per hoc enim et rei

---

[1] Cf. S. 230 and Appendix A. 1. for P.'s *alimenta,* and the
"alimentary tables" of Nerva and Trajan in S. 435 and S. 436
(the Table of Veleia).

[2] *i.e.* 6 per cent per annum: more than the 5 per cent at
Veleia, but only half the interest on private loans (X. 54. 1).

Consequently I do not regret my practice; experience has taught me its great advantages, and I am so far from being deterred by the idle comments of the people you quote that I should like you to suggest something else I can do. Nothing can satisfy my desire for perfection; I can never forget the importance of putting anything into the hands of the public, and I am positive that any work must be revised more than once and read to a number of people if it is intended to give permanent and universal satisfaction.

XVIII

To Caninius Rufus

You want my advice on what provision to make for securing now and after your death the money you have offered to our native town to pay the cost of an annual feast. It is an honour to be consulted, but difficult to give an immediate opinion. You might hand over the capital to the town, but there is a danger of its being dissipated. Or you might make a gift of land, but it would be neglected as public property always is. Personally I can think of no better plan than the one I adopted myself. I had promised a capital sum of 500,000 sesterces for the maintenance of free-born boys and girls,[1] but instead of paying this over I transferred some of my landed property (which was worth considerably more) to the municipal agent, and then had it reconveyed back to me charged with an annual rent payable of 30,000 sesterces.[2] By this means the principal is secured

publicae sors in tuto nec reditus incertus, et ager
ipse propter id quod vectigal large supercurrit, sem-
4 per dominum a quo exerceatur inveniet. Nec ignoro me plus aliquanto quam donasse videor ero-
gavisse, cum pulcherrimi agri pretium necessitas
5 vectigalis infregerit. Sed oportet privatis utilitatibus publicas, mortalibus aeternas anteferre, multoque diligentius muneri suo consulere quam facultatibus. Vale.

XIX

C. Plinius Prisco Suo S.

1 Angit me Fanniae valetudo. Contraxit hanc dum
adsidet Iuniae virgini, sponte primum (est enim ad-
2 finis), deinde etiam ex auctoritate pontificum. Nam
virgines, cum vi morbi atrio Vestae coguntur excedere, matronarum curae custodiaeque mandantur.
Quo munere Fannia dum sedulo fungitur, hoc dis-
3 crimine implicita est. Insident febres, tussis in-
crescit; summa macies summa defectio. Animus
tantum et spiritus viget Helvidio marito, Thrasea
patre dignissimus; reliqua labuntur, meque non
4 metu tantum, verum etiam dolore conficiunt. Doleo
enim feminam maximam eripi oculis civitatis, nescio
an aliquid simile visuris. Quae castitas illi, quae
sanctitas, quanta gravitas quanta constantia! Bis
maritum secuta in exsilium est, tertio ipsa propter

for the town, the interest is certain, and the property will always find a tenant to cultivate it because its value greatly exceeds the rent charged. I am well aware that I appear to have paid out more than the sum I have given, seeing that the fixed rent charge has reduced the market value of a fine property, but one ought to make personal and temporary interests give place to public and permanent advantages, and consider the security of a benefaction more than one's own gains.

XIX

To Neratius Priscus

I am very worried about Fannia's illness. She contracted it while nursing Junia, one of the Vestal Virgins, a duty she undertook voluntarily at first (Junia being a relative of hers) and then by order of the pontiffs. (For when sickness compels the Virgins to leave the hall of Vesta, they are always committed to the care and authority of a married woman.) This service Fannia was faithfully performing when she fell a victim to her present illness. Her fever never leaves her, her cough grows worse, and she is painfully thin and weak. There remain only the courage and the spirit worthy of her husband Helvidius and her father Thrasea: in every other way she is failing, and my anxiety on her behalf is coupled with grief, grief that so great a woman will be lost to the sight of her country when her like may not be seen again; such are her purity and integrity, her nobility and loyal heart. Twice she followed her

5 maritum relegata. Nam cum Senecio reus esset
quod de vita Helvidi libros composuisset rogatumque
se a Fannia in defensione dixisset, quaerente minaci-
ter Mettio Caro, an rogasset respondit: " Rogavi ";
an commentarios scripturo dedisset: " Dedi "; an
sciente matre: " Nesciente "; postremo nullam
6 vocem cedentem periculo emisit. Quin etiam illos
ipsos libros, quamquam ex necessitate et metu temporum abolitos senatus consulto, publicatis bonis
servavit habuit, tulitque in exsilium exsili causam.
7 Eadem quam iucunda quam comis, quam denique
(quod paucis datum est) non minus amabilis quam
veneranda! Eritne quam postea uxoribus nostris
ostentare possimus ? Erit a qua viri quoque fortitu-
dinis exempla sumamus, quam sic cernentes audien-
8 tesque miremur, ut illas quae leguntur ? Ac mihi
domus ipsa nutare, convulsaque sedibus suis ruitura
supra videtur, licet adhuc posteros habeat. Quantis
enim virtutibus quantisque factis adsequentur, ut
9 haec non novissima occiderit ? Me quidem illud
etiam adfligit et torquet, quod matrem eius, illam
(nihil possum inlustrius dicere) tantae feminae matrem, rursus videor amittere, quam haec, ut reddit
ac refert nobis, sic auferet secum, meque et novo

---

¹ See Index, Helvidius Priscus (ii) and Herennius Senecio.
² The younger Arria. See Introduction, p. xiv.

husband into exile, and a third time was banished herself on his account.[1] For when Senecio was on trial for having written a life of Helvidius, and said in his defence that he had done so at Fannia's request, Mettius Carus then demanded in a threatening tone if this was true. She replied that it was. Had she lent Senecio her husband's diaries? "Yes." Did her mother know of this? "No." Not a word in fact did she utter through fear of danger. Moreover, although the Senate was driven through fear of the times to order the destruction of the books in question, she managed to save them when her possessions were confiscated, and took them with her into the exile they had caused.

At the same time she has such friendliness and charm, the rare gift, in fact, of being able to inspire affection as well as respect. Will there be anyone now whom we can hold up as a model to our wives, from whose courage even our own sex can take example, and whom we can admire as much as the heroines of history while she is still in our midst? To me it seems as though her whole house is shaken to its very foundations and is tottering to its fall, even though she may leave descendants; for how can their deeds and merits be sufficient to assure that the last of her line has not perished in her?

A further and more personal pain and grief for me is my feeling that I am losing her mother[2] again—to whom I can pay no higher tribute than by calling her the famous mother of a great woman. The mother was restored to us in her daughter, but soon will be taken away with her, leaving me the pain of a re-opened wound to bear as well as this fresh blow.

527

10 pariter et rescisso vulnere adficiet. Utramque colui
utramque dilexi: utram magis nescio, nec discerni
volebant. Habuerunt officia mea in secundis,
habuerunt in adversis. Ego solacium relegatarum,
ego ultor reversarum; non feci tamen paria atque eo
magis hanc cupio servari, ut mihi solvendi tempora
11 supersint. In his eram curis, cum scriberem ad te;
quas si deus aliquis in gaudium verterit, de metu non
querar. Vale.

XX

C. PLINIUS TACITO SUO S.

1 LIBRUM tuum legi et, quam diligentissime potui,
adnotavi quae commutanda, quae eximenda arbitrarer. Nam et ego verum dicere adsuevi, et tu
libenter audire. Neque enim ulli patientius reprehenduntur, quam qui maxime laudari merentur.
2 Nunc a te librum meum cum adnotationibus tuis
exspecto. O iucundas, o pulchras vices! Quam me
delectat quod, si qua posteris cura nostri, usquequa-
qua narrabitur, qua concordia simplicitate fide
3 vixerimus! Erit rarum et insigne, duos homines
aetate dignitate propemodum aequales, non nullius
in litteris nominis (cogor enim de te quoque parcius
dicere, quia de me simul dico), alterum alterius
4 studia fovisse. Equidem adulescentulus, cum iam

---

¹ Either the *Dialogus* or a volume of the *Histories*. See
VIII. 7 and note.

I honoured and loved them both—I cannot say which
the more, nor did they wish a distinction to be drawn.
My services were at their command alike in pros-
perity and adversity; I was their comfort in exile
and their champion after their return. I could never
make them an adequate return, and so I am all the
more anxious for Fannia's life to be spared to give
me time to pay my debt. These are my troubles at
the time of writing to you; but, if one of the gods will
turn them to joy, I shall make no complaint about
my present fears.

XX

To Cornelius Tacitus

I have read your book,[1] and marked as carefully as
I could the passages which I think should be altered
or removed, for if it is my custom to tell the truth, you
are always willing to hear it; no one accepts criticism
so readily as those who best deserve praise. Now I
am awaiting the return of my book from you, with
your comments: a fair exchange which we both
enjoy. I am delighted to think that if posterity
takes any interest in us the tale will everywhere be
told of the harmony, frankness, and loyalty of our
lifelong relationship. It will seem both rare and
remarkable that two men of much the same age and
position, and both enjoying a certain amount of
literary reputation (I can't say much about you when
it refers to me too), should have encouraged each
other's literary work.

I was still a young man when you were already

529

tu fama gloriaque floreres, te sequi, tibi " longo sed proximus intervallo " et esse et haberi concupiscebam. Et erant multa clarissima ingenia; sed tu mihi (ita similitudo naturae ferebat) maxime imita-
5 bilis, maxime imitandus videbaris. Quo magis gaudeo, quod si quis de studiis sermo, una nominamur, quod de te loquentibus statim occurro. Nec desunt
6 qui utrique nostrum praeferantur. Sed nos, nihil interest mea quo loco, iungimur; nam mihi primus, qui a te proximus. Quin etiam in testamentis debes adnotasse: nisi quis forte alterutri nostrum amicissimus, eadem legata et quidem pariter accipimus.
7 Quae omnia huc spectant, ut invicem ardentius diligamus, cum tot vinculis nos studia mores fama, suprema denique hominum iudicia constringant. Vale.

XXI

C. PLINIUS CORNUTO SUO S.

1 PAREO, collega carissime, et infirmitati oculorum ut iubes consulo. Nam et huc tecto vehiculo undique inclusus quasi in cubiculo perveni et hic non stilo modo verum etiam lectionibus difficulter sed abstineo,
2 solisque auribus studeo. Cubicula obductis velis opaca nec tamen obscura facio. Cryptoporticus

---

¹ *Aeneid*, V. 320.
² *e.g.* in the will of Dasumius in 108 (*CIL* VI. 10229, line 17).

winning fame and glory, and I aspired to follow in
your footsteps and be " far behind but still the
nearest "[1] to you in fact and in repute.   There were
at the time many other distinguished men of talent,
but a certain similarity in our natures made me feel
that you were the person I could and should try to
imitate.   So I am all the happier to know that whenever conversation turns upon literature, our names
are mentioned together, and that my name comes up
when people talk about you.   There may be writers
who are ranked higher than either of us, but if we are
classed together our position does not matter; for
me the highest position is the one nearest to you.
You must also surely have noticed in wills that unless
someone has been a particular friend of one or the
other of us we are left legacies of the same kind and
value.[2]   All this shows that our love should be still
warmer, seeing that there are so many ties to bind
us in our work, character and reputation, and, above
all, in the last wishes of our friends.

XXI

To Cornutus Tertullus

I obey, dear colleague, and I am seeing to my eye
trouble as you bid me.   I travelled here in a closed
carriage with the light completely excluded, so that I
might have been at home in bed, and now that I
am here I am neither writing nor reading—no easy
sacrifice, but I have made it—and am working only
by ear.   I can darken my rooms by drawing the
blinds, without making them too dark, and the light in

quoque adopertis inferioribus fenestris tantum um-
brae quantum luminis habet. Sic paulatim lucem
3 ferre condisco. Balineum adsumo quia prodest,
vinum quia non nocet, parcissime tamen. Ita adsuevi, et nunc custos adest.

4   Gallinam ut a te missam libenter accepi; quam satis
acribus oculis, quamquam adhuc lippus, pinguissimam
vidi. Vale.

XXII

C. Plinius Falconi Suo S.

1   Minus miraberis me tam instanter petisse, ut in
amicum meum conferres tribunatum, cum scieris
quis ille qualisque. Possum autem iam tibi et nomen
indicare et describere ipsum, postquam polliceris.
2 Est Cornelius Minicianus, ornamentum regionis
meae seu dignitate seu moribus. Natus splendide
abundat facultatibus, amat studia ut solent pauperes.
Idem rectissimus iudex, fortissimus advocatus, ami-
3 cus fidelissimus. Accepisse te beneficium credes,
cum propius inspexeris hominem omnibus honoribus,
omnibus titulis (nihil volo elatius de modestissimo
viro dicere) parem. Vale.

the roofed arcade is reduced by half when the lower windows have their shutters closed. By this means I am gradually reaccustoming myself to full daylight. I take baths, as they do me good, and wine, which can do no harm, but only very sparingly; this has always been my way, and now I am under supervision. I was delighted to receive the pullet, especially as it was a gift from you. My eyes may still be inflamed, but they were sharp enough to see how plump it was.

XXII

To Pompeius Falco

You may have felt that I was rather pressing in my request for you to confer a military tribunate on a friend of mine, but you will be less surprised when you know who and what he is. Now that I have your promise I can give you his name and a full description. He is Cornelius Minicianus, in rank and character the pride of my native district. He is well born and rich, but cares for literature as a poor professional might; and he is remarkable too for his justice on the bench, courage at the bar, and loyalty in friendship. You will feel that it is you who are receiving the favour when you come to know him more intimately and find that he is equal to any official position or distinction; I don't want to say more in praise of the most modest of men.

XXIII

C. Plinius Fabato Prosocero Suo S.

1   Gaudeo quidem esse te tam fortem, ut Mediolani occurrere Tironi possis, sed ut perseveres esse tam fortis, rogo ne tibi contra rationem aetatis tantum laboris iniungas. Quin immo denuntio, ut illum et domi[1] et intra domum atque etiam intra cubiculi limen exspectes. Etenim, cum a me ut frater diligatur, non debet ab eo quem ego parentis loco observo, exigere officium quod parenti suo remisisset. Vale.

XXIV

C. Plinius Gemino Suo S.

1   Ummidia Quadratilla paulo minus octogensimo aetatis anno decessit usque ad novissimam valetudinem viridis, atque etiam ultra matronalem modum 2 compacto corpore et robusto. Decessit honestissimo testamento: reliquit heredes ex besse nepotem, ex tertia parte neptem. Neptem parum novi, nepotem familiarissime diligo, adulescentem singularem nec iis tantum, quos sanguine attingit, inter propinquos 3 amandum. Ac primum conspicuus forma omnes sermones malignorum et puer et iuvenis evasit, intra quartum et vicensimum annum maritus, et si

---

[1] domi γ: Comi *M, Stout.*

---

[1] Milan. Cf. VII. 16 and 32.

XXIII

To Calpurnius Fabatus, his Wife's Grandfather

I am delighted to hear that you are feeling well enough to meet Tiro at Mediolanum,[1] but I must ask you to conserve your strength and not take upon yourself a burden too heavy for your years. In fact I insist that you wait for him at home, indoors and without leaving your bedroom; for as I love him like a brother, he must not demand from one I honour as a father an attention which he would not expect his own father to show.

XXIV

To Rosianus Geminus

Ummidia Quadratilla is dead, having almost attained the age of seventy-nine and kept her powers unimpaired up to her last illness, along with a sound constitution and sturdy physique which are rare in a woman. She died leaving an excellent will; her grandson[2] inherits two-thirds of the estate, and her granddaughter the remaining third. I scarcely know the latter, but the grandson is a close friend of mine. He is a remarkable young man who inspires a sort of family affection among people in no way related to him. In the first place, though conspicuous for his good looks, he spent his youth and early manhood untouched by scandal; then he married before he was twenty-four and would have been a

[2] The promising young man of VI. 11.

deus adnuisset pater. Vixit in contubernio aviae
delicatae severissime, et tamen obsequentissime.
4 Habebat illa pantomimos fovebatque, effusius quam
principi feminae convenit. Hos Quadratus non in
theatro, non domi spectabat, nec illa exigebat.
5 Audivi ipsam cum mihi commendaret nepotis sui
studia, solere se, ut feminam in illo otio sexus, laxare
animum lusu calculorum, solere spectare pantomimos suos, sed cum factura esset alterutrum, semper se
nepoti suo praecepisse abiret studeretque; quod mihi
non amore eius magis facere quam reverentia videbatur.
6   Miraberis, et ego miratus sum. Proximis sacer-
dotalibus ludis, productis in commissione pantomimis,
cum simul theatro ego et Quadratus egrederemur, ait
mihi: " Scis me hodie primum vidisse saltantem
7 aviae meae libertum? " Hoc nepos. At hercule
alienissimi homines in honorem Quadratillae (pudet
me dixisse honorem) per adulationis officium in
theatrum cursitabant exsultabant plaudebant mira-
bantur ac deinde singulos gestus dominae cum canticis reddebant; qui nunc exiguissima legata, theatralis
operae corollarium, accipient ab herede, qui non
8 spectabat.   Haec, quia soles si quid incidit novi non
invitus audire, deinde quia iucundum est mihi quod
ceperam gaudium scribendo retractare. Gaudeo

father had his prayers been granted. He lived in his grandmother's house, but managed to combine personal austerity with deference to her sybaritic tastes. She kept a troupe of pantomime actors whom she treated with an indulgence unsuitable in a lady of her high position, but Quadratus never watched their performances either in the theatre or at home, nor did she insist on it. Once when she was asking me to supervise her grandson's education she told me that as a woman, with all a woman's idle hours to fill, she was in the habit of amusing herself playing draughts or watching her mimes, but before she did either she always told Quadratus to go away and work: which, I thought, showed her respect for his youth as much as her affection.

This incident will surprise you as it did me. The last Sacerdotal Games were opened by a performance of mime, and as we left the theatre together Quadratus said to me: " Do you realize that today was the first time I have seen any of my grandmother's freedmen dancing? " So said her grandson; but meanwhile people who were nothing to Quadratus were running to the theatre to pay their respects to her—though " respect " is hardly the word to use for their fawning attentions—jumping up and clapping to show their admiration, and then copying every gesture of their mistress with snatches of song. Today there is only a tiny bequest as a gratuity for their hired applause, which they will receive from the heir who never watched them perform.

I have told you this because you are usually glad to hear of any news, and also because I like to dwell on my pleasure by writing about it. It is a joy to

enim pietate defunctae. honore optimi iuvenis;
laetor etiam quod domus aliquando C. Cassi, huius
qui Cassianae scholae princeps et parens fuit, serviet
9 domino non minori.   Implebit enim illam Quadratus
meus et decebit, rursusque ei pristinam dignitatem
celebritatem gloriam reddet, cum tantus orator inde
procedet, quantus iuris ille consultus.   Vale.

XXV

C. Plinius Rufo Suo S.

1   O quantum eruditorum aut modestia ipsorum aut
quies operit ac subtrahit famae!   At nos eos tantum
dicturi aliquid aut lecturi timemus, qui studia sua
proferunt, cum illi qui tacent hoc amplius praestent,
2 quod maximum opus silentio reverentur.   Expertus
scribo quod scribo.   Terentius Iunior, equestribus
militiis atque etiam procuratione Narbonensis provinciae integerrime functus, recepit se in agros suos,
paratisque honoribus tranquillissimum otium praetu-
3 lit.   Hunc ego invitatus hospitio ut bonum patrem
familiae, ut diligentem agricolam intuebar, de his
locuturus, in quibus illum versari putabam;   et
coeperam, cum ille me doctissimo sermone revocavit

---

[1] There were two Schools of Jurisprudence, the Cassian and
the Proculian, represented in P.'s day by Javolenus Priscus,
and Neratius Priscus and Titius Aristo (for whom, see Index).

witness the family affection shown by the deceased and the honour done to an excellent young man, and I am happy to think that the house which once belonged to Gaius Cassius, the founder of the Cassian School of jurisprudence,[1] will have a master no less distinguished. For my friend Quadratus will adorn it by his presence and restore its former grandeur, fame, and glory by issuing from it to be as great an orator as Cassius was a jurist.

XXV

To Caninius (?) Rufus

What a number of scholars are hidden and lost to fame through their own modesty or retiring habits! And yet when we are about to make a speech or give a reading we are nervous only of those who parade their learning, whereas the others who say nothing prove themselves superior by paying a noble effort the tribute of silence. I can illustrate this from my own experience.

After Terentius Junior had held the military posts open to a knight and had also served as procurator in the province of Gallia Narbonensis, his conduct being irreproachable throughout, he retired to his estates, preferring a life of peace and leisure to the offices which could have been his. I looked upon him as a good father of his household and a hard-working farmer, so when he invited me to visit him I intended to talk on the subjects with which I imagined he was familiar; but when I began to do so the scholarly

4 ad studia. Quam tersa omnia, quam Latina, quam
Graeca! Nam tantum utraque lingua valet, ut ea
magis videatur excellere, qua cum maxime loquitur.
Quantum ille legit, quantum tenet! Athenis vivere
5 hominem, non in villa putes. Quid multa? Auxit
sollicitudinem meam effecitque ut illis quos doctis-
simos novi, non minus hos seductos et quasi rusticos
6 verear. Idem suadeo tibi: sunt enim ut in castris
sic etiam in litteris nostris, plures cultu pagano quos
cinctos et armatos, et quidem ardentissimo ingenio,
diligenter scrutatus invenies. Vale.

XXVI

C. Plinius Maximo Suo S.

1 Nuper me cuiusdam amici languor admonuit, optimos esse nos dum infirmi sumus. Quem enim in-
2 firmum aut avaritia aut libido sollicitat? Non amori-
bus servit, non adpetit honores, opes neglegit et
quantulumcumque, ut relicturus, satis habet. Tunc
deos tunc hominem esse se meminit, invidet nemini,
neminem miratur neminem despicit, ac ne sermonibus quidem malignis aut attendit aut alitur: balinea
3 imaginatur et fontes. Haec summa curarum, summa votorum mollemque in posterum et pinguem, si

trend of his conversation led me back to literary
topics. Everything he says is expressed in well-
turned phrases in excellent Latin or Greek, and his
proficiency in both languages is such that he always
seems to speak best the one he happens to be using.
He reads and remembers an immense amount; you
would think Athens his home, not a country house.
In short, he has increased my nervousness and made
me respect these retired somewhat countrified people
as much as the persons I know to be learned scholars.
You should do likewise, for in the field of letters, as of
battle, there are men who may be rustic in appearance, but are found on closer inspection to be well
armed and equipped and full of spirit and fire.

XXVI

To Valerius (?) Maximus

The poor health of a friend of mine has lately
reminded me that we are never so virtuous as when
we are ill. Has a sick man ever been tempted by
greed or lust? He is neither a slave to his passions
nor ambitious for office; he cares nothing for wealth
and is content with the little he has, knowing that he
must leave it. It is then that he remembers the gods
and realizes that he is mortal: he feels neither envy,
admiration, nor contempt for any man: not even
slanderous talk can win his attention or give him food
for thought, and his dreams are all of baths and cool
springs. These are his sole concern, the object of all
his prayers; meanwhile he resolves that if he is lucky

541

contingat evadere, hoc est innoxiam beatamque
4 destinat vitam. Possum ergo quod plurimis verbis
plurimis etiam voluminibus philosophi docere conan-
tur, ipse breviter tibi mihique praecipere, ut tales
esse sani perseveremus, quales nos futuros profitemur
infirmi. Vale.

XXVII

C. Plinius Surae Suo S.

1 Et mihi discendi et tibi docendi facultatem otium
praebet. Igitur perquam velim scire, esse phantas-
mata et habere propriam figuram numenque aliquod
putes an inania et vana ex metu nostro imaginem
2 accipere. Ego ut esse credam in primis eo ducor,
quod audio accidisse Curtio Rufo. Tenuis adhuc et
obscurus, obtinenti Africam comes haeserat. Inclinato die spatiabatur in porticu; offertur ei mulieris
figura humana grandior pulchriorque. Perterrito
Africam se futurorum praenuntiam dixit: iturum
enim Romam honoresque gesturum, atque etiam cum
summo imperio in eandem provinciam reversurum,
3 ibique moriturum. Facta sunt omnia. Praeterea
accedenti Carthaginem egredientique nave eadem
figura in litore occurrisse narratur. Ipse certe im-

---

[1] In the version given by Tacitus (*Ann.* XI. 21–2) Rufus is
the son of a gladiator and *sectator quaestorius* (*i.e.* on the staff
of the governor's assistant).

enough to recover he will lead a gentle and easy life in future, that is, a life of happy innocence.

So here for our guidance is the rule, put shortly, which the philosophers seek to express in endless words and volumes: in health we should continue to be the men we vowed to become when sickness prompted our words.

XXVII

To Licinius Sura

Our leisure gives me the chance to learn and you to teach me; so I should very much like to know whether you think that ghosts exist, and have a form of their own and some sort of supernatural power, or whether they lack substance and reality and take shape only from our fears. I personally am encouraged to believe in their existence largely from what I have heard of the experience of Curtius Rufus.[1] While he was still obscure and unknown he was attached to the suite of the new governor of Africa. One afternoon he was walking up and down in the colonnade of his house when there appeared to him the figure of a woman, of superhuman size and beauty. To allay his fears she told him that she was the spirit of Africa, come to foretell his future: he would return to Rome and hold office, and then return with supreme authority to the same province, where he would die. Everything came true. Moreover, the story goes on to say that as he left the boat on his arrival at Carthage the same figure met him on the shore. It is at least certain that when he fell

plicitus morbo futura praeteritis, adversa secundis
auguratus, spem salutis nullo suorum desperante
proiecit.

4 Iam illud nonne et magis terribile et non minus
5 mirum est quod exponam ut accepi? Erat Athenis
spatiosa et capax domus sed infamis et pestilens.
Per silentium noctis sonus ferri, et si attenderes
acrius, strepitus vinculorum longius primo, deinde e
proximo reddebatur: mox adparebat idolon, senex
macie et squalore confectus, promissa barba horrenti
capillo; cruribus compedes, manibus catenas gere-
6 bat quatiebatque. Inde inhabitantibus tristes dirae-
que noctes per metum vigilabantur; vigiliam morbus
et crescente formidine mors sequebatur. Nam interdiu quoque, quamquam abscesserat imago, memoria imaginis oculis inerrabat, longiorque causis
timoris timor erat. Deserta inde et damnata solitudine domus totaque illi monstro relicta; proscribe-
batur tamen, seu quis emere seu quis conducere
7 ignarus tanti mali vellet. Venit Athenas philosophus Athenodorus, legit titulum auditoque pretio,
quia suspecta vilitas, percunctatus omnia docetur
ac nihilo minus, immo tanto magis conducit. Ubi
coepit advesperascere, iubet sterni sibi in prima
544

ill he interpreted his future by the past and misfortune by his previous success, and gave up all hope of recovery although none of his people despaired of his life.

Now consider whether the following story, which I will tell just as it was told to me, is not quite as remarkable and even more terrifying. In Athens there was a large and spacious mansion with the bad reputation of being dangerous to its occupants. At dead of night the clanking of iron and, if you listened carefully, the rattle of chains could be heard, some way off at first, and then close at hand. Then there appeared the spectre of an old man, emaciated and filthy, with a long flowing beard and hair on end, wearing fetters on his legs and shaking the chains on his wrists. The wretched occupants would spend fearful nights awake in terror; lack of sleep led to illness and then death as their dread increased, for even during the day, when the apparition had vanished, the memory of it was in their mind's eye, so that their terror remained after the cause of it had gone. The house was therefore deserted, condemned to stand empty, and wholly abandoned to the spectre; but it was advertised as being to let or for sale in case someone was found who knew nothing of its evil reputation.

The philosopher Athenodorus came to Athens and read the notice. His suspicions were aroused when he heard the low price, and the whole story came out on inquiry; but he was none the less, in fact all the more, eager to rent the house. When darkness fell he gave orders that a couch was to be made up for him in the front part of the house, and asked for his

domus parte, poscit pugillares stilum lumen, suos omnes in interiora dimittit; ipse ad scribendum animum oculos manum intendit, ne vacua mens audi-
8 ta simulacra et inanes sibi metus fingeret. Initio, quale ubique, silentium noctis; dein concuti ferrum, vincula moveri. Ille non tollere oculos, non re-mittere stilum, sed offirmare animum auribusque praetendere. Tum crebrescere fragor, adventare et iam ut in limine, iam ut intra limen audiri. Respicit,
9 videt agnoscitque narratam sibi effigiem. Stabat innuebatque digito similis vocanti. Hic contra ut paulum exspectaret manu significat rursusque ceris et stilo incumbit. Illa scribentis capiti catenis insona-bat. Respicit rursus idem quod prius innuentem, nec
10 moratus tollit lumen et sequitur. Ibat illa lento gradu quasi gravis vinculis. Postquam deflexit in aream domus, repente dilapsa deserit comitem. Desertus herbas et folia concerpta signum loco ponit.
11 Postero die adit magistratus, monet ut illum locum effodi iubeant. Inveniuntur ossa inserta catenis et implicita, quae corpus aevo terraque putrefactum nuda et exesa reliquerat vinculis; collecta publice sepeliuntur. Domus postea rite conditis manibus caruit.
12 Et haec quidem adfirmantibus credo; illud ad-firmare aliis possum. Est libertus mihi non inlittera-

notebooks, pen, and a lamp. He sent all his servants to the inner rooms, and concentrated his thoughts, eyes and hand on his writing, so that his mind would be occupied and not conjure up the phantom he had heard about nor other imaginary fears. At first there was nothing but the general silence of night; then came the clanking of iron and dragging of chains. He did not look up nor stop writing, but steeled his mind to shut out the sounds. Then the noise grew louder, came nearer, was heard in the doorway, and then inside the room. He looked round, saw and recognized the ghost described to him. It stood and beckoned, as if summoning him. Athenodorus in his turn signed to it to wait a little, and again bent over his notes and pen, while it stood rattling its chains over his head as he wrote. He looked round again and saw it beckoning as before, so without further delay he picked up his lamp and followed. It moved slowly, as if weighed down with chains, and when it turned off into the courtyard of the house it suddenly vanished, leaving him alone. He then picked some plants and leaves and marked the spot. The following day he approached the magistrates, and advised them to give orders for the place to be dug up. There they found bones, twisted round with chains, which were left bare and corroded by the fetters when time and the action of the soil had rotted away the body. The bones were collected and given a public burial, and after the shades had been duly laid to rest the house saw them no more.

For these details I rely on the evidence of others, but here is a story I can vouch for myself. One of my freedmen, a man of some education, was sleeping in

547

tus. Cum hoc minor frater eodem lecto quiescebat.
Is visus est sibi cernere quendam in toro residentem,
admoventemque capiti suo cultros, atque etiam ex
ipso vertice amputantem capillos. Ubi inluxit, ipse
circa verticem tonsus, capilli iacentes reperiuntur.
13 Exiguum temporis medium, et rursus simile aliud
priori fidem fecit. Puer in paedagogio mixtus pluribus dormiebat. Venerunt per fenestras (ita narrat)
in tunicis albis duo cubantemque detonderunt et
qua venerant recesserunt. Hunc quoque tonsum
14 sparsosque circa capillos dies ostendit. Nihil notabile secutum, nisi forte quod non fui reus, futurus, si
Domitianus sub quo haec acciderunt diutius vixisset.
Nam in scrinio eius datus a Caro de me libellus inventus est; ex quo coniectari potest, quia reis moris
est summittere capillum, recisos meorum capillos
depulsi quod imminebat periculi signum fuisse.
15   Proinde rogo, eruditionem tuam intendas. Digna
res est quam diu multumque considores; ne ego
quidem indignus, cui copiam scientiae tuae facias.
16 Licet etiam utramque in partem (ut soles) disputes,
ex altera tamen fortius, ne me suspensum incertum-
que dimittas, cum mihi consulendi causa fuerit, ut
dubitare desinerem. Vale.

---

[1] See III. 11. 2–3 and IV. 24. 4–5.

the same bed as his younger brother when he
dreamed that he saw someone sitting on the bed and
putting scissors to his hair, even cutting some off the
top of his head. When day dawned he found this
place shorn and the hair lying on the floor. A short
time elapsed and then another similar occurrence
confirmed the earlier one. A slave boy was sleeping
with several others in the young slaves' quarters.
His story was that two men clad in white came in
through the window, cut his hair as he lay in bed, and
departed the way they had come. Daylight revealed that his head had also been shorn and the hair
was scattered about. Nothing remarkable followed,
except perhaps the fact that I was not brought to
trial, as I should have been if Domitian (under whom
all this happened) had lived longer.[1] For among the
papers in his desk was found information laid against
me by Carus; from which, in view of the custom for
accused persons to let their hair grow long, one may
interpret the cutting of my slaves' hair as a sign that
the danger threatening me was averted.

So please apply your learned mind to this question;
it deserves your long and careful consideration, and
I too am surely not undeserving as a recipient of your
informed opinion. You may argue both sides of the
case as you always do, but lay your emphasis on one
side or the other and do not leave me in suspense
and uncertainty; my reason for asking your opinion
was to put an end to my doubts.

XXVIII

C. Plinius Septicio Suo S.

1 Ais quosdam apud te reprehendisse, tamquam amicos meos ex omni occasione ultra modum laudem.
2 Agnosco crimen, amplector etiam. Quid enim honestius culpa benignitatis? Qui sunt tamen isti, qui amicos meos melius norint? Sed, ut norint, quid invident mihi felicissimo errore? Ut enim non sint tales quales a me praedicantur, ego tamen beatus
3 quod mihi videntur. Igitur ad alios hanc sinistram diligentiam conferant; nec sunt parum multi, qui carpere amicos suos iudicium vocant. Mihi numquam persuadebunt ut meos amari a me nimium putem. Vale.

XXIX

C. Plinius Montano Suo S.

1 Ridebis, deinde indignaberis, deinde ridebis, si
2 legeris, quod nisi legeris non potes credere. Est via Tiburtina intra primum lapidem (proxime adnotavi) monimentum Pallantis ita inscriptum: " Huic senatus ob fidem pietatemque erga patronos ornamenta praetoria decrevit et sestertium centies quinquagies,
3 cuius honore contentus fuit." Equidem numquam

---

¹ For Pallas, see Index and Tacitus, *Ann.* XII. 53, Suetonius, *Claud.* 28. Dio (LXII. 14. 3) says he was worth 400 millions at his death.

XXVIII

To Septicius Clarus

You say that people have criticized me in your hearing for taking any opportunity for exaggerated praise of my friends. I accept the charge, in fact I welcome it, for there can be no more honourable fault than warmth of heart. But who are these people who know my friends better than I do myself? And, even if they do, why grudge me happiness in my delusion? My friends may not be all I proclaim them, but it makes me happy to think that they are. Let these people transfer their misplaced attentions to someone else; they will find all too many who think it a sign of good judgement to disparage their friends, but they will never persuade me to believe that I love mine too much.

XXIX

To Montanus

You will think it a joke—or an outrage, but a joke after all—if you read this, which has to be seen to be believed. On the road to Tibur, less than a mile from Rome, as I noticed the other day, there is a monument to Pallas[1] with the following inscription: "To him the Senate decreed in return for his loyal services to his patrons, the insignia of a praetor, and · the sum of fifteen million sesterces, but he thought fit to accept the distinction only."

Personally I have never thought much of these

sum miratus quae saepius a fortuna quam a iudicio
proficiscerentur; maxime tamen hic me titulus
admonuit, quam essent mimica[1] et inepta, quae interdum in hoc caenum, in has sordes abicerentur, quae
denique ille furcifer et recipere ausus est et recusare,
atque etiam ut moderationis exemplum posteris pro-
4 dere. Sed quid indignor? Ridere satius, ne se
magnum aliquid adeptos putent, qui huc felicitate
perveniunt ut rideantur. Vale.

XXX

C. PLINIUS GENITORI SUO S.

1 TORQUEOR quod discipulum, ut scribis, optimae
spei amisisti. Cuius et valetudine et morte impedita
studia tua quidni sciam? cum sis omnium officiorum
observantissimus, cumque omnes quos probas effusis-
2 sime diligas. Me huc quoque urbana negotia perse-
quuntur; non desunt enim qui me iudicem aut
3 arbitrum faciant. Accedunt querelae rusticorum,
qui auribus meis post longum tempus suo iure abutun-
tur. Instat et necessitas agrorum locandorum,
perquam molesta: adeo rarum est invenire idoneos
4 conductores. Quibus ex causis precario studeo,
studeo tamen. Nam et scribo aliquid et lego; sed
cum lego, ex comparatione sentio quam male scribam,

---

[1] mimica *Mi, Budaeus*: inimica γa.

---

[1] In IX. 37. 2 P. says that they were let for periods of five
years. He writes from Tifernum.

honours whose distribution depends on chance rather
than on a reasoned decision, but this inscription more
than anything makes me realize what a ridiculous
farce it is when they can be thrown away on such dirt
and filth, and that rascal could presume to accept and
refuse them, all with a show of setting posterity an
example of moderation. But it isn't worth my
indignation; better to laugh, or such people will
think they have really achieved something when
their lucky chance has brought them no more than
ridicule.

XXX

To Julius Genitor

I am deeply distressed to hear that you have lost a
pupil of such promise, and, knowing your readiness
with kindly attentions and generous affection for
anyone of whom you think highly, I cannot but feel
that his illness and death have interfered with your
own work.

As for me, I am pursued by city business even here,
for there is no lack of people wanting me to act as
judge or arbitrator, and then there are the peasants
who claim their right after my long absence to vex
my ears with their complaints. The necessity of
letting my farms [1] is also becoming urgent and giving
a good deal of trouble, for suitable tenants can rarely
be found. Consequently I can only beg a moment
here and there for my own work, though I *am* working, for I write a little and read; though comparison
with my reading only makes me realize how badly I

licet tu mihi bonum animum facias, qui libellos
meos de ultione Helvidi orationi Demosthenis κατὰ
5 Μειδίου confers. Quam sane, cum componerem
illos, habui in manibus, non ut aemularer (improbum
enim ac paene furiosum), sed tamen imitarer et
sequerer, quantum aut diversitas ingeniorum maximi
et minimi, aut causae dissimilitudo pateretur. Vale.

XXXI

C. Plinius Cornuto Suo S.

1 Claudius Pollio amari a te cupit dignus hoc ipso
quod cupit, deinde quod ipse te diligit; neque enim
fere quisquam exigit istud nisi qui facit. Vir alioqui
rectus integer quietus ac paene ultra modum (si
2 quis tamen ultra modum) verecundus. Hunc, cum
simul militaremus, non solum ut commilito inspexi.
Praeerat alae miliariae; ego iussus a legato consulari rationes alarum et cohortium excutere, ut magnam quorundam foedamque avaritiam, neglegentiam
parem, ita huius summam integritatem, sollicitam
3 diligentiam inveni. Postea promotus ad amplissimas
procurationes, nulla occasione corruptus ab insito ab-
stinentiae amore deflexit; numquam secundis rebus

---

[1] The speech delivered in early 97; see IX. 13.
[2] It was exceptional, though not impossible at this period
to start military service in command of a number of cohorts
(*alae*) instead of a single one (*praefectura cohortis*).

write, however much you encourage me by comparing
my speech in vindication of Helvidius [1] with Demosthenes' speech against Meidias. I admit that I had
this by me while I was writing my own speech, not
with any idea of rivalling it—it would be madness to
presume so far—but treating it as a model to follow
as closely as the diversity of subject permitted, and
the difference between my own small talent and
Demosthenes' genius allowed.

XXXI

To Cornutus Tertullus

Claudius Pollio is anxious for your friendship,
which he deserves for that very reason, and also
because he has a real affection for you himself—for
few people expect this from others if they do not first
feel it themselves. He is besides a man of honour
and integrity, retiring and modest almost to excess,
if that were possible. We did our military service
together, when I came to know him more intimately
than just as a fellow soldier. He was in command of a
cavalry division,[2] while I had been ordered by the
consular legate to audit the accounts of the cavalry
and infantry divisions; in several cases I found a
great deal of shocking rapacity and carelessness
equally bad, by contrast with his accounts which had
been kept with scrupulous care and complete honesty.
On his subsequent promotion to important administrative posts [3] he could never be tempted out of his

[3] He was procurator of the Graian Alps and head of the
Inheritance-tax office (ILS 1418).

intumuit; numquam officiorum varietate continuam laudem humanitatis infregit, eademque firmitate animi laboribus suffecit, qua nunc otium patitur. 4 Quod quidem paulisper cum magna sua laude intermisit et posuit, a Corellio nostro ex liberalitate imperatoris Nervae emendis dividendisque agris adiutor adsumptus. Etenim qua gloria dignum est, summo viro in tanta eligendi facultate praecipue placuisse! 5 Idem quam reverenter, quam fideliter amicos colat, multorum supremis iudiciis, in his Anni Bassi gravissimi civis, credere potes, cuius memoriam tam grata praedicatione prorogat et extendit, ut librum de vita eius (nam studia quoque sicut alias bonas artes 6 veneratur) ediderit. Pulchrum istud et raritate ipsa probandum, cum plerique hactenus defunctorum 7 meminerint ut querantur. Hunc hominem adpetentissimum tui, mihi crede, complectere adprehende, immo et invita, ac sic ama tamquam gratiam referas. Neque enim obligandus sed remunerandus est in amoris officio, qui prior coepit. Vale.

---

[1] By the *lex Cocceia*; cf. Dio, LXVIII. 2. 1.

deep-rooted dislike of personal gain; success never went to his head, and, in all the various posts he held, he preserved intact his reputation for humanity while applying the same strength of purpose to all his duties, as he now shows in his present retirement. He did indeed once (to his greater glory) return temporarily to active life when he was chosen by our friend Corellius to assist him in the purchase and distribution of land made possible through the generosity of the Emperor Nerva:[1] and there could be no higher honour than to be the special choice of so great a man from such a wide field for selection.

You can also be assured of Pollio's respect and loyalty for his friends by the dying wishes of many people, among them Annius Bassus whose merit is well known, and whose memory Pollio preserves and perpetuates in the grateful tribute of a published biography; for he cultivates literature as he does every honest pursuit. Such splendid conduct deserves praise for its very rarity, seeing that the majority of people remember their dead friends only to complain about them. This, then, is the man who so much desires your friendship, so that you should, if you will trust me, welcome him with open arms, or rather summon him to your side with affection as though returning a favour. For, according to the code of friendship, the one who takes the initiative puts the other in his debt and owes no more until he is repaid.

XXXII

C. Plinius Fabato Prosocero Suo S.

1 Delector iucundum tibi fuisse Tironis mei adventum; quod vero scribis oblata occasione proconsulis plurimos manumissos, unice laetor. Cupio enim patriam nostram omnibus quidem rebus augeri, maxime tamen civium numero: id enim oppidis 2 firmissimum ornamentum. Illud etiam me non ut ambitiosum sed tamen iuvat, quod adicis te meque et gratiarum actione et laude celebratos. Est enim, ut Xenophon ait, ἥδιστον ἄκουσμα ἔπαινος, utique si te mereri putes. Vale.

XXXIII

C. Plinius Tacito Suo S.

1 Auguror nec me fallit augurium, historias tuas immortales futuras; quo magis illis (ingenue fatebor) 2 inseri cupio. Nam si esse nobis curae solet ut facies nostra ab optimo quoque artifice exprimatur, nonne debemus optare, ut operibus nostris similis tui scrip- 3 tor praedicatorque contingat? Demonstro ergo quamquam diligentiam tuam fugere non possit, cum sit in publicis actis, demonstro tamen quo magis credas, iucundum mihi futurum si factum meum, cuius

---

[1] See VII. 16 and 23.
[2] *Memorabilia*, II. 1. 31.
[3] The *acta diurna*; cf. V. 13. 8.

XXXII

To Calpurnius Fabatus, his Wife's Grandfather

I am glad you enjoyed my friend Tiro's visit,[1] and particularly pleased to hear that you took the opportunity of his presence with a governor's authority to liberate a number of your slaves. I am always anxious for the advancement of our native place, and above all through the increasing numbers of her citizens, for that is a tribute which sets a town on the surest of foundations.

One other thing pleases me I confess, not that I am courting popularity; you go on to say that you and I were both warmly praised in a vote of thanks, and, as Xenophon says, "praise is the sweetest thing to hear,"[2] especially if it is felt to be deserved.

XXXIII

To Cornelius Tacitus

I believe that your histories will be immortal; a prophecy which will surely prove correct. That is why (I frankly admit) I am anxious to appear in them. We are usually careful to see that none but the best artists shall portray our features, so why should we not want our deeds to be blessed by a writer like yourself to celebrate them? So here is an account of an incident which can hardly have escaped your watchful eye, since it appeared in the official records;[3] but I am sending it so that you may be the more assured of my pleasure if this action of mine,

559

gratia periculo crevit, tuo ingenio tuo testimonio
ornaveris.

4 Dederat me senatus cum Herennio Senecione
advocatum provinciae Baeticae contra Baebium
Massam, damnatoque Massa censuerat, ut bona eius
publice custodirentur. Senecio, cum explorasset
consules postulationibus vacaturos, convenit me et
" Qua concordia " inquit " iniunctam nobis accusationem exsecuti sumus, hac adeamus consules petam-
usque, ne bona dissipari sinant, quorum esse in cus-
5 todia debent." Respondi: " Cum simus advocati
a senatu dati, dispice num peractas putes partes nostras senatus cognitione finita." Et ille: " Tu quem
voles tibi terminum statues, cui nulla cum provincia
necessitudo nisi ex beneficio tuo et hoc recenti; ipse
6 et natus ibi et quaestor in ea fui." Tum ego: " Si
fixum tibi istud ac deliberatum, sequar te ut, si qua
7 ex hoc invidia, non tantum tua." Venimus ad consules; dicit Senecio quae res ferebat, aliqua subiungo.
Vixdum conticueramus, et Massa questus Senecionem
non advocati fidem sed inimici amaritudinem im-
8 plesse, impietatis reum postulat. Horror omnium;
ego autem " Vereor " inquam, " clarissimi consules,

---

[1] In 93; see III. 4. 4: VI. 29. 8 and Tac. *Agr.* 45.

[2] His property was not confiscated, and would not have been
sold up unless Massa failed to repay his debts (cf. the case of
Classicus, III. 9. 17). Senecio evidently feared that Massa
might remove some of the moveable property.

which gained interest from the risks attending it, shall be distinguished by the testimony of your genius.

The Senate had instructed me to act with Herennius Senecio as counsel for the province of Baetica against Baebius Massa,[1] and after Massa's conviction had passed the resolution that his property should be kept in official custody. Senecio then discovered that the consuls would be willing to hear Massa's claims for restitution, so sought me out and proposed that we should continue to act in unity as we had done in carrying out the prosecution entrusted to us: we should approach the consuls and ask them not to allow the dispersal of the property which they were responsible for holding in custody.[2] I pointed out that we had acted as counsel by appointment of the Senate, and asked him to consider whether perhaps we had come to the end of our role now that the case was over. "You can set what limit you like to your own responsibilities," he said, "for you have no connexion with the province except the recent one of the services you have rendered, but I was born in Baetica and served as quaestor there." "If your mind is made up," I said, "I will act with you, so that if any ill-will results, you will not have to face it alone."

We went to the consuls. Senecio said what was necessary and I added a few words. We had scarcely finished speaking when Massa complained that Senecio had displayed the animosity of a personal enemy rather than a professional counsel's honour, and demanded leave to prosecute him for treasonable conduct. Amidst the general consternation I began to speak: "Most noble consuls, I am afraid that by

561

ne mihi Massa silentio suo praevaricationem obiec-
erit, quod non et me reum postulavit." Quae vox
et statim excepta, et postea multo sermone cele-
9 brata est. Divus quidem Nerva (nam privatus quoque attendebat his quae recte in publico fierent)
missis ad me gravissimis litteris non mihi solum,
verum etiam saeculo est gratulatus, cui exemplum
10 (sic enim scripsit) simile antiquis contigisset. Haec,
utcumque se habent, notiora clariora maiora tu facies;
quamquam non exigo ut excedas actae rei modum.
Nam nec historia debet egredi veritatem, et honeste
factis veritas sufficit. Vale.

not including me in his accusation Massa's very silence has charged me with collusion with himself." These words were acclaimed at once and subsequently much talked about; indeed, the deified Emperor Nerva (who never failed to notice anything done for the good of the State even before he became Emperor) sent me a most impressive letter in which he congratulated not only me but our generation for being blessed with an example so much (he said) in the best tradition.

Whatever the merit of this incident, you can make it better known and increase its fame and importance, but I am not asking you to go beyond what is due to the facts. History should always confine itself to the truth, which in its turn is enough for honest deeds.

CENTRAL AND NORTHERN ITALY

SCALE OF MILES
25   0   25   50   75   100

Comum
Vercellae
TRANSPADANI
Mediolanum *Vicentia* VENETIA
Ticenum *Brixia* *Verona* *Altinum*
Patavium

R. PO

LIGURIA
GALLIA CISALPINA

UMBRIA

ETRURIA

Arretium *Tifernum* PICENUM
Perusia *Firmum*
Asisium
Hispellum
Amenia
L. Vadimon *Narnia* SAMNIUM
Ocriculum
Centumcellae *Tibur*
Alsium ROME *Praeneste*
Ostia *Tusculum* CAMPANIA
Laurentum
LATIUM
Formiae NAPLES Mt.
Baiae Vesuvius
Misenum *Pompeii*
Capreae *Stabiae*

Nola
NAPLES
Baiae Mt.
Vesuvius
Misenum *Herculaneum*
Pompeii
Stabiae
Surrentum
Capreae
MILES
0   10